Neodomestic American Fiction

Neodomestic American Fiction

Kristin J. Jacobson

 THE OHIO STATE UNIVERSITY PRESS • COLUMBUS

Copyright © 2010 by The Ohio State University.
All rights reserved.

Library of Congress Cataloging-in-Publication Data
Jacobson, Kristin J., 1973–
  Neodomestic American fiction / Kristin J. Jacobson.
     p. cm.
  Includes bibliographical references and index.
  ISBN-13: 978-0-8142-1132-8 (cloth : alk. paper)
  ISBN-10: 0-8142-1132-1 (cloth : alk. paper)
  ISBN-13: 978-0-8142-9231-0 (cd-rom)
   1. Domestic fiction, American—History and criticism. 2. American fiction—20th century—History and criticism. 3. American fiction—21st century—History and criticism. 4. Home in literature. I. Title.
  PS374.D57J33 2010
  813'.609355—dc22
                          2010014420

This book is available in the following editions:
Cloth (ISBN 978-0-8142-1132-8)
CD-ROM (ISBN 978-0-8142-9231-0)
Paper (ISBN: 978-0-8142-5646-6)
Cover design by Mia Risberg
Type set in Adobe Minion Pro by Juliet Williams

*In recognition, appreciation, and love:
to my parents, Paul and Bev, my big brother, Kurt,
and my new sister, Karen*

Housekeeping ain't no joke.
                                —*Louisa May Alcott,* Little Women

And feminism, with its inherently undomesticated place—neither at home nor away from—is uniquely placed to engage in productive forms of domestic deconstruction. The results will never be tidy, but they will always be different.
                                —Rachel Bowlby, "Domestication"

Either way, I guessed this could be called cultural progress, the new day as played out in neo-domestic neo-realism across the land.
                                —Frederick Barthelme, Natural Selection

Contents

Acknowledgments   xi

Introduction	Recycling Domesticities: Contemporary American Fiction's Domestic Geographies	1
Chapter 1	Remapping Domestic Fiction: Neodomestic Geographies	15
Chapter 2	Recycling Feminine Domesticity: Rewriting Conventional Domestic Fiction	41
Chapter 3	Remodeling Home: Redesigning Conventional Domestic Space	77
Chapter 4	Mapping Gendered Genres: Domestic Masculinity, Suburban Fiction, and the Antidomestic	114
Chapter 5	Performing Domesticity: Anxious Masculinity and Queer Homes	153
Chapter 6	Conclusions: The Territory Ahead	182

Appendix   203
Notes   205
Works Cited   219
Index   233

Acknowledgments

Not all books and scholars emerge from happy homes. The various places I have inhabited, especially during the time spent working on this book, have blessed me with the time, encouragement, and knowledge to write.

My work on contemporary domestic novels began in the English department at the Pennsylvania State University as my dissertation. My acknowledgments must begin by thanking my dissertation director, Deborah Clarke. Her dedication to this project and me comes in many forms—too many to detail here. So, I will simply write—with all my heart—thank you, Deb. Ralph Rodriguez's outstanding guidance also supported my project from start to finish. My thanks as well to the other members of my dissertation committee, Robin Schulze and Lorraine Dowler. Their feedback set me on the road to publication.

Numerous colleagues and friends read, commented on, and otherwise supported this work through its various stages. Many thanks to Holly Flint, Lori Ween, Beth Capo, Janet Holtman, Brandon Kempner, Erika Spohrer, Carissa Turner, KarenDe Herman, Susan K. Harris, Kathryn Hume, Cheryl Glenn, and Liz and Philip Jenkins. Thanks also to the readers and editors at The Ohio State University Press for their insightful reading and thoughtful suggestions. I am especially indebted to Vorris Nunley. His patient listening and willingness to read helped me overcome countless writing woes: I owe him at least a nickel.

My Stockton colleagues and students provide a place that is not only intellectually habitable but also a truly good place to be. I am especially thankful for the encouragement and friendship offered by Laura Zucconi, Katherine Panagakos, Kory Olson, and Michael Cronin. I also wish to express my heartfelt appreciation for the generous support provided by my Literature program colleagues, particularly my mentors Tom Kinsella, Deborah Gussman, Ken Tompkins, Lisa Honaker, and Marion Hussong. I also want to acknowledge Beth Olsen (director of Stockton's Grants Office), who led me through numerous applications. Deans Rob Gregg and Jan Colijn, as well as the wonderful staff of the Arts and Humanities office, were also instrumental in ushering this project to its conclusion; their support of my research made all the difference.

The Richard Stockton College of New Jersey and the Faculty Resource Network at New York University provided valuable summer research support. My fellow summer 2009 scholars-in-residence at NYU energized my editing and final research work. My gratitude also goes to the Northeast Modern Language Association and their readers for selecting my manuscript as their Book Award winner.

Last but not by any means least, I want to acknowledge my most reliable source of funding and support: Mom and Dad. This work is dedicated to them for giving me the best home.

The advice, resources, and support that I received greatly contributed to my work. I hope that this study advances our understanding of domestic fiction and, more broadly, American literature and culture. My friends, colleagues, students, and family: thank you. "Mi casa es su casa."

PORTIONS OF CHAPTERS are revised versions of previously published articles. I am grateful to the following journals and editors for granting permission to use selections from previously published essays:

"The Neodomestic American Novel: The Politics of Home in Barbara Kingsolver's *The Poisonwood Bible*," from *Tulsa Studies in Women's Literature* 24.1 (Spring 2005), 105–27.

"Renovating *The American Woman's Home*: American Domesticity in *Extreme Makeover: Home Edition*," from *Legacy: A Journal of American Women Writers* 25.1 (2008): 105–27, by permission of University of Nebraska Press.

"Imagined Geographies," from *Seeds of Change: Critical Essays on Barbara*

Kingsolver, edited by Priscilla V. Leder, by permission of University of Tennessee Press (2010).

"Anxious Male Domesticity and Gender Troubled *Corrections*," from *Pimps, Wimps, Studs, Thugs and Gentlemen: Essays on Media Images of Masculinity* ©2009, edited by Elwood Watson, by permission of McFarland & Company, Inc., Box 611 Jefferson, NC 28640 http://www.mcfarlandpub.com.

Introduction

Recycling Domesticities

Contemporary American Fiction's Domestic Geographies

The privately owned, single-family home epitomizes the American dream. This ideal persists despite longstanding disparities in housing access and equity. For example, according to the U.S. Census Bureau only 46 percent of blacks and 48 percent of Hispanics currently own their own homes, whereas Caucasian homeownership remains steady at 75 percent (Callis and Cavanaugh 8). Homeownership rates for Asians are slightly higher than for other minorities, 59 percent, but still well below whites (Kochhar i). Black householders, furthermore, have a median net worth of only $5,446, and without home equity, $1,102; in comparison, non-Hispanic white householders' median net worth is $87,056, and without home equity, $19,079 (Gottschalck 13). Additionally, only 25 percent of female-headed households could afford a modestly priced house in 2004; in contrast, 36 percent of male-headed households and 70 percent of married couples could afford the same moderately priced home (Savage 4). Finally, the downturn in the American housing market and the rise in nationwide foreclosures since 2005 have had disproportionate effects on minorities, erasing gains made in the previous ten years: "From 1995 through the middle of this decade, homeownership rates rose more rapidly among all minorities than among whites. But since the start of the housing bust in 2005, rates have fallen more steeply for two of the nation's largest minority groups—blacks and native-born Latinos—than for the rest of the population" (Kochhar i).

These discrepancies and the rising foreclosure rates suggest the need to remodel America's "domestic geographies," the multifaceted territories that compose American housing and domestic ideology. As an emblem of American success (especially in terms of financial stability) and as a prime location for identity formation, the material and ideological American home presents a critical site for feminist redefinitions and activism. *Neodomestic American Fiction* explores how novels written after 1980 responded to and shaped America's understanding of home in the midst of the recent boom and bust housing market. In traditional American literary history, women generally write "domestic fiction," a term that conventionally refers to nineteenth-century novels written by and for women, novels in which the dramatic action focuses on homemaking. *The Oxford Companion to Women's Writing in the United States* clarifies that domestic fiction is "didactic and exemplary fiction centered in the 'women's sphere' and focusing on the concerns of women's lives" (Forcey 253). *Neodomestic American Fiction* explores the extent to which writing about the home remains women's work in the twenty-first century and how the generic and political practices of contemporary American novelists are defined within the domestic sphere. This book defines and analyzes a critical mass of late twentieth-century and early twenty-first-century novels that renovate the ideal home's usual depiction by positioning instability—as opposed to stability—as a key structure of quotidian American home life.

When authors, critics, and general readers label a text "domestic fiction," political questions are in play. The genre's shifting terms speak to its contested terrain. The collection of nineteenth-century women's novels that are generally defined as domestic fiction may also be labeled "women's fiction," "family romance," "domestic romance," "domestic sentimentalism," and "sentimental fiction." Today "chick lit" joins the generic labels used to describe and define a range of texts, including domestic fictions. Looking at twentieth-century literature, Deborah Philips crafts a definition of the "Aga-Saga" that sharpens our understanding of domesticity's gendered contours. As Philips explains, the Aga-Saga's "generic requirements . . . are that it should center on a female protagonist (middle- or upper middle-class, and middle-aged), that the domestic is fore-grounded and, as in most romantic fiction, that the setting should be rural" (48). Susan J. Schenk's article "Protest or Pathology: The Politics of Madness in Contemporary Domestic Fiction" likewise connects domestic fiction with women's experiences. She defines contemporary domestic fiction as "the 'mad housewife' novel [that] explores the ways in which this very flexible label is applied to the female protagonists who deviate from social norms" (231).

Domestic novels authored by or focused on men are also assigned various labels ("romances," "social novels," and "suburban fictions"). Conspicuously absent from the men's list is the label "domestic fiction." While domestic genres are often divided according to the author's and/or the protagonist's gender, there are some exceptions. If the story—whether written by or focused on a man or a woman—features a haunted house, the narrative generally falls under the rubric of "gothic fiction." These generic descriptors, as Michael Kowalski argues about the terms "domestic romance" and "domestic fiction," are sometimes used interchangeably while they also describe specific genres with unique characteristics.

Neodomestic American Fiction sorts various genres and subgenres, selecting novels that feature domestic spaces and protagonists who are concerned with the processes of making home. Whereas traditionally only those novels written by and focused on women are labeled "domestic fiction," *Neodomestic American Fiction* revises this custom and identifies a new subgenre, neodomestic fiction, which has distinctive spatial characteristics. I use the term "neodomestic fiction" to differentiate from earlier fiction about the home this related but distinct collection of post-1980 novels that exhibit unconventional domestic topographies.

A list of major neodomestic authors and novels is included in the appendix. I found Frederick Barthelme's use of the term "neodomestic" in *Natural Selection* (1990) after using the term and drafting the bulk of this project. The narrator in this suburban novel remarks, "Either way, I guessed this could be called cultural progress, the *new day* as played out in neo-domestic neo-realism across the land" (60; emphasis in original). While I do not necessarily relate neodomesticity to "cultural progress," the narrator and I both utilize the term to mark a new age for domesticity.

Neodomesticity's distinctive spatiality marks a new era and ideology for the genre of domestic fiction while simultaneously recognizing its dynamic connections to earlier domestic literatures and traditions. Both domestic and neodomestic novels feature a self-consciousness about the home's physical space and the project of homemaking, highlighting domestic instability in positive and negative ways; however, neodomestic fiction—emerging after second-wave feminism and responding to a return to "family values"— marks a paradigm shift: neodomestic fiction advances a politics of domestic instability, particularly emphasized through its distinctive domestic spaces and conclusions. Neodomestic novels intentionally demonstrate the exclusions associated with the single-family, privately-owned home. While nineteenth- and early twentieth-century domestic fiction also invokes domestic uncertainty and works to elicit social change on issues as diverse as women's civic and private roles, slavery, and temperance, its didactic and spatial politics—which are tied to its own sociohistorical domestic culture—demand separate consideration. As Rachel Blau DuPlessis argues, "It is the project of twentieth-century women writers to . . . replace the alternate endings in marriage and death that are their cultural legacy from nineteenth-century life and letters by offering a different set of choices" (4). Post-1980 neodomestic novels continue this project in ways that are distinct from their predecessors.

Explicating neodomestic fiction's distinct spatial narrative is especially important to establishing and understanding this neo-genre. In Henri Lefebvre's terms, "a revolution that does not produce a new space has not realized its full potential" (54). The neodomestic novel's spatiality specifically exhibits three features: (1) relational (as opposed to oppositional) domestic space, which self-consciously emphasizes the home's connection to "outside" environments; (2) domestic mobility, which is the notion that home, as both an ideology and a physical space, can occupy and blur the boundaries of multiple domestic locations; and (3) domestic renovation and redesign of the conventional material and ideological model home, which refers to the privately owned single family structure that represents financial, physical, and psychological security to its owners.[1] In short, neodomestic fiction interrogates and expands on the nineteenth-century domestic novel's legacies.

Neodomestic fictions' distinct spatiality and frequently inconclusive endings especially revise the genre's conventional politics. In *Desire and Domestic Fiction: A Political History of the Novel*, Nancy Armstrong clarifies domestic fiction's traditional politics: "I believe it [eighteenth- and nineteenth-century domestic fiction] helped to formulate the ordered space we now recognize as the household, made that space totally functional, and used it as the context for representing normal behavior" (23–24). Michael Kowalski agrees, suggesting that the domestic romance often worked at "cross purposes: the arousal of sentiments for change and the reassurance of cosmic justice, social criticism, and the affirmation of the status quo" (65). Domestic fiction, in other words, largely works its revolution from within the confines of what Audre Lorde calls the "master's house." Conversely, neodomestic fiction represents and promotes a politics of instability and heterogeneity. It is not so much situated outside the master's house. Rather, it attempts to occupy—as I will discuss in greater detail in the next chapter—an ideological and physical space defined by various contemporary cultural critics: what bell hooks calls the "margin," what Toni Morrison describes as being "'both snug and wide open'" and having "'a doorway never needing to be closed'" ("Home" 9), what Homi Bhabha labels a "third space," what Michel Foucault describes as "heterotopia," and what feminist geographers frequently describe as "relational space."

While Armstrong's claim focuses on English literature and other scholars have since complicated her arguments, her analysis that the development of the ideal or model home constitutes a stable, normative, and protected location remains the dominant rhetorical model.[2] The rise and development of the domestic novel and of conduct and household manuals in the nineteenth century supports Armstrong's thesis that nineteenth-century domestic texts helped establish the conventional model of American domesticity as white, Protestant, middle class, and heterosexual. The reinforcement of the heteronormative aspects of home and family continues today in much domestic literature and culture; multimedia empires such as Martha Stewart Living Omnimedia continue to sell a model of American domesticity that is predominantly white, conservative, middle class, and privately owned. Today's representations of the American home often present a narrow model that nonetheless enjoys as strong of a cultural currency now as it did a hundred years ago. The dream houses featured on *Extreme Makeover: Home Edition*, for example, can be read as supersized versions of the ideal cottage described in 1869 by Harriet Beecher Stowe and Catharine E. Beecher's the *American Woman's Home*.[3]

Given the model's powerful longevity, what accounts for the renewed attention to and attempts to renovate model domesticity in the 1980s? Michael A. Griffith clarifies what the revitalized interest implies: "What returned to fashion in 1984 was not the family, but 'The Family.' Reaganite conservatism had ushered 'Family' back into prominence as a political catchword, and evangelists had adopted the (presumed) disintegration of 'traditional family values' as a rallying cry" (94). Important novels focus on the home and homemaking in order to illustrate the ways in which the model fails the protagonists. These neodomestic stories challenge the conventional politics of American culture and the novel. While Ann Hulbert has suggested that the novel's form itself encourages conservatism—that the novel strengthens "the bourgeois institution of the family"—neodomestic novels complicate, if not refute, Hulbert's suggestion about the novel's form (Hulbert 36). Homeownership is likewise associated with more conservative political practices. Richard Harris and Chris Hamnett report, "Most of the rather limited evidence . . . does indicate that an association between ownership and conservatism is the general rule" (175). The following chapters map how domestic and neodomestic fiction resolve tensions surrounding homeownership differently. Building on the domestic fiction that precedes it, neodomestic fiction recycles domestic tensions and structures to produce alternative geographies of home.

Neodomestic American Fiction recognizes that in the nineteenth century a range of authors appropriated conventional domestic ideals and complicated, if not challenged outright, the model home and domestic fiction's gendered definition, broadening both to include such outsiders as men, single women, and nonwhites. Counterhegemonic spaces encoded in nineteenth-century women's fiction include Harriet Jacobs's "loopholes of retreat" (437–40), Louisa May Alcott's domestic performance spaces in *Little Women*, and Mary E. Wilkins Freeman's churches and barns. We see the appropriation of domestic space by nineteenth-century male writers in novels such as *Moby-Dick*, *The House of Seven Gables*, *Walden*, *The House Behind the Cedars*, and *Washington Square*.[4] Significantly, as Lora Romero points out in *Home Fronts*, these male-authored and male-focused novels are not generally considered domestic fiction. This double standard reveals domestic fiction's gendered definitions. The spatial definition of domestic fiction mapped in this project joins Romero and other recent scholarship in questioning this literary history that largely excludes male writers and protagonists.[5] Furthermore, my spatial definition opens new doors for scholars who are reconsidering the genre's earlier incarnations in the nineteenth and early twentieth centuries.

Recent modernist studies of domestic fiction also emphasize domestic multiplicity and instability: "Mobility, agency, and mutability were central to urban homes in ways that the literary historical narrative of separate spheres has obscured" (Klimasmith 8). In the modern period, writers such as Gertrude Stein, following the call to "make it new," crafted new modes of representing domesticity.[6] Nevertheless, the impetus to stabilize the domestic environment—to produce a stable home or to escape a domestic trap—spans the literature through much of the nineteenth and twentieth centuries. Betsy Klimasmith's study of urban domesticity in the late nineteenth and early twentieth centuries reveals, for example, how the novel during that period "became a testing ground for examining relationships between urban spaces and the development of an unsettled and unsettling modern subjectivity" (5). Yet, while the urban domestic literature of this early modern period challenges the separate spheres of a male public and a female private (domestic) space and stability, the home continues to be "deployed rhetorically, linguistically, and physically to help order the potential chaos" (Klimasmith 7–8). Thus, both nineteenth- and twentieth-century domestic fictions often ultimately resolve domestic instability. Stability remains the American home's dominant, idealized feature in domestic literature, space, and culture.

Neodomestic fiction intensifies attempts to theorize or model alternatives to the stable home. The exploration of the literary and cultural significance of this shift from traditional stability to a "productive instability" is this book's central project. As I have begun to suggest, neodomestic fiction does not represent a full break from its literary predecessors. Neodomestic fiction is a recycled or revised neo-genre, not a completely different form. The analysis of the literary and cultural domestic histories in the chapters that follow reveals that neodomestic novels represent an *intensification* and *rearrangement* of tensions and characteristics present at the time of domestic fiction's inception in the nineteenth century and its continued development in the twentieth century.

Neodomestic fiction's revisions rearrange domestic fiction's conventional boundaries. Consequently, this book remaps the generic study of domestic fiction in three ways: (1) it extends the genre's time period through the twentieth century and establishes a significant revision of and resurgence in domestic fiction beginning in the 1980s, (2) it includes male as well as female authors, and (3) it provides a primarily spatial rather than plot- or character-based analysis.[7] Utilizing a spatial analysis more readily extends domestic fiction through the twentieth century and to authors and stories focused on men as well as women. Domestic fiction particularly concentrates on the home's geography and homemaking processes—"spatial narratives" that focus on place and the practices that define location.[8] This analysis of domestic geographies, thus, includes the home's material and nonmaterial borders and the processes involved in establishing and maintaining this space. Following the lead of cultural geographers such as David Harvey, I read domestic space as a social process.[9] This methodology allows me to address not only what constitutes a "house," but also what practices and social forces make a "home."

In addition to covering expanded territory, this study of neodomestic fiction also reveals entrenched boundaries. Men especially constitute the subject matter of this contested terrain. This revised map of domestic fiction adds to recent separate sphere scholarship that questions the strict boundaries between private/public and feminine/masculine spaces. While significant research has been completed that problematizes the so-called separate spheres, little discussion has taken place about how such reevaluations of gendered, classed, and raced space influence the construction and evaluation of literary genres. Domestic fiction in particular continues to reflect a strict separate spheres mentality—there is women's fiction and there is men's fiction. According to this conventional generic definition, men in particular do not write domestic fiction or serve as domestic fiction's protagonists.

Upon closer examination we see that two distinctly gendered traditions exist in both contemporary and nineteenth-century domestic fiction. Briefly, the distinguishing characteristics include discrete views of the home's spiritual geography and distinctive homemaking habits, or the particular practices deemed necessary to keep the home functioning within the domestic novel. *Masculine* domestic fictions, for example, frequently build their narratives from property relations and disputes and focus on a male protagonist. *Feminine* domestic fictions tend to deemphasize ownership or property disputes and focus on a female protagonist. Masculine and feminine domestic fictions also frequently carry distinct social currencies in the public sphere.

As much as these two gendered traditions clash, they simultaneously produce what Jennifer Haytock has described in relation to modernist domestic and war fiction as "a system of literary interdependence" (Haytock xviii). Romero makes a similar point in reference to the nineteenth century's celebratory and antidomestic cultures (1–8). Neodomestic fiction contends with America's gendered domestic contexts and frequently mixes these gendered literary and cultural traditions, reflecting both changing gender roles and longstanding gendered divisions in American culture. Milette Shamir describes this split in nineteenth-century fiction in terms of "divided plots." Shamir argues, "The example of the domestic division plot shows the romance and sentimental traditions to be competing over the same space [the home], albeit from different angles and perspectives" (431). Shamir's description of the romance (masculine) and the sentimental (feminine) novel offers another way to characterize the gendered spatial tensions among the masculine and feminine domestic fictions that I map in the following chapters. However, I do not use these frequently gendered literary traditions (the romance and the sentimental novel) as synonymous with domestic fiction because not all romances and sentimental novels are spatial narratives. For example, a romance might not qualify as a spatial narrative to the same degree as a work of (neo)domestic fiction, which sustains an intense focus on the physical home and homemaking. As a result, geography—particularly feminist geography—provides the crucial mapping tool for this highly spatial literature.

Geography, like literary studies, wrestles with the interpretation of the economic, racial, and gendered forces that produce America's inequitable domestic geographies, such as those outlined at the beginning of this introduction. This project also takes seriously Harvey's suggestion in *Spaces of Hope* that the novel provides a valuable space for exploring social change and his recognition of the significant number of female authors doing this work (189). Cultural geography helps us to gauge literary constructions of domestic space by providing tools to (re)design literary discourse so that it moves between fictional spaces and the real worlds that men and women inhabit. It is particularly helpful in narrowing the range of novels that fall under neodomesticity's rubric.

While I am interested in a range of domestic geographies, I am not suggesting that every contemporary novel that features the home and homemaking could be or should be labeled neodomestic fiction. The spatial novels included in this study posit the home as a key location for narrative action and feature homemaking as a central component of the plot. As the following chapters explore in greater detail, neodomestic fiction's three characteristics (mobility, relational space, and renovation) frame a distinctive neo-genre. In subtle and obvious ways, neodomestic fiction emphasizes that *place shapes the characters as much as the characters shape place.* The home in neodomestic fiction may speak or otherwise interact with the characters, as in the haunted house in Toni Morrison's *Beloved* (1987) and the talking island at the conclusion of Gloria Naylor's *Mama Day* (1988). Such elements emphasize that domestic geographies are not neutral or mere reflections of characters' traits or desires.[10] In feminist geographer Doreen Massey's terms, neodomestic space is relational; its identity "derives, in large part, precisely from the specificity of its interactions with 'the outside'" (Massey 169). As Sister Salt describes in Leslie Marmon Silko's *Gardens in the Dunes*, walls do not define a house (438). Home is a space determined by the interaction between "inside" and "outside."

Like the neodomestic novels that we will encounter in the following pages, feminist geographers do not insist on an isolated, stable definition of home. That is, rather than studying home as a place that is *not* public, feminist geographers understand the private home and public space in "relational" terms, where public and private space interact and are not mutually exclusive: "Rather than a static site, home may be conceptualized in relation to other places (for example, offices), and the social relations appropriate to different places analyzed in terms of power and authority" (Al-Hindi 154). Relational space rejects "negative counterposition" (Massey 169) and "forces us to recognize our interconnectedness" (Massey 170). Neodomestic fiction likewise uses relational space to present a distinctive architecture of the American home.

Feminist geographers' argument for a relational understanding of space parallels in many respects the questions that historical and literary studies have posed about whether the public and private spheres are actually separate. That is, a relational view of space sees that a home may be physically separate yet not discursively isolated. Feminist geographer Linda McDowell clarifies in *Gender, Identity, and Place* how relational space specifically affects the domestic sphere: "a focus on the social relations within a domestic space crosses the boundary between the private and the public, between the particular and the general, and is not, as often incorrectly asserted, a focus on the 'merely' domestic or the private sphere" (72–73). For instance, Loida Maritza Pérez's *Geographies of Home* (1999) subtly highlights the neodomestic home's unique physical and ideological structure with passages that describe the home's physical state and the characters' psychological connections and reactions to the home's changing structure and appearance.

Iliana's mother in Pérez's *Geographies of Home* observes that her home, fashioned after the middle-class ideal, actually embodies instability, not stability:

> Stepping from the couch, she noticed that one of the floor's marble tiles had cracked. She then imagined that the slightest disturbance might topple furniture, collapse shelves, detach the chandelier. That she and her husband had managed to purchase all these things as well as their own home had often been offered as proof to their children of the stability in their lives. Only now did she concede that nothing was stable—nothing. The earth itself might give out under their feet, their house burn down, madness take root, evil unfold into their lives. (Pérez 293)

The home's cracked tile provokes this reverie. Iliana's mother concedes in this passage that the American dream, which is represented by material possessions and especially the home, hardly provides stability for her Dominican American family: nothing is secure. This instability is home.

Possessions, in particular, do not assure solidity. In an age when Americans are told by their president to go shopping when faced with national tragedy and insecurity, *Geographies of Home* exposes the instability of America's consumer culture.[11] How the characters arrive at and cope with this realization in *Geographies of Home* composes much of the novel's plot. Thus, *Geographies of Home* provides one example, with a particularly appropriate title, of late twentieth-century neodomestic writing that destabilizes the conventional home, questioning and refashioning its economic and social worth. Its politics also distinguishes neodomesticity from neoliberalism, which has developed during the same period but thwarts rather than advances the "downward redistribution of economic, political, and cultural resources" (Duggan 40). Unlike neoliberalism, neodomesticity seeks "A sustainable opposition . . . [that] connect[s] culture, politics, and economics; identity politics and class politics; universalist rhetoric and particular issues and interests; intellectual and material resources" (Duggan 41). Neodomestic fiction engages in this project by exploring rather than quelling domestic instability.

The novels included in this study survey a range of genders, sexualities, ethnicities, races, and classes. These neodomestic novels literally and/or symbolically remodel the conventional home's material and social structures, incorporating instability and individual and social histories as part of the fictional homes' physical designs. The home's (in)stability, specifically in regard to the model white, middle-class, Protestant home, is a central concern. This criterion for neodomestic fiction is key because, although they are not the focus of this study, more traditional versions of domestic fiction continue to be written. Contemporary conventional domestic novels, such as Robert Morgan's *Gap Creek* (1999), are not included in the following chapters because they frequently reproduce and romanticize the traditional domestic geography of the single-family, heterosexual, patriarchal home rather than attempt to redesign and destabilize its singular dominance within the American landscape. I have intentionally selected fiction that represents a wide range of domesticities in order to explore this shared instability while recognizing historical, material, and social differences among the narratives and the cultures from which they emerge.

While domestic fiction's extensions, migrations, and transformations since 1980 form my primary focus, this investigation of late twentieth- and early twenty-first-century domestic fiction still addresses key concerns that Cathy N. Davidson and Jessamyn Hatcher's edited collection *No More Separate Spheres!* raises in regard to moving "beyond the separate spheres," apprehensions relevant to nineteenth-, twentieth-, and twenty-first-century studies of American literature and culture broadly and domestic and women's fiction in particular. Specifically, my analysis demonstrates how opening the genre to both male and female authors and protagonists still provides "a potent organizing metaphor" and "a source within the dominant culture for legitimizing" interest in women's history and literature, while it simultaneously "complicate[s] the binary model of men versus women" (Davidson and Hatcher 9; 11–12). While female protagonists and such women writers as Toni Morrison, Barbara Kingsolver, and Leslie Marmon Silko dominate neodomestic fiction, male protagonists and authors are increasingly—even if, as Jonathan Franzen demonstrates, sometimes reluctantly—redefining our understanding of the domestic sphere and literature.

Although *Neodomestic American Fiction* focuses on the American home's post-1980 fictional geographies, physical homes play a key role, too. Like Nancy Armstrong, I "regard fiction . . . both as the document and as the agency of cultural history" (*Desire* 23). Grounded in an awareness of America's twentieth-century housing discrepancies and histories, *Neodomestic American Fiction* addresses literature's presentation of and intervention in this crisis.[12] Following the model of Harriet Beecher Stowe's *Uncle Tom's Cabin*, the literature, in other words, serves representational (aesthetic), political, and theoretical ends. My methodology draws specifically from David Harvey's paradigm described in *Justice, Nature and the Geography of Difference*, in which an understanding of spatial tactics necessarily involves two basic assumptions: categories like the home are social constructions and thus unstable, and the politics of space involve three equally interrelated spheres—materiality, representation, and imagination (320–24). As a result, the following chapters analyze the interrelated realms of material history, the home's representations in fiction, and domesticity's physical manifestations and theoretical models. Thus, this feminist literary and cultural study of the American home seeks to accomplish what domestic fiction's didacticism and much interdisciplinary work in American literature and women's studies aims to do: revitalize individual disciplines and gain support for initiatives that can affect American's lives, especially the lives of American women.

Key to *Neodomestic American Fiction*
Chapter Overviews

Chapter 1, "Remapping Domestic Fiction: Neodomestic Geographies," outlines the project's theoretical and historical parameters: it traces and extends domestic fiction's time period into the twenty-first century; it identifies the spatial lens with which to define and interpret this genre, providing an alternative to the plot or character-based definition of the fiction; and finally, it redefines the genre to include male as well as female authors and protagonists. This chapter also explains a shift in the politics of home from stability to instability. I locate this shift in the 1980s, pointing to the threshold neodomestic novels *Housekeeping* (Marilynne Robinson) and *The House on Mango Street* (Sandra Cisneros) as landmark works that mark neodomestic fiction's emergence out of both the feminist movement and significant housing changes.

Chapter 2, "Recycling Feminine Domesticity: Rewriting Conventional Domestic Fiction," features neodomestic novels that self-consciously rewrite nineteenth-century domestic fiction and what Amy Kaplan terms "manifest domesticity." The chapter includes extended close readings of Leslie Marmon Silko's *Gardens in the Dunes* and Barbara Kingsolver's *The Poisonwood Bible*, which I have chosen for their extensive revisions of the genre. I open the chapter with *Gardens in the Dunes* to explore neodomestic fiction's three primary characteristics: mobility, home renovation or redesign, and relational domestic space. The section that follows examines how neodomestic novels self-consciously invoke and revise nineteenth-century domestic fiction's tropes, particularly those of mobility, the stable home, and the selfless woman.

Chapter 3, "Remodeling Home: Redesigning Conventional Domestic Space," demonstrates that rather than ultimately constructing the home as a trap or a haven, neodomestic fiction deconstructs, recycles, and finally explodes the conventional house-home dichotomy, enacting neodomestic ideology through its experimentation with an elusive but productive domestic instability. I examine various homes' geopolitics, especially residents' gendered and raced housekeeping styles and renovations. African American spatial politics as defined by bell hooks and John Michael Vlach ground my spatial analysis of several representative domestic locations in Morrison's *Beloved* and *Paradise*.

The next two chapters focus more exclusively on domestic masculinity in fiction by writers such as Michael Cunningham, Richard Ford, and Jane Smiley. Chapter 4, "Mapping Gendered Genres: Domestic Masculinity, Suburban Fiction, and the Antidomestic," continues the argument presented in the introduction that masculinity has always been and remains a key component within domestic fiction. This chapter primarily focuses on the antidomestic tradition, in which suburban literature frequently falls, and on the neodomestic novels that are especially engaged in recycling these conventionally masculine features. The chapter briefly defines conventional domestic masculinity vis-à-vis Washington Irving's "Rip Van Winkle" and William Dean Howells's *Suburban Sketches*. Mark Twain's portrayal of "lighting out for the territory" in *The Adventures of Huckleberry Finn* also provides a key trope for defining conventional domestic masculinity's "beset manhood" (Baym 130). This largely antidomestic tradition is compared and contrasted with several contemporary suburban novels, such as John Edgar Wideman's Homewood trilogy, Don DeLillo's *White Noise*, Ford's *Independence Day*, and Andre Dubus III's *House of Sand and Fog*. While the antidomestic tradition is still very much alive in contemporary fiction, this chapter focuses on the novels attempting to rework the complexly gendered structures undergirding the domestic novel.

Chapter 5, "Performing Domesticity: Anxious Masculinity and Queer Homes," primarily examines Jonathan Franzen's *The Corrections*, Michael Cunningham's *A Home at the End of the World*, and Chang-rae Lee's *A Gesture Life* for the unique ways they recycle the domestic novel. The chapter features the cultural and literary reception of *The Corrections* in order to examine the role of white, domestic masculinity in the American public sphere. An extended reading of queer domesticities, both literal (as seen in such novels as *A Home at the End of the World*) and figurative (as seen in such novels as *A Gesture Life*), concludes this chapter, bringing home my argument that neodomestic novels do not erase gender distinctions but rather attempt to "trouble"—in the Judith Butler sense—their stability.

Chapter 6, "Conclusions: The Territory Ahead," provides more in-depth commentary on (neo)domestic texts other than the novel, such as artwork by photographer Clarissa Sligh, innovative design work by the Rural Studio at Auburn University, and the popular ABC reality television program *Extreme Makeover: Home Edition*. This chapter connects literary representations of American domesticity to other types of houses and attitudes about home and family that have appeared in the late twentieth century.

Thus, this study maps the development of American domestic fiction written by women and men after 1980 and its resonance with earlier domestic novels. Following Cathy N. Davidson and Jessamyn Hatcher's model from *No More Separate Spheres!* I seek to demonstrate "how domesticity is saturated by and dependent on a range of factors, terms, and agents imagined to lie outside its domain" (18). Masculinity, including male-authored and male-focused novels, along with the ideological and physical constructions of the "nation" and the "foreign," are key agents generally considered outside American domestic fiction. Therefore, my work also contributes to the conversation about American domesticity as set out by Amy Kaplan's essay "Manifest Domesticity" and her larger work *The Anarchy of Empire in the Making of U.S. Culture* (2002). Neodomestic fiction seeks to avoid reproducing "manifest domesticities."

The following chapters emphasize the intimate connections between "foreign" and "domestic" as well as between "masculinity" and "femininity." The individual chapter divisions reflect American domestic culture's gendered structures while the chapters simultaneously relate to and bleed across these physical and ideological distinctions. The chapters, like relational space, converse with one another, demarcating physical and ideological boundaries that are in constant negotiation. This relational methodology and organization seeks to underscore my overall argument about the study of neodomestic fiction: the key to understanding neodomestic fiction and its radical project of recycling and reinventing American domesticity is to recognize such seemingly separate, "foreign" entities—like masculine and queer domesticities—as members of the family.

1

Remapping Domestic Fiction

Neodomestic Geographies

Domestic fiction seemingly hit a dead end in the late nineteenth century. Nina Baym states that the changes women's fiction underwent "in the late 1860s and 1870s . . . signify the fact that the genre [domestic fiction] had run its course" (*Woman's Fiction* 13). The rise of the new woman and modernism are often understood as launching domestic fiction's demise. Blythe Forcey's entry "Domestic Fiction" in *The Oxford Companion to Women's Writing in the United States* clarifies, "While the genre has never died out, it became an object of near-constant disdain in the first half of the twentieth century as it was made the icon of everything that modern literature strove *not* to be" (253; emphasis in original). Suzanne Clark in *Sentimental Modernism* makes a similar argument: "Modernism inaugurated a reversal of values which emphasized erotic desire, not love; anarchic rupture and innovation rather than the conventional appeals of sentimental language. Modernism reversed the increasing influence of women's writing, discrediting the literary past and especially that sentimental history" (1). Countering this interpretation of literary history, Susan Edmunds in *Grotesque Relations* argues that modernism did not ring the death knell for the domestic novel: "the cultural legacy of sentimental domesticity was not rejected, killed off, or supplanted in this period. Instead, it was rearticulated, making the sense of a revolutionary break with the past shared by modern domestic subjects an important but untrustworthy guide for later critics" (10). Whether described as a force for reversal or rearticulation, modernist critics were not the first or the last to critique domestic fiction. From Nathaniel Hawthorne's caustic statement in 1855 against "a d—d mob of scribbling women" to Jonathan Franzen's disparaging remarks in 2001 about Oprah's Book Club, domestic fiction and its predominately female writers and readers have long been pushed to the back roads of American literature and culture (Hawthorne 304).

Despite receiving sustained critical censure, the home, in all of its diverse and vibrant configurations, occupies a central position in much contemporary American fiction, confirming that domestic fiction has not disappeared or reached the end of its road. Rather, the array of novels that focus on the domestic sphere in late twentieth-century American fiction testifies to the genre's continued, if reconfigured, importance. The assortment of domestic geographies in the late twentieth century includes the exiled homes in Lan Cao's *Monkey Bridge* (1997), Cristina Garcia's *Dreaming in Cuban* (1992), and Leslie Marmon Silko's *Gardens in the Dunes* (1999); the "perfect" yet unsuccessful homes in Chang-rae Lee's *A Gesture Life* (1999) and David Wong Louie's *The Barbarians Are Coming* (2000); the migrant home in Helena María Viramontes's *Under the Feet of Jesus* (1995); the divorced father's suburban home in Richard Ford's *Independence Day* (1995); the patriarchal and matriarchal homes in Toni Morrison's *Paradise* (1997) and Barbara Kingsolver's *The Poisonwood Bible* (1998); the lost homes in John Edgar Wideman's Homewood trilogy (1981; 1983; 1988); the queer homes in Leslie Feinberg's *Stone Butch Blues* (1993) and Michael Cunningham's *A Home at the End of the World* (1990); the stolen homes in Joy Williams's *Breaking and Entering* (1981); and the postmodern expanding and contracting home in Mark Z. Danielewski's *House of Leaves* (2000). These novels with their diverse domestic terrains testify to an ongoing renaissance in domestic fiction.

This chapter addresses how literature that focuses on the space of the home and the practices of homemaking reemerges in the late twentieth century to self-consciously reflect on where the genre has been and what the future may hold for this conventionally nineteenth-century genre with revolutionary as well as imperial, class-biased, and racist origins.[1] This chapter outlines a revised way to define all domestic fiction in addition to mapping neodomestic fiction's emergence in the 1980s and its distinctive features. Until now, the pioneering scholarly works on domestic fiction primarily define the genre according to plot and character analysis; as a result, they also tend to privilege (white) women's experiences. We might productively understand these novels as "spatial narratives" (stories that sustain a focus on the space and place of the home) in order to use domestic fiction's geography as a prime means for defining the genre and mapping its travel across the past one hundred years. "Queer" and "recycled domesticities" form two concepts that are central to remapping domestic fiction and to understanding neodomestic space and fiction.

Defining Neodomestic Space
Queer and Recycled Domesticities

Neodomestic fiction emphasizes queer and recycled homes and homemaking. Queer in this context defines various domestic spaces and practices rather than exclusively homosexual households. Queer domesticity refers to homemaking practices that produce "an alternative articulatory space of gender and sexuality" (Parikh 863). Like Nayan Shah in *Contagious Divides*, I define queer domesticity as a category identified by its aims and effects rather than by its sexual makeup: "Rather than viewing the term *queer* as a synonym for homosexual identity, I use it to question the formation of exclusionary norms of respectable middle-class, heterosexual marriage. The analytical category of queer upsets the strict gender roles, the firm divisions between public and private, and the implicit presumptions of self-sufficient economics and intimacy in the respectable domestic household" (Shah 13–14; emphasis in original). In this light, queer domesticity includes renting and other economic relationships outside of conventional ownership. While Willie and Liberty in Joy Williams's *Breaking and Entering* are heterosexual, for instance, their homemaking is queer. By squatting in other people's lavish houses, the couple upsets conventional domesticity, especially our notion of private homeownership. Their childlessness, or lack of reproductive sexuality, also marks them as queer.[2]

Such "alternative articulatory spaces" reform—in both senses of physically reshaping and ideologically revising—fictional domestic space (Parikh 863). In Rosemary Marangoly George's terms, neodomestic fiction "recycles" or self-consciously reuses domestic structures. George explains,

> narratives and practices that responsibly recycle domesticity perform two tasks: first, they effect transformations that are attentive to the materials and the debris of past domestic edifices. Second, in being attentive to the material and historical factors that have enabled domesticity to flourish, such recycling narratives make the domestic a site from which countertheorizations about seemingly "larger" and unrelated institutions and ideologies can be produced. ("Recycling" 2–3)

George posits two conditions necessary for the effective recycling of domestic fiction: historical consciousness and "countertheorization." The first recycling protocol demands that domestic history must help determine what and how contemporary domestic fiction recycles. For example, recycling the domestic novel's historical privileging of single-family, privately owned homes must take into account that not everyone has equal access to this type of home. In the most extreme cases, as I discuss in chapter 2, authors literally rewrite nineteenth-century domestic fictions.

George's second tenet demands that historical consciousness produce what I have labeled a queer or destabilized domestic site—a location for "countertheorizations." This space has been described by a range of cultural theorists and geographers. Neodomestic, relational spaces can be seen as illustrations and theorizations of Michel Foucault's concept of "heterotopia" and a modified form of Homi Bhabha's theorization of "third space." Kevin Hetherington defines "heterotopia" as "spaces of alternate ordering. Heterotopia organize a bit of the social world in a way different to that which surrounds them. That alternate ordering marks them out as Other and allows them to be seen as an example of an alternative way of doing things" (qtd. in Harvey, *Spaces of Hope* 184). Neodomesticity's emphasis on instability also marks it as "Other" and "an alternative way of doing things." David Harvey describes heterotopia's uses and limitations: "The concept of 'heterotopia' has the virtue of insisting upon a better understanding of the heterogeneity of space but it gives no clue as to what a more spatiotemporal utopianism might look like. Foucault challenges and helps destabilize (particularly in the realm of discourse) but provides no clue as to how any kind of alternative might be constructed" (*Spaces of Hope* 185). Neodomestic fiction theorizes—by producing fictional homes—such alternative spaces.

Bhabha's "third space" also describes neodomestic space. Third space, especially when put to use by feminist principles, can create "alternative geographies which bring together space, politics and hybrid identities" (Jeffery 274). According to Craig Jeffery's entry on third space in *A Feminist Glossary of Human Geography*, "geographers have focused particularly on third space as a location of knowledge and resistance" (274). He sees the concept's strengths "as lying in the fact that it elaborates the 'grounds of dissimilarity' on which dualisms are based; acknowledges that there are spaces beyond dualisms; and accepts that third space itself is fragmented, incomplete and the site of struggle for meaning and representation" (Jeffery 274). Neodomestic spaces, similarly, complicate conventional dualistic epistemologies, such as public-private and male-female, to produce hybrid geographies.

Bhabha emphasizes that hybridity cannot "trace two original movements from which the third emerges" and "this third space displaces the histories that constitute it, and sets up new structures of authority, new political initiatives"; neodomesticity, by contrast, maintains clear traces of its conventional origins in order to produce "a new area of negotiation" (Bhabha, "The Third Space" 211). Neodomestic instability, furthermore, also emphasizes space's fragmentation and its relational "struggle for meaning and representation." The characters in *Breaking and Entering*, for instance, violate the private sphere by breaking into homes, but they do not steal anything except the otherwise empty space of the uninhabited home. The luxurious vacation homes would simply sit empty if the characters did not squat in them. The squatters learn about the homeowners' intimate lives and then drift to the next house. The space that they inhabit is both home and not home; the stolen homes are more suitable than the home that they rent, yet the stolen houses are never their permanent homes. Their "perverse skill of inhabiting the space others had made" constitutes a third space that resists such dualities as private-public and lawful-unlawful (Williams 28). Outlining domestic fiction's generic definitions and literary histories clarifies further how neodomestic space and literature differs from its predecessors. Examining the origin and history of the term "domestic fiction" also clarifies how domestic fiction emerged as a legible genre largely to the exclusion of masculine domesticity.

Defining Domestic Fiction
Shifting and Resisting Terminologies

Whether focused on men's or women's lives, and whether set in rural, urban, or suburban locations, all domestic fictions share a focus on the home's physical and ideological spaces. Nina Baym explains in *Woman's Fiction*, "The term 'domestic' for this [nineteenth-century] fiction generally means that the content is largely descriptive of events taking place in a home setting" (26). Significantly, the term "domestic fiction" itself is of fairly recent vintage and emerges from second-wave feminist scholarship that worked to revalue the space of the home and American women's writing; it is a product of feminists working to recover and reassess nineteenth-century fiction by women. The term "domestic fiction" was most likely coined by Baym "so as to avoid calling the genre I worked with 'sentimental fiction'":[3]

> Other scholars . . . used the term domestic sentimentalism (i.e., Gillian Brown) or wrote about the novelists as sentimental domestics (Mary Kelley). And then there's the term "domestic feminism," a term applied by con-

temporary historians for the kind of feminism that was rooted in women's supposed connection with the home. (Baym, "Re: Query")

In all cases, the adjective "domestic" is "a coinage of second-wave feminism" (Baym "Re: Query"). While "domestic fiction" is not the only generic descriptor of women's writing, the term reflects both its deeply rooted history and the critical reception of its texts.

Labeling this separate sphere of literature originally served to demarginalize these frequently forgotten or undervalued nineteenth-century women's voices. As Catherine Jurca points out in her study of suburban fiction, our generic definitions still tend to reflect a separate sphere approach to literature about the home and domesticity: "Literary scholarship on the home has continued to be confined almost exclusively to nineteenth-century texts and contexts and to the experience of women" (9). Domestic fiction conventionally denotes women's fiction and writing. Masculinity, which is conventionally considered to be outside of domesticity, heightens attention to domestic fiction's gendered genre status and the practices that define it as such. How domesticity is gendered influences which novels historically wear the label "domestic fiction." Outlining the characteristics of domestic masculinity and domestic femininity clarifies their distinctive but interdependent literary and spatial traditions.

Outlining Gendered Terrain
Domestic Masculinity and Domestic Femininity

Where domestic femininity traditionally celebrates homemaking, domestic masculinity attempts to escape it. White domestic masculinity, from Washington Irving's "Rip Van Winkle" to its contemporary forms in novels such as John Updike's *Rabbit, Run*, often presents the home as a trap. Judith Fetterley argues in "'Not the Least American': Nineteenth-Century Literary Regionalism" that this antidomestic masculine tradition often generates a "national narrative that valorizes violence, that defines masculinity as the production of violence and defines the feminine and the foreign as legitimate recipients of such violence" (893). Similarly, Baym describes such stories (for example, the fiction by "Poe, Melville, Hawthorne, and James" as well as Thoreau, Kerouac, Updike, and Bellow [Baym 128; 132]) as "Melodramas of Beset Manhood." In the early twentieth century, the "new woman" frequently appropriated this masculine story and likewise presented the home as a trap to be escaped (as in Elizabeth Stuart Phelps's *The Story of Avis*, Edith Wharton's *The House of Mirth*, and, more recently, Erika Lopez's *Flaming Iguanas*).

Contemporary literature that focuses on domestic masculinity narrates a range of experiences and perspectives, including those of the genre's hallmark, the disenchanted or alienated white male (for example, Jonathan Franzen's *The Corrections* and Richard Ford's *Independence Day*); equally disenchanted female protagonists (Sandra Tsing Loh's *If You Lived Here, You'd Be Home by Now* and *A Year in Van Nuys*); African American families making community (John Edgar Wideman's Homewood trilogy and Gloria Naylor's *Linden Hills*); and stories of a young man's spiritual rebirth (Anne Tyler's *Saint Maybe*). Suburban fiction constitutes the dominant masculine domestic model, from William H. Whyte's *The Organization Man* (1956) to John Updike's Rabbit novels and Gabrielle Zevin's *The Hole We're In* (2010).

Representations of white domestic masculinity, like representations of domestic femininity, not only reflect but also challenge the domestic sphere's gendered definitions and ideals. As I have begun to argue, American literary history emphasizes that domestic masculinity frequently presents narratives of "beset manhood"; it also often understands home as property. Homeownership, closely associated with successful masculinity, often symbolizes a male's ability to protect and provide for his family. Significantly in this regard, Richard Ford's protagonist Frank Bascombe shifts from being a fiction writer, to being a sportswriter (*The Sportswriter*), and finally, after his divorce and the death of his son Ralph, to being a real estate agent (*Independence Day* and *The Lay of the Land*). Frank's job as a real estate agent epitomizes domestic masculinity's connections to the formal domestic economy.

By contrast, homemaking, not homeownership and the formal domestic economy, takes precedence and more frequently symbolizes a female character's ability to produce a loving, safe, and comfortable environment. For instance, the Convent women in Morrison's *Paradise* never bother to obtain official ownership of their home, nor do they follow others' notions of conventional domestic propriety. In Kingsolver's *The Poisonwood Bible*, the mother Orleanna initially hoards her domestic property; after her daughter's death, Orleanna gives it all away. She, too, eventually rejects the premise of domestic property and ownership. *The Poisonwood Bible* also ends with the possibility for redemption. In contrast, Andre Dubus III's *House of Sand and Fog* revolves around homeownership and concludes from an alienated space, with Kathy in jail silently signaling to another inmate for a cigarette and three other characters dead due to the dispute over who legally owns the property.

The presence of ghosts or the evocation of spirits—what Kathleen Brogan defines as "cultural haunting"—frequently distinguishes masculine and feminine domesticities. Brogan explains, "To be haunted in this literature is to know, viscerally, how specific cultural memories that seem to have disappeared in fact refuse to be buried and still shape the present, in desirable and in troubling ways" (Brogan 16). Domestic masculinity tends to resist this haunting, especially when the story is written by and focused on white men; domestic femininity tends to embrace ghostly presences. For instance, while Behrani in *House of Sand and Fog* assures his married daughter, to whom he writes his suicide note, "Your mother and I await you upon your return," he closes with the postscript, "Soraya-joon, live here if you like but if you sell it take no less than one hundred thousand dollars" (Dubus 337). Behrani does not expect to haunt the house he leaves behind—nor has he given up his desire to provide for his family by making the contested house turn a profit.

The masculine and feminine domesticities that I have begun to outline here demonstrate how key gendered and racial distinctions remain operative within American literature and culture. In the following chapters, I analyze these approaches to the home's geography in greater detail to flesh out further the suggestive differences between the various strands of domestic fiction and their influence on our mapping of neodomestic fiction. Given domestic fiction's historical and literary connections to a feminine domesticity, there are advantages and disadvantages to reviving this generic terminology in the twenty-first century.

Redefining Domestic Fiction
(Neo)Domestic Terminology and Spatial Fictions

(Re)claiming domestic fiction for twenty-first-century novels and for women's fiction, in particular, becomes a fraught proposal when we consider previous criticism that argues against this generic moniker for nineteenth-century women's fiction. Domestic fiction's literary history emerges from a cultural anxiety about domesticity and women writers. Like their nineteenth-century predecessors, writers of domestic fiction today struggle against accusations of "excess"—of too much "heart" or sentiment (Harris 5). These features supposedly make them popular but not necessarily "authentic" or "literary" American writers; "literary" authors do not always enjoy the same degree of popular acclaim, but they supposedly write aesthetically superior novels (Harris 5). Certainly, the presence of neodomestic *powerhouse* authors such as Toni Morrison suggests that domestic fiction's status has changed. However, Jonathan Franzen's remarks about Oprah Winfrey's book club, as I explore in chapter 5, remind us of readers' continued anxiety about domestic themes and the negative connotations associated with producing women's fiction and masculine domesticity. Without a doubt, patriarchy depends on strict gender codes and imbues them with gravity as a means to solidify gender, race, and class hierarchies.

Even domestic fiction's advocates are sometimes reluctant to use the term. Both Nina Baym and Susan K. Harris, for instance, caution against the label "domestic fiction" to describe nineteenth-century women's fiction. Baym explains, "the term 'domestic' is not a fixed or neutral word in critical analysis. For many critics, domesticity is equated with entrapment—in an earlier critical generation, of men by women and, more recently, of women by a pernicious ideal promulgated (so the worm turns!) by men" (*Woman's Fiction* 26). In turn, Harris specifically rejects "domestic fiction" as the appropriate descriptor for nineteenth-century women's fiction because the term restricts rather than enhances our understanding of the texts: "My objection to 'sentimental,' 'women's,' and 'domestic' as genre descriptives is that the terms themselves encourage us to continue approaching women's novels of the mid-nineteenth century within a particular hermeneutic that focuses on the social/sexual context and that, consequently, restricts our access to the novels' verbal, structural, and thematic adventures" (Harris 20). Harris goes on to clarify that, unlike Baym, the form that she describes is not exclusively a woman's genre; male writers employ the "exploratory" as well (Harris 20). More recently, Amy Kaplan's term "manifest domesticity" has also raised questions about American domesticity's positive resonance, linking domesticity and the domestic novel with imperialism.

Both Baym and Harris offer cogent arguments against using domestic fiction as an exclusive category to define nineteenth-century women's novels. Kaplan, in turn, reminds us of its imperial connotations. While domesticity's negative and limited connotations should not be ignored or propagated, we also should not underestimate domesticity's continued centrality to American identity and literature. In response to Biddy Martin and Chandra Talpade Mohanty's landmark question about feminist politics—"What's home got to do with it?"—feminist politics and contemporary fiction still have much to do with home.[4] Home contributes to our physical, mental, and economic well being. As Dana Heller writes of the contemporary family romance, domestic fiction also offers feminists "a tool for rewriting and reconnecting with feminist history" (230). Domesticity's fraught connotations need to be engaged and recognized; neodomestic fiction shares this goal. The label "neodomestic" helps mark significant changes in the genre's history while recognizing connections to its literary roots. The term "neodomestic" responds to the criticisms leveled against the label "domestic" by distinguishing the structural differences that characterize the home in narratives that may be removed from one another by more than a century. Therefore, rather than suggest a postfeminist or postgender world, neodomestic fiction's spatial definition and inclusion of male and female writers and protagonists offers opportunities to examine contemporary gender hierarchies.

In essence, I am arguing that a critical emphasis on spatiality should converge with the temporal or plot considerations that have long been a part of the study of American domestic fiction. During the mid-nineteen-eighties, the same period during which neodomestic fiction emerged, Foucault argued in "Of Other Spaces" that "we are at a moment, I believe, when our experience of the world is less that of a long life developing through time than that of a network that connects points and intersects with its own skein" (22).[5] This understanding of time-space relationships resembles some non-Western worldviews, which frequently also do not understand space, narrative, and time as separate concepts. Reading domestic fiction as a spatial narrative takes into account space's influence on and reflection of domestic culture and incorporates non-Western narrative strategies. The shared space of the home and the focus on homemaking, or "the processes by which diverse subjects imagine and make themselves at home in various geographic locations," more than a specific plot sequence, connect these novels (Espiritu 2).

There are several advantages to redefining the genre according to its geographic focus. A focus on "domestic geographies," or various broadly defined "home spaces" and self-conscious homemaking practices, more easily connects a range of domesticities across time and cultures. For instance, domestic practices change with time; specific historical and cultural circumstances frequently merit attention to particular plots. Historical and literary changes, furthermore, make following a common plot across the span of a century or more difficult, if not impossible. When radically different domestic plots emerge—for instance, those that write the home as haven, as seen in Louisa May Alcott's *Little Women* (1868), versus those that depict the home as a trap, as seen in Edith Wharton's *The House of Mirth* (1905)—the domestic plot may be seen to change so dramatically as to not merit a common genre. Hence, a plot-based lens generally affirms domestic fiction's disappearance soon after the Civil War. However, a spatial analysis reveals that the home as haven or trap represents two sides of the same coin: both rely on domestic security.

Moreover, the novel's form changes from largely omnipotent, realistic nineteenth-century narratives to frequently multivocal, (post)modern experiments. As a result of these aesthetic changes in novelistic form, the plot may be less linear in twentieth- and twenty-first-century novels. What remains, despite these aesthetic changes, is a collection of novels that feature a domestic setting and the processes involved in making home. A spatial lens reveals that these novels, like their nineteenth-century predecessors, use the local domestic setting to engage their audiences for "political or moral purposes by (re)presenting political struggles neither in the theater of political institutions (Congress or court) nor in the public arena (the press, town meetings) but in conversations between husbands and wives, parents and children, masters and servants" (Berman 22). This spatial understanding of the genre of domestic fiction provides the foundation for further distinctions and interpretations.

Writing and analyzing domestic literary history from this spatial perspective allows us to consider the links and disjunctions among a range of authors writing about the construction of home during the same period as well as across centuries and cultures. A spatial approach includes female and male writers and protagonists and centers the African American women's novels that Claudia Tate analyzes in *Domestic Allegories of Political Desire: The Black Heroine's Text at the Turn of the Century*. The resistance initiated by women of color, as Iris Marion Young argues, is "integral to modern political theory and is not an alternative to it" (306). Herein lie the generic taproots of what eventually becomes neodomestic fiction. That is, such "alternative" narratives—when read in the context of contemporary neodomestic fiction—are not *marginal* but rather are *central* to domesticity's reconfigurations.

The domestic novel, after all, did not die after the Civil War but underwent a renaissance within African American women's literature. Tate demonstrates in her study how African American women writers deployed domestic fiction "to promote the social advancement of African Americans" after the Civil War (Tate 5). Where many white women writers changed domestic plots after the Civil War, black women writers appropriated the white domestic form for their own enfranchisement. Along these lines, Kate McCullough argues that Pauline E. Hopkins recycled the domestic novel for her own ends: "Rewriting an erased history specifically through figures of African-American womanhood—primarily mulatto members of the bourgeoisie but also the working-class business woman—Hopkins produced a new version of African-American womanhood and simultaneously made it clear that 'America' had always included her, even if in an elided form" (94). While some critics understand Hopkins's use of the domestic form as "a sell-out to white America encoded in the white bourgeois genre of the sentimental novel," McCullough and others place Hopkins "in a line of

African-American writers—Hopkins's contemporary Frances Harper or her predecessors Harriet Wilson and Harriet Jacobs, for instance—who use sentimental forms as a means of cultural intervention" (McCullough 98; 99).[6] African American writers like Hopkins have not simply reproduced domestic fiction's conventional ideology; rather, they have been among the first to recycle and revise it for their own political ends.

Nineteenth-century African American women writers' adoption of the sentimental, domestic form emphasizes that neodomestic fiction represents an intensification of narrative practices and tensions that have been present since domestic fiction's inception. A character like the tomboy Jo in *Little Women* signals that even during the nineteenth century, a narrow model of domesticity produced tensions that white domestic fiction had to resolve. Alcott complicates the home as a separate sphere and as a space that follows conventional domestic ideology lockstep when she transforms the home into temporary performance spaces and, through the Pickwick Club's newsletter, makes it a "news worthy" place. Such examples emphasize that nineteenth-century writers like Pauline E. Hopkins and Louisa May Alcott did not simply produce domestic fiction; they used its ideology for their own political ends. Neodomestic fiction eventually emerges from such sustained efforts by writers ranging from Pauline E. Hopkins, María Amparo Ruiz de Burton, and Louisa May Alcott in the nineteenth century to Edith Wharton, Gertrude Stein, Ann Petry, and Paule Marshall in the early twentieth century. Neodomesticity's distinct ideology and spatiality materializes from these nineteenth- and early twentieth-century domestic novels.

Neodomestic Fiction
A Distinct Ideological Map

While they share domestic settings and a concern with homemaking, neodomestic novels craft distinctive model homes. Conventional domestic prose specifies white Protestant domesticity as the ideal domestic model and seeks to stabilize and produce this model in the midst of American diversity. Barbara Welter clarifies that the "four cardinal virtues—piety, purity, submissiveness and domesticity"—define True Womanhood and domestic ideals (if not realities) in the nineteenth century (21). Finding the proper home frequently stabilizes the protagonist's identity and her domestic life. The home, in this sense, serves as a metaphor for the protagonist's development. If she is successful, she is rewarded with a home and marriage, or at least the promise of such, as seen in the conclusion of Susan Warner's *The Wide, Wide World*

(1850). While domestic fiction such as *The Wide, Wide World* may begin in or move through positions of instability, its heroine ultimately seeks some type of domestic stability. Warner's novel offers a quintessentially feminine domestic tale focused on a single young woman's struggle to find and make home.

Nearly as popular in the nineteenth century as Harriet Beecher Stowe's *Uncle Tom's Cabin* (1852), *The Wide, Wide World* follows the experiences of the orphaned Ellen Montgomery.[7] Her search for home is a lesson in Christian selflessness and patience as well as in proper American homemaking. At the story's conclusion, Ellen is living with Scottish relatives, and we understand that she eventually marries John. While we do not get a marriage in the novel, the novel's conclusion is written so as to set the reader's mind at ease about Ellen's future: "In other words, to speak intelligibly, Ellen did in no wise disappoint" (Warner 569). By contrast, death and the denial of home function as a punishment; or, on occasion, an ideal woman is brought "home" to God through death. The deaths of Ellen's mother in *The Wide, Wide World* and of Beth in *Little Women* function as the latter.[8]

Nineteenth-century domestic fictions emerge from a cultural context in which slavery, immigration, and America's expanding borders granted special urgency to the need to stabilize and "unionize" the American family. America's shifting demographics and national borders in the nineteenth century simultaneously expanded the home and produced anxiety about the "foreign" bodies that were newly incorporated into the national union. Kaplan explains that the ideal of "economical, healthful, beautiful, and Christian homes" was bound up in a project of "manifest domesticity," in which American imperialism and model domesticity worked hand-in-hand: "Adherence to [the] woman's sphere guarantees adhesion to the larger family of the Union" (Kaplan 24). The feminine, orderly home, thus counters the disorder created by such forces as the annexation of new territories, slavery, and immigration.

The ideology of the conventional model seeks to stabilize and homogenize diverse bodies and homemaking practices. Ann Romines agrees, suggesting that housekeeping, which often takes on a "godlike status" in nineteenth-century domestic fiction, provides women with a means of control (10). Jennifer Haytock also agrees with this characterization of conventional domesticity (xii). These frequently "illusory" notions of a stable model domesticity do not end with the nineteenth century and the rise of modernism (Haytock xii). Even novels that mark the emergence of the new woman and new domestic forms frequently continue to emphasize stability. For example, the conclusion to *Ruth Hall* (1855) sets the protagonists on the road but also assures the reader that "life has much of harmony yet in store for you" (Fern 211).

The modern period represents a significant transitional point in portrayals of the home and domestic ideology. As Thomas Foster explains in *Transformations of Domesticity in Modern Women's Writing*, "Modernist women's writing . . . should be read as a transitional moment between nineteenth-century domestic ideologies and postmodern concepts of space, when those two sets of assumptions about space and gender can still be read in relation to one another" (3). Modern domestic fictions form an "interspace"—a place between conventional and neodomestic ideologies. The modern period encompasses both the freedoms associated with the jazz age and the repressions tied to the red scare.

The persistent power of conventional domesticity in the first half of the twentieth century is apparent in the names of popular Sears mail-order houses. The names continue to "speak of the desire for assimilation" and the need for broader, more diverse conceptions of model domesticity. "'The Yale,' 'The Franklin,' 'The Portsmouth,' 'The Hamilton,' and 'The Atterbury' might be modest bungalows, colonials, or Cape Cods, but they had upper-class white Anglo-Saxon Protestant names. In the 1919 Aladdin catalog, even the small garages had names such as 'The Peerless,' 'The Winton,' 'The Maxwell,' and 'The Packard'" (Hayden, *Building Suburbia* 106; 110). These names indicate how conventional domesticity is threatened by the uncertainty and instability that diversity fosters, especially as familial diversity allegedly threatens "the good influence of society" (Bush) in the twenty-first century or "the refinements of high civilization" (Beecher and Stowe 441) in the nineteenth century.[9]

The lasting and powerful influence of conventional American domesticity is further demonstrated by the fact that white women have been the leading domestic icons of the nineteenth, twentieth, and twenty-first centuries. The New England domestic ideals promoted by Catharine E. Beecher and Harriet Beecher Stowe in the nineteenth century live on in the model domesticity televised by fellow New Englander Martha Stewart. Emily Jane Cohen emphasizes, "As the cradle of American civilization, New England was every American's home. It was the birthplace of our first cookbook, of the domestic school of romance, and of the science of home economics, which tried to give housekeeping a respectable name" (655–56). Hortense Spillers further explains model domesticity's patriarchal and racial traits: "Domesticity appears to gain its power by way of a common origin of cultural fictions that are grounded in the specificity of proper names, more exactly, a patronymic, which, in turn, situates those persons it 'covers' in a particular place" (72). This patriarchal domesticity practices "the *vertical transfer* of a bloodline, of a patronymic, of titles and entitlements, of real estate" and, as a result, "becomes the mythically revered privilege of a free and freed community" (Spillers 74; emphasis in original). Model American domesticity, thus, reveals and promotes white privilege: "Physical and psychological security of place is . . . a rare and privileged fate that many women have never experienced" (Gathorne-Hardy 125). Contemporary culture's continued psychological and material investment in the model domesticity represented by popular domestic icons exposes its literal and figurative investment in "white houses"—the domestic spaces, practices, and ideals buttressed by or dependent on white privilege. Rather than seeking access to this model, neodomestic fiction "gain[s] the *insurgent* ground" (Spillers 80; emphasis in original).

What makes neodomestic fiction unique is that it recycles these longstanding tensions in ways that promote, rather than attempt to resolve, instability and heterogeneity. Neodomestic fiction's distinct ideology and geography tend to maintain instability. The home's characteristic instability can be broken down into three interrelated traits or specific spatial practices that define the neodomestic narrative: (1) "mobility," bell hooks's notion that home is not one place but locations (*Yearning* 148); (2) "relational space," an understanding that the domestic sphere depends on "outside" or "foreign" relations and vice versa; and (3) "renovation" or "redesign," the active construction and (re)design of the (conventional) domestic sphere and its concomitant effects on community and the self. These distinctive features highlight how neodomestic novels redesign what architectural historian Dolores Hayden describes in *Redesigning the American Dream* as the "architecture of gender" (34). The "architecture of gender" refers to how the home's spatial design, or in this case its narrative design, prescribes restrictive gender roles for both men and women. Neodomestic novels, furthermore, expand Hayden's paradigm to explore the genre's architectures of gender, race, sexuality, and class.

Neodomestic novels map a revised generic conception of domesticity that self-consciously addresses the ways in which various Americans have been (dis)enfranchised. As a result, instability becomes an ideological and architectural attribute. The protagonists in both *Housekeeping* and *Breaking and Entering*, for example, remain drifters. They are not recontained within conventional domestic norms, which also means there is no guarantee at the end of these novels that "life has much . . . harmony in store" (Fern 211). Neodomestic fiction also highlights the home's social relations rather than (re)inscribing stable divisions between public and private spaces. For example, the Puente's converted warehouse home in Cristina Garcia's *Dreaming in*

Cuban (1992) combines commercial space and private residence, and Sylvie's homemaking in Marilynne Robinson's *Housekeeping* (1981) breaks down the barriers between the natural and domestic worlds. Sylvie's methods prepare the home for "wasps and bats and barn swallows" as well as for human occupants (Robinson 74).[10]

In Loida Maritza Pérez's *Geographies of Home* (1999), we also see how instability develops as an ideology and as an architectural feature. In *Geographies of Home*, the female protagonist's family home is "stable" because it is comforting and recognizable: "This was home: safe and familiar" (Pérez 27). The home is also profoundly "unstable" because it is the location where the protagonist's mentally disturbed sister sexually assaults her (Pérez 292–94). The neodomestic home remains politically charged: neither fully a haven nor a trap, these spaces explore and explode conventional binary oppositions.

Domestic fiction in the nineteenth century also responds architecturally and structurally to the domestic problems that produce instability. As Kaplan notes, "Many domestic novels open at physical thresholds—such as windows or doorways—to problematize the relation between interiors and exteriors" (43). These transitional, unstable beginnings position domesticity's turmoil within the architecture of the home and within the plot's structure. Neodomestic protagonists reconfigure these domestic thresholds; rather than becoming recontained by the domestic narrative's structure and the home, neodomestic protagonists embrace and invent "spaces of radical openness" (hooks, *Yearning* 148). "For me," bell hooks writes, "this space of radical openness is a margin—a profound edge. Locating oneself there is difficult yet necessary. It is not a 'safe' place. One is always at risk" (*Yearning* 149). The threshold becomes a homeplace: "One's homeplace was the one site where one could freely confront the issue of humanization, where one could resist" (hooks, *Yearning* 42). The neodomestic protagonist seeks to construct what hooks names the "margin," what Morrison calls "home," and what Gloria Anzaldúa describes as the "borderlands." Thus, rather than eliminate or stabilize the crossroads—the narrative's literal and figurative thresholds—neodomestic fiction seeks "a place 'already made for me, both snug and wide open. With a doorway never needing to be closed'" (Morrison, "Home" 9).

Neodomestic politics, as a result, play up the home's relational, unstable nature (rather than its homogenizing properties) and recycle the genre's didacticism. Kingsolver's statement in *Small Wonder*, "Home is where all justice begins," can be seen as a recycled version of nineteenth-century didacticism and notions about domesticity and the home's political place (201). Carolyn Vellenga Berman summarizes domestic fiction's political force: "Domestic novels . . . reshaped political communities both by their structures of address and by their content. By modeling and critiquing contemporary modes of sexual and family life, family-orientated fictions established not only who belonged in the (national) community they addressed but also how the (national) community would reproduce itself" (Berman 19–20). The neodomestic home experiments with open security. Neodomestic fiction's first novels help us understand this seemingly contradictory architecture of home.

Neodomestic Thresholds
Housekeeping and *The House on Mango Street*

Two threshold neodomestic novels from the early 1980s are Marilynne Robinson's *Housekeeping* (1981) and Sandra Cisneros's *The House on Mango Street* (1984). Up until this point, domestic fiction tended to categorize the home as either a haven or a trap, a dichotomy predicated on domestic stability. Robinson's novel presents one of the first American domestic novels to reject strongly conventional domestic stability. The novel's title together with the orphan girls in search of a home emphasize *Housekeeping*'s rewriting or recycling of conventional domestic ideology and fiction. Sylvie's unconventional homemaking and the resulting domestic geography emphasize its status as an unusual domestic fiction.

In *Housekeeping*, Sylvie takes over the care of Ruth and her younger sister Lucille after their father abandons them, their mother commits suicide, their grandmother dies, and two other relatives seek to be relieved of their young charges. With Sylvie at the head of the household, the family home changes from an ordered space of "habit and familiarity" to a disordered space that blurs the boundaries between inside and outside, where "leaves began to gather in the corners" of the rooms (Robinson 28; 73). Sylvie's housekeeping exhibits subversive, comic, and tragic features. The kitchen, for example, has a scorched curtain that was "half consumed by fire once when a birthday cake had been set too close to it. Sylvie had beaten out the flames with a back issue of *Good Housekeeping*" (Robinson 87). Sylvie's "antihousekeeping" creates both freedom and a potentially dangerous instability for the two young girls: "But it was not the pleasures of home at suppertime that lured us back to Sylvie's house. Say rather that the cold forced me home, and that the dark allowed Lucille to pass through the tattered peripheries of Fingerbone unobserved" (Robinson 85). This passage hints that the young girls do not feel loved and secure; they have too much freedom and instability. Lucille eventually seeks domestic security and regularity by moving in with her home economics teacher. Ruth follows Sylvie's lead and becomes a transient, helping Sylvie set fire to the house before hitting the road. The fire "puts an end to housekeeping," a result that seems liberatory because of the ways that domestic responsibilities can entrap women; yet the ending also suggests a darker side to leaving the home-as-haven behind (Robinson 179).

Housekeeping's status as a threshold neodomestic text becomes more apparent when we consider how the novel questions the antidomestic promise of emancipation. The novel complicates the haven-trap binary. Leaving housekeeping behind does not ensure a better life. Christine Caver's essay tempers celebratory readings of the novel's resistant qualities, arguing that Ruth, *Housekeeping*'s narrator, ends the story not as a liberated outsider but instead as someone with an "ontologically uncertain status—socially, if not literally, dead" (133).[11] Ruth and Sylvie's indeterminate status at the end of the novel leaves open the possibility that they are not "drifting" through the countryside but rather are dead at the bottom of the lake (Robinson 180). The fact that the ending is not clearly positive or freeing, however, does not disqualify *Housekeeping* from initiating the neodomestic novel.

Housekeeping exhibits all the hallmarks of the neodomestic novel. A significant portion of the narrative takes place in the home, and that home exhibits domestic instability and a rewriting of conventional homemaking through Sylvie's transient housekeeping and the characters' mobility. Once Sylvie comes to live with the girls, the home exhibits a relational construction with the outdoors—blurring the boundaries between the natural and domestic worlds. The ways in which Sylvie's housekeeping renovates conventional methods, furthermore, changes the home's physical structure: "it seemed that if the house were not to founder, it must soon begin to float" (107). The home is unstable. These qualities, together with the novel's self-conscious construction of the home and homemaking, introduce neodomestic fiction's defining features of domestic instability and recycling. Significantly, Sylvie's and Ruth's transience marks their privileges as white women. Like the protagonists in *Breaking and Entering*, their transience is voluntary rather than forced. They consciously leave behind a physical home.

Following on the heels of *Housekeeping*, *The House on Mango Street* also exhibits neodomesticity's major tenets and a critical self-awareness of the exclusions produced by the conventional single-family home. The narrator's imaginative home destabilizes the domestic trap constructed by patriarchal notions about women. The house, for example, has "windows so small you'd think they were holding their breath. . . . [A]nd the front door is so swollen you have to push hard to get in" (4). The home is both difficult to gain entry into and, once inside, difficult to escape. *Mango Street*'s narrator, Esperanza, represents the one who might break a cycle of female disenfranchisement and entrapment. Such women can inhabit the threshold without being recontained by the home; they can freely move between worlds. This ideal space embodies a safe fluidity between inside and outside.

Housekeeping complicates the domestic freedom and security binary; the house on Mango Street, likewise, is portrayed as both a haven and a trap. The narrator's assessment of her house on Mango Street reveals the economic and social improvements that the house represents to her Chicano family, but her remarks also expose how the house falls short of her family's dream home: "But the house on Mango Street is not the way they told it at all" (Cisneros 4). Homeownership does not result in the achievement of the American dream. Written as a response to Bachelard's poetics of space, *The House on Mango Street* crafts a spatial poetics relevant to its Chicana protagonist.[12] Mango Street's name, as Julián Olivares notes, marks the narrator's "circumscribe[d] . . . neighborhood . . . [for] its Latino population of Puerto Ricans, Chicanos and Mexican immigrants" (162). This raced, less-than-ideal home is contrasted with the home Esperanza hopes to inhabit someday. Her model "real house," however, does not simply modify conventional domesticity (Cisneros 5): "the narrator transgresses both against the norms for women that prevail within her community as well as against the myth of the American dream" (Salazar 393). Esperanza rewrites the dream home.

The House on Mango Street ultimately offers a more clearly positive outlook for conventional domesticity's redefinition than *Housekeeping*. Esperanza, the protagonist, openly embodies hope. "Esperanza" means "hope" as well as "waiting" in Spanish (Cisneros 10–11). As an embodiment of hope, Esperanza is determined not to live in the same homes as the women around her, who lead such trapped and contained lives that they are always standing in doorways and peering out windows (Cisneros 11; 23–4; 79; 81; 102). These women spatially and thematically recall the conventional domestic protagonists who frequently appear in doorways and thresholds in nineteenth-century novels.[13] Esperanza also occupies a metaphorical threshold; she dreams of a house that she will not be ashamed to admit is hers and that will not force her to conform to the Chicano patriarchal notions of femininity that many of the other women in the narrative exemplify.

Esperanza, like many of her nineteenth-century predecessors, is on a journey to find home—what Inés Salazar calls "a metaphysical journey, undertaken through her writing" (394). While her model home remains in an imaginary realm—unrealized like Selina's ideal home in Paule Marshall's *Brown Girl, Brownstones* (1959)—the novel presents a strong indication that her dreams will not only be realized but that she has returned for those left behind: "I have gone away to come back. For the ones I left behind. For the ones who cannot out" (Cisneros 110). The use of the past tense marks her return. The "ones" seem to refer to the trapped women whom the narrative introduces, such as Alicia (31–32), Rafaela (79–80), Sally (81–83; 92–93; 101–2), and Minerva (84–85).

Selina in Marshall's *Brown Girl, Brownstones*, in fact, represents the narrative mother or grandmother for later female neodomestic protagonists such as the narrator in *The House on Mango Street*. Like *Mango Street*, *Brown Girl, Brownstones* explores the theme of homeownership and the American dream amid a young girl's coming of age story. Like Esperanza, Selina experiences her home as a trap. When she escapes her home's bounds, for example, "Selina knew. She had finally passed the narrow boundary of herself and her world. She could no longer be measured by Chauncey Street or the park or the nearby school. 'Lord,' she whispered behind her hand, 'I'm free'" (56). As a young woman, Selina feels trapped by her domestic surroundings and by the domesticated life that she seems doomed to live. Selina sees her fate—in her sister's menstruation pains and her mother's household management—and attempts to find routes out of this trap. The novel's final image of the torn-down brownstones sears a haunting picture in the reader's imagination.

When Selina tosses one of her signature bangles into a brownstone, which is being leveled for a new city housing project, we can understand this gesture as Selina's homage to her imperfect community. The wrecked buildings represent those within the Barbadian community, like her mother, who are the most trapped and broken. Selina imagines "seeing the bodies of all the people she had ever known broken, all the familiar voices that had ever sounded in those high-ceilinged rooms shattered—and the pieces piled into this giant cairn of stone and silence" (Marshall 310). Selina's bangle makes "A frail sound in that utter silence," suggesting that she may go on to create and experience a different end by giving voice to this silence (Marshall 310).

Esperanza's narrative picks up where Selina's ends. Esperanza speaks in the language of a community-based domestic ideology, narrating a clear plan for her revised home and homemaking. She will take in homeless people, for example, and not reproduce the private, exclusionary, single-family dwelling: "One day I'll own my own house, but I won't forget who I am or where I came from. Passing bums will ask, Can I come in? I'll offer them the attic, ask them to stay, because I know how it is to be without a house" (Cisneros 87). When Esperanza achieves her private, single-family dwelling, she will recycle its properties to fit her own needs and those of her community. She clearly plans to achieve "the adaptation of suburban house forms to new uses" that Dolores Hayden calls for in *Redesigning the American Dream* (222–224). She envisions a plan to recycle the privately owned, single-family dwelling in ways that will better respond to the crisis in affordable and accessible housing. Thus, Esperanza represents the girls who will get out of the patriarchal domestic trap; the house on Mango Street represents "the house I belong but do not belong to" (Cisneros 110). Esperanza is not possessed; rather, she controls her domesticity.

The overwhelming critical response to both *Housekeeping* and *The House on Mango Street* indicates a collective desire for and an anticipation of novels that write women beyond both the domestic trap and haven. This longing may be framed in the question Christine Caver poses: "how long will it be until women who flee an abusive or repressive system are allowed to escape the last frame alive?" (133). Toni Morrison's *Paradise* picks up on this longing, beginning its story with the "final frame" of women fleeing for their lives. In *Paradise*'s real conclusion, as in *Housekeeping* and *Breaking and Entering*, the women's physical status is unclear. Are they alive or are they ghosts? Although focused on a male protagonist, Chang-rae Lee's *A Gesture Life* also ends similarly unresolved; the novel concludes with Franklin "Doc" Hata at a border, on the "outside looking in . . . Come almost home" (356). *The Poisonwood Bible*'s conclusion, moreover, questions whether the Congolese village of Kilanga even existed. From Esperanza's ideal home to the haunted house in *Beloved*, such "ghostly" or spiritual geographies emphasize that neodomestic novels often highlight instability through such inconclusive conclusions. Out of what cultural context do these ambivalent endings and neodomestic fiction more generally emerge?

(Neo)Domesticity's Cultural Foundations

The dual explosion in attention to domesticity in the nineteenth and early twenty-first centuries helps explain domestic fiction's twin renaissances. It also provides opportunities to compare what constitutes the model home and to what extent homeownership, a key symbol of the American dream's achievement, has changed. The nineteenth century, for example, saw the rise of domestic fiction and domestic science. The late twentieth century marks a steep rise in home improvement shows and networks, cooking personalities and networks, the sustained success and growth of shelter magazines, and the expansion of big-box home improvement outlets. Additionally, the crisis in family values that Catharine E. Beecher describes in the conclusion of *American Woman's Home* resembles our own so-called "crisis of the family" (463–70). A resurgence in "traditional" family rhetoric began in the 1980s and continues through the present moment. Where Beecher worried about the harmful effects of woman's rights conventions and free love, our own communities and government officials debate abortion and gay marriage. Furthermore, the anxieties that Beecher, Stowe, and other nineteenth-century domestic authors have expressed about foreign families and servants resonates in our own age in which foreign(er) and terror(ist) are closely aligned. Just as in the nineteenth century, a significant nexus of literary and cultural events have intensified in post-1980 American culture, including neoconservatism, neoliberalism, the new urbanism movement, and the aftermaths of 9/11 and Hurricane Katrina. The rise and aftereffects of second-wave feminism also provide the context for the proliferation of neodomestic fictions.

While the first- and second-wave feminist movements inaugurated significant changes in gender roles, domestic fiction's continued status as a gendered genre reflects our gendered lives. Today, for example, studies indicate that the majority of women who work outside the home start a second shift when they return home, functioning as the family's primary caregiver and domestic laborer. According to one survey, "married women spend forty hours a week on household chores, compared to seventeen for men" (Domosh and Seager 2). Such statistics continue to speak to the need to rethink gender roles, especially as they play out in the domestic sphere. These statistics also help account for why many women writers remain invested in the domestic sphere and its informal economy.

Conventional domesticity's twenty-first-century revival, furthermore, continues the promotion of stereotypical roles related to gender, sex, class, and race. For example, while denying marriage to homosexual couples, the second Bush administration concurrently promoted marriage for heterosexuals, especially for low-income couples. Emerging after the racist and sexist "welfare queen" rhetoric that intensified during the latter half of the twentieth century with the Clinton administration's efforts to reform welfare, this argument claims that Christian marriage improves the lives of unmarried, low-income Americans—especially poor, unmarried mothers. Building on controversial research that demonstrates "married people experience less poverty than single people, and that children of two-parent households tend to fare better overall than children of single-parent households," the marriage initiative earmarked $1.5 billion for "counseling services, public awareness campaigns and marriage enrichment courses intended to foster 'healthy marriages' among the poor" (Zeller 4.3).

Before contemporary welfare programs, nineteenth-century Christian women had the "peculiar" domestic privilege and responsibility "to lift up the fallen, to sustain the weak, to protect the tempted, to bind up the broken-hearted, and especially to rescue the sinful" (Beecher and Stowe 433). Today the institution of heterosexual Christian union, bolstered and policed by the U.S. government, similarly aims to build a better America among the impoverished: "'If you have a single mom making good choices and she marries a good man,' said the Rev. Ted Haggard, president of the National Association of Evangelicals, 'then it's not long before they're driving a better car and living in a better home and the child is better off and they become an asset to society rather than a drain on society'" (qtd. in Zeller 4.3). According to this logic, the model Christian home structures American culture and strengthens the nation's economic health.

Notably, Haggard's narrative does not challenge conventional gender or sex roles: women remain primary caregivers, men act primarily as economic providers, and financially beneficial unions can only take place within a legal, heterosexual marriage. Haggard's narrative fails, too, to recognize that women—regardless of economic status—are most at risk for violence within their own homes. Ostensibly, healthy-marriage training alleviates such risk factors; however, as Doreen Massey and Pat Jess write, "For many women . . . the home is a site of hard work and perhaps physical and sexual abuse; for some, only by leaving such homes can they find a place in which to belong" (90). Real-life, single mothers can now make temporary "until better times do us part" cohousing arrangements at CoAbode, a nonprofit matchmaking service for single mothers (Pace, qtd. in Ydstie).[14] The redesigned alliances that conclude neodomestic novels also invent or recycle alternatives out of the conventional (white) heterosexual marriage as well as represent and theorize "real life" alternatives.[15]

Neodomestic fiction emerges out of a cultural landscape marked by a crisis in access to affordable housing. The 1980s inaugurated an especially dark period for many seeking homeownership: "After 50 years of steady and uninterrupted progress, the percentage of blacks who own their homes suddenly and unexpectedly declined in the 1980s. A continuation of this trend would reinforce the position of America's blacks at the margin of America's propertied society" ("Decline" 19). Such setbacks, combined with the developments within domestic fiction during the modern period and the rise of homelessness under the Reagan administration, help contextualize the cultural landscape out of which neodomestic fiction emerges.

Suburban development in the nineteenth and twentieth centuries is also significant to the emergence of neodomestic fiction because it helped solidify the American ideal of a privately owned, single-family dwelling. The popularity of gated communities, furthermore, emphasizes the strong hold oppositional spatial politics continue to have on American housing practices and desires, especially since 1980: "In the 1980s, upscale real estate speculation and the trend to conspicuous consumption saw the proliferation of gated communities around golf courses that were designed for exclusivity, prestige, and leisure. The decade also marked the emergence of gated communities built primarily out of fear, as the public became increasingly preoccupied with violent crime" (Blakely and Snyder 4–5).[16] As Witold Rybczynski points out in *Last Harvest*, gated communities still account for only a small percentage of communities and most of the time the gates are left open (132). Nevertheless, their rise in popularity in the 1980s supports my argument that this period marks a watershed moment for American domesticity. While oppositional spatial politics such as segregation and exclusionary housing practices are present throughout the nineteenth and twentieth centuries, we see once again in the 1980s a renewed intensification of longstanding domestic fears and a renewed desire for a safe home. As D. A. Leslie suggests, the era is marked by a "New Traditionalism."

Neodomestic fiction reflects, provokes, and theorizes distinctive responses to conservative visions of the contemporary home and family. Notably—but not surprisingly, given the historical and cultural context I have briefly outlined—when such neodomestic recycling appears, it is frequently perceived as un-American. For example, Mrs. Nguyen's "refugee" housekeeping in Lan Cao's *Monkey Bridge* (1997) seems so different from the conventional American model that her daughter does not even recognize it as American. Mrs. Nguyen's daughter describes her mom's "un-American" housekeeping:

> Our apartment was so different. My mother wanted it maintained as a mere way station, rootlessly sparse since the day of our arrival. . . . She had even taken American disposability a step backward with her special kind of twist. Plastic spoons and knives, picnic plates and Ziploc bags, tin foil and Styrofoam cups, these were all modern-day inventions my mother had decided to reinvent, the refugee way.
>
> Why should something be discarded just because it's designed to be disposable? In our kitchen, my mother hand-washed plastic forks and knives. She saved used clingwraps and aluminum foil. (91–92)

Mrs. Nguyen recycles, literally and figuratively. She recycles Beecher and Stowe's call for thrift—a principle largely lost in America's contemporary emphasis on materialism. According to Beecher and Stowe, "a child should be brought up with the determined principle, never to *run in debt*, but to be content to live in a humbler way, in order to secure that true independence, which should be the noblest distinction of an American citizen" (285; emphasis in original). Mrs. Nguyen transforms this Protestant ideal into a mobile, "refugee" style of homemaking.

We see a similar scene of recycling the flotsam of white American domesticity in Leslie Marmon Silko's *Gardens in the Dunes*. At the beginning of this novel, the narrator describes the housekeeping practices of the matriarchal family of Grandma Fleet, Mama, and Mama's two daughters, Sister Salt and Indigo. In addition to gathering grains and grasses for subsistence and basket weaving, Grandma Fleet and her granddaughter Indigo

> walk though the town dump, where they surveyed the refuse and Indigo scrambled down the sides of the garbage pits to retrieve valuables the townspeople carelessly threw away. String, paper, scraps of cloth, glass jars and bottles, tin cans, and bits of wire—they washed their discoveries in the shallows of the river and reused them. Grandma Fleet saved seeds discarded from vegetables and fruits to plant at the old gardens when they returned; she poked her stick through the debris in garbage piles behind the café and hotel. (22)

The scene demonstrates how those living at the margins of dominant society survive. Grandma Fleet and Indigo literally live off the white community's trash, which highlights the community's wastefulness and the Sand Lizard's ingenuity. Their homemaking also marks them as not fully American; hence the "need" to send Native children to boarding schools and away from "dangerous" domestic habits.

Dorothy Allison's *Bastard Out of Carolina* (1992) similarly features a scene that involves literal recycling (Allison 180–87). In this scene, members of the protagonist's "white trash" family troll the river that passes Aunt Raylene's house for useable items. Some things Aunt Raylene keeps and others are cleaned and patched and sold during the weekend on the side of the road. Like the Sand Lizard family, Bone's "white trash" family occupies society's margins and lives off its trash. The community also considers them "trash." When Aunt Raylene proclaims that "trash rises. . . . Out here where no one can mess with it, trash rises all the time," she speaks of the literal trash that rises out of the bend in the river and also of her family that lives at society's margins (Allison 180). The margin affords a certain amount of freedom that Aunt Raylene as well as the other characters embrace when they engage in recycling. Domestic thrift and living on the margin both empowers these characters and marks them as outsiders.

Thus, conventional domesticity's call for thrift should not be overidealized. It remains distinct from neodomestic forms of both recycling and questioning the dominant domestic consumer culture. As Hayden reminds us, "Beecher also became an early advocate of household consumption as necessary to a capitalist economy, recommending the use of multiple consumer goods, or 'superfluities,' in order 'to promote industry, virtue and religion' by keeping people employed in diverse kinds of production" (*Building Suburbia* 41–2). In contrast, Mrs. Nguyen models an alternative to rampant American consumerist consumption and its disposable domesticity. The fastidious recycling and stance against clutter produce an alternative domestic aesthetics that is "rootless" or mobile while also reasserting a kind of financial and environmental stability by stopping (or at least reducing) the cycle of disposable domesticity. This cycle causes her daughter to label Mrs. Nguyen's housekeeping un-American, and the same cycle keeps the Sand Lizard and "white trash" families relegated to outsider status. They live as refugees in their own lands; their largely forced domestic mobility has empowering and oppressive characteristics.

Neodomestic fiction emerges out of such historical and contemporary contexts, exposes conventional domesticity's limitations, and seeks alternatives to the prevailing model. Where conventional domestic ideology—whether expressed in the nineteenth or twentieth century—consistently responds to instability by homogenizing homemaking and patrolling domestic borders, neodomesticity experiments with instability and porous margins. It theorizes and represents a distinctive set of alternative domestic modes. Where conventional domestic discourses about union mask some exclusions (such as those associated with white privilege) and clarify other exclusions (such as the prohibition against the "foreign bodies" of homosexuals), neodomestic discourses self-consciously consider the historical and contemporary factors contributing to the home's definition and its associated privileges. Orleanna's question in *The Poisonwood Bible* is an example of this self-consciousness, which white women writers and privileged Americans increasingly encounter: "There's only one question worth asking now: How do we aim to live with it?" (Kingsolver 9). Orleanna asks: how do we live with this conventional ideal, given its exclusions and its pervasiveness in American culture? As I explore in the next chapter, historically conscious recycling constitutes one response. Neodomestic fiction theorizes and represents alternatives to a homogenizing union—to the continued production of a conventional domesticity to the exclusion of other domesticities and people.

2

Recycling Feminine Domesticity

Rewriting Conventional Domestic Fiction

All domestic fictions agree with the March family housekeeper's tidy summation in *Little Women*: "Housekeeping ain't no joke" (Alcott 114). As I outlined in the previous chapter, how the serious business of keeping house plays out in individual novels reflects the novels' distinct historical milieus as well as reveals significant generic and ideological connections and revisions. This chapter further demonstrates that, although domestic fiction's politics shift in the 1980s, useful links emerge when we compare the domestic cultures and fictions of the nineteenth century with those of the twenty-first century. The domestic cultures and novels of these periods invite "a network that connects points and intersects with its own skein" (Foucault, "Of Other Spaces" 22). This domestic palimpsest layers domestic history—literary and cultural—in the narrative and in the physical space of the home. We see this palimpsest in the ways that neodomestic fiction rewrites domesticity's narrative tropes. Responding to the genre's imperial and racist histories as well as to the revived interest in conservative family definitions and politics, neodomestic fiction recycles domestic fiction's didactic turn and its gendered protagonists, ideology, and settings for its own ideological ends. Neodomestic fiction self-consciously reshapes the ways domestic space and fiction function. The sum total of these revisions produces a distinct subgenre, which in its most extreme form figuratively and literally rewrites nineteenth-century domestic texts, crafting reconfigured narrative spaces.

How neodomestic novels rewrite this generic space is the focus of this chapter. The chapter features Leslie Marmon Silko's *Gardens in the Dunes* and Barbara Kingsolver's *The Poisonwood Bible* because of their hyper-revising of nineteenth-century domestic fiction and culture. This chapter also primarily focuses on women's novels, or fiction written by and primarily focused on female protagonists. The focus on women's (neo)domestic fiction allows us to examine the specific shared and distinctive characteristics of this traditionally gendered genre. It also reflects women writers' continued investment in women's experiences and in the genre of women's fiction and how gender remains an important and distinctive lens for understanding domestic fiction and American literature and culture more broadly.

Neodomestic Fiction
A Blueprint for Recycling

Novels written after 1980 are by no means the first to recycle and revise domestic models. Domestic space in the nineteenth and twentieth centuries offers a theater for a highly charged battle to more firmly establish or unseat white Protestant domesticity. In the nineteenth and early twentieth centuries, Native American women, such as Sarah Winnemucca Hopkins (*Life among the Piutes: Their Wrongs and Claims*, 1883) and Zitkala-Sa (*American Indian Stories*, 1921), narrate the exacting costs of acculturating to white American domestic norms, and African American women, such as Harriet Jacobs (*Incidents in the Life of a Slave Girl*, 1861), describe the barriers erected against access to American domestic ideals.[1] Pauline E. Hopkins and María Amparo Ruiz de Burton also negotiated responses to dominant white domesticity. Such "alternative" voices struggled against being subsumed by the dominant American domestic ideology and culture that often denigrated other domesticities in order to establish and advance white domesticity.

Leslie Marmon Silko's novel *Gardens in the Dunes* continues this tradition developed by women of color by reimagining conventional narrative frames. Silko's novel epitomizes the notion of recycling "past domestic edifices" (George, "Recycling" 2) by crafting a literal return to the nineteenth century and revising the period's popular genres. Angelika Köhler, in fact, describes Silko's novel according to this neodomestic formula: "Silko's characters are in search of their individual homes, the places where historical rootedness and modern awareness intersect" (242). Set at the turn of the century (circa 1893), *Gardens in the Dunes* revisits a crucial moment in American domesticity and domestic policy, especially for Native Americans.

Like much nineteenth-century domestic fiction, furthermore, *Gardens in the Dunes* is structured as a journey home. Divided into ten sections with a third-person narrator who focuses on multiple perspectives, *Gardens in the Dunes* encompasses several settings that reverse an imperial East-West frontier narrative. The novel begins in the American Southwest and then moves east to Long Island, England, and the Mediterranean before returning west. Because of the multiple story lines and circular emplotment, the novel ultimately defies a strictly linear plot in both chronological and spatial terms. Characters' stories overlap and flashbacks abound.

The storylines primarily concern two character sets. The first involves two Sand Lizard sisters, Indigo and Sister Salt. The Sand Lizards are a fictional, southwestern, indigenous people who share similarities with Laguna culture. Early in the novel, police separate the sisters from each other and their family. Indigo's story focuses on her quest to return to her family and ancestral home in the dunes after being forcibly sent to the Sherman Institute in Riverside, California. Sister Salt, the elder sister, is judged to be too old for boarding school and is left under custody of an Indian agency in Parker, Arizona. Indigo escapes from boarding school and hopes to reunite with her sister; however, while trying to find her way home she is found by Hattie Palmer, a thwarted religious scholar, and her husband, Edward, a collector of exotic plant specimens for European and American companies.

The Palmers' story composes the novel's other principal narrative. They take Indigo in under the guise that Hattie will train her for domestic service. The Palmers take Indigo along on a trip east to Long Island and then to England and eventually the Mediterranean. During these travels Hattie loses her home as well due to her husband's illegal plant-collection activities, his poor financial management skills, and their eventual divorce. The novel juxtaposes Indigo's and Sister Salt's experiences with Hattie's struggles to find her place in the world. In the end, both Hattie and Indigo find their way back home: Indigo, reunited with her sister, returns to the old gardens in the sand dunes; Hattie returns to her Aunt Bronwyn's house in Bath, England. She remains a friend to Indigo and her sister, sending money to assist the women's independence.

From this brief plot synopsis, we can begin to see that the novel rewrites several popular nineteenth-century genres, including travel and captivity narratives, the Victorian children's novel, and domestic and sentimental fiction. Its diverse cast of characters, likewise, addresses several key nineteenth-century issues: (1) nineteenth-century American imperialism—for example, through Edward's collection expeditions and his approach to the cultures and people that he encounters on his travels (Silko 129–51); (2) the place of Native American peoples at the turn of the century—especially the role of Native American land claims and Indian schools, which forcibly separate Indigo and Sister Salt from their mother and grandmother (Silko 64–74); (3) (white) female education—Hattie's liberal education (Silko 95) and her "hysteria" (Silko 231), for example; and (4) Christianity's patriarchal nature—as exhibited in its suppression of Coptic scrolls that demonstrate Mary Magdalene was an apostle in the early church (Silko 97–104; 268). This list only scratches the surface, as the novel also incorporates federal development projects, such as Parker Canyon's dam construction (Silko 207), conflicts in Mexico (Silko 356), and Celtic mysticism (Silko 250–69). Such diverse, historically grounded plot elements demonstrate that this narrative is keenly aware of nineteenth-century conventions and concerns.

Additionally, this contemporary Native American text incorporates Western and non-Western domestic spatial and narrative practices. Silko explains that in her cultural tradition (Laguna Pueblo), all narratives are spatial narratives, or stories deeply connected to the land. This tenet holds true for many indigenous cultures and for the fictional Sand Lizards. Silko defines the deep connections between story and place in her introduction to her collection of essays, *Yellow Woman and a Beauty of the Spirit*:

> This book of essays is structured like a spider's web. It begins with the land; think of the land, the earth, as the center of a spider's web. Human identity, imagination and storytelling were inextricably linked to the land, to Mother Earth, just as the strands of the spider's web radiate from the center of the web. (21)

The image of the spider web positions narrative as a web, rather than a linear plot line. Pueblo people, furthermore, "never conceived of removing themselves from the earth and sky. . . . Viewers are as much a part of the landscape as the boulders they stand on" (*Yellow Woman* 27). Silko's remarks begin to describe an interdependent relationship with the landscape and how space takes precedence over time in the Pueblo oral tradition. Silko goes on to say, "The precise date of the incident often is less important than the place or location of the happening" (*Yellow Woman* 33). Thus, location (more than a specific moment in time) possesses priority.

Significantly, in this regard, *Gardens in the Dunes* contains clues to the time period in which it takes place but does not give precise dates. The novel's beginning, for example, emphasizes mythic time rather than locating the story in a specific historical moment. The novel's initial paragraphs describe the sisters laughing naked in the rain and invoke an Eden-like setting where the sisters live in peace. At the same time, the narrative grounds itself in historical references to locate the contemporary reader within the story's specific temporal-spatial politics, but does not pace the narrative so it matches dates precisely. For example, we know that the assassination of King Umberto I took place on July 29, 1900, and that the Spanish-American War occurred from April 21, 1898 (U.S. declaration made retroactive to April 21) to December 10, 1898 (Silko 276). As a result, the novel's reference to the Parker Dam's construction, which begin in 1934, presents a historical rupture. Rather than evaluate the novel as a loose or even inaccurate portrayal of history, its Laguna framework emphasizes location. In other words, it is more important that these events occurred in the same landscape rather than that they occurred at exactly the same time.

Furthermore, rather than providing one version of the story, the characters' multiple perspectives present a "communal truth, not an absolute truth": "For [ancient Pueblo people] this truth lived somewhere within the web of differing versions, disputes over minor points, and outright contradictions tangling with old feuds and village rivalries" (*Yellow Woman* 32). The multiple snake stories produce an example of the "communal truth" Silko describes in *Yellow Woman*. Hattie begins to realize the significance of the multiple, competing narratives while traveling through Europe: "Hattie drifted off to sleep recalling the pictures and statues of the Blessed Virgin Mary standing on a snake. Catechism classes taught Mary was killing the snake, but after seeing the figures in the rain garden, she thought perhaps the Virgin with the snake was based on a figure from earlier times" (Silko 306). Indigo and Sister Salt's competing stories about snakes add another layer of significance. When the sisters return to the old gardens at the end of the novel, they notice that someone killed the old rattlesnake. They make amends by giving the rattlesnake's bones a proper burial. The novel concludes with the snake in the garden—but not as an image of temptation and human sin. A rattlesnake welcomes Indigo and Sister Salt back to the old gardens, suggesting that a balance has returned and that ecological relationships have been mended. The rattlesnake's return represents ecological and domestic harmony: "Old Snake's beautiful daughter moved back home" (479). Before the sisters and Hattie reach this moment and find their respective homes, each embarks on a journey. Domestic mobility is key to understanding (neo) domesticity. In *Gardens in the Dunes*, historically conscious journeys seeking home contribute to the novel's deconstruction of conventional domestic rhetoric.

Neodomestic Mobility
Home's Locations

Whether literal or metaphoric, the basic plot for much nineteenth-century domestic fiction involves the process of making or finding home. In Susan Warner's *The Wide, Wide World* (1850), this journey is literal. Ellen, the protagonist, travels from place to place in search of a home. In *Little Women*, the journey is more metaphoric. The March girls' behavior structures their search for home. The neodomestic novels' use of mobility follows bell hooks's notion that "home is no longer just one place. It is locations" (*Yearning* 148). Adopting this "postmodern" definition of home does not overlook material factors. For example, distinctions exist between a homeless person, an itinerate person who may lay claim to homes in various locations, and a multimillionaire who owns several homes or may have dual citizenship. Comparing and contrasting the domestic mobility of white women and Sand Lizard women clarifies these politics.

Mobility, a by-product of both dispossession and privilege, enters Silko's novel at several levels. The sisters' separation from each other and from the rest of their family dispossesses them of their known home and forces them to construct new ones as they attempt to reunite. Hattie, Indigo's guardian, loses her home as a result of her husband's illegal activities, their eventual divorce, and her own resistance to conventional white womanhood: "Hattie realized, oddly enough, she was the one who no longer had a life to return to. Although they would welcome her, she could not return to her parents' house" (Silko 439). *Gardens in the Dunes* creates various comparisons between Indigo's and Hattie's experiences involving issues of women's domestic mobility and dispossession.

Hattie's and Indigo's stories about dispossession demonstrate that both are trapped by conventional domesticity and that both exhibit key differences in how this trap functions. For example, *Gardens in the Dunes* opens with stories about how the Sand Lizard people move to escape persecution by the whites (15–20). Controlling the Sand Lizard's mobility and the location of their homes becomes tantamount to the American government: "the new orders stated all Indians must leave their home places to live on the reservation at Parker" (19–20). The Indian schools attempt to retrain Native girls to follow conventional (white) domesticity. When indigenous bodies cannot be retrained or contained to produce docile domestic subjects, they are frequently killed: "All those who were not killed were taken prisoner. Grandma Fleet lost her young husband to a bullet; only the women and children remained, captives at Fort Yuma" (18). Indigo's pet parrot, Rainbow, serves as a symbol of her captivity and colonialism. The parrot is an exotic pet associated with the Victorian era. Indigo loves the parrot, so when the parrot bites Indigo, it is as though the parrot says, "Then let me out of the cage" (196). Conversely, Hattie and Edward enjoy freedom of movement, represented in their grand tour through Europe and across the United States and its territories. Unlike Indigo, Sister Salt, and Rainbow, they freely trespass borders—at least until Edward's illegal citron collection gets them in trouble with Spanish police (323–32).

Hattie is a woman trapped by conventional domesticity and notions about a (white) woman's place in society. She is, after all, a queer woman and foreshadows the New Woman of the early twentieth century: "housekeeping chores bored her" (76). Her (proto)feminist intellectual pursuits—she is labeled a heretic after arguing that "Jesus had women disciples and Mary Magdalene wrote a Gospel suppressed by the church"—set her apart (79). Her frustrations, as in Charlotte Perkins Gilman's "The Yellow Wallpaper" (1892), escalate to visible mental and physical problems. The doctor "pronounced her condition female hysteria" and prescribes for Hattie "complete rest and above all no books" (Silko 231). American patriarchal forces have vested interests in keeping her, like the Sand Lizard people, contained.

We can begin to see how mobility may be a transgressive and imperial feature of the home's structure and function in the community; its multiple locations may be liberating or a result of dispossession. Hattie and Indigo also demonstrate home's preferred locations. Bath, England, becomes Hattie's preferred home, and the gardens in the sand dunes are Indigo's and Sister Salt's ideal home. During their travels in Europe, Hattie, Edward, and Indigo confront various homes and homemaking strategies—frequently symbolized through the different types of gardens people cultivate. The characters that successfully integrate or diversify their gardens end the novel at home. Edward, who attempts to colonize space by stealing plant cuttings, meets difficulties that bring about his demise. In contrast, Hattie and Indigo demonstrate a relational interaction with their environments.

Neodomestic Relational Space
The Home's Contexts

Hattie and Indigo practice what feminist geographers define as a relational interaction with their environments. That is, rather than attempt to conquer space or set up oppositional dichotomies, they attempt to create diversity. Relational space demarcates neodomesticity's refusal to reinscribe separate spheres or other hierarchical binaries. This view recognizes, for example, that home is not exclusively private or isolated. Rather, it is defined by its associations with the community and other spaces in its vicinity. Rather than figured as an idealized feminine space (as in Charlotte Perkins Gilman's *Herland*), as a dystopian trap (as in Edith Wharton's *The House of Mirth* and many other works of feminine domestic fiction), or as a site from which boys and men must flee (as in Mark Twain's *Huckleberry Finn* and many other works of masculine antidomestic fiction), neodomestic fiction portrays homes with shifting (ideological) locations and meanings, which are relative to their present and historical relationships with surrounding communities. In Doreen Massey's terms, neodomestic fiction rejects the "culturally masculine" tendency that exhibits the "need for the security of boundaries, the requirement for such a defensive and counterpositional definition of identity" (7). Relational space produces "open security" through blurred rather than oppositional boundaries.

Silko explains in an interview that *Gardens in the Dunes* follows a philosophy best described as relational: "Those who would make the boundary lines and try to separate them, those are the manipulators.... We can be our best selves as a species, as beings with all the other living beings on this earth, we behave best and get along best, without those divisions" (qtd. in Arnold 170–71). In *Gardens in the Dunes*, Sister Salt explains, "'A house' means a circle of stones, because spirits don't need solid walls or roofs; but it must have two hearths, not one, to be the Lord's house" (438). "Two hearths" implies community. In other words, Sister Salt's and Silko's descriptions of relational space emphasize the cliché that "no man, (or woman), is an island." As seen in Cisneros's *The House on Mango Street*, relational space translates into a welcoming home to "outsiders"—Esperanza's "bums in the attic." Sister Salt and Indigo, for instance, share their home with Vedna and Maytha, the twin sisters Sister Salt befriends. The twins do the same. In *Gardens in the Dunes*, the relational home also extends to an ecological relationship with nature.

Often, as I described in chapter 1, these alternative, relational, or third spaces foster hybrid identities (Jeffery 274). Hybrid identities blur boundaries that are usually considered sacrosanct—boundaries such as race, gender, and class. Hybridity enters *Gardens in the Dunes* in multiple ways. For example, both Sister Salt and Indigo are of mixed race. Sister Salt also has relationships with both black and Mexican men; Big Candy, an African American, fathers her child. Racist notions about cross-racial relationships emerge in the text only to be defeated (Silko 211), even when practiced among indigenous peoples: "Some of the other tribes used to smother their half-breed babies because they were afraid of them" (Silko 204). This theme of beneficial diversity is also paralleled in discussions and examples of hybrid flowers and other plant life. Where Indigo and many of the other characters she encounters on her journey freely share seeds (Indigo saves and plans to transport them to the old gardens), Edward collects plants for profit and illegally attempts to obtain *Citrus medica* cuttings; he also finds himself on an expedition attempting to secure equally sought-after rubber tree seedlings resistant to a blight that is "destroying Britain's great Far Eastern rubber plantations" (131).

Edward engages in oppositional spatial practices that lead to violence and his eventual death: "His ambition was to discover a new plant species that would bear his name, and he spent twenty years of his life in this pursuit before their marriage" (Silko 80). Edward invokes patriarchal, colonial, and imperial powers and oppositional spatial practices. Edward's interest in Indigo, for instance, emerges when he believe that she, too, is a rare specimen for his collection: "He was intrigued with the notion that the child might be the last remnant of a tribe now extinct, perhaps a tribe never before studied by anthropologists" (Silko 113).

By contrast, Indigo's relational spatial practices result in a literal and figurative fecundity. The gardens and Indigo's life at the end of the novel are flourishing. Unlike the controlled Western gardens portrayed in the novel—especially the gardens of Hattie's sister-in-law, Susan—the Sand Lizards' garden in the dunes represents not just beauty but also utility. For example, the hybrid gladioli that Indigo brings back from Aunt Bronwyn's garden nourish the eye and body: "Those gladiolus weren't only beautiful, they were tasty!" (478). Hattie by the novel's end participates in her Aunt's Celtic mysticism and gardening practices that honor the land's spirits. Aunt Bronwyn has "gone native" in Edward's mind because she protects stones that "dance and walk" at night (239).

Sister Salt, Indigo, and Hattie also clearly demonstrate the limits of sharing their home and of following an uncritical understanding of relational space—especially in the face of racism and sexism. When the nearby town floods but leaves the land owned by Maytha and Vedna safe and dry, Maytha remarks, "If we leave for even one night, the flooded people will call our place abandoned and move in" (438). Later, when Hattie joins Sister Salt and Indigo on the riverbank south of Needles where they are dancing, she also brings white soldiers and her father: "Hattie realized the police and soldiers came to break up the Indian gathering because of her—because they came looking for her there" (472). While ideally Hattie, Sister Salt, and Indigo should be able to live together, conditions do not allow for this to happen, especially if their homemaking practices follow Native American, rather than Western, traditions. Their ideal home cannot exist outside of relationships with the larger community. The model home—especially in a novel set nearly one hundred years ago—requires further renovations.

Neodomestic Renovation and Redesign
Remodeling the Model Home

Neodomesticity resonates with and differs from the conventional heterosexual home by way of renovation and redesign. While the single-family, heterosexual home continues to dominate domestic culture, neodomestic renovations and redesigns broaden the geography of domestic fiction to include more diverse family structures and domestic settings. Neodomestic fiction reveals and recovers "queer space" as a vital part of domestic fiction's architecture. As I outlined in chapter 1, the term "queer space" in this context broadly describes homes that "deviate" from the single-family, heterosexual norm:

> In the context of feminism, ["queer"] most commonly refers to the "deconstruction" by literary critics, artists and, increasingly, social scientists, working in a postmodern or post-structuralist framework, of oppressive binarisms, especially those related to gender, sexuality and the sex–gender system (most notably the homosexual–heterosexual binarism). (Knopp 225)[2]

In line with relational spatial practices, queer space rejects "counterpositional definition[s] of identity" and space (Massey 7).

Literal home renovations, as I discuss in greater detail in chapter 3, also take place within neodomestic fiction. *Gardens in the Dunes* presents both physically and ideologically different or "queer" homes. That is, it renovates our understanding of home through the indigenous homemakers' distinct practices and housing locations and situations. Sister Salt and Indigo, for instance, model Sand Lizard homemaking. Sister Salt in particular challenges Western conventions regarding female sexuality and domesticity, especially nineteenth-century Protestant expectations: "Sex with strangers was valued for alliances and friendships that might be made" (204). Although she lives with Big Candy, her African American boyfriend, Sister Salt earns money by selling beer and engaging in sex work along a construction route: "Sister Salt took her choice of the men willing to pay a dime for fun in the tall grass along the river" (220). From Sister Salt's perspective, "sex with strangers was advantageous because it created a happy atmosphere to benefit commerce and exchange with strangers" (220). Big Candy, furthermore, does not mind: "He was making good money and busy himself. Her body belonged to her—it was none of his business" (220). Their transient housing, open relationship, and her sexuality present a clear contrast to the conventional monogamous heterosexual marriage. Even Hattie and Edward's marriage does not fit within this conventional definition; the couple never consummate their marriage.

We can read the ending of *Gardens in the Dunes* as an ideological revision of *Little Women*'s conclusion and depiction of the model home and homemaking. Unlike *Little Women*, which concludes during the fall harvest, *Gardens in the Dunes* concludes in the spring. Rather than end the novel with the characters reaping the rewards of the fall harvest and of their individual successful journeys to home and marriage, the Sand Lizard sisters remain single, fertile, and independent. By returning Hattie to live in Bath with her Aunt, furthermore, *Gardens in the Dunes*—in a more subtle fashion than *Almanac of the Dead*—sends the white population "back home." An older spatial order is restored in the conclusion of *Gardens in the Dunes*. The narrative comes full circle, back to the idyllic gardens with which the narrative began. While the homemaking practices in *Little Women* and *Gardens in the Dunes* are worlds apart, both novels conclude with characters celebrating their domesticity. In both cases, the home provides a sanctuary.

A sanctuary, of course, implies a kind of stability or haven that neodomestic fiction resists. Morrison's notion of home is instructive here; home is a place that is safe but open (Morrison, "Home" 9). *Gardens in the Dunes*, after all, presents a world where even the stones "dance and walk" (Silko 239). The old gardens represent "a place 'already made for me, both snug and wide open. With a doorway never needing to be closed'" (Morrison, "Home" 9). The sense of timelessness and emphasis on the space of the gardens reflect neodomestic principles by challenging conventional Western notions of a "good home." Edward, for example, feels "reassured to know the time; one of the worst parts of the Brazilian ordeal had been the sensation time disappeared with the white men" (Silko 314). When Edward literally and figuratively leaves his place in the world (represented by the disappearance of white men), he is ill-equipped to survive. The contemporary reader, furthermore, knows the sense of stability in the gardens will not last. We know the challenges faced by American Indians at the turn of the century did not end as happily as they do in *Gardens in the Dunes*. The cycle of dispossession begins again.

Far from nostalgic in its presentation, *Gardens in the Dunes* portrays realistic consequences for women who attempt to remodel the home and redefine their place within American culture in the nineteenth century. Hattie, for example, is raped, robbed, and left for dead when she travels alone (458–60). Indigo and Sister Salt endure many setbacks before they finally reunite. Silko cannot rewrite the violence associated with Western expansion and sexism, but she can retell the story in such a way that questions the ways other narratives uncritically valorize the taming of women's and indigenous people's bodies and the West. In the sections and chapters that follow, I discuss in greater detail domestic remodeling, recycling, and instability's costs, advantages, and consequences by exploring, for instance, Toni Morrison's, Barbara Kingsolver's, Chang-rae Lee's, and Jonathan Franzen's domestic fiction. The next section examines neodomestic fiction's revision of nineteenth-century domestic fiction in greater detail, primarily focusing on another novel that consciously returns to the genre and recycles it: *The Poisonwood Bible*.

Recycling Nineteenth-Century Domestic Tropes

Where Silko's novel returns to the nineteenth century, Kingsolver's *The Poisonwood Bible* is set in the mid-twentieth century. Nevertheless, this novel also self-consciously rewrites nineteenth-century domestic fiction. The ways that *The Poisonwood Bible* (1998) recycles the domestic novel can be seen when we compare it to *Little Women* (1868). Both stories are set in the "women's sphere" of the home and narrate the women's domestic travails. The Price family in *The Poisonwood Bible* loosely but distinctly parallels the March family from *Little Women*. Both stories have minister fathers and families with four girls. The Price girls' character flaws especially coincide with the March daughters' failings that set *Little Women*'s narrative in motion.[3] Rachel Price mirrors her precedent Meg March, who thinks too much of her looks and hates to work.[4] Both Leah Price and Jo March are tomboys who long to be somewhere else, and Adah Price and Amy March are similarly selfish, "defective" girls. Amy endures ridicule due to her nose, and Adah's noticeable birth defect sets her apart physically and emotionally.[5] Void of moral or physical defects, the family favorites, Ruth May Price and Beth March, die tragically young. With its missionary family, *The Poisonwood Bible* also invokes the Protestant morality promoted in *Little Women*. The rich ways such parallels jumble together—Meg March, for example, ultimately represents a woman of domestic faculty whereas Rachel Price commercializes faculty for profit—provide an extreme example of how neodomestic novels revise nineteenth-century domesticity and fiction.[6]

The connections with *Little Women* suggest that *The Poisonwood Bible* self-consciously plays with domestic fiction's generic features in both subtle and literal ways. Set during the Civil War, *Little Women* follows the March girls' transition from practicing homemaking as daughters to producing domesticity as wives and mothers. The Price's recycled story begins in 1959 in Bethlehem, Georgia, as this Baptist family prepares to leave for a mission in the Belgian Congo. The father's ego and attendant difficulty in converting the community, the family members' culture shock, communication problems, environmental disasters, the political uprising, and Ruth May's death all conspire against the mission's success. What began as a year-long pilgrimage to the Congo turns into three decades of stories mapping the aftermath of the family's experiences in Kilanga, the fictional Congolese community where the Price family moves. Unlike *Little Women*, there is not an omniscient narrator. All the Price women take turns narrating the events. The novel's structure—similar to *Gardens in the Dunes*' multiple focal points—thus promotes narrative and ideological instabilities because different voices with distinct perspectives narrate the same incidents.

While not an explicit rewriting of *Little Women*, *The Poisonwood Bible* consciously echoes the significant features of Alcott's novel. On her publisher's Web site, Kingsolver says, "Certainly I considered that other famous family of 'little women,' as I was writing this. It was one of the most beloved books of my childhood. But the parallels don't go too far. Louisa May Alcott didn't put any snakes in her book" (Kingsolver, "Barbara Kingsolver FAQ"). Kingsolver's remark about snakes provides a figurative distinction between conventional domesticity and neodomesticity. Neodomesticity emphasizes the American home's problems (read "snakes") as well as its potential.

Kingsolver's innovative recycling is not always as historically conscious as it could be. The problematic recycled narrative in *The Bean Trees* revolves around an illegally adopted Native American child. After publication of *The Bean Trees*, Kingsolver admits,

> I realized with embarrassment that I had completely neglected a whole moral area when I wrote about this Native American kid being swept off the reservation and raised by a very loving white mother. It was something I hadn't thought about, and I felt I needed to make that right in another book. Otherwise I don't think I would want to write a sequel. I would just start from scratch. (qtd. in Perry 165)

As Mary Jean DeMarr points out, "People living in the Southwest are familiar with cases of well-meaning white families adopting Native American infants who are later wanted back by their tribes" (94). Turtle's adoption becomes the main focus of *Pigs in Heaven*, the unplanned sequel to *The Bean Trees*. This example reminds us that recycled narratives should be carefully examined for their problems as well as for their potential in envisioning alternative domesticities. The following sections examine the ways that neodomestic fiction critically recycles domestic fiction's common tropes, including its protagonists, journey plots, ideologies, and spaces of domestic privilege.

Revised Protagonists and Domestic Ideology
Selfless, Benevolent Women

Nineteenth-century domestic fiction requires, at least according to the conventional definition, a selfless female protagonist. In Carolyn Vellenga Berman's words, "Not every domestic novel features a good wife as a major character, but if a novel cannot teach us what would make a good wife, even by counterexample, then it is probably not a work of domestic fiction" (22). The protagonist that (eventually) represents conventional domestic ideology usually reaps marriage or its promise as her reward. Ellen, for example, must gain her Aunt Fortune's respect in *The Wide, Wide World* through Christian tenets of female selflessness.[7] *The Wide, Wide World* implies that women's moral, Christian education relies on "dispossession," or a letting go of self. For instance, when Ellen questions the logic of her mother's impending death, her mother responds, "'Perhaps he [God] sees, Ellen, that you never would seek him while you had me to cling to'" (Warner 41). Ellen achieves success when she finally disciplines herself to be selfless.

Morrison's Sethe in *Beloved* specifically recycles the selfless domestic protagonist by embodying a "self-less" woman. Unlike Ellen, Sethe must "re-member" herself. Rather than ultimately embodying an idealized, selfless woman, neodomestic women continue to exhibit a range of flaws and beneficent personality traits. When looking at the broad range of characters presented in nineteenth-century fiction, alternatives and complications also appear; for example, Aunt Fortune in *The Wide, Wide World* models an alternative domesticity in contrast to Ellen's pious selflessness. Nevertheless, neodomestic heroines (and heroes) are not as one-dimensional as those that Baym describes as significant to the study of nineteenth-century women's fiction, where the heroines by the novel's conclusion tend to be either "flawless" or "flawed" (Baym 35). For instance, Sethe's capacity for love—an advantageous trait, especially in the sentimental and domestic traditions—is also her Achilles heel. Sethe and her literary contemporaries accentuate such inconsistencies.

Where the domestic heroine generally stabilizes her identity and environment, the neodomestic protagonist learns to cope with her volatile domestic setting. Ellen in *The Wide, Wide World* and Jo in *Little Women*, for example, must give up their contrary ways. The quintessential neodomestic protagonist, whether male or female, learns to reconcile but not necessarily eliminate his/her contradictions. Iliana in *Geographies of Home*, for example, embraces instability at the novel's conclusion. When she prepares to leave home once again, Iliana vows, "She would leave no memories behind. All of them were her self. All of them were home" (Pérez 321). At the end of the novel's journey, she seeks neither an escape nor a safe haven. She creates a home that is not dependent on such dichotomies. Iliana ultimately embraces her home's instability and contradictions: "All of them were home" (321).

In (neo)domestic fiction, the characters' actions frequently represent some aspect of domestic ideology. The nineteenth century's "cult of true womanhood" requires helping others successfully produce white middle-class domesticity. In Alcott's *Little Women*, the March women's charity work furthers this aim, adding benevolence to womanhood's virtues of domesticity and piety. The March women embody "THE WOMEN OF AMERICA, In Whose Hands Rest the Real Destinies of the Republic," to which Catharine E. Beecher and Harriet Beecher Stowe dedicated their domestic handbook, *American Woman's Home* (1869). Beecher and Stowe explain that a (white) woman's domestic teaching and example should demonstrate, "the peculiar privilege of woman in the sacred retreat of a 'Christian home,'" which is "to lift up the fallen, to sustain the weak, to protect the tempted, to bind up the broken-hearted, and especially to rescue the sinful" (Beecher and Stowe 433). To these ends, the March family assists local foreign and destitute families, thereby furthering their Christian and patriotic missions. For example, early in the novel they take a poor German family under their wing and informally adopt the motherless Laurie (17–19). Such acts of Christian charity promote the cult of true womanhood, making the March women good Christians and good American citizens.

The March women embrace their "peculiar privilege" by (re)producing a stable Christian home and community. The Price women in Kingsolver's *The Poisonwood Bible*, in turn, produce a poor imitation at best. For example, the Price family also adopts a child—a local boy, Nelson. However, they ultimately depend more on the aid provided by Nelson and Mama Tataba, (a local woman who assists Orleanna with the cooking and housekeeping) than the

Congolese depend on and benefit from their relationship with the Price family (Kingsolver 90–98).[8] In the end, the Price women form their own "Circus mission" that highlights the failure of American domesticity in the Congo (271).

Analyzing the mother's role of promoting the cult of true womanhood provides further insight into the novels' reproduced and recycled protagonists and domestic ideologies as they affect white privilege. As mothers, Orleanna and Mrs. March share the "peculiar" responsibility of modeling domesticity for their daughters. Mrs. March self-assuredly takes up this role, explaining that following one's duty produces happiness: "'I gave my best to the country I love. . . . Why should I complain, when we both [referring to her husband] have merely done our duty and will surely be the happier for it in the end?'" (84). *The Poisonwood Bible* also presents the mother as an exceptional character. Like her nineteenth-century counterpart, Orleanna serves as a fundamental source of knowledge. Orleanna enjoys a "complete" historical consciousness—she always narrates from the present—whereas her daughters narrate their stories chronologically. Orleanna's reflections faintly echo the confident, fully formed wisdom that Mrs. March shares with her girls. However, Orleanna lacks Mrs. March's righteousness and Christian confidence. Whereas Mrs. March turns to God to legitimize her actions (84–85), Orleanna does not use faith as her justification. As a result, Orleanna exhibits less confidence about her homemaking and parenting. Where Mrs. March understood her "peculiar privilege" as her Christian duty, Orleanna wrestles with how to live with white privilege—with the legacies and realities of what Amy Kaplan terms "manifest domesticity."[9]

Orleanna, however, is not Mrs. March's complete opposite or a failed mother. She models a compelling recycled ideology that negotiates American domesticity's imperial past, present, and possible future incarnations. Orleanna does not cleanly reproduce the rhetoric of manifest destiny or domesticity, and yet she recognizes its power and deep, relational connections to "foreign" powers. Our suspicions about Orleanna's abilities to recycle old discourses are piqued when she compares her situation with her husband, Nathan, to that of a colonized country, specifically the Congo: "To resist occupation, whether you're a nation or merely a woman, you must understand the language of your enemy" (383). "In the end," explains Orleanna, "my lot was cast with the Congo" (201). Like Africa, Orleanna contends that she was an occupied country. As a result, Orleanna implores her readers to judge her fairly: "My talents are different from those of the women who cleave and part from husbands nowadays—and my virtues probably unrecognizable. But look at old women and bear in mind we are another country" (383).

The conflation between Orleanna and the Congo could be read as an appropriative gesture. Furthermore, the African villagers with whom the Prices live and work are heard only through the women's narrations. Kimberly Koza critiques *The Poisonwood Bible*, "because [Kingsolver's] Congolese characters never speak for themselves, she seems to deny them agency in their own history" (288). However, as much as Orleanna identifies with the colonized Congo, she also understands the limitations of their similar situations. To the extent that privilege is a function of race—as well as gender and class—truly moving out of the site one is often born into is an extremely difficult, if not impossible, task. Orleanna powerfully articulates her inability to relinquish privilege completely and why it is important to recognize this aspect of white privilege.

Reflecting on her family tragedies and her personal losses, Orleanna understands that despite her troubles she still has the "peculiar privileges" afforded her by her birthplace and her race. She explains,

> You'll say I walked across Africa with my wrists unshackled, and now I am one more soul walking free in a white skin, wearing some thread of the stolen goods: cotton or diamonds, freedom at the very least, prosperity. Some of us know how we came by our fortune, and some of us don't, but we wear it all the same. There's only one question worth asking now: How do we aim to live with it? (9)

Orleanna questions her family's role and her own role in the Belgian Congo, complicating duty's connection to privilege and to the domestic. The passage demonstrates Orleanna's awareness of her geopolitical privilege and a concomitant uncertainty about her role. Orleanna's questioning epitomizes neodomestic ideology's emphasis on historical consciousness (as opposed to Christian duty) and instability (as opposed to stability) as a central feature of the domestic sphere. Orleanna's recognition of her privileged position, a position dependent on "stolen goods," also acknowledges the Africanist presence, which domestic novels by white women historically tend to conceal. Her plea suggests that white American women can no more eliminate their privilege than they can shed their white skin. While metaphorically shackled to her husband, Orleanna draws a distinction in this passage between her patriarchal oppression and African and African American suffering as a result of imperialism and slavery. Her references to cotton and diamonds invoke two key resources picked and mined by African American and African slave labor, respectively. The passage concludes with a key question about how to construct homes that are critical and mindful of the varying forces that (re)produce privilege.

Orleanna's closing question in the passage pinpoints the problem that white women struggle with in neodomestic fictions: *How can one move beyond imperial history without forgetting or ignoring it?* How will and how should (white) Americans negotiate their privilege on domestic and global scales? Seyla Benhabib in her essay "Sexual Difference and Collective Identities: The New Global Constellation" poses a similar question about the construction of home. She asks, "Can we establish justice and solidarity at home without turning in on ourselves, without closing our borders to the needs and cries of others? What will democratic collective identities look like in the century of globalization?" (Benhabib 355).[10] Orleanna suggests that the goal of eliminating white privilege fails to take adequate account of the present and historical factors that form (white) privilege. Unable to reproduce or eliminate white privilege, she must recycle it.

When "things fall apart" in Kilanga, the Price family cannot be put together again just as they were. The Price women recycle to survive. For instance, Orleanna gives away much of what the family owns (371–72) and finally gathers the courage to leave her husband and Kilanga. In this symbolic and material act, Orleanna relinquishes the material trappings of her house of privilege: "My household would pass through the great digestive tract of Kilanga and turn into sights unseen" (382). The Price women unpack white privilege, a key step in the shift from *reproducing* to *recycling* home. While they cannot eliminate white privilege, they can change how they carry it. Balancing their respective ideological and material burdens informs the Price women's exit from Kilanga and functions as part of the process of deconstructing white privilege and the model American home.

The Prices' domestic breakdowns during their journey—both before and after Ruth May's death—highlight rather than attempt to mask American domesticity's connections to imperialism. Furthermore, the lost sense of home that results from their repeated domestic failures forces the Price women to recycle American domesticity, crafting homemaking strategies that remodel their positions within their family, the village of Kilanga, and—more broadly—their positions as American citizens and exiles in Africa. Unpacking white privilege requires that the Price women find ways to live responsibly with their privileges and histories. They need new homemaking strategies.

While Orleanna successfully distributes a portion of her material possessions, her redemptive act cannot so simply produce a more egalitarian society. Leah understands her mother's actions as a "farewell gift to Kilanga. . . . My pagan mother alone among us understood redemption" (456). However, the limited extent of this "redemption" reveals itself through the burdens that the Price women carry out of Kilanga. When the women leave, they are traveling much lighter than they were when they arrived. Rosemary Marangoly George, using Jurgen Joachim Hesse's essay about Canadian immigrant writers, explains that "immigrant novels themselves suggest that traveling light or arriving with luggage are both serviceable ways of entering the new location" (*Politics* 173). In *The Poisonwood Bible*, however, both cases are equally ineffective. The section "What We Carried Out" emphasizes that traveling with less material luggage and incorporating new domestic and traveling strategies does not eliminate the Price women's imperial loads.

In Leah's case, adopting new traveling modes initially produces clear benefits. As she leaves Kilanga, Leah implements the Congolese women's carrying method, placing her burden on her head. She had never tried this before: "What a revelation, that I could carry my own parcel like any woman here! After the first several miles I ceased to feel the weight on my head at all" (390). Her sense of weightlessness contrasts sharply with the burdens that weigh down the family upon their arrival. The weightlessness, however, is not permanent. As Adah says, Leah's "religion *is* the suffering" (442; emphasis in original). Even her husband Anatole's love does not mitigate Leah's burdens: "But even his devotion can't keep this weight off my shoulders" (456). Whatever scruples her sister Rachel lacks, Leah appears to take on. Part of Leah's burden is her guilt and loss over Ruth May's death. Leah especially shares this weight with her mother, although all her sisters carry the burden of Ruth May's death. Adah says of her mother's millstone, "She will put down that burden, I believe, on the day she hears forgiveness from Ruth May herself" (493). And Adah herself reveals, "What I carried out of [the] Congo on my crooked little back is a ferocious uncertainty about the worth of a life" (443). Adah struggles to reframe her existence with the recognition of such instability. As the section "What We Carried Out" emphasizes, traveling with less luggage did not necessarily lighten the Price women's loads. The balancing of their individual and collective burdens informs the Price women's reterritorializations—their struggles to recycle domesticity responsibly. How will the Price women live now that "Africa has slipped the floor out from under [their] righteous house"? (443). To understand this, we must look at the houses they inhabit.

Recycling the Model American Home
A Neodomestic Approach

The recycled houses in Kingsolver's domestic fiction offer various ways of dealing with white American privilege, modeling homemaking practices that answer the "needs and cries of others" (Benhabib 355). Mona Domosh and Joni Seager in *Putting Women in Place: Feminist Geographers Make Sense of the World* remind us that in the nineteenth century, "middle-class notions of proper domesticity were often considered essential to the 'Americanizing' project, not only in American cities but also on the recently established reservations for Native Americans in the West" (21). As a missionary family in the Congo, the white Price family in *The Poisonwood Bible* continues this imperial tradition. An awareness of places and homes that exist beyond the characters' locations and needs eventually enables the white female protagonists to recycle homes and homemaking practices that are not limited to their individual homes and nations.

Geographer Doreen Massey clarifies what is at stake when we begin to pay attention to home's locations: "There is, then, an issue of whose identity we are referring to when we talk of a place called home and of the supports it may provide of stability, oneness and security" (167). American (neo)domestic literature provides a clear case study to flesh out Massey's remarks because of its embrace of (in)stability. Examining the notion of a "stable" home to find its racial, gender, and class contours reveals more about how neodomestic fiction critically revises conventional domesticity.

The lost sense of home that the Price women experience when their conventional American homemaking proves more and more inadequate leads to the development of postcolonial homemaking strategies, methods that address the knotty relationship between imperialism and Western white feminism. A primary difference, for example, between Kingsolver's *The Poisonwood Bible* and Alcott's *Little Women*—and domestic and neodomestic fiction generally—is that unlike the March family, the Price women do not successfully reproduce a stable home. *Little Women* ends triumphantly with the fall harvest, in which Mrs. March symbolically reaps the fruits of her parenting. The final tableau of her three surviving daughters' happy marriages celebrates Mrs. March's successful reproduction of model American domesticity. At the conclusion Mrs. March sees her married daughters and exclaims that she "never can wish [for them] a greater happiness than this!" (502). While the Price women initially share this goal of creating a secure home, they are ultimately less successful in fulfilling it. *The Poisonwood Bible* does not repeat *Little Women*'s happy family tableau. In fact, Orleanna asks at the novel's outset, "What do we know, even now? Ask the children. Look at what they grew up to be" (10). Orleanna's children are scattered across the globe, and her knowledge of them is uncertain.

This reversal of fortunes may be seen in part as a product of the Price's displacement, but it also suggests that the novels have fundamentally different views of the white, middle-class, American home's redemptive possibilities and benign status as a model for all. *The Poisonwood Bible*'s revised protagonists and ideology distinguish it as "a text that speaks from within 'Western feminist discourse' and attempts to expose the bases and supports of privilege even as it renegotiates political and personal alliances" (Martin and Mohanty 296). The Price's domestic breakdown similarly highlights rather than attempts to mask American domesticity's connections to imperialism. Amy Kaplan in "Manifest Domesticity" clarifies these connections: "Domesticity is more mobile and less stabilizing; it travels in contradictory circuits both to expand and contract the boundaries of home and nation and to produce shifting conceptions of the foreign" ("Manifest Domesticity" 583). The Price home emphasizes domesticity's "expansionist logic" by destabilizing conventional dichotomies between the domestic and the foreign (Kaplan 602).[11] Rather than functioning as oppositional constructions, these spaces encroach on each other's territory throughout the novel. In particular, *The Poisonwood Bible*'s setting unmoors stable domesticity, exposing its imperial drive and intimate connections with the foreign.

Where nineteenth-century domestic novels tend to mask what Toni Morrison terms the "Africanist presence" within American literature, *The Poisonwood Bible* sets Africa at its most visible center, as its "foreign" destination (Morrison, *Playing* 6).[12] Placing its portrayal of American homemaking in the Belgian Congo and the Jim Crow South, *The Poisonwood Bible* locates the Africanist presence within its narrative in order to tease out American domesticity's connections to imperialism. Conversely, conventional domesticity in part reproduces American imperialism and white privilege by *displacing* the Africanist presence. In Amy Kaplan's words, the Africanist presence "is intimately bound to the expansionist logic of domesticity itself" (602). *Little Women*, for example, does not foreground the Africanist presence even though it spurs the March's homemaking projects. For example, the Civil War necessitates the father's absence, but the slavery question remains an unspoken text. *Little Women* also does not explore the imperial implications of Hannah's largely invisible domestic labor or Mr. Laurence's desire for his grandson Laurie to become an "India merchant," but these details expand the March's ability to reproduce domesticity and to stabilize their domain (148). Rather than repeating this lacuna, the neodomestic novel accounts directly for domesticity's expansionist history and its ties to an Africanist presence. In addition to setting the novel in the Belgian Congo and the Jim Crow South, *The Poisonwood Bible* highlights domestic ideology's hidden connections to an Africanist presence by deconstructing homemaking's promotion of good works.[13]

The following sections illustrate that there is not a true "model" home among the Price women—at least in the sense of successfully constructing an idealized, perfect haven from the "outside" world or a home that fully allows them to "move out" of their privileged positions. As mentioned previously, such a goal fails to take adequate account of the present and historical factors that form (white) privilege. The Price women's homes, especially Orleanna's, Adah's, and Leah's homes, imagine alternative homemaking practices that remain conscious of their historical and present locations. Rachel's and Leah's homes and homemaking practices especially interrogate the American home's alluring pleasures (like security) and damning injustices (such as exclusion), thereby offering a critical rethinking of American homemaking in a postcolonial, translocal context.

The Prices of Stable Homes
Rachel's and Leah's Recycled Homes

Constructed after the Price women leave Kilanga, Rachel's "bad" commercial hotel and Leah's "good" charitable home appear to provide two contrasting models that apparently realign *The Poisonwood Bible* with conventional domestic ideology and its stable setting. Conventional domesticity constructs a sacred, stabilizing dichotomy that sets commercial concerns against domestic ones. The cult of true womanhood frequently places the home against commercial culture: "Domesticity is set forth as a value scheme for ordering all of life, in competition with the ethos of money and exploitation that is perceived to prevail in American society" (Baym, *Woman's Fiction* 27). The Marchs' stable, happy home and genteel poverty constructs itself in opposition to commercial culture. *The Poisonwood Bible* seems to follow this critique because commercial American culture's burdens contribute to the Price's failed Kilanga home.[14] Rachel's and Leah's distinctive homemaking practices also appear to promote this tenet of conventional domesticity.

Rather than reestablishing the commerce/domesticity dichotomy, Rachel's and Leah's homes ultimately undercut it. Their homes demonstrate that the home's material security cannot be decoupled from its emotional security and vice versa. While neodomesticity clearly favors Leah's noncommercial homemaking, it also demonstrates that as long as Rachel and Leah share the same goal—domestic security—neither presents a genuine choice. Their distinctive homes emphasize domestic security's two sides: one economic and the other emotional. In this sense, their recycled search for a safe retreat demonstrates what Judith Williamson calls "the supreme trick of bourgeois ideology," which "is to be able to produce its opposite out of its own hat" (100). Their homemaking practices connect domestic stability to imperialism and white privilege, teasing out economic and emotional security's appeal, costs, and consequences.

Were she a character in a conventional domestic novel, Rachel would be tragically flawed for refusing to renounce her materialism. Unlike Jo March, Rachel never realizes the error of the personal pursuit of money and power (Alcott 354). Rachel, sinning against a fundamental tenet of the cult of true womanhood, profits by seeking individual gain. Within the neodomestic novel's context, Rachel's character flaws turn conventional domesticity against itself, connecting imperialism, commercial culture, and American domesticity. In true colonial form, Rachel describes her home and business as a "little *country*":[15]

> Then why not go back [to America]? Well, now it's too late, of course. I have responsibilities. First there was one husband and then another to tie me down, and then the Equatorial, which isn't just a hotel, it's like running a whole little *country*, where everybody wants to run off with a piece for themselves the minute you turn your back. (512; emphasis in original)

Rachel's remarks suggest that she understands how imperialism works. She recognizes, in typical colonial fashion, that the land and its resources are up for grabs. She takes advantage of her situation and builds a home for personal financial gain. Aptly named the Equatorial, her hotel-home reflects Rachel's "central" position as an American running a business abroad, a position that she gains at the expense of the Congolese.

Ironically, her failure as a true woman (to put others before herself) underscores the deep connections between commercialism, imperialism, and domesticity that conventional domesticity attempts to mask. Rachel's domestic practices and ideology represent the worst in American domestic and foreign policy: she couches her individual economic gain as a cultural improvement. Jo March builds a school with her inheritance, and Rachel correspondingly incorporates commercial culture into her hotel-home. However, where Jo instructs for community good, Rachel clearly works for personal profit. She explains,

> The restaurant is for paying guests only, which is, needless to say, whites, since the Africans around here wouldn't earn enough in a month to buy one of my *prix-fixe* dinners. But I certainly am not one to leave anyone sitting out in the rain! So I built them that shelter, so they wouldn't be tempted to come in and hang about idly in the main bar. (461–62)

Positioned as the center of Rachel's universe, the Equatorial is a refurbished plantation for whites only. Rachel attempts to skirt her racist practices by translating into economic terms her refusal to treat blacks and whites equally; she will serve the black Congolese only if they stay out of the main bar. As a result, Rachel replicates segregated Georgia in her miniature empire through her "separate but equal" exploitative services. Rachel's racist practices may also be a reproduced version of apartheid; after leaving Kilanga she moves to Johannesburg, South Africa, where she lives for at least four years (from about 1960–64). Rachel thus reproduces white privilege in her colonial retreat's construction. In fact, she conflates the aims of capitalist enterprise and aid organizations when she complains, "Mother's group has never raised one red cent for me, to help put in upstairs plumbing at the Equatorial, for example" (476). Rachel's "imperial" hotel serves herself and other whites.

Significantly, Rachel idealizes American life in ways that fail to recognize her privileged position as an American. Her nationalist, "America is best" attitude voices a romanticized 1950s image of American home and family. Rachel begins the novel a young woman "whose only hopes for the year were a sweet-sixteen party and a pink mohair twin set" (28). She also assumes that the Congolese regard her pale skin and blonde hair with envy: "Of course, everyone kept staring at *me*, as they always do here. I am the most extreme blonde imaginable" (47; emphasis in original). Rachel grossly misreads their stares; the Congolese nickname her "termite" (208). Rachel is so vain that when driver ants invade Kilanga, she grabs her most prized possession, her mirror (301–2). Of course, she is *only* a teenager at this point in the novel. But perhaps her teenage narcissism—which she never outgrows—is exactly what characterizes American domesticity: it is beautiful, charming, selfish, and protected at all costs.

Thus, Rachel's "dumb blonde" characteristics—hypervisual whiteness, child-like innocence, and sexual attractiveness and vulnerability—mark her as a privileged domestic figure.[16] In other words, her place may be the home, but she reigns there as the bourgeois trophy wife or mistress and not as the mother and certainly not as the housekeeper. Later, when she takes over the Equatorial, for the first time in her life she is not directly defined and controlled by her father, a "husband," or some other male authority figure. In Rachel's words, "Not to boast, but I have created my own domain. I call the shots" (511). Nevertheless, she cannot simply define herself. Money and power do not protect her absolutely.

The Poisonwood Bible presents a witty critique of Rachel's subservience to a patriarchal eye while it simultaneously criticizes her attempts to stabilize her precarious position, a stability that she hopes to gain by increasing her separation from black Congolese culture. The cult of true womanhood punishes women's entrance into commercial spheres by questioning their morality. Jo, for example, learns this lesson when she writes "sensation stories" (353–69). Before too long, Jo reflects, "They *are* trash, . . . I've gone blindly on, hurting myself and other people, for the sake of money" (365; emphasis in original). The cult of true womanhood haunts Rachel, too. Unlike Jo, who takes personal responsibility for her actions, Rachel places the blame on the viewer:

> Every so often a group of fellows will stop by in the afternoon on a sightseeing tour, and receive a mistaken impression of my establishment. . . . And guess what: they'll take me for the madam of a whorehouse! Believe you me, I give them a piece of my mind. If this looks like a house of prostitution to you, I tell them, that just shows the quality of your own moral fiber. (514–15)

Rachel abnegates personal responsibility for her business's outward appearance and the history that informs why men may misinterpret her occupation. Rachel questions the viewer's moral fiber, not her own—or the patriarchal social constructions that associate single businesswomen with sexual promiscuity. While Rachel may not escape a patriarchal, imperial gaze that often views independent women as sexual objects, she still benefits from her place within the system: "I'm making a killing," she brags (512). Unlike her girlfriends in Georgia, Rachel has "opportunities as a woman of the world" (514). Her economic and racial privileges ultimately promote her success.

Rachel's knack for brushing off moral qualms also helps her construct a retreat from the outside world. Combined with her economic capital, her colonial amnesia allows her to retreat from "bad luck" (465). For example, when Rachel learns about diamond mines, she thinks, "Gee, does Marilyn Monroe even know where they come from? Just picturing her in her satin gown and a Congolese diamond digger in the same universe gave me the weebie jeebies. So I didn't think about it anymore" (127). The last sentence underscores Rachel's domestic logic; she refuses to think about troubling issues: "If there's ugly things going on out there, well, you put a good stout lock on your door and check it twice before you go to sleep. You focus on getting your own one little place set up perfect, as I have done, and you'll see. Other people's worries do not necessarily have to drag you down" (516). Rachel assumes that everything that happened in Kilanga was simply a result of "bad luck": "What happened to us in the Congo was simply the bad luck of two opposite worlds crashing into each other, causing tragedy. . . . I'd made my mind up all along just to rise above it all. Keep my hair presentable and pretend I was elsewhere" (465). The fact that she is able to repress or deny much of this history—to imaginatively rise above it—reveals her special dispensation as an American.

Rachel's homemaking practices highlight the historical amnesia required to carry out American domesticity's inequitable economic and imperial agendas. Notably, Rachel keeps forgetting that Leah and Anatole's children are her kin. The racism of this passage is hard to ignore; just prior to making a remark about Leah and Anatole's children, she says, "After all this time I can certainly work with the Africans as well as anybody can, mainly by not leading them into temptation. But to *marry* one? And have children? It doesn't seem natural" (464; emphasis in original). The "natural" in this case actually refers to racist cultural constructions. Rachel defines herself as the prototypical imperial American woman (the self-confident white female who lives at the expense of the African colonial subject), denying the African presence that nonetheless exists within the social construction of herself.

In *Animal Dreams*, Kingsolver refers to this distinctive American quality of selective memory: "That's the great American disease, we forget" (316). Or more accurately in Rachel's case, we refuse to remember. Rachel thus represents white privilege's "luck" with her conscious ability to forget and her economic means to lock herself away. Luck, in this case, functions as a synonym for colonialist opportunity. Her neocolonial retreat resembles a gated compound, requiring constant surveillance to assure that no one can "run off with a piece for themselves the minute you turn your back" (512).

This indictment of Rachel, however, fails to take into account the ways in which she also resists, or at least complicates, a neocolonial model of American domesticity. Her posture as the Price family's "dumb blonde" fails to give her credit for recognizing the family's precarious position as soon as she steps off the airplane in Africa: "We are supposed to be calling the shots here, but it doesn't look to me like we're in charge of a thing, not even our own selves" (22). Another of Rachel's remarkable qualities is her use of language. At once demonstrating her "dumb blonde" mentality *and* her precise understanding of Africa and herself, her malapropisms are humorous and often express larger truths.[17] For example, upon arriving in Africa, Rachel remarks, "Already I was heavy-hearted in my soul for the flush commodes and machine-washed clothes and other simple things in life I have took for *granite*" (23; my emphasis). Africa truly shakes Rachel's "granite" foundation, and it takes all her might (and a few drinks at the bar) to restore her confidence.

The above condemnation, additionally, does not account for how Rachel's nostalgic longing for America changes after Ruth May's death: "Until that moment I'd always believed I could still go home and pretend the Congo never happened.... The tragedies that happened to Africans were not mine. We were different, not just because we were white and had our vaccinations, but because we were simply a much, much luckier kind of person" (367). Prior to Ruth May's death, "luck" in Rachel's lexicon—like "duty" in Mrs. March's worldview—ultimately justifies her racial, class, and national privileges. After Ruth May's death, however, Rachel realizes that luck may not always be on her side. Her lot in life leads Rachel to understand that "sometimes life doesn't give you all that many chances at being good" (515). Rachel knows, furthermore, that she can never go home again because she no longer fits in: "My long tramp through the mud left me tuckered out and just too worldly-wise to go along with the teen scene" (513). While she still does not concern herself with the material factors that might influence luck or her "peculiar privilege," she knows from personal experience that sometimes all possible choices are bad.

Additionally, if Rachel had really "risen above it all," she would not keep trying to justify her decision to remain in Africa and would not be so defensive about her exiled position. We must remember that as Orleanna and her daughters were trying to leave Kilanga, Rachel was effectively handed over to the colonialist mercenary Axelroot, who takes her to Johannesburg, South Africa, and promptly gives her a venereal disease that leaves her infertile. Rachel's experiences—both in terms of her upbringing and the cultural moment—lead her to believe that her survival hinges on her ability to latch onto (white) men. In this sense, Rachel's experiences are perhaps closer to her mother's than those of her younger sisters. Like her mother, Rachel is representative of "another country" of women (383). However, Rachel manipulates men for her own benefit, whereas her mother is presented as a more passive and guileless woman.

This examination of Rachel Price reveals that Kingsolver's novel fails to reproduce a clean copy of what George refers to as "the authoritative American woman." Rachel's shifts between facile and astute understandings resist straw (wo)man constructions. Rachel is not simply evil. Her likeable qualities and keen insights prevent us from dismissing her offhandedly. Her Americanisms make her especially difficult to ignore. Rachel says, "The way I see Africa, you don't have to like it but you sure have to admit it's out there" (516). This passage suggests that she, too, ultimately recognizes the Africanist presence within her own narrative. As readers, we don't have to like Rachel, but we sure have to admit she's out there.

Leah's character also explores a recycled version of the benevolent American, particularly true womanhood's self-sacrifice for a greater good. Echoing

Mrs. March's remarks about duty (84), Leah values her marriage not only for its individual and family comforts but for its "worldly" effects as well. For example, Leah hopes that her marriage, despite its difficulties, means something in the world: "But hasn't our life together *meant more to the world* than either of us could have meant alone?" (473; my emphasis). Leah's homemaking recycles Mrs. March's philosophy, but her unorthodox family undercuts conventional domesticity. Thus, Leah also resembles fellow tomboy Jo March, who balks at traditional gender roles throughout *Little Women* and makes an unconventional marriage.

Jo and Leah both marry men who are ethnically different, resisting the cultural taboos against mixed marriages. This textual wrinkle underscores *Little Women*'s gender and ethnic complexities. Although Jo eventually marries the German professor Friedrich Bhaer, and is thereby recontained by conventional narrative expectations, her marriage—like Leah's—is unconventional. Even as the story marks Professor Bhaer's speech and demeanor as ethnically different, it also demonstrates how this unique match benefits both Jo and Professor Bhaer. This older man—he is forty while Jo is still in her twenties when they marry—takes Jo's "improprieties" in stride. Furthermore, their school, like Leah and Anatole's relief work, provides stimulating work for them both (Alcott 494–97). *Little Women* thus reinforces conventional, stable domesticity, but it should not be dismissed as a simple reproduction of patriarchal and racist ideologies.

Likewise, Leah does not blindly recreate the conventional home. She resists its imperial and commercial roots, recycling an alternative model home. Even before Ruth May's death, Leah questions her own privileged position and begins to break away from traditional gender roles that would confine her to the home. For example, Leah's participation in a Congolese hunt—a practice reserved for boys and men—challenges Congolese gender roles (335–42; 348–49). Her "feminist" participation also may be read as a stereotypical white American woman's cultural insensitivity to local practices. Later, her biracial family hints at waging a significant mutiny against white privilege and other legacies of imperial history. Her children, furthermore, are documents of possible redemption, proof that whiteness and by extension imperialism will not endure. Observing her children, Leah remarks, "I look at my four boys, who are the colors of silt, loam, dust, and clay, an infinite palette for children of their own, and I understand that time erases whiteness altogether" (526). The fact that her children appear fairly well adjusted to their lives in the United States and Africa attests to her hope's veracity.[18]

Ruth May's observation about whiteness helps us understand Leah's statement about the erasure of whiteness. Ruth May observes that whiteness in the Congo does not last: "Anything that ever was white is not white here. That is not a color you see. Even a white flower opening up on a bush just looks doomed for this world" (50). I understand Leah's comment about her children as fitting in along these same lines. Her whiteness—coded as sin— will not be erased, but her children represent possible redemption, proof that whiteness (colonialism) will not last in the Congo. Leah flips white privilege's familiar script: "[I] work my skin to darkness under the equatorial sun" (526). Rachel, on the other hand, accuses Leah of being brainwashed by Communists (503). In Rachel's mind, Communists and Leah share the desire to dissolve national, racial, and class boundaries.

A less generous reading might suggest that Leah simply engages in "cultural impersonation"; she borrows, in other words, "the identity of the Other in order to avoid not only guilt but pain and self-hatred" (Martin and Mohanty 306).[19] Leah's self-conscious awareness of her position as a white American, however, disproves or at least weakens this argument. After all, Leah and Anatole's sons are all named for men lost to war (497). History lives within their household. Unlike Rachel, Leah does not attempt to mask her white privilege or use her home for personal profit. She does not construct security behind a door with stout locks. Rachel, like conventional domestic ideology, masks fissures to achieve stability. Leah, practicing neodomestic ideology, recognizes how the historic and present forces of cultural and economic capital converge to form privilege.

For example, describing her residence in Kinshasa in 1974, Leah explains, "Our house is sturdy, with a concrete floor and a tin roof. We live in what would be called, in America, a slum, though here it's an island of relative luxury in the outskirts of *la cité*, where the majority have a good deal less in the way of roofing, to say the least" (446). Contrasting American slums with the Kinshasa housing illustrates Leah's ability to distinguish the cultural and economic differences between the two urban environments and notions of a good home. Leah consciously makes key distinctions between similar economic housing conditions. Nevertheless, she still often retreats to a model of security and stability. Leah will attempt extreme acts to achieve a "safe retreat": "But in my dreams I still have hope, and in life, no safe retreat. If I have to hop all the way on one foot, damn it, I'll find a place I can claim as home" (506). While Leah, like Jo, finds a good partner, she is not as successful in finding her place in the world. Therefore, despite their distinct homemaking practices, Rachel and Leah ultimately share a core definition of home. Both seek security.[20]

Where Rachel frequently defines home according to material comforts like running water, her sister understands home as a place of emotional security. For example, Leah describes their house in the Kimvula District of Zaire as follows: "Our house here is mud and thatch, plenty large, with two rooms and a kitchen shed. A happier place, for sure, than the tin-and-cement box that packaged us up with all our griefs in Kinshasa" (501). While the home depends on both discursive and material elements, Leah's experiences emphasize that "in all societies . . . the home is much more than a physical structure" (McDowell 92). Rachel struggles to fabricate a sense of security through conscious forgetting and material hotel improvements. Leah struggles to construct a family and home able to withstand a nomadic life. While this house is "a happier place," Leah still does not feel at home on the insecure border: "But our life in this village feels provisional. We have one foot over the border into the promised land, or possibly the grave" (501).

Where Rachel pursues financial control and security by running her business, Leah seeks emotional security for herself and her family. The time that Leah's family spends in the United States demonstrates the complex ways in which economic and cultural, specifically racial, politics influence one's sense and experience of home and security. Where Rachel replicates segregation, her sister and her biracial family suffer from its legacies. In America, their home's material comforts are beyond what Leah's family has ever experienced. Living in "married-student housing, a plywood apartment complex set among pine trees" (468), Leah and Anatole have trouble adjusting to American ideas about home:

> The singular topic of conversation among our young neighbors was the inadequacy of these rattletrap tenements. To Anatole and me they seemed absurdly luxurious. Glass windows, with locks on every one and two on the door, when we didn't have a single possession worth stealing. Running water, *hot*, right out of the tap in the kitchen, and another one only ten steps away in the bathroom! (468; emphasis in original)

Modern conveniences like hot water from the tap seem "luxurious" considering the home Leah and Anatole recently left behind in Africa. Their experience demonstrates that material comforts and physical security—in the form of window and door locks—do not successfully produce a safe home or even a safe retreat. While their physical housing improves in America, Leah's family still experiences racial prejudice, which prevents them from feeling comfortable. Leah explains, "The citizens of my homeland regarded my husband and children as primitives, or freaks. On the streets, from a distance, they'd scowl at us, thinking we were merely the scourge they already knew and loathed—the mixed-race couple, with mongrel children as advertisement of our sins" (468–69). Anatole's warrior markings on his face present another problem—further pushing him to the outer extremes of being an outsider in America (469). Racism against biracial families prevents Leah's family from feeling at home.

Part of Leah's problem is that she does not seem to belong anywhere, which holds true when the family decides to return to Africa (468–74). Anatole's arrest upon reentry forces Leah to make a home without him: "Cloaked in my *pagne* and Anatole, I seemed to belong. Now, husbandless in this new neighborhood, my skin glows like a bare bulb" (472). Alone, Leah does not feel at home in Kinshasa either. Nevertheless, she understands her Kinshasa neighbors' reserved manner: "They know just one thing about foreigners, and that is everything we've ever done to them" (472). Leah recognizes the historical justification behind her Kinshasa neighbors' behavior, and she dreams "to leave my house one day unmarked by whiteness" (504).

Leah and Rachel's mutual search for a safe retreat may be traced back to their lost American home—once again we see "the materials and debris of past domestic edifices" recycled in their homes (George, "Recycling" 2). Feminist geographer Doreen Massey best contextualizes their search for security: "Those who today worry about a sense of disorientation and a loss of control must once have felt they knew exactly where they were, and that they *had* control" (Massey 165; emphasis in original). Massey goes on to clarify, "There is, then, an issue of whose identity we are referring to when we talk of a place called home and of the supports it may provide of stability, oneness and security" (Massey 167). In Sanza Pombo, for example, Leah struggles to get her students to plan for the future: "I ought to understand. I've been as transient in my adult life as anyone in our cooperative" (524). Leah seems to forget that prior to adulthood she knew security. Being nomadic for most of one's adult life is not the same as living "homeless" in one's own country for generations. Leah still seeks control. However, Leah's final chapter in book 6 suggests that she eventually strikes a balance between a safe retreat and access to the privileges that she desires for others: "There's the possibility of balance" (522). Significantly, *Little Women* also points to balance as a mark of domestic success (121). However, neodomestic balance is not predicated on stasis but rather on movement. Leah finally understands her mother's wisdom: "As Mother used to say, not a thing stands still but sticks in the mud" (526).

Neodomestic Homes in America
Orleanna's and Adah's Recycled Homes

Orleanna articulates most clearly how neodomesticity's instability can be productive. According to Orleanna, if we can embrace change and let go of our need to conquer space and people, then we will experience "the only celebration we mortals really know" (385). Unlike Mrs. March, Orleanna does not rejoice in domestic stability. In fact, she suggests that the desire for stability will not only eventually cause colonialists to fail but will ultimately curse all of humanity (384). Orleanna explains, "In perfect stillness, frankly, I've only found sorrow" (385). When we insist on domestic stability, we experience sorrow. Orleanna does not hold these views throughout the novel. She initially practices conventional homemaking. The changes in Orleanna's conventional homemaking begin just prior to the women's exodus out of Africa.

Orleanna's homemaking practices follow an interesting trajectory. She begins with the traditional, protective home model. When the family arrives in Kilanga, Orleanna follows an oppositional model and uses their home as a traditional shelter against outside dangers. Orleanna seeks to construct a safe haven for her girls. Near the middle of the novel, as she grows increasingly frustrated with their situation, she makes a 180 degree turn. Adah describes this change in "Judges":[21]

> Our mother, the recent agoraphobe, who kept us pumpkin-shelled indoors through all the months of rain and epidemic and Independence, has now turned on her protector: she eyes our house suspiciously, accuses it of being "cobwebby" and "strangling us with the heat." She speaks of it as a thing with will and motive. Every afternoon she has us put on our coolest dresses and run away from our malignant house. (276–77)

Orleanna attempts to cope with the home-abroad by first trying to replicate the American domestic sphere abroad and then trying to invert this model, turning her daughters loose outdoors and breaking the barriers between the patriarchal Price home—likened to the nursery rhyme about female containment—and the "undomesticated" Congo. Finally, back in America, she sets up two transformed homes—homes that defy conservative bourgeois values—while never taking her eyes off Africa.

Orleanna's fixation on Africa keeps her historically grounded and accountable. She situates her neodomestic homemaking within a translocal framework. Similar to her daughter Rachel who looks toward America without ever returning, Orleanna continues to look toward Africa with an anxious gaze. Unlike Rachel, Orleanna does not look back with nostalgia. Her gaze fails to contain Africa; Africa shifts under it, "refusing to be any place at all, or any thing but itself" (10). Upon her return to Georgia, Orleanna becomes an exile in her own country. Africa hounds her, reminding her of the price that she paid to gain her wings and fly from her gilded cage: "I'd lost my wings. Don't ask me how I gained them back—the story is too unbearable" (201). The story that she cannot tell (but that her daughters do tell) is the story of how Ruth May died, how Orleanna pawned Rachel to a colonialist mercenary, and how Orleanna left a sick Leah behind in Africa.[22] This series of events finally leads to and allows for Orleanna to leave her husband and return to America with one child in tow, her disabled daughter Adah.

Orleanna and Adah do not return home to Georgia in heroic glory; they also do not pick up where they left off in 1959. Without their requisite patriarch breadwinner, they are literally without a home (407). In a hometown that presumes they are insane heathens, Orleanna initially rents a small cabin on the town's outskirts and begins a fantastic flower garden—something her husband Nathan never allowed.[23] She later moves to a rented apartment in Atlanta and marches for civil rights. Not surprisingly, she never remarries: "Nathan Price was all the marriage I needed" (531). Her African colonial existence as Nathan's wife directly shapes her own postcolonial exile in America. Such changes document her refusal to return to the gilded cage after her flight back to America (201) and her self-chosen position on the margin of (white) American society.

Like her mother, Adah lives on the margin by rejecting marriage, but she does so for "different reasons" (531): "Eros is not so much an eyesore, it turns out, as just too much noise" (532). One might argue that Adah seeks security by not risking the "noise" or instability produced by depending on loved ones. Adah leaves home, as it were, almost the moment that she returns to America. She goes to college and eventually sets up house alone in Atlanta. Adah describes her changed view of home: "Africa has slipped the floor out from under my righteous house, my Adah moral code" (443). Like Rachel, she no longer takes life for "granite." From her new position, Adah builds a life based on her work, not a husband and family: "I don't have cats or children, I have viruses" (530). Like Orleanna, Adah keeps her eyes on Africa but at the microscopic level.

In her work on God's "housecleaning," Adah seeks not so much to find a cure for the diseases she studies, but to understand more clearly their histories and the balance they create in the world: "The race between predator and prey remains exquisitely neck and neck" (529). Remembering the driver ants that invaded Kilanga and almost cost Adah her life helps her understand:

"This is what we learned in Kilanga: move out of the way and praise God for the housecleaning" (529). Adah connects domesticity and balance with nothing less than cosmology. Her minimalist homemaking similarly seeks to maintain this balance between loss and salvation: "My life is satisfying and ordinary. I work a great deal, and visit my mother on Sanderling Island once a month. . . . Sometimes I play chess with one of my colleagues, an anchorite like myself, who suffers from post-polio syndrome" (530–32). In this sense, Adah maintains a nomadic lifestyle to the extent that she refuses to construct a home, at least in any traditional manner with a conventional family: "I don't think of the viruses as my work, actually. I think of them as my relations" (530).

While Adah's home represents an alternative to a patriarchal construction, I imagine that it fails to resonate with many readers. Her sterile approach to creating a home lacks comfort. As Witold Rybczynski remarks, "Hominess is not neatness" (Rybczynski 17). In this light, Leah's self-righteous homemaking practices render her home and character the least appealing and interesting—whereas Rachel, for all her faults, seems the most human and, in that sense, likable. Their homemaking strategies all fail in some respect to reconcile the conflict between comfort and equitable access. As a result, while Orleanna, Adah, and Leah all give up stable, patriarchal homes, the extent to which these individual changes produce decisive consequences for the "governing principles of exclusions and inclusions" remains limited (George, *Politics* 200). These individual women are not able to single-handedly wipe out white privilege. Nevertheless, their journeys and struggles to construct home provide rich terrain for inquiry. All the women's descriptions of the various houses that they occupy reveal the extent to which a sense of home requires more than adequate shelter. Individuals within particular historical and cultural contexts experience home differently. Additionally, the variety of their homemaking strategies reveals that no single, monolithic model can work for everyone.

Various strategies of "responsible recycling" can be seen in the individual homes that Orleanna, Adah, and Leah construct after leaving Kilanga. These characters do not create traditional homes. Even Rachel opts for a home that is unconventional, though it is not particularly radical. Deviating too far from socially acceptable homemaking practices carries too high a price. In all fairness, we must also recognize the novel's historicity and the constraints that this realism entails. To suggest that these women could have solved such problems would demean Kingsolver's project to inform her readers about America's destructive involvement in Africa. Thus, rather than measure the worth of the characters' homes according to the degree of radical change that they signify or produce, we must consider how these "personal histories that are themselves situated in relation to the development within feminism of particular questions and critiques" interrogate the boundaries between first-world inclusion and third-world exclusion (Martin and Mohanty 294). *The Poisonwood Bible* commands the respect that Rosemary Marangoly George argues should be granted to texts that "acknowledge the seductive pleasure of belonging in homes and in communities and in nations—while working toward changing the governing principles of exclusions and inclusions" (*Politics* 200). The novel's representations of the Price women, specifically regarding their feelings about and constructions of home, complicate or destabilize what George calls the "authoritative American woman," or the self-confident white female produced at the expense of the African colonial subject. What emerges out of these revisions is a clearly identifiable spatial genre tied together by three common features: mobility, relational space, and renovation and redesign.

While there ultimately may be no "outside" to the American home's trappings, which would account for why neodomestic fiction relies on recycling rather than invention, neodomestic fiction generates a politics of home that focuses attention on the home's relational nature, on its fundamental instability. Neodomestic protagonists reconfigure domestic thresholds; rather than becoming recontained by the domestic narrative's structure, neodomestic protagonists embrace and invent "spaces of radical openness" (hooks, *Yearning* 148). The neodomestic novel, thus, does not offer a magic solution to American domestic inequalities; however, it does attempt to destabilize conventional domesticity by revising, recycling, and remodeling alternatives that are cognizant of the past and the present.

Recycling Conclusions

We need fictional maps based on geopolitical realities to navigate contentious material realities. For white American subjects—especially women, who are traditionally associated with the home—this necessarily constitutes moving away from conventional homes founded on racism and sexism. As David Harvey and Rosemary Marangoly George suggest, those who imagine or otherwise engage in utopian or fictional constructions of space must eventually confront such material realities: "Any contemporary struggle to envision a reconstruction of the social process has to confront the problem of how to overthrow the structures (both physical and institutional) that the free market has itself produced as relatively permanent features of our world" (Harvey, *Spaces* 186). Kingsolver and Silko actively produce such maps, which are key components in their activist, neodomestic fiction.

Their maps reveal that just as the various meanings of the word *bangala* depend on the word's pronunciation—one referring to "something precious and dear" and one referring to the name of the poisonwood tree—the American home depends on at least two seemingly contradictory forces: the need to create emotional and economic security for oneself and the desire to share this security with others (Kingsolver, *Poisonwood* 276). *The Poisonwood Bible* and *Gardens in the Dunes*, along with neodomestic novels more generally, suggest that American homes—in their ideological and material manifestations—can change for the better as well as continue on well-worn destructive paths. Domestic stability serves as the linchpin.

Not surprisingly, when the model American home undergoes scrutiny, Americans bristle. Critiquing the American home brings the American dream—in essence the very ideology that *is* America—under question. But we risk more by placing stout locks on this ideal. Gwendolyn Wright, in "Prescribing the Model Home," describes the problems that result when the model American home remains a singular proposition: "Confronting the problems of those for whom 'home' is lost or denied can intensify the potency of this ideal, making one's own 'perfect home' seem all the more essential and precarious. This fear prompts large numbers of Americans to turn away from the injustice they see around them" (Wright 223). She cautions that the American model home can become a "form of bondage" when it fails to fit a variety of family types (Wright 223). Rachel Price in *The Poisonwood Bible* demonstrates the traits that Wright describes; Rachel never returns to the United States because she cannot meet traditional American domestic expectations. Likewise, Leah Price's search for a safe retreat threatens to doom her ability to experience "the only celebration we mortals really know" (385). The homes that the female characters build in *Gardens in the Dunes* and *The Poisonwood Bible* represent America's "poisonous" as well as "precious" domestic spaces and provide tenuous model neodomestic homes. As the next chapter explores, the ways that neodomestic fictions remodel home further reveal the model home's "form[s] of bondage" (Wright 223) and provide blueprints of "doable" alternatives (Morrison, "Home" 3–4).

3

Remodeling Home

Redesigning Conventional Domestic Space

> What I am determined to do is to take what is articulated as an elusive race-free paradise and domesticate it.
>
> —Toni Morrison, "Home"

According to Harvard University's Joint Center for Housing Studies, Americans doubled the amount they spent on home improvement between 1995 and 2007; by 2008 a sluggish housing market and falling real estate prices contributed to a nearly 16 percent drop in renovations by the third quarter of 2008 (Joint Center 3; 8). While the recent drop is significant, so is the growth that has been recorded over the last ten years or so; in 1995 remodeling expenses hovered at $149 billion, and by 2007 Americans were spending $326 billion on remodeling (Joint Center 3). Daniel McGinn in *House Lust* points out that while some of this remodeling is simply replacing the things, like roofs, that wear out, "More than half of Americans' home improvement spending . . . [goes] toward 'discretionary' remodels that let older homes boast some of the features—like family rooms and master bathrooms—that either didn't exist when they were built, or were considered proper amenities for only upper-class housing" (89–90). Whether we remodel out of necessity, desire, or some combination of both, renovation is part of the homeownership experience.

The booming remodeling period that characterized the early years of the twenty-first century figured in other areas of the era's domestic culture. The late twentieth century saw a steep increase in the number of home improvement shows and networks, the sustained success and growth of shelter magazines, and the expansion of big-box home improvement outlets such as Home Depot and Lowe's. This widespread commercial growth coincided with a sustained interest in domestic laborsaving technologies and rising interest in green design. As Anita Gates points out in regard to the large variety of home makeover television programs, "It's not hard to understand the genre's popularity. Combine the traditional importance of home with a hunger for security in the post–Sept. 11 era and a growing middle-class sense of entitlement, and you get a huge potential audience eager for home betterment" (E1). Home renovation both maintains and redesigns model domesticity; the home's shifting ideal architectures reveal entrenched and changing ideas about the social construction of the American family, particularly regarding gender, race, class, (dis)ability, and sexuality.

Remodeling in American literature involves both literal renovation projects within the storyline as well as generic and symbolic restructuring. Redesigning the domestic novel carries bold potential, as it simultaneously asks us to remodel our understanding of the American family and, by extension, our national identity. Key to neodomestic fiction's literal and generic remodeling projects is how race and gender shape the American home's physical and ideological contours. This chapter examines the geopolitical roles that race and gender play in the home's material and ideological structures. Through a series of "careful and effective reversals," neodomestic fictions condemn homes that violently construct oppositional boundaries (Martin and Mohanty 306). This chapter appraises the American home's physical and ideological space by surveying several (neo)domestic novels' gendered and raced spaces and their literal and metaphorical remodeling projects.

The various homes in Toni Morrison's *Beloved* and *Paradise* focus especially on the ways that race, gender, and sexuality influence domestic geopolitics. The residents' unique styles of housekeeping and renovation and the characters' fundamental notions about what constitutes home provide important case studies in how recycled and renovated domestic spaces affect female character development and notions of security. Following the lead of scholars like bell hooks, I am interested in the special investment African American women have in domestic space: "Since sexism delegates to females the task of creating and sustaining a home environment, it has been primarily the responsibility of black women to construct domestic households as spaces of care and nurturance in the face of the brutal harsh reality of racist oppression, of sexist domination" (hooks, *Yearning* 42). *Beloved* and *Paradise* provide ideal novels for this analysis because both sustain attention to the relationship between their female protagonists and the home as a safe haven. Additionally, unlike Morrison's first novel, *The Bluest Eye* (1970), *Beloved* and *Paradise* exhibit the three key tropes of neodomestic fiction: mobility, home renovations, and relational domestic space.[1] Following neodomestic ideology, the novels' remodeling emphasizes the dangers associated with oppositional, patriarchal space and the benefits of following relational, feminist spatial practices.

Remodeling the Race House
Morrison's *Beloved* and *Paradise*

The American home is raced as well as gendered. Traditionally, both paradigms frame the house as either a haven or a trap. For example, *Beloved* (1987) and *Paradise* (1997) may appear at first glance to reproduce the American home's faults—its traps, exclusions, and the very real physical dangers associated with unstable housing—rather than remodel domesticity in ways that "domesticate," in Toni Morrison's words, "an elusive race-free paradise" ("Home" 8). For instance, homes become sites of violence in both novels. The house in *Beloved*, 124 Bluestone Road, fails to protect the "crawling already baby." The Convent in *Paradise* should epitomize a safe haven for its female residents, but it instead traps them during a blaze of gunfire. However, these initial impressions of the novels' domestic geographies do not tell the whole story. Rather than ultimately constructing the home as a trap (or as a haven), both novels deconstruct and remodel the conventional house-home dichotomy, materializing neodomestic ideology through their experimentation with an elusive but productive domestic instability.

Uncritical and oppositional constructions of home explain the folly of the residents' actions in *Beloved* and *Paradise*. The novels address how "the pursuit of safe places and ever-narrower conceptions of community relies on unexamined notions of home, family, and nation" (Martin and Mohanty 293). In both novels the residents attempt to construct a safe home and community, but their isolated homes promote precisely the violent relations that they had wished to avoid. Biddy Martin and Chandra Mohanty have made keen observations about Minnie Bruce Pratt's critical construction of home that also apply to *Beloved* and *Paradise:* "The tension between the desire for home, for synchrony, for sameness, and the realization of the repressions and violence that make home, harmony, sameness imaginable, and that enforce it, is made clear in the movement of the narrative by very careful and effective reversals which do not erase the positive desire for unity, for Oneness, but destabilize and undercut it" (306). This domesticated violence is the type of brutality that Morrison spoke about in an interview with Claudia Tate: "There's a special kind of domestic perception that has its own violence in writings by black women—not bloody violence, but violence nonetheless" (Morrison, qtd. in Tate 162). This is a violence infused in everyday life; this is the violence of conventional, oppositional constructions of home. Morrison's domestic fiction, thus, incorporates both subtle and extreme manifestations of the home's violent aspects and attempts to remodel this space.

Placing Morrison's theoretical conceptions of "house" and "home" in conversation with other historical and theoretical paradigms before turning to the novels themselves helps to unpack the relationships between power and place. An examination of Morrison's essay "Home" clarifies what is at stake when she distinguishes between house and home, then deconstructs and remodels this dichotomy in her fiction. Additionally, "Home" clarifies how Morrison's fiction realizes neodomestic principles. Morrison writes, "I am determined to concretize a literary discourse that (outside of science fiction) resonates exclusively in the register of a permanently unrealizable dream" ("Home" 8). Morrison's essay and neodomestic fiction bring to fruition what David Harvey defines in *Spaces of Hope* as "spatiotemporal utopias"—fictional maps grounded in present and historical realities.

Pouring the Foundation
Morrison's "Home"

As the epigraph to this chapter implies, Morrison's fiction "domesticates" three elements crucial to this study: history, present realities, and spatial theory. The present and historical experience of home for African Americans shapes domestic fiction's geopolitics in particular ways. Four salient moments in American history come immediately to mind when considering the significance of home for African Americans: (1) slavery; (2) dispossession in the wake of Reconstruction (1865–1877) and *Plessy v. Ferguson* (1896); (3) the Great Migration north during the first half of the twentieth century (roughly 1910–1930); and (4) the perpetuity of low African American homeownership rates during the twentieth century. During the 1980s, African American homeownership rates declined after steadily increasing for fifty years ("Decline in Black Home Ownership" 19). According to data released by the U.S. Census Bureau, "After 50 years of steady and uninterrupted progress, the percentage of blacks who own their homes suddenly and unexpectedly declined in the 1980s. A continuation of this trend would reinforce the position of America's blacks at the margin of America's propertied society" ("Decline"19). In 1980, blacks were 36 percent less likely than whites to own their own home ("Decline" 20). Discouragingly, affordability for a modestly priced house in 2004 remained low for African Americans, especially for black renter families. (The Census Bureau defined "affordability" as the ability to buy a home with cash or "qualify for a conventional, 30-year mortgage with a 5-percent down payment" [Savage 1].) According to the U.S. Census Bureau, in 2004, "about 1 out of 5 non-Hispanic White married couples who rented could qualify to buy a modestly priced home, while 1 in 10 Black married couples who rented could buy a home" (Savage 4).

The material, ideological, and fictional home for African Americans emerges from this history of disenfranchisement and repeated resettlement. Furthermore, the violence lodged within this domestic geography contextualizes the frequency and significance of the reconstruction and renovation of home and community as significant themes within African American literature broadly and Morrison's novels specifically.[2] As historian Andrew Wiese writes, "space and spatial struggle" are central to African American life (288): "In the face of white racism, expressed through extraordinary efforts to limit their [African Americans'] freedom to occupy, use, or even move through space, they battled to defend and expand the territory available to them" (291). As bell hooks has written, "Many narratives of resistance struggle from slavery to the present share an obsession with the politics of space, particularly the need to construct and build houses" ("Black Vernacular" 397).

Toni Morrison's novels not only share a focus on domestic space but also situate the American home within each of the above landmark struggles. *Beloved* addresses the denial of home and family brought about by slavery, drawing special attention to slavery's geopolitics through the haunting of 124. Set in the 1680s, *A Mercy* (2008) goes back further to map the building of colonial America; portions of the story are literally written on the walls of an empty house. *Song of Solomon*, *Paradise*, and *Love* take up African American dispossession and segregation following Reconstruction and *Plessy v. Ferguson*, tracking their legacies into the twentieth century. *Jazz* follows its characters from the rural South to the urban North during the Great Migration when about one million southern blacks moved north. Set in the fall of 1941, in the wake of a national decline in homeownership that occurred in 1940, *The Bluest Eye* accurately portrays disparities between black homeowners (as represented by Geraldine) and black renters (like the Breedlove family), highlighting that homeownership issues for the black community have not changed much throughout the twentieth century.[3] Additionally, *Sula* (1974) is set during a period of rampant suburban growth (1919–1965). Not coincidentally, *Sula* tells the story of the Bottom's inhabitants, locating the story in an African American neighborhood that no longer exists because it was removed "to make room for the Medallion City Golf Course" (3). Finally, the contemporary setting in *Tar Baby* (1981) considers the longstanding relationship between African American domestic servants and white employers.

Morrison repeatedly uses the home setting to "domesticate" or "bring home" her message for her readers. While domestic fiction is not the only genre that defines Morrison's oeuvre, her experimentation with this form situates it as a central rather than marginal literary genre—within her own body of work and within contemporary American literature generally, as Morrison is one of the major American authors of our time. Especially in *Beloved* and *Paradise,* home remodeling and the search for community address the violent historical legacies and present realities described above.

To use Michel Foucault's terminology, the recycled, renovated, and relational domestic spaces in *Beloved* and *Paradise* record a "history of *powers.*" Connecting historical and theoretical concerns regarding space, Foucault argues that "a whole history remains to be written of spaces—which would at the same time be the history of *powers*" (*Power/Knowledge* 149; emphasis in original). Significantly, both novels locate home and community at the margins; the novels' geopolitics address the construction of African American communities that are frequently required to make homes on the periphery. Therefore, while Geoffrey Bent claims that Morrison in *Paradise* "undermines her talent for characterization by making the protagonist a place—for a piece of real estate to have a personality" (a criticism that also could have easily been made about *Beloved* and its haunted house), I argue that the intense focus on the home in both of these novels moves beyond prosaic personification (Bent 149).

Morrison's fictional dwellings—like Kingsolver's and Silko's homes—historicize and emphasize the "racial project" of moving "the job of unmattering race away from pathetic yearning and futile desire; away from an impossible future or an irretrievable and probably nonexistent Eden to a manageable, doable, modern human activity" ("Home" 3–4). Her didactic structures teach us much about our own participation in the maintenance of what Morrison calls the "race house," which contributes to home's Edenic qualities. Adding her own voice to the growing chorus of criticism concerning the domestic spaces that appear in her fiction, Morrison describes in her essay "Home" the difference between "house" and "home." Drawing directly from descriptions of dwellings in her novels, Morrison describes a "home" as where "one can imagine safety without walls, can iterate difference that is prized but unprivileged, and can conceive of a third, if you will pardon the expression, world 'already made for me, both snug and wide open, with a doorway never needing to be closed'" (12). Significantly, a portion of this passage first appeared in *Jazz* as the narrator's description of home: "I want to be in a place already made for me, both snug and wide open. With a doorway never needing to be closed, a view slanted for light and bright autumn leaves but not rain" (221). In *Paradise*, one of the men set on murdering the women at the Convent also describes home in these terms, further complicating and destabilizing Morrison's definition of home (*Paradise* 8–9; "Home" 9–10). These textual repetitions demonstrate that Morrison's essay draws from and reflects on her fictional portrayals and interrogations of home.

The borderless home—imagined but not impossible—contrasts with the "race house," which embodies the ideological structures that keep racism alive in American culture ("Home" 8). Frequently acting as symbolic structures of racism and sexism, houses in Morrison's novels prompt readers to police themselves in a Foucauldian manner. In his chapter on the panopticon, Foucault explains that the efficiency of the "house of certainty" is its ability to make the subject self-policing: "He inscribes in himself the power relation in which he simultaneously plays both roles; he becomes the principle of his own subjection" (*Discipline* 202–3). Along similar lines, Morrison states at the end of her essay that we must "recognize [our] own participation in the maintenance of the race house" (12). Institutional racism materializes in the race house. This transformation connects social forces with individuals' behavior. In Foucauldian terms, the race house functions as a state apparatus made visible through the vehicle of fiction. Where Morrison's description of the race house builds on Foucault's notion of discipline, her definition of home resembles bell hooks's conception of home: "Home is that place which enables and promotes varied and everchanging perspectives, a place where one discovers new ways of seeing reality, frontiers of difference" (hooks, *Yearning* 148). Like hooks's characterization of home, Morrison describes home as radically open. For Morrison, there are no walls or doors that need closing ("Home" 12). She defines the "house" primarily as an "oppositional space" and the "home" primarily as a "relational space."

Morrison's and hooks's conceptions of home link well with feminist geographers' ideas about relational space. Like relational space, home for Morrison and hooks emphasizes the *interaction* between spaces rather than their *opposition*. Although Carolyn M. Jones does not refer to relational space in her discussion of landscape in Morrison's fiction, she suggests that place both shapes and is shaped by people: "We shape and, finally, return to land, mark it with our work and our being, even as the land marks us" (46). This give and take is a hallmark of relational space and of the domestic geography in *Beloved* and *Paradise*. While the houses in *Beloved* and *Paradise* are located at the margins of society, domestic space often shifts between alienation from and reintegration into a larger community.

My reading here diverges from Patricia McKee's understanding of how the home functions in *Paradise*. While we both turn to bell hooks who, like Morrison, understands that home cannot be a "secure or fully-constructed place" (McKee 204), McKee argues in "Geographies of *Paradise*" that hooks constructs a "dialectics of center and margin" and, therefore, *Paradise's* "claims are not quite marginal, since they produce no secure or significant border" (212). McKee's reading productively describes how the Convent women "practice a geography of replacement rather than displacement" (208). However, my understanding of hooks's conception of the margin stresses its flexibility and multiplicity over its function as a clear boundary marker—although certainly borders and margins can and do function in those ways.

In *Justice, Nature and the Geography of Difference*, human geographer David Harvey offers a similar critique of hooks's essay "Choosing the Margin as a Space of Radical Openness." He questions whether appropriating the margin can serve as a source of agency. Harvey points out that hooks's discourse appears to move "from a real 'space' one might call 'home' . . . to a metaphorical 'place' that is to open a different kind of becoming" (*Justice* 104). Where Harvey critiques this movement from a "real space" to a "metaphorical place," feminist geographer Doreen Massey refutes Harvey and understands such "metaphorical" places as "relational," not unrealistic or dangerously nonmaterial. That is, she rejects Harvey's insistence—which McKee's reading also seems to follow—on place's *bound* nature.

According to Massey, geographers like Harvey depend on "negative counterpositions" to define places like the home (Massey 167–68). Harvey's position requires concrete distinctions between house and home. In contradistinction, Massey argues for a more fluid, relational definition of home in her essay "A Place Called Home?" and in her interpretation of hooks's notions of the home and the margin. The homes and communities in *Beloved* and *Paradise* interrogate the viability and dangers of embracing the margin as home and of constructing home as a relational space. Additionally, the home's "spiritual geography," which offers another way of mapping home's relational characteristics, is fundamental to the imaginative and historically grounded homes located in Morrison's fiction and in neodomestic fiction more broadly.

Inés Salazar describes three roles that spiritual geographies play in African American and Chicana literature and culture that apply to Morrison's novels and to neodomestic fiction generally, but especially to those fictions that are focused on characters who are members of minority groups:

The first is personal affirmation outside the framework of western cultural paradigms. Secondly, cultural and geographical dislocation requires a nonmaterial means to maintain historical remembrance and cultural continuity in the face of potential erasure. Finally, and perhaps most importantly, the emphasis on the spiritual signals a process of transformation that signifies the always unfolding negotiation between the collective and subject; and between the preservation of the past and the requirements of the present. (400)

Salazar's description resonates with the neodomestic spatial practices that I describe in this and previous chapters. Neodomestic space also emphasizes historical and cultural specificity as well as the relational nature of the individual's private sphere with the larger community. I explore spiritual geography's particular significance to neodomestic fiction in greater detail in chapters 4 and 5. The following sections focus on the significance of relational space in Morrison's novels, especially regarding how the characters remodel the home in ways attentive to the past and the present and to individual and communal needs.

Thus Morrison's essay "Home"—especially when placed in conversation with Foucault, hooks, Harvey, Massey, and Salazar—articulates the tensions among material dwellings, theoretical interpretations of domestic space, and, as we will now consider in more detail, representations of home in fiction. While Morrison's essay "Home" makes clear distinctions between houses and homes, the distinctions in her fiction are not always as clear. Morrison even writes in "Home" that she has abandoned her search for the "elusive sovereignty" known as home (4). However, this admission does not mean that she has yielded to the race house. Rather, the relational, recycled structures in Morrison's fiction articulate an ongoing struggle to "domesticate"—or bring to physical reality—the relational "elusive race-free paradise" ("Home" 8). She is no longer searching for an oppositional haven—a "sovereignty"—but rather a "race-specific yet nonracist home" ("Home" 5). The domestic structures in *Beloved* and *Paradise* in particular demonstrate qualities of both the race house and the ideal home.

Slavery's Domestic Geographies:
Remodeling the Big House in *Beloved*

A geopolitical analysis of the house at 124 Bluestone Road in *Beloved* reveals that its design contains elements of both the race house and the idyllic home.

In *Beloved*, we see further support for hooks's characterization of the home as a "site of resistance and liberation struggle" for African American women (*Yearning* 45). In fact, such resistance within domestic spaces has roots in slavery. By remodeling her fictional dwellings, Morrison demonstrates an African American woman's power to change domesticity's traditional geopolitics by destabilizing the house-home dichotomy and remaking home.

John Michael Vlach in *Back of the Big House: The Architecture of Plantation Slavery* explains that one means of resistance utilized by slaves was the (re)appropriation of space. Such resistance centered on the plantation's domestic sphere:

> The spaces that slaves claimed and modified for their own domestic purposes provided them with their own sense of place. In these locations they were able to develop a stronger sense of social solidarity, a feeling of community that would serve as a seedbed not only for further resistance but also for the invention and maintenance of a distinctive African American culture. (Vlach 236)

Slaves gained agency, according to Vlach, by appropriating places on the plantation (169). While these domestic spaces were still strongholds of oppression, slaves effectively made spaces like the kitchen or the slave quarters so "black" that their white owners entered them reluctantly (Vlach x–xi). Vlach notes that after emancipation, slaves often remained on the plantation. Rather than indicating dependency, this behavior illustrates the true extent to which slaves appropriated plantation space, calling and claiming it their own. For example, in a collective petition sent to President Andrew Johnson, a group of emancipated slaves "protested the restoration of plantation lands to their former owners, declaring, 'This is our home. We have made these lands what they are'" (Vlach ix). This appropriation of domestic space by (former) slaves plays an important role in understanding Baby Suggs's motivation to remodel 124 as well as in understanding the particular ways in which she changes the house on Bluestone Road.

The house at 124 Bluestone shares external and internal similarities to slave plantation architecture. According to Vlach, typical buildings on slave plantations included the big house, slave quarters, yard, kitchen, smokehouse, barn, and a collection of outbuildings. While the 124 property does not have separate housing for slaves, the house does have a designated sleeping area for the hired help (*Beloved* 207). Additionally, the property has a yard and a small collection of outbuildings: the privy, a detached kitchen that later becomes the woodshed and toolroom where the "crawling already baby" dies, and a cold house where Paul D eventually sleeps with Beloved (29). Baby Suggs creates an attached storeroom after she removes the back door. The location and layout of 124 also evoke plantation design because the house is surrounded by eighty acres of land (*Beloved* 259). Slave quarters were often located at the margins of "civilized" space on the plantation (Vlach 229). Located near the border between slave states and free states, 124 likewise is set in the wilderness outside of the town (*Beloved* 3). Considering that the house's design and location bear so many similarities to a plantation, it is not surprising that Baby Suggs remodels 124 Bluestone Road shortly after moving in. Two major renovations take place: she moves the kitchen inside the house, and she boards up the back door. By moving the kitchen inside and eliminating the back door, Baby Suggs abolishes two architectural features that are characteristic of slave plantations.

In slave plantations, the location of the kitchen was deeply symbolic. Vlach notes that moving kitchens outside and to the back of the big house "established a clearer separation between those who served and those who were served. . . . The detached kitchen was an important emblem of hardening social boundaries and the evolving society created by slaveholders that increasingly demanded clearer definitions of status, position, and authority" (Vlach 43).[4] Although it remained a clear symbol of slavery, the plantation's kitchen still served as an empowering space for slaves. Vlach relates, "The cook at the Merrick plantation in Louisiana not only ran the kitchen but determined who could have access to it" (15). While denied ownership of their bodies, slaves like the Merrick's cook could occasionally control their domestic workspaces.

Similarly, Baby Suggs's refusal to conform to white housing design standards for the placement of the kitchen emphasizes her appropriation of domestic space. Baby Suggs doesn't pay any mind to the "visitors with nice dresses [who] don't want to sit in the same room with the cook stove and the peelings and the grease and the smoke" (*Beloved* 207). Moreover, by boarding up the back door, Baby Suggs ensures that everyone enters and leaves the house through the front door, regardless of race. Baby Suggs logically remodels 124 to eliminate slave space, although people might say that she illogically turned the house (read "white space") into a cabin (read "black space") (*Beloved* 207). White outsiders may not understand her design because, as Vlach notes, appropriated domestic spaces often became unreadable to white slave owners (Vlach 14). By extension, a black community that is enmeshed in white ideology and attempting to live in a world dominated by white supremacy—a reality of the race house of American culture—might also misread her renovations.

Furthermore, Baby Suggs's refusal to accept slave plantation spatial design initially provides her with a source of power. In this space she is able to feed the black community spiritually and physically (*Beloved* 135–38). She crafts a home "without losing or denying racial identity" (Wiese 292). After its occupants become alienated from the surrounding black community, however, the isolated remodeled home cannot safeguard its residents. Designed to keep danger outside of her home, the remodeled kitchen and the elimination of the back door fail to keep schoolteacher out of Baby Suggs's yard. While the yard is technically not a part of the house, it does constitute an important part of the home, especially within African American culture. As bell hooks notes, "Often, exploited or oppressed groups of people who are compelled by economic circumstance to share small living quarters with many others view the world right outside their housing structures as liminal space where they can stretch the limits of desire and the imagination" ("Black Vernacular" 398). Home's flexible or relational territory includes the space beyond a house's four walls; in this case, it also includes the yard.

According to Andrew Wiese, the garden and yard are key parts of African American domestic space: they extend the home's territory, provide a means of economic enrichment through food production, and create domestic focal points for African American culture. In *A Raisin in the Sun* (1959), Lorraine Hansberry represents these aspects of the African American home (and its rural, southern ideal) in the character Mama, who wants "a little old two-story somewhere, with a yard where Travis could play in the summertime" and "a little garden in the back" (44, 45). Mama says, "Well, I always wanted me a garden like I used to see sometimes at the back of the houses down home" (53). Her dream home includes a modest house, yard, and garden—an alternative to the "rat trap" house that she has lived in for years and that does not even allow enough sun in the window to grow a "little old plant" (44; 52–53). Thus, we can begin to see that gardens and yards are significant spaces in African American homes.

In *Beloved*, Denver's fear of leaving the yard demonstrates the relational aspects the house, the yard, and her initial oppositional spatial politics: "Whatever it is, it comes from outside this house, outside the yard, and it can come right on in the yard if it wants to. So I never leave this house and I watch over the yard, so it can't happen again and my mother won't have to kill me too" (205). Denver's oppositional spatial politics require that she guard her house and yard against the forces "outside." She eventually understands that her family is "locked in a love that wore everybody out" (243). As a result, one warm spring day she gathers the courage to face the outside and enact a relational spatial politics by reconnecting with the community beyond her yard: "She stood on the porch of 124 ready to be swallowed up in the world beyond the edge of the porch. Out there where small things scratched and sometimes touched" (243). Denver hesitates on this threshold: "Denver stood on the porch in the sun and couldn't leave it. Her throat itched; her heart kicked" (244). Baby Suggs's spirit eventually encourages her. Still frightened of what's "out there," Denver responds:

> But you said there was no defense.
> "There ain't."
> Then what do I do?
> "Know it, and go out the yard. Go on." (244)

Denver embraces insecurity and ventures into territory beyond her isolated home.

While 124 initially shelters and rewards its inhabitants, once the inhabitants are alienated from the black community, the property fails to protect and the house becomes haunted. As Denise Rodriguez observes, "The house becomes a site of isolation that carries traces of the other structure looming ominously in the narrative's background, Sweet Home" ("'Where the Self'" 44). The reference to Sweet Home clarifies that one person's shelter—or "home, sweet home"—is frequently another person's slavery: the race house and the conventional, idealized home constitute each other. Furthermore, the property's failure to protect its inhabitants emphasizes the interrelated aspects of a productive neodomestic instability. If remodeling alone could successfully produce a safe haven, for instance, Rachel Price in *The Poisonwood Bible* would have been better able to fortify her hotel. In fact, Rachel's hotel demonstrates that giving too much attention to remodeling can isolate individuals rather than connect them to the home's translocal communities.

The relational aspects of 124 are clear: home depends on the ways in which it relates to the community. When the house at 124 Bluestone becomes temporarily isolated from the African American community, we see that choosing the margin as a site of resistance requires support from a community; remodeling the home is not enough. Baby Suggs recognizes her community's withdrawal of support just before schoolteacher arrives: "And then she knew. Her friends and neighbors were angry at her because she had overstepped, given too much, offended them by excess" (138). This passage implies that the black community fails to notify Baby Suggs of the approaching slave catchers because of their anger. A dozen years later, Denver takes the necessary steps beyond 124's yard and successfully reintegrates the household; by doing so, she eventually brings about Beloved's expulsion from 124 (*Beloved* 245). Paul D remarks on the change in the house when he returns to 124 at the end of the novel: "Something is missing from 124. . . . He can't put his finger on it, but it seems, for a moment, that just beyond his knowing is the glare of an outside thing that embraces while it accuses" (270–71). Paul D's description suggests that the surrounding black community provides the accusing embrace. After all, Paul D recognizes that the absence is not related to "Beloved or the red light" (*Beloved* 270–71). The community "embraces" as well as "accuses," implying individual and community obligations to one another. The house's dependence on the black community supports bell hooks's observation that choosing the margin as a site of resistance relies on community: "One needs a community of resistance" (*Yearning* 149). One cannot live alone on the margin—at least not if one wishes to resist successfully the forces of white supremacy.

At the novel's conclusion, 124 appropriates, with the help of the black community, the margin of American culture. Although at the close of the novel Mr. Bodwin plans to sell 124 as soon as possible (*Beloved* 264), the house returns to the black community—a marginal location that hooks would call strategic. As hooks notes, this strategic space on the margin is not secure: "Locating oneself there is difficult yet necessary. It is not a 'safe' place. One is always at risk" (*Yearning* 149). As Paul D points out, the threat of losing their house remains, but "anybody got the money don't want to live out there" (264). Just like the places Vlach describes that were made so "black" that white slaveholders were reluctant to enter them, 124 holds no attraction to those (presumably white) people who could buy it. Another key factor to 124's potential for successful resistance from the margin deals with the inhabitants' agency. There is a difference between *choosing* the margin and *being forced* to live on the margin, bell hooks argues: "I make a definite distinction between that marginality which is imposed by oppressive structures and that marginality one chooses as site of resistance" (*Yearning* 153). While the characters' choices are circumscribed by slavery's legacies in *Beloved*, the characters can nonetheless choose how to live on the margin. In this vein, Charles Scruggs argues in "The Invisible City in Toni Morrison's *Beloved*" that Morrison's geopolitics aim to move African American domestic space out of the slave quarters—to move, in other words, African Americans from an oppressive margin to an appropriated margin.

What is true for 124 holds potential for individual characters. If Sethe, like 124, can return to the community, she will not suffer the same demise as Baby Suggs, who dies isolated from the black community (*Beloved* 179; 201). The repositioning of the house within the black community hints that Sethe will likewise repossess herself. In this space Sethe—like hooks—will not "pass on" (*Beloved* 274–75) the "remembrance of the past, which includes recollections of broken tongues giving us ways to speak that decolonize our minds, our very beings" (hooks, *Yearning* 150). Indeed, the "broken tongues" in section 2 (210–217) of *Beloved* suggest that this decolonization process has already successfully begun. If Sethe chooses to embrace fully the margin, she will empower herself and her experiences will not be passed over or forgotten, even if 124 is sold: "She thus moves from the position of the 'defined' to that of the 'definer'—to borrow School Teacher's terms" (Rodriguez, "'Where the Self'" 49; *Beloved* 190). Significantly, Sethe ends the novel in the storeroom built by Baby Suggs. She is temporarily stored and resting when Paul D comes to take her off the shelf and help her back into the world. Rather than emphasize individual agency, Morrison concludes the novel by highlighting the need to accept help from others.

The house at 124 Bluestone, therefore, stands as a "race house," structured by white and black actions that construct and maintain racist ideologies. The dwelling also represents a remodeled home. The house features the haunted structures of slavery and occupies a peripheral position in the white and black communities. The haunting unfixes the structure—materializing the negative and positive aspects of domestic instability. As Michael Hogan notes, "It is a site riddled by paradox: both white house and black house, safe house and slaughterhouse" (168). As a house located on the border between free states and slave states, between city and country, and as a dwelling that shifts between safe haven and haunted house, 124's fluctuations into and out of the community contribute to and are part of its ambivalent design. The ambivalent design suggests the home's ability to resist oppression but not to forget history. Denise Rodriguez holds similar optimism for *Beloved's* productive, albeit ambivalent, conclusion: "The characters' growing awareness of the historical factors that inform familial life leads to a reshaping of families and to the emergence of a new domestic narrative" (45).

The "new domestic narrative" includes 124's contradictory architectural features and location that render it a strong but unstable structure. Like the table leg that Paul D mends, making the table stronger than before it was broken, 124's structural fractures produced by the race house hold the potential to heal stronger than the original design (*Beloved* 64). In this light, Michael Hogan's pessimistic assessment of 124 is perhaps too harsh, granting too much agency to the race house and not enough power to the remodeled home: "As a free-standing American house, it promises protection; as home to African-American slaves, the disenfranchised and dehumanized, it cannot possibly deliver" (174). The house at 124 Bluestone questions the status of the "free-standing American house," its promised protection and isolation from the community. Charles Scruggs offers a more optimistic reading of 124's paradoxical features in relation to the female protagonists: "Morrison's female characters often evince strong attachments to houses, even those that seem cursed, and instead of rejecting the house as an image of confinement or entrapment, as white women writers have often done, in her fiction Morrison shows a desire to redeem the house and to reintegrate it into the community" (99). The recycled relational space that Morrison creates "eventually defines home as communal . . . [and] bind[s] the domestic to the external world" (Rodriguez, "'Where the Self'" 49). The recycled narrative that redeems domesticity depends on Baby Suggs's remodeling and on 124's relationships with its local community.

Paradise Refurbished
Restoring (African) American Home and Community

The characters in *Paradise* also struggle to balance a life on the margin that redesigns the race house and gender house while attempting to maintain some connection to supportive communities. *Paradise* sketches this struggle from two community's perspectives: from the standpoint of a patriarchal black community attempting to preserve its racial purity (as represented in the "8-rock" families who found Haven, Oklahoma, and later Ruby, Oklahoma) and from the standpoint of the renegade women who form a haphazard community at the Convent, located at Ruby's outskirts and considered a "white's house" by some of Ruby's residents (*Paradise* 198). Where Baby Suggs remodels her home to produce a space so "black" that whites will be reluctant to enter, the 8-rock families attempt to construct an all-black town that will likewise discourage outsiders and protect its residents. In contrast, the Convent, as its name implies, becomes a space associated with women from various racial, ethnic, and economic backgrounds. As when communication breaks down between 124 and the black community in *Beloved*, violence also erupts when relations between the Convent and the black community disintegrate in *Paradise*. Magnifying Haven's and Ruby's gendered geopolitics, the Convent emphasizes how traditional, oppositional home constructions rely on violence.

Chronologically, *Paradise* takes up where *Beloved* leaves off, mapping the migration of rural southern blacks westward as Reconstruction ends and terrorism against African Americans in the South pushes blacks to seek homes along an increasingly distant margin of American life: the frontier. *Paradise*'s narrative present primarily takes place from the mid-1960s to 1976, the year when the men raid the Convent and America celebrates its bicentennial.[5] The 8-rock story told in *Paradise* fictionalizes the Oklahoma version of the Exoduster migration, the first major migration north and west by ex-slaves.[6] Scholars thus far have used *Paradise*'s version of this migration and the subsequent establishment of the all-black towns Haven and Ruby to critique the American dream and nationalism. For many readers, *Paradise* seems to be Morrison's version of the American jeremiad.[7] An examination of the novel's engagement with local and national histories has provided rich terrain for scholars interested in *Paradise*'s communities and sense of home.[8] Viewing this narrative through a spatial lens provides additional insight into the novel's complex framing of the relationships between (African) American history, home, and community. In fact, an examination of the novel's spatial politics—especially important in this ambivalent, postmodern novel notorious for its refusal to reveal its roman à clef—reveals a key that unlocks the geopolitical dynamics of the 8-rock and Convent communities.[9]

The information we learn about the creation of Haven and Ruby reveals that the 8-rock community's insistence on isolation and an oppositional construction of space contributes to Haven's failure and causes Ruby's violence. Given that black homeownership consistently registers well below the national average, a generous reading may interpret the fierceness with which the men defend Ruby against outsiders, especially against the Convent, as a response to the lack of access to housing—the violence is a specific domestication of the race house. In addition to drawing from the spatial politics of dispossession in the aftermath of Reconstruction and *Plessy v. Ferguson*, Morrison's representations of domestic space in *Paradise* may have contemporary foundations as well. The novel's present roughly covers a span of about twenty years, from the 1960s to July 4, 1976. While individual states may have had black homeownership levels that were above national averages, the only uniformity to these individual instances is that rural areas tended to have better percentages than metropolitan locations. Kansas and Iowa, for example, boasted black homeownership at or above 60 percent in 1950, but by 1990 both states' black ownership rates dropped dramatically to 43 percent and 39 percent, respectively (U.S. Census Bureau, "Historical Census"). As African Americans historically and currently experience lower homeownership rates and often inferior housing quality, these national averages emphasize the *myth* of home and the *reality* of the race house for African Americans during the latter half of the twentieth century. However, even given this historical and material "justification," the men's actions against the Convent are not endorsed by *Paradise*'s narrative.

The original title, *War*, emphasizes the tactics employed by the 8-rock men, especially the Morgan twins, to maintain their power and sovereignty. *War* also highlights the ideological conflicts between the patriarchal town of Ruby and the matriarchal Convent. Pallas, in fact, says that the Convent "felt permeated with a blessed maleleness, like a protected domain, free of hunters" (*Paradise* 177). The title *Paradise*, in turn, encompasses the search for (a lost) home, a search shared by the residents of Haven, Ruby, and the Convent. The narrative attempts to materialize or "domesticate" an elusive safe haven or home. Mapping the search for home and subsequent home-making practices highlights Morrison's decisive endorsement of remodeled domesticity and relational space, neither of which promise an easy way to attain home.

The Geopolitics of Oppositional Isolation
Founding a Haven in 8-Rock

Scholars examining *Paradise* have not overlooked the patriarchal aspects of Haven and Ruby.[10] Michael K. Johnson, for example, argues, "In *Paradise*, Morrison casts a critical eye at the desire to create a black patriarchy (even as a defense against white oppression) in the West" (247). Additionally, Therese E. Higgins frames Ruby as a representative patriarchy and the Convent as a matriarchy (131). Ellen G. Friedman describes the Convent as a "woman's utopia" and Ruby as a "black utopia" (703). The novel fairly straightforwardly lays out the towns' patriarchal control: we need only to review the towns' primary landmarks to see the numerous ways in which the (religious) patriarchy functions within these towns. Patriarchal control at various geopolitical levels remains necessary in order to patrol the boundaries between men and women, "good" and "bad" women, and between insiders (8-rock families) and outsiders (non-8-rock families). Thus, 8-rock patriarchal control becomes synonymous with oppositional space, where territories must be clearly distinguished from each other. Patriarchal space, furthermore, constructs gendered hierarchies among its oppositional spaces. We can also see that patriarchal space often works in tandem with the race house, which similarly insists on hierarchal control and segregated space. Finally, the religious or spiritual geography of both Ruby and the Convent spreads across these patriarchal and matriarchal spaces. *Paradise* self-consciously deploys spiritual geographies in its interrogation of home.

Ruby's layout, for instance, demonstrates extreme spatial partitioning that is suggestive of the various ways in which the town attempts to police its inhabitants. The town's streets, for example, follow a strict grid. The main street, Central Avenue, has four east side streets, named after the Gospels. The streets' names announce that the town is organized within a Christian structure. As Ruby grew, west side streets were added: "Although these newer streets were continuations of those on the east—situated right across from them—they acquired secondary names. So St. John Street on the east become [sic] Cross John on the west. St. Luke became Cross Luke. The sanity of this pleased most everybody, Deek especially" (*Paradise* 114). The street names underscore the importance of distinguishing between original lines (or streets) and the tributaries that come along later. The naming practices also emphasize the town's closed, incestuous nature. No new names are used: "St. Luke became Cross Luke" (114). Additionally, they emphasize paternal, not maternal, lines; there are no streets named after women. Endemic of the founders' monitoring of pure bloodlines, the genealogy of the town's streets reveals the town's patriarchal religious foundations.

However, the town's "blood rules" do not stay as neatly organized and distinct as the names of the streets might suggest (*Paradise* 196). As a result, some spaces must be left unnamed or unmarked. As the town's unofficial genealogist and historian, Patricia Best Cato, points out, women rarely have recorded last names; presumably, the town did not deem the women's last names worthy to be recorded or remembered. These "lost" names facilitate informal appropriations: "A young widow might take over a single man's house. A widower might ask a friend or a distant relative if he could take over a young girl who had no prospects" (*Paradise* 196). A space or person not claimed through a last name, after all, can become someone else's territory. At best confused, at worst incestuous, the resulting bloodlines create unusual familial relationships that ultimately defy legible mapping. Patricia explains, "Billy's mother was wife to her own great-uncle. Or another way: my husband's father, August Cato, is also his grandmother's (Bitty Cato Blackhorse's) uncle and therefore Billy's great-granduncle as well" (196). Patricia's genealogy "should delineate branching paths along which 'bloodlines' travel through time and through bodies. But the 'lines' Pat discovers circle back, cross one another; and some branches are left out, where light-skinned people have come in" (McKee 203).

In the face of this confusion, the 8-rock men nevertheless aim to arrange the women just as they have arranged the streets. The fact that the men preside over town business—including the conflict between KD and Arnette when Arnette's father says, "I'll arrange her mind" (*Paradise* 61)—provides additional evidence of the town's patriarchal and religious organization. Billie Delia, in fact, observes that the conflict between KD and Arnette was really about male control of women and children: "The real battle was not about infant life or a bride's reputation but about disobedience, which meant, of course, the stallions were fighting about who controlled the mares and their foals" (150). Significantly, both "stallions"—Senior Pulliam and Reverend Misner—have scripture on their sides (150). At stake, as Billie Delia explains, is whether "history" or the "future" will win out: "Senior Pulliam had scripture and history on his side. Misner had scripture and the future on his. Now, she supposed, he was making the world wait until it understood his position" (*Paradise* 150).

Thus, named and unnamed territories hold deep significance in *Paradise*. While Ruby's name pays tribute to Deacon and Steward Morgan's sister who died shortly after the "new Haven" was founded, Ruby also signifies a patriarchal idolization of women that ultimately confines more than liberates women: "The men of Ruby devote themselves to the ideal of the black woman as a racially pure figure who must be protected both from white men and from other (impure) African American men. The necessity of protecting the 'sleepless woman' justifies the establishment of homosocial bonds" (Johnson 64). When with "God at their side, the men take aim. For Ruby," they are not only defending the town; they are also defending the virtue of idealized black Christian women—a virtue that they believe the Convent women threaten (*Paradise* 18).

The 8-rock community's appropriation of the Oven also testifies to the group's insistence on patriarchal control, on the one hand, and to the power of community, on the other. Michael Johnson also notes, "The Oven itself is a female symbol taken over and controlled by men" (Johnson 62). When transferred into the public sphere, "the oven" (traditionally a feminine symbol of hearth and home) becomes "the Oven" (a part of the men's domain). The following passage describes the Oven's glory days in the first town, Haven, where it once provided the community with literal and metaphoric nourishment because of its ability to keep black women out of white kitchens and its ability to foster community connections:

> In 1910 there were two churches in Haven and the All-Citizens Bank, four rooms in the schoolhouse, five stores selling dry goods, feed and foodstuffs—but the traffic to and from the Oven was greater than to all of those. No family needed more than a simple cookstove as long as the Oven was alive, and it always was. Even in 1934 when everything else about the town was dying; when it was clear as daylight that talk of electricity would remain just talk and when gas lines and sewers were Tulsa marvels, the Oven stayed alive. (15)

The Oven outlasts numerous changes in the community. To Haven's original founding fathers, the "thinking that made a community 'kitchen' so agreeable" appealed to their pride: "They were proud that none of their women had ever worked in a white-man's kitchen or nursed a white child. Although field labor was harder and carried no status, they believed the rape of women who worked in white kitchens was if not a certainty a distinct possibility—neither of which they could bear to contemplate" (*Paradise* 99). So, the Oven keeps the 8-rock wives from having to work in white kitchens—freeing them for other labors. Keeping black women out of the kitchen was a means to honor and respect their wives and to protect their way of life. The narrative reverses expectations and historical privileges: fieldwork is better than housework and dark skin is better than light.

Gradually, however, the Oven's use declines. In Ruby, "A utility became a shrine" (*Paradise* 103). The men carry and rebuild the Oven, brick by brick, when they move: "The women nodded when the men took the Oven apart, packed, moved and reassembled it. But privately they resented the truck space given over to it—rather than a few more sacks of seed, rather than shoats or even a child's crib. Resented also the hours spent putting it back together—hours that could have been spent getting the privy door on sooner" (103). The women's resentment clarifies that the Oven no longer functions to keep the women out of the kitchen. Instead, the Oven has become a status symbol for the men. Furthermore, "What was needed back in Haven's early days had never been needed in Ruby" (*Paradise* 103). Rather than function as a community gathering place and communal kitchen, the Oven in Ruby becomes a contested symbol detached from material worth or use.

The women's flower gardens and the resulting "garden battles" also emphasize a shift from practical "use value" to ornamental, "symbolic value": "The garden battles—won, lost, still at bay—were mostly over. They had raged for ten years, having begun suddenly in 1963, when there was time" (89). Changes in domestic technology help bring about this shift from use value to symbolic value: "The humming, throbbing and softly purring gave the women time" to propagate flower gardens (89). As a result, "the dirt yards, carefully swept and sprinkled in Haven, became lawns in Ruby until, finally, front yards were given over completely to flowers for no good reason except there was time in which to do it.... The women kept on with their vegetable gardens in back, but little by little its produce became like the flowers—driven by desire, not necessity" (89–90). The "husbands complained of neglect and the disappointingly small harvest of radishes, or the too short rows of collards, beets" (89). Like the gardens in *The Poisonwood Bible* and

Gardens in the Dunes, these beautiful but unfruitful gardens characterize Ruby and its problems.[11] The emphasis turns to a "frenetic land grab" based on control, where suddenly doors need to be locked against something: "Dovey was sure theirs was the only locked door in Ruby. What was he [her husband] afraid of?" (90). The fight over the Oven's meaning clarifies the fear at the heart of the men's control.

Just as they fight over how to resolve the dispute between KD and Arnette, the men fight over the Oven's meaning. Is the motto it bears "Beware" or "Be the Furrow of His Brow"? The disputes reflect a desire to control meaning and space—not so much to find the Oven's "true meaning," which as Patricia Best points out, was designed "to have multiple meanings: to appear stern, urging obedience to God, but slyly not identifying the understood proper noun or specifying what the Furrow might cause to happen or to whom" (195). Rather than embrace multiple, flexible meanings, the men insist that there can only be one.

The stories describing the towns' establishment also reverberate with patriarchal cosmogony. Several scholars have noted that Haven's mythologized founding echoes America's Puritan establishment as a "city upon a hill." Likewise, the town's condemnations of the Convent women parallel the Salem witch trials.[12] We recall the founding fathers of the American Revolution when we learn that Haven's founders are known as the "Old Fathers" and Ruby's founders are called the "New Fathers" (*Paradise* 99; 194).[13] Haven's and Ruby's founding as cities upon a hill, led and governed by a pioneering group of men, establish the towns as patriotic, nationalist, and patriarchal communities. Haven's and Ruby's oppositional spatial politics, which can be appraised by comparing the towns' histories and locations, underscore their patriarchal roots and functions. At the same time, *Paradise* refuses to construct a patriarchal house of straw ready to be blown away by the matriarchal wolves residing in the Convent. The all-black towns of Ruby and Haven present compelling homes, albeit inherently flawed ones, by (re)establishing African Americans as actors within an idealized American mythos—not just as victims of an American nightmare.[14]

The towns' spatial politics solidify patriarchal rule while simultaneously correcting the marginality of the African American experience related in the conventional telling of the westward expansion narrative. While clear parallels exist between the specific founding of all-black towns and the white American patriarchal mythos upon which the country was founded and expanded, African American contributions to the "broader" American foundation have been largely excluded or lost. The dominant narratives of westward expansion set white American cowboys against American Indians.

Paradise recovers a lost history of African American pioneers while simultaneously critiquing the frontier's patriarchal foundations. Peter Widdowson similarly locates Ruby at the crossroads of the recognition of African American experience and of the critique of (white) patriarchal power. Because of the ways that the 8-rock men "replicate the conservative values at the heart of white America," Widdowson sees Ruby as "not just an isolated black small town—'deafened by its own history'—but America at large by the end of its second century of independence" (326). Widdowson explains,

> What the town of Ruby seems to represent, then, is a distillation of all the abuses and failures of the American democratic experiment in respect of its black population: it is at once the extreme of an enforced siege or ghetto mentality and the extreme of a cherished racial separatism. In this respect, Ruby is both a chilling indictment of white America (the failures of the Declaration, Reconstruction, twentieth-century reforms), and a celebration of black resilience, independence and honour (a triumph of the Exoduster spirit). (324)

The construction of the all-black towns of Haven and Ruby critiques African Americans' denied access to the American dream while simultaneously replicating conservative white values. As Audre Lorde might have said, the 8-rock men use the "master's tools" (the very same used to construct the race and gender houses) to build their communities. Policing its women and their children, the 8-rock community's reversal of the one-drop rule provides a case in point. Reverend Misner points out the danger of the "blood rule": "Separating us, isolating us—that's always been *their weapon*. Isolation kills generations. It has no future" (210; my emphasis). Examining the margin's geopolitical functions in this narrative clarify further how the towns' geopolitics work at the crossroads of recognition and critique.

Significantly, Haven's and Ruby's founding fathers choose the margin—the extreme western frontier—as the location for their communities. The historical justification for Haven's marginal location begins with the Exoduster experience. Like many Exodusters traveling to Kansas and Oklahoma in the late nineteenth century, the 8-rock families came from the lower Mississippi Valley, specifically Zechariah Morgan and Juvenal Du Pres from Louisiana and Drum Blackhorse from Mississippi (*Paradise* 193).[15] Nell Irving Painter describes the motivation for the Exoduster migration as dependent on two factors: economics (especially "access to land and the terms of tenant farming and sharecropping") and terrorism (namely "anti-black terrorism") (ix). *Paradise* makes several pointed allusions about black migration to Oklahoma as a result of these factors (13–14; 193–94). The story also lists the prominent all-black towns in Kansas and Oklahoma that Haven's founding fathers planned to visit during their trip: "Boley, Langston City, Rentiesville, Taft, Clearview, Mound Bayou, Nicodemus" (108).[16] Like the historical Exodusters, the fictional 8-rock families "got to the place described in advertisements carefully folded into their shoes or creased into the brims of their hats" (*Paradise* 194). However, the streets of these all-black towns were not paved with gold. *Paradise*, in fact, includes a quotation from the *Langston City Herald*: "Come Prepared or Not At All" (*Paradise* 13).[17]

The 8-rock legend emphasizes the fact that some all-black towns in Oklahoma, Langston City in particular, "actively discouraged poor blacks from coming to Langston and to Oklahoma" (Hamilton 104). Kenneth Marvin Hamilton explains that one of Langston City's promoters, Edward P. McCabe, "realized from his prior experience in Nicodemus [an all-black town in Kansas] that only blacks with capital could stimulate the growth of Langston, which would in turn provide the promoters with increased profits" (104). In fact, "When the paper [the *Herald*] learned that three hundred destitute blacks, en route to the Cheyenne and Arapaho areas of the Oklahoma Territory, had arrived in Fort Smith, Arkansas, it attempted to deter them from entering Oklahoma, reporting 'common labor is not in demand, the supply is already too great'" (Hamilton 104).[18] *Paradise* fictionalizes the historical discouragement into the "Disallowing." The 8-rock families are "shooed away" by the all-black towns they visited (*Paradise* 194). As a result, they form their own town rather than join an existing one.

The intense focus on property and ownership emphasizes how economics structures the all-black towns in *Paradise*. Furthermore, "In the aftermath of the Civil War, property ownership was indissolubly linked with freedom in the aspiration of former slaves. Throughout the late nineteenth and early twentieth centuries, property ownership persisted among the chief values of blacks in the rural South" (Wiese 84). The 8-rock families clearly illustrate this value. Yet instead of emphasizing class concerns, the 8-rock mythology frames the rejection by the all-black towns as primarily a result of the 8-rock families' dark skin.[19] Like *Beloved*, *Paradise* emphasizes the oppositional space constructed by the "race house."

In *Paradise*, the separation is not between black and white but between light- and dark-skinned blacks. The 8-rock families "saw a new separation: light-skinned against black. Oh, they knew there was a difference in the minds of whites, but it had not struck them before that it was of consequence, serious consequence, to Negroes themselves. . . . The sign of racial purity they had taken for granted had become a stain" (*Paradise* 194). Emerging from slavery with dark skin initially generated pride in the 8-rock families; however, the Disallowing presents a "new" racial hierarchy to the 8-rock families who apparently were used to being discriminated against by every other group but not by their fellow African Americans: "Turned away by rich Choctaw and poor whites, chased by yard dogs, jeered at by camp prostitutes and their children, they were nevertheless unprepared for the aggressive discouragement they received from Negro towns already being built" (*Paradise* 13). The sting of this rejection fosters a consolidation of 8-rock blood, where the unwritten rule was against marrying outside of the founding families (that is, "light-skinned blacks"). Haven's founding represents an absolute circling of the wagons to protect and secure a home for its rejected residents.

Paradise provides historical reasons for Haven's founding, but the novel does not present an irreproachable account of the characters' motivations. The 8-rock families embody both the rhetoric of American exceptionalism and the reality of American empire. One of the more subtle ways that *Paradise* registers its critique of Haven's patriarchal, imperial foundation emerges in how the town's land was secured. The spatial ramifications of the Disallowing push Haven to "unassigned lands." The novel hints that the land upon which the 8-rock families build Haven is not free. Dispossessed or otherwise forced from the South, the 8-rock Exodusters seem to have few qualms about squatting on Native American lands. During the nineteenth century, the Oklahoma Territory was largely reserved for displaced Native Americans, specifically those members of the so-called Five Civilized Tribes (the Cherokees, Choctaws, Chickasaws, Creeks, and Seminoles).[20] The 8-rock families travel through Arapaho territory, see members of the Choctaw, and barter with the Creek (*Paradise* 14). Haven was built on land that belonged to the Creek Nation and "which once upon a time a witty government called 'unassigned land'" (*Paradise* 6). *Paradise* recognizes that Haven's founding required stealing land, an act that centralizes the town's marginal position. The Convent's status as a school for Indian girls also marks the American Indian's displacement and dispossession within Oklahoma.

The 8-rock community's isolation—historically "justified" and fiercely defended—ultimately has destructive consequences. One of the most condemning features of the community's isolation is that it is not productive, especially after its move to Ruby. Literally, the residents have trouble reproducing. As I discussed previously, the lack of interaction with outside communities results in incestuous intermarriages across generations, an ultimate sign of both Haven's and Ruby's dangerous isolation. Incestuous communities often fail to organize against white supremacy. As seen in the discussion about *Beloved*, successfully resisting from the margin requires community support. However, the 8-rock families do not resist: "Just as the original wayfarers never sought another colored townsite after being cold-shouldered at the first, this generation joined no organization, fought no civil battle. They consolidated the 8-rock blood and, haughty as ever, moved farther west" (*Paradise* 194). Ruby's insistence on "pure blood" cements rather than dissolves the race house's foundation. Instead of seeking justice, the families seek to be left alone. Their actions contribute to rather than deconstruct the race house. Living on the margin without community ties results in an incestuous isolation without resistance against the internal and external forces that structure the race house.

The community's continued isolation and reliance on an oppositional construction of space contributes to Haven's failure.[21] The second "Disallowing" occurred after World War II (*Paradise* 194). Soldiers returning to Haven note the emasculation and economic stagnation of black men—"the missing testicles of other colored soldiers; . . . medals being torn off by gangs of rednecks and Sons of the Confederacy"—and decide to move farther west (*Paradise* 194). Once again, antiblack terrorism and economic need instigate migration to a more distant margin, a place fortified against the outside world. As seen in *Beloved*, venturing beyond the confines of the town invites the terrorism of "Out There, where your children were sport, your women quarry, and where your very person could be annulled; where congregations carried arms to church and ropes coiled in every saddle. Out There where every cluster of whitemen looked like a posse, being alone was being dead" (*Paradise* 16). So great is the fear of the outside that Sloane Morgan believes her sons are safer fighting in war than living in "any city in the United States" (*Paradise* 101): "Safer than anywhere in Oklahoma outside Ruby" (*Paradise* 100).

Where other all-black towns "merged with white towns" or "shriveled into tracery," Ruby emerges and persists in defiant opposition (5–6). However, the same mistakes that contribute to Haven's failure are replicated in Ruby: "The men of Ruby identify so strongly with the ideology and actions of the Old Fathers that they try to replicate rather than imitate their ancestors' accomplishments, establishing Ruby on the model of Haven, painstakingly rebuilding the Oven" (Johnson 62). In other words, the men attempt to rebuild home—symbolized here in the rebuilt community Oven—without renovating or seeking to improve otherwise on the original structure, or even assure that the new town and its services account for the present needs of its inhabitants. Their actions suggest that a resistance to change, an inability to negotiate new borders, contributes to the race house. McKee suggests that the ways in which the residents rewrite history and religious myth—such as in the Christmas play that mixes the Christian story of Jesus's birth with the

Disallowing—"poses no challenge to 'claims of cultural supremacy and historical priority,' as [Homi] Bhabha suggests, except to make those claims on behalf of different people" (207). The 8-rock families, therefore, reproduce rather than recycle home, still focusing on exclusion in their construction of a secure home.

Ruby, therefore, can only delay the need to move again. However, with no more frontiers at their disposal, the men see no other choice but to stand their ground and to defend violently their way of life. Backed against their chosen margin, the 8-rock men not surprisingly emerge with guns blazing in an attempt to reestablish their town. Ruby's extreme isolation, its lack of frontier space, and its oppositional, patriarchal construction of space conspire to produce the town's destructive violence. Drawing from Walter Benjamin's "Theses on the Philosophy of History," Rob Davidson understands Ruby's isolation as key to understanding the subsequent "crisis" situations that elicit action by the Old and New Fathers: "the perpetual 'state of emergency' is one of their chief tactics for retaining power, as it justifies—in their minds, at least—practically any course of action" (359). In this light, Davidson argues, the 8-rock men "execute the Convent women not for moral reasons but as a show of strength" (368). Just as I described in the previous chapter where Rachel Price in *The Poisonwood Bible* epitomizes the worst in American foreign policy, so too do the 8-rock men exhibit the "culture of fear" that can drive government policy.[22] Ruby's oppositional space requires constant surveillance and, when "necessary," a violent defense of the boundaries against threatening others or outsiders. A closer look at how Ruby's residents and the Convent define home helps unpack the conflict and the cause of the violence against the Convent by Ruby's 8-rock men.

The Geopolitics of a "True Home"
Defining Home in *Paradise*

How the residents create home provides a useful lens for analyzing Haven, Ruby, and the Convent. As the analysis above suggests, the founding of Haven and Ruby as safe spaces against "Out There" challenges us to revise traditional definitions of home (*Paradise* 16). As in *Beloved*, the cost of these safe spaces is too great. One seemingly alternative vision of home emerges when two of Ruby's resident outsiders—the Baptist minister Richard Misner and the unofficial historian Patricia Best Cato—disagree about what constitutes home. Richard Misner is an outsider because he moves to Ruby to serve the Baptist congregation; thus, he does not have an 8-rock ancestry. Additionally, he is associated with stirring up the young people and encouraging them to participate in a world larger than the confines of Ruby. The light-skinned Patricia also occupies a position outside the tight 8-rock bloodline because her light-skinned mother was, according to Steward Morgan, "the dung we leaving behind" (*Paradise* 201).

The narrative sets up these insiders/outsiders as uniquely positioned to reflect on the meaning of home in Ruby. During her conversation with the Reverend Misner, Patricia observes, "Home is not a little thing" (213). Misner responds, "I'm not saying it is. But can't you even imagine what it must feel like to have a true home?" (213). A "true home," according to Misner, is an "earthly home," not heaven (213). His definition can be understood as emblematic of *Paradise*'s examination of the traditional definition of home and Morrison's project to domesticate the "elusive race-free paradise" ("Home" 8).

Misner's definition of the "true home" reveals "very careful and effective reversals which do not erase the positive desire for unity, for Oneness, but destabilize and undercut it" (Martin and Mohanty 306). Misner's definition contains clear contrasts to the ways in which the 8-rocks have constructed home in Haven and Ruby. The "true home," he says, is

> not some fortress you bought and built up and have to keep everybody locked in or out. A real home. Not some place you went to and invaded and slaughtered people to get. Not some place you claimed, snatched because you got the guns. Not some place you stole from the people living there, but your own home, where if you go back past your great-great-grandparents, past theirs, and theirs, past the whole of Western history, past the beginning of organized knowledge, past pyramids and poison bows, on back to when rain was new, before plants forgot they could sing and birds thought they were fish, back when God said Good! Good!—there, right there where you know your own people were born and lived and died. (*Paradise* 213)

Home, in contrast to Haven and Ruby, is neither stolen nor a fortress. Misner's true home is not a place "snatched because you got the guns" (another line crafted to distinguish the true home from Ruby's patriarchal and imperial homemaking practices). This definition of a true home shares some of the features of a relational definition of home—specifically, the claim that home is not a "fortress" that keeps "everybody locked in or out."

Rejecting isolationism, Misner finds Afrocentrism attractive and feels a deep connection to Africa. In fact, he claims that "Africa is our home" (210). In contrast, Pat says that she is "really not interested" in Africa: "I just don't believe in some stupid devotion to a foreign country" (210). Rob Davidson understands Pat's rejection of Misner's true home as a reversion to "isolationism" (366). However, one can never truly return and live in Misner's true African home, which is no more "true" or "real" than the "pure blood" that the 8-rock families isolate themselves to maintain. Pat's skepticism does not necessarily realign her with 8-rock patriarchal ideology.

Reverend Misner's true home also reproduces several key features of the traditional definition of the ideal American home, sharing traits, if not the letter of the law, with the 8-rock ideology. Misner and the 8-rock community agree that they cannot steal a true home; doing so would only taint it. Rather, a true home is inherited from ancestors whose racial and cultural claims are indisputable. Given these similarities between 8-rock ideology and Misner's definition of the true home, I disagree with Philip Page's suggestion that Misner's home is a fully viable alternative to the 8-rock configuration. Page argues that Misner's portrayal of the true home presents an alternative to the "materialistic, acquisitive pursuit of a worldly home" (647). Page contends, "Through their new prophets—Richard Misner and Consolata—they [the novel's characters] begin to imagine a spiritual home that transcends their efforts to establish material homes" (646). While I agree that spiritual geography plays an important role in the novel's construction of neodomesticity, Page fails to take into consideration Africa's participation in colonialism. Additionally, Misner's true home appears to be paradise before Adam and Eve were banished from the garden. Unlike the opening and closing of *Gardens in the Dunes*, *Paradise* does not suggest that we can return to this earthly paradise. While this true home in the mind may open a productive imaginative space, it does not adequately deal with or recycle the historical and material realities encountered by (African) Americans constructing home in the United States.

Pride in one's connections to African cultures can ground a character spiritually and psychologically; however, locating one's true home in a single place may demand excluding other origins and refusing to acknowledge hybrid identities. A focus on pure origins, as the 8-rock story also emphasizes, fails to consider adequately the community's present needs and realities. Home, as bell hooks writes, is frequently "no longer just one place. It is locations" (*Yearning* 148). In contrast to Page's support of Reverend Misner's definition, Peter Widdowson argues that "the novel does not side with either Misner's dream of 'a true home' to be rediscovered at some pre-historical time, 'past the whole of Western history' [213], or Pat's 'real' history of slavery and its aftermath" (328). "But what it does seem to confirm," Widdowson suggests, "is that the purity, exclusivity, intolerance and isolation of Ruby is a kind of living death" (328). I would add that the specific ways Morrison associates 8-rock ideology with the true home of Afrocentrism emphasizes a critique of any definition of home based on a purity of cultural origins. Thus, the Convent women's "impure," unknown, or uncertain origins, in addition to their renegade position as a collection of women without men, clearly threaten Ruby's patriarchal foundations and test the viability of a home not based on pure origins. More so than Misner's ideological and spiritually authentic African home, the Convent materially and spiritually experiments with a viable alternative to the traditional, detached American home of pure origins represented and critiqued in Haven, Ruby, and Misner's true home.

A look at the Convent's history illustrates how Morrison continues to destabilize and recycle traditional notions about home in *Paradise*. Originally, the Convent was not a convent; rather, it was the mansion of a wealthy embezzler (*Paradise* 3). The mansion's phallic shape highlights its overall masculine design: "Shaped like a live cartridge, it curved to a deadly point at the north end" (71). Filled with ornate, lascivious ornamentation and strategically placed windows and doors, the mansion was designed as a fortress against the original owner's enemies and as a playground for his guests (*Paradise* 71). Comparable to the 8-rock families, the embezzler fears the outside world: "Fright, not triumph, spoke in every foot of the embezzler's mansion" (71). Like Sethe and 124 in *Beloved*, the design and location of the embezzler's mansion does not protect him. The embezzler apparently has no community invested in protecting him. During his first party, the embezzler is captured (71). Capitalizing on the embezzler's misfortune, nuns purchase the mansion and attempt to remove, or at least rub out, the unusual decor, including the "nipple-tipped doorknobs" and penis-shaped faucets (72). Playing with the virgin-whore binary, Morrison constructs a dwelling that shifts from a house of ill repute to a house of God.

When viewed in tandem with Haven's and Ruby's histories and Misner's definition of a true home, the Convent's history thus far illustrates the shared foundations of the race house, the gender house, and the idealized American home. Violence and separation are traditionally fundamental to these constructs. The race house and the gender house police boundaries through racism and sexism, respectively. As Biddy Martin and Chandra Mohanty remind us, "the desire for home" frequently demands "repressions and violence that make home, harmony, sameness imaginable, and that enforce it" (306). Although gated communities today more clearly operate along class lines, such spaces crystallize the traditionally shared foundation between house and home—emphasizing the home's exclusionary qualities.

The Convent's school further emphasizes the conventional American home's homogenizing goals. Misnamed "the Convent" by locals, Christ the King School for Native Girls aims to convert its Arapaho scholars; however, the nuns are only able to renovate partially the building's and the girls' most superficial aspects (*Paradise* 224). The nuns' partially successful refurbishing efforts attempt to eliminate excess: "The ornate bathroom fixtures, which sickened the nuns, were replaced with good plain spigots, but the pricey tubs and sinks, which could not be inexpensively removed, remain coolly corrupt" (4). Like Geraldine's fanatical cleaning in *The Bluest Eye*, the house's new owners fail to sanitize the Convent or to rid the girls of their "funk": the nuns "could not wipe out what [they] ruled out-of-place" (McKee 210).

"Funk" in Morrison's fiction, as Susan Willis points out, "is really nothing more than the intrusion of the past in the present" (41). Furthermore, "As often happens in Morrison's writing, sexuality converges with history and functions as a register for the experience of change, i.e., historical transition" (Willis 34). These sexual and historical aspects of funk frighten the men who attack the Convent after the school closes. When the school initially closes, Connie, Sister Roberta, and Mother Mary Magna spend the "winter waiting, then not waiting, for some alternative to retirement or a 'home'" (241). After Sister Roberta goes to a nursing home, Connie takes care of Mother and sells produce and baked goods to the community. At this point, Connie opens the Convent to various women who need a place to stay, and funk erupts in ways that are intolerable to Ruby's residents.

The 8-rock men fear the Convent women's funk partially because of the 8-rock women's "loss of spontaneity and sensuality" (Willis 35). That is, the Convent women represent a return of a past and largely lost sensuality and fertility. The men liken the Convent women's funky housekeeping to "slack" and are disgusted by the bathroom that foregrounds the women's fertility with a "Modess box" and "a bucket of soiled things" (*Paradise* 5; 9). As in *The Bluest Eye*, rather than siding with the men's critiques, Morrison writes "against the privatized world of suburban house and nuclear family," where women have assimilated to a (white) bourgeois culture that demands order and fights against funk (Willis 34).

The Ruby women also criticize the Convent women for "dancing nasty" and wearing inappropriate clothing at KD and Arnette's wedding reception (158). The impression of overt sexuality also condemns Billie Delia (203). Moreover, Anna's unstraightened hair embodies a dangerous, disordered funk for many of Ruby's residents: "The subject [her unstraightened hair] summoned more passion, invited more opinions, solicited more anger than that prostitute Menus brought home from Virginia" (*Paradise* 119). Thus, funk includes a variety of behaviors and appearances deemed uncivilized or beyond the bounds of conventional suburban order. Women as well as men participate in the policing of funk.

This embrace of and revulsion to funk helps illustrate that oppositional space may cloak itself under a variety of ideologies. The spatial practices of patrolling and controlling boundaries trump more superficial homemaking principles. For example, the embezzler (through his careful construction of the mansion as a fortress) and the nuns (through their efforts to erase sexuality) patrol and attempt to manipulate the structure of the Convent to fit their individual purposes and ideas about home. Their similar spatial tactics make them more alike than their opposing lifestyles and houses might suggest. Patricia McKee makes a similar argument about the homes in *Sula*, noting that Eva and Helene Wright are "primarily occupied, then, with controlling, or even patrolling, boundaries in order to control the definition of their own selves" ("Spacing" 11). That is, despite the fact that Eva's house is messy and Helene's house is neat, the "difference between the two is less than such oppositions suggest, since the primary concern of each woman seems to be her capacity to control and manipulate boundaries" (McKee, "Spacing" 11).

However, do all spaces have to be defined according to these negative binary oppositions (what Massey terms "negative counterpositions")? The Convent women add a third, funky term to the mix, exploding the binary. For example, after the school closes, the Convent becomes a safe house for wayward and wounded women from Ruby and abroad. Connie counters oppositional spatial logic when she says, "Scary things not always outside. Most scary things is inside" (39). Kidnapped from South America in 1925, Connie (née Consolata) is perhaps the school's most conventionally successful student—at least until 1954 "when she met the living man" and had an affair with the married Deacon Morgan (*Paradise* 223; 225). Connie's unique homemaking practices ultimately recycle spiritual power, funk, and strong mothering, thereby remodeling the ideal home.

The home Connie builds not only heals its inhabitants but also allows the women to come and go freely. The Convent women do not refurbish the home, but they do eventually add paintings to the basement floor, an action that heals the house's residents: "the Convent women were no longer haunted" (266). Not being haunted by their pasts, however, does not mean that they have forgotten them. Like Sethe, the Convent women must come to terms with their pasts. Additionally, while they may leave at any time, the women realize "that they could not leave the one place they were free to leave" (262). This statement begins to define home in a relational sense—as a place where you can and perhaps do leave but do not want to abandon. It is also a place open to others—a place you may claim as your own but not a place that is secured in order to exclude outsiders. For a short period, the Convent provides a safe residence and retreat for a variety of women. Even the fierce disagreements between Mavis Albright and Gigi (née Grace) settle into the Convent's structure. But Ruby's residents storm the Convent, reminding us of the building's historical and continued failure to protect its inhabitants.

One way of understanding the attack on the Convent is to focus on *Paradise*'s critique of the 8-rock patriarchal order: "The women in the Convent become the scapegoats for the town's crisis of identity" (Johnson 66). Placing the men's violence in the context of other frontier narratives, Michael Johnson writes,

> While such works as Roosevelt's *The Winning of the West* and Cooper's *The Deerslayer* justify acts of violence by linking them to the protection of womanhood, Morrison reveals that male violence, which the frontier narrative so often celebrates, is more likely to be employed against (rather than in protection of) women. Through the attack on the Convent, Morrison makes visible the contradiction usually concealed in the trope of transformative violence—the irony of trying to achieve a civilized goal (protecting womanhood) through savage (violent) actions. (68)

The attack on the Convent reveals the violence embedded in oppositional patriarchal spatial constructions. The rhetoric of safe space within an oppositional construction requires aggressive reinforcement of the boundaries between protected and unprotected space.

Shifting our focus to the Convent and relational space, the attack reinforces the idea that home extends beyond a single physical structure and depends on community relationships. The Convent represents relational space's potential and problems. The Convent confirms that the identity of a place "derives, in large part, precisely from the specificity of its interactions with 'the outside'" (Massey 169). When residents fear the outside, problems often arise. Oppositional space, instead of continually negotiating the terrain between home and the outside, responds to these fears by either constructing higher and higher walls of protection or by turning to violence. Reading heaven as oppositional space, Geoffrey Bent claims that "One of paradise's shortcomings as a concept is that it's too schematic, a place that's all of this and none of that. Morrison's new novel falls prey to this same exclusivity" (148). However, Bent's schematic characterization of *Paradise* offers yet another example of what feminist geographers such as Doreen Massey critique; Bent's reading relies on and reproduces negative counterpositions—

strict boundaries and either/or constructions. Actually, by exaggerating the supposed differences between home and the race house, the novel highlights the failure of a schematic understanding of domesticity and emphasizes the importance of space's relational nature.

Critics of relational space may argue that it does not adequately account for history. That is, by emphasizing current relationships, relational space does not account for past wrongs. Following this logic, the 8-rock men could evoke their own violent history of dispossession as a way of justifying their preemptive strike against the Convent. As Massey points out, however, a relational understanding of home "does not mean that the past is irrelevant to the identity of place. It simply means that there is no internally produced, essential past" (171). In this sense, the Convent embodies "the ever-shifting geography of social relations present and past" (Massey 172). Reading the concept of "paradise" or "home" as a continual negotiation between inside and outside, between past and present, reveals the crux of the novel's spatial politics. The 8-rock community's resistant, oppositional relationship with the outside and the Convent's relational, open associations with Ruby illustrate that relational space may not eliminate violence, but oppositional space will produce violence every time. Even Billie Delia constructs an oppositional geopolitics as she critiques it, hoping the Convent women are "out there" and will return to seek justice against the "backward noplace ruled by men whose power to control was out of control and who had the nerve to say who could live and who not and where" (308). Does the Convent women's history give them any more right to "take aim"?

Thus despite all her attention to the home in her novels, Morrison may agree—at least in one respect—with Daphne Spain who suggests that "modifying the interior of houses may be the least important form of spatial intervention because less time is spent in the home now than in the past" (236). Morrison's reworking of home likewise cannot be completely bound by its physical barriers or structure. *Paradise* rewrites the conventional domestic narrative that frequently places its female protagonists at thresholds only to recontain them in the home. There must be open doors or windows: "Whether through a door needing to be opened or a beckoning window already raised, what would happen if you entered? What would be on the other side? What on earth would it be? What on earth?" (*Paradise* 305). The Convent's invitation to embrace neodomesticity beckons. These routes establish connections with the outside. Home is locations. In fact, the women, who may be ghosts at the end of *Paradise*, leave the Convent and occupy various types of spaces.

Significantly, Morrison's turn to a spiritual geography at *Paradise*'s conclusion, which is also seen in Barbara Kingsolver's conclusion to *The Poison-*

wood Bible, sets up a key difference between many feminine and masculine domestic fictions. Feminine domestic fiction's frequent embrace of spiritual geography emphasizes nonmaterial, relational spatial relations. "Spiritual reality," according to Kathryn Hume, "invites readers to reconsider the validity and human efficacy of the strictly phenomenal explanation" (113). Largely absent in masculine domestic fiction, this spiritual geography, or "spiritual reality," recycles the domestic novel's traditional religious or spiritual basis. However, rather than reproduce an absolute moral authority, the neodomestic novel's spiritual geography invites a deep comfort with—a faith in—instability: "What on earth would it be?" (*Paradise* 305). This same faith in instability takes Denver beyond her yard. Additionally, as Salazar points out, spiritual geographies are embedded in historical context, they negotiate individual and community relationships, and they affirm non-Western paradigms (400).

Instability unflaggingly recycles and renovates conventional domesticity in *Paradise*. For example, the Convent women embrace their marginality, accepting "dispersal and fragmentation as a part of the construction of a new world order that reveals more fully where we are, who we can become, an order that does not demand forgetting" (hooks, *Yearning* 148). Unlike the (ghost) woman in *Beloved* who needs to be exorcised from 124, these (ghost) women reconcile their pasts without haunting. The Convent opens passage to radical constructions of home and identity—what Patricia McKee describes as "radical geographical imaginaries," which depend on "multiple occupations of space" ("Geographies" 197; 198). Such radical constructions focus on the home's relational nature and the prospects produced by renovation and instability.

By deemphasizing the home's and the women's physical borders (the women, as ghosts, are literally disembodied), the novel suggests a means of demolishing the race house and the gender house. Remodeling the traditional notions of home offers liberatory potential. If we are to understand spatial politics and ultimately try to change them, we must first understand, as Massey argues, that "a proportion of the social interrelations will be wider than and go beyond the area being referred to in any particular context as a place" (169). Haven, Ruby, and the Convent, therefore, cannot isolate themselves without destroying themselves or one another; negative counterpositions demand such violence because they require characters to constantly define the self against the Other. Placing these spatial relationships in a specific historical context, Johnson writes, "Although sympathetic with the desire to establish a space protected from white violence, Morrison is critical of excesses committed in the name of black solidarity" (60). While the novel allows the Convent and the towns' home spaces to heal these wounded and rejected people, it does not ultimately allow the characters' desire for unity to segregate them from the larger community. Once again, some balance between these contradictory drives must be forged for a productive instability to exist and flourish.

Relational spaces, especially in conjunction with structural renovations that are targeted at oppressive race and gender structures, hold the potential to produce fruitful negotiations among places and communities, creating relationships beneficial to multiple parties. Mavis and Gigi's ability to live together despite hating each other provides a hopeful (and certainly not idealized) picture of relational space's potential. Benign skirmishes may occur but negotiations are not allowed to escalate to dangerous levels. By donning fatigues, the women seem to be preparing for battle at the novel's conclusion; however, their attire may be camouflage of a different sort.[23] Rather than suggesting that they are preparing to fight the men of Ruby, the women's camouflage may allow them to move undetected between spaces and to choose when to reveal themselves to their loved ones. What we, as readers, desire for the women ultimately tells us more about how close we are to achieving an "elusive race-free paradise" than if Morrison wrote a decisive ending about the women's fates.

Conclusions
Open Doors and Windows

Recognized as a historical battleground by Vlach, hooks, and Morrison, the home appropriately figures as a troubled space for the protagonists in these novels. In *Beloved* the haunted house engages the spatial history of slavery as a means to exorcise (but not forget) this specter. Haven, Ruby, and the Convent in *Paradise* outline the dangers of exclusion and separatism, which have conventionally been understood as necessary components of home and, at times, as viable solutions to racism and sexism. Carolyn M. Jones, writing about *Beloved* and *Song of Solomon*, observes that the home can be a place where "irreconcilable opposites" will destroy each other "to make home homogenous, or they can be complementary forces that yield, caress, express, and enrich our creative possibilities" (46). Jones goes on to say, "Even when it works, however, home is not paradise" (46). By appraising the novels' dwellings and their gendered, racial, social, and historical relations, I have tried to highlight the ways in which the structures' physical and spiritual (relational) frameworks and interior designs reveal authentic cultural constructions of race and gender as well as exhibit "imagined" or alternative constructions of

(African American) identity and home. Understanding Morrison's domestic fiction in light of its interrelated theoretical, historical, and material worlds illuminates what the "manageable, doable, modern human activity" looks like—a domestication that composes one of the fundamental projects of her fiction and of neodomestic fiction more broadly ("Home" 4).

IN PREVIOUS CHAPTERS I discussed the Africanist presence necessary to the foundation of the American home and American domestic literature. Where critics of Barbara Kingsolver's *The Poisonwood Bible* question Africa's role within her novel—suggesting that it presents local color, not serious history or cultural context—Kimberlé Williams Crenshaw points out in her work on critical race and legal studies that the African American woman more often than not fails to function as a "universal" model in American culture. This certainly rings true for the formation of domestic literature, which tends to privilege white women's experiences as "universal." Crenshaw's groundbreaking article "Demarginalizing the Intersection of Race and Sex: A Black Feminist Critique of Antidiscrimination Doctrine, Feminist Theory, and Antiracist Politics" looks at the ways in which "Black women are theoretically erased" because of the failure of the legal and social systems to view the intersections of race and gender (23). Countering this line of critique, this chapter demonstrates that Morrison's novels are both culturally specific and universally applicable for the study of American domestic fiction and American literature more generally. Grounded in the specifics of African American culture and history, Toni Morrison's domestic fiction defines the range and breadth of neodomesticity's varied forms. Morrison's fiction helps us "to grasp the importance of Black women's intersectional experiences, . . . [and to recognize the] unique compoundedness of their situation and the centrality of their experiences to the larger classes of women and Blacks" (Crenshaw 29).

Therefore, my first three chapters' juxtapositions of Silko's, Kingsolver's, and Morrison's neodomestic fictions demonstrate that the novels endorse neither "either/or" nor "white/black" constructions—rather, these chapters together demonstrate neodomesticity's "both/and" relational nexus. The following chapters continue this mapping of neodomesticity's relational nexus, focusing more extensively on masculine domesticity. These succeeding chapters also emphasize that the neodomestic novel locates itself translocally— encompassing both locally grounded histories and sociopolitical relations beyond the individual at home. The neodomestic novel locates interrelated local and global spheres and, when successfully crafted, brings this story home.

4

Mapping Gendered Genres

Domestic Masculinity,
Suburban Fiction, and the Antidomestic

> *Houses can have this almost authorial power over us, seeming to ruin or make perfect our lives just by persisting in one place longer than we can. (In either case it's a power worth defeating.)*
>
> —Frank Bascombe from Richard Ford's Independence Day

Richard Ford's Pulitzer Prize–winning *Independence Day* (1995) explores homemaking from a man's perspective. Like the domestic fiction that I have discussed in previous chapters, Ford's suburban novel takes homemaking as its topic and situates home as a central feature of the novel's geography. Similar to Toni Morrison's *Paradise*, Ford's *Independence Day* uses the Fourth of July as a motif to explore American domesticity and "the sacrifices people are willing to make to protect themselves and their property" (Jurca 171). Like Morrison's novel, various domestic geographies and dispossessions compose this exploration—though in *Independence Day*, dispossession primarily results from divorce. As a real estate agent, furthermore, Frank Bascombe earns a living through the transfer of property rather than suffering from its exchange. Such differences between the novels highlight important gender and racial disparities. Furthermore, Ford's centering of a male protagonist— men are conventionally considered to be outside of domestic fiction—and the novel's call to defeat home's power heighten attention to domestic fiction's status as a gendered genre and prompt us to ask what practices define it as such. After all—even given its focus on the home—what does it mean to label *Independence Day* "domestic fiction"?

The question is partly political. Male-authored and male-focused novels like *Independence Day* challenge conventional approaches to domestic fiction, approaches that often assume that domestic fiction is predominantly, if not exclusively, written by and about women. Clearly, men write domestic fiction, too. By rereading and reconceiving domestic fiction's literary history, we can account for the ways in which masculinity and men's fiction have always been a part of domestic culture and literature. The chapter begins by outlining and accounting for domestic masculinity's distinct literary history, particularly through the genre of suburban fiction. As in the previous chapters, a spatial reading allows for comparisons across home-centered fictions that are not often considered in relation to one another. This chapter and the next address the politics of the creation and maintenance of gendered fictions about the home, mapping more precisely the degree to which American authors write gendered domestic fictions and promote distinctly gendered ideologies and spaces.

Building on Judith Butler's notion of "gender performance," I examine the construction of gendered genres by identifying the key tropes that a text "performs" to produce a gendered identity. The performative features reveal the complexly gendered structures undergirding domestic fiction; the same performative features allow neodomestic fiction to interrogate such structures. By focusing on domestic fiction's gendered tropes rather than on the author's gender, I reject an essentialist view of biology, though I do not deny that the protagonist's gender and the author's gender do shape domesticity and the construction of domestic fiction (although biographical criticism is not the focus of my analysis). Sorting texts (rather than authors) according to gendered categories allows an analysis of the gendered roles assigned to both authors and texts, however socially or biologically determined, within American literature. As novels themselves are rhetorical and fictional constructions, they especially lend themselves to a socially constructed analysis of gender. Their fictional worlds provide insight into how "real" gender matters, particularly as it shapes and is constructed by social formations.

Mapping domestic fiction's gendered contours emphasizes that many gendered domestic roles—and the gendering of genres—have not changed dramatically through the course of the nineteenth and twentieth centuries. Female authors generally write a feminine form of domestic fiction (focused on female protagonists and feminized housekeeping activities), and male authors likewise tend to create a masculine form (focused predominately on male protagonists and masculine domestic duties). My own largely gendered chapter divisions reflect these tendencies. In part the correlation between genre and gender reflects men and women's longstanding labor and spatial divisions.¹ Like our gendered genres, domestic roles remain traditionally divided.

Today, for example, most of the women who work outside the home still start a second shift when they return home, functioning as the family's primary caregiver and domestic laborer. According to data collected in 2005 by the University of Michigan Institute for Social Research, "women, of all ages with no children, on average do 10 hours of housework a week before marriage and 17 hours of housework after marriage. Men of all ages with no children, on the other hand, do eight hours before marriage and seven hours afterward" (Mixon par. 6). While women do less housework today (seventeen hours per week in 2005 compared to twenty-six hours per week in 1976), men's weekly averages remain lower than women's, even as they have increased since the mid-1970s (six hours in 1976 compared to thirteen hours in 2005) (Mixon par. 13). As Kris Frieswick points out, the discrepancies "made sense, sort of, back when women's occupations were limited to variations on caring for other people, usually the ones living at home with them. But it makes no sense today" (30). Today, in fact, "women, who compose 49 percent of the American workforce, are now outearning their husbands in 32.6 percent of American married couples, up from 23.7 percent in 1987" (Frieswick 30). As women contribute more financially, however, their husbands' housework contributions have decreased (Frieswick 30). Same-sex couples, by comparison, "tended to share the burdens [related to housework, sex, and money] more equally" (Parker-Pope F1). Such trends among same-sex couples emphasize gender's inequitable and socially constructed power dynamics more than its firm biological roots. These gendered divisions and revisions appear in and shape our understanding of contemporary fiction, too.

This chapter's epigraph hints at the nature of literary domesticity's gender divide. Frank Bascombe's proposal that the home's power is "worth defeating" endorses a more masculinist, oppositional framing in regard to the home (Ford 106). Unlike Morrison's *Paradise*, Kingsolver's *The Poisonwood Bible*, or Silko's *Gardens in the Dunes*, Ford's *Independence Day* seeks to demystify the home's spiritual geography rather than reinscribe or promote it. Frank Bascombe's remarks, as a result, do not endorse the same type of historically grounded spatial tactics. Thus, while the overarching theme of "productive instability" is the hallmark of neodomestic fiction, gendered differences among neodomestic fictions regarding homemaking practices and views of the home's spiritual geography mark residual gendered practices that survive both the recycling process and the "third space" produced by neodomestic fictions. These gendered differences, moreover, hold significance for neodomestic fiction's politics. While "masculine" and "feminine" neodomestic novels both provide viable alternatives to domestic stability, my reading in this and the next chapter demonstrates why novels that nourish spiritual geographies more clearly reflect feminist and antiracist politics. Tracing domestic masculinity's emergence in early American fiction provides a historical and cultural context for contemporary domesticity's gendered qualities.

Suburban Fiction
American Domestic Masculinity's Literary History

Domestic masculinity is a construct that the conventional gender dichotomy considers already hybrid: if domesticity is implicitly and explicitly gendered feminine, then something or someone that is both masculine and domestic is, by definition, a gendered mix.[2] Traditionally, domestic masculinity has been categorized separately from domestic fiction—especially in distinct and arguably more "universal" literary categories such as the romance or the social novel. In the twentieth century, suburban fiction became a primary genre for domestic masculinity. Often focused on a male protagonist and written by men (and in these ways its definition is similar to that of its feminine counterpart, domestic fiction), suburban literature includes fictions focused on suburban space and suburban domesticity. The home as haven and trap appears in these masculine domestic fictions, too. Such shared features begin to suggest that suburban fiction, such as Ford's *Independence Day*, "requires us to revise our current understanding of the home as a gendered [feminine] fixture in American literature and literary criticism" (Jurca 9). By repositioning several representative suburban texts as domestic fictions, I aim to flesh out the suggestion that, like the rhetoric of separate spheres, divisions among men and women who write about the home have historically been overstated, oversimplified, or simply undertheorized. Analyzing domestic masculinity's literary history continues the reversionary work advanced by scholars such as Catherine Jurca and Lora Romero and clarifies neodomestic fiction's recycling efforts.

Domestic masculinity has a long American literary history. In its earliest literary forms, the home frequently symbolizes an oppressive feminine space that threatens masculinity and male freedom. For instance, in "Rip Van Winkle" (1819), generally considered the first American short story, Rip escapes oppressive domesticity by fleeing his home and falling asleep for several years. When he wakes up and conveniently finds his wife dead,

Rip enjoys a life free of domestic duties: "Having nothing to do at home, and being arrived at that happy age when a man can be idle with impunity, he took his place once more on the bench at the inn-door, and was reverenced as one of the patriarchs of the village, and a chronicle of the old times 'before the war'" (Irving 47). When Rip awakes, not only does he find America free of England's shackles, but he also discovers perfect domestic tranquility without a wife to nag him.

Rip's literary legacy of the home as a trap to be escaped, rebelled against, or dominated appears throughout the nineteenth and twentieth centuries, where male characters flee the home and "light out for new territory." Judith Fetterley, referring to Washington Irving's "The Legend of Sleepy Hollow," argues, "Irving suggests that the quintessential American story will be a tall tale circulated among men for the purpose of establishing dominance" (891). Mark Twain's *The Adventures of Tom Sawyer* (1876) and *The Adventures of Huckleberry Finn* (1885) follow in this tradition that Nina Baym aptly describes as "melodramas of beset manhood" (130). These foundational masculine antidomestic dramas imagine women as "entrappers and domesticators" and present the domestic sphere as an impediment to male development and comfort (Baym 133). Peggy Cooper Davis and Carol Gilligan, building on the work of Nancy F. Cott, clarify that such "flights from relationship are grounded in what we call the logic of patriarchy" (58). Patriarchal logic discourages relational and egalitarian interactions in favor of competition, dominance, and hierarchy.

Rip's "beset manhood" becomes a key trope for American domestic masculinity. Significantly, not only does this seminal melodrama position a male character's flight from domesticity, but it also "can be taken as representative of the [male] author's literary experience, his struggle for integrity and livelihood against flagrantly bad best-sellers written by women" (Baym 130). According to this logic, Rip's "beset manhood" is not dissimilar to the male author's struggle against domesticity and domestic fiction or women's writing in particular. The next chapter takes up this theme in greater detail, looking at how Jonathan Franzen's remarks about Oprah's Book Club relate to this long history of anxiety about feminine writing. In this section focused on the literary origins and history of domestic masculinity, I wish to build on this foundational trope to reread and revise domestic fiction's formation as an exclusively feminine genre. Tracing suburban fiction's emergence as a masculine genre reveals narratives of men's flights from and to the home.

Women are also central to suburban fiction; however, suburban literature traditionally comes out of a male-authored and male-focused tradition.[3] Steven M. Gelber suggests in "Do-It-Yourself: Constructing, Repairing and

Maintaining Domestic Masculinity" that masculinity's strong relationship to suburban (domestic) space results from "the creation of a male sphere *inside* the house" that emerged with the rise of suburbia (73; emphasis in original). Gelber explains, "the do-it-yourself movement . . . brought men back into the home by turning their houses into hobbies" (104). The suburban home, in other words, became a domestic space where one could securely assert or perform masculinity. While today women are increasingly performing these same do-it-yourself tasks, the rise of suburbia in the first half of the twentieth century carved out a space for domestic masculinity.[4] Suburban fiction reflects this masculine focus.

Suburban fiction is perhaps best known for narrating (white) men's alienation. Catherine Jurca suggests that the twentieth century's suburban "domestically oriented male identity" is a remarkably modern paradox that compels writers to "treat paradise . . . as though it were purgatory" (168). Jurca identifies the contemporary suburban novel's central paradox as a rejection of the home that grants the (white) characters their privilege: "Literary representations of the suburb propose that white middle-class identity is not grounded in safe havens or homes but in its alienation from the very environments, artifacts, and institutions that have generally been regarded as central to its affect and identity" (7).[5] Jurca identifies this paradox as a dominant trope that has changed little since the 1920s and probably will not change in the twenty-first century (171).[6] However, modern suburban literature's hallmark masculine irony and domestic alienation connects to earlier American literary traditions, linking suburban literature to both the nineteenth century's antidomestic male and domestic female literary traditions.

Twentieth-century white male suburban "sentimental dispossession" (Jurca 7) harkens back to nineteenth-century narratives of "beset manhood" and to turn-of-the-century novels written primarily by white women that also posit the home as a trap. For instance, contemporary white male suburban fiction often narrates a masculine version of the conventional (feminine) domestic trope of the home as a trap. The "veneer stripping" and "exposé" (Jurca 161) aspects of the (suburban) home's constrictive qualities connect the twentieth-century male suburban tradition to white women's own literary exposé of the home. Where the masculine tradition may emphasize alienation (especially in the modern period), the feminine tradition frequently focuses on isolation. Such distinctions emerge from distinct cultural milieus represented by William H. Whyte's *The Organization Man* (1956) and the alienation from labor it represents for (primarily white) men and masculinity; whereas Betty Friedan's *The Feminine Mystique* (1963) emphasizes (primarily white) women's isolation produced by a career in homemaking.[7] Additionally, white men frequently enjoy greater mobility to escape these traps; although, as Jurca argues, in the twentieth century men's alienation "from the suburban home in the popular novel expresses the *desire for* domestic familiarity" rather than a desire to escape such "familiarity" (11; emphasis in original). Significantly, race and class considerations also shape the alienation-isolation dichotomy. As Ann Petry's novel *The Street* (1946) reminds us, the alienation-isolation described is arguably most applicable to the experiences of middle-class whites. Her own "*desire for* domestic familiarity" and inability to achieve it as well as the novel's invocation of "home as the measure of the characters' loss" speak to distinct gendered, raced, and classed experiences from her white male and female contemporaries (Jurca 11).

While the alienation from home remains a dominant theme within (white) masculine domestic fiction, the home as a haven appears in masculine domestic fiction as well. William Dean Howells's *Suburban Sketches* (1872) is particularly interesting because of the groundwork it lays for suburban literature and neodomestic themes, its historical placement at the beginning of the development of suburban space in America, and its literary presentation of Charlesbridge, a suburb of Boston, as both "a kind of Paradise" and a suburban trap (Howells 12). Like the nineteenth-century domestic advice books and female-authored and female-focused domestic fiction that I discussed in previous chapters, *Suburban Sketches* clearly advances a domestic politics of stability. It also simultaneously celebrates American mobility. In *Suburban Sketches* the domestic haven-trap dilemma appears in conjunction with the promotion of the single-family dwelling and the development of suburbia.

Suburban Sketches marks the emergence and development of suburban space in the nineteenth century. It describes an ideal "picturesque enclave" that "architects and landscape architects began to design . . . in the 1850s" (Hayden, *Building Suburbia* 45). *Suburban Sketches* describes its setting as a haven, or an ideal combination of city and country: "We were living in the country with the conveniences and luxuries of the city about us. The house was almost new and in perfect repair; and, better than all, the kitchen had as yet given no signs of unrest in those volcanic agencies which are constantly at work there, and which, with sudden explosion, make Herculaneums and Pompeiis of so many smiling households" (Howells 12–13). The home's newer condition sets chaotic remodeling projects—especially the project of remodeling the kitchen—at bay. *Suburban Sketches* promotes American suburban space as a secure domestic sphere—a haven from the city without the complete isolation of the country.

Dolores Hayden's description of the early suburban "borderland" or "edge" in *Building Suburbia* echoes Howells's description of the Charlesbridge home. Hayden writes, "The edge was neither rural nor urban. It formed a distinctive gateway zone between city and country" (22). Howells writes, "The neighborhood was in all things a frontier between city and country" (13). Suburban space's role as a "gateway zone" ostensibly offers a utopian balance between these two worlds. However, living on this chosen borderland also frequently proves isolating for many residents. Additionally, the narrator valorizes his new home for its lack of history rather than its potential for longevity as a home. The narrator has not yet worn out or outgrown this home—although his initial description suggests this inevitable fate. Thus, we can begin to see the trap embedded in the suburban "frontier" haven.

Regarding the suburban home's isolation, *Suburban Sketches* relates the trouble that the family has in finding a housekeeper because most of the Irish "gairls doesn't like [sic] to live so far away from the city" (Howells 16). While this isolation from the city makes finding household help more difficult, this problem also curiously centers the sketch's otherwise marginalized domestic figures. For example, *Suburban Sketches*'s first sketch, "Mrs. Johnson," describes the narrator's new black housemaid and cook. The difficulty of finding a housekeeper leads the family into the black quarter of the city in search of African American help, because black women are presumably less picky about their employers than are Irish women. This domestic problem opens a space for the narrator to ruminate on racial difference. He distinguishes Mrs. Johnson, for example, from Anglo-Saxon New Englanders: "It was only her barbaric laughter and her lawless eye that betrayed how slightly her New England birth and breeding covered her ancestral traits, and bridged the gulf of a thousand years of civilization that lay between her race and ours" (Howells 20–21). The contrasts that the narrator draws between his own household—which clearly depends on this "outside," "foreign" labor—and the "sympathetic" portraits of the Irish and black servants control access to suburbia's "gateway zone" or domestic "frontier."

Thus, the sketch suggestively begins with the narrator's oblique indication that such "volcanic agencies" are foreign traits that are also necessary for the household to function smoothly (Howells 13). They hold the power to quell or produce kitchen chaos. *Suburban Sketches* begins by incorporating and distinguishing these "foreign" elements from the "native" residents of the domestic frontier. Beginning with the "Mrs. Johnson" sketch emphasizes suburbia's literal and metaphoric negative space—its central but potentially unsettling Africanist presence upon which the American home depends. The narrator, for example, states, "We were conscious of something warmer in this old soul than in ourselves, and something wilder, and we chose to think it the tropic and the untracked forest" (Howells 29). This portrait of a not fully domesticated Mrs. Johnson presents her "barbaric" qualities as local color; her features amuse and sometimes frustrate but never truly pose a danger to the household. For example, her son's constant presence around the house constitutes an annoyance but never a real threat for the narrator and his wife: "We could formulate no very tenable objection to all this, and yet the presence of Thucydides in our kitchen unaccountably oppressed our imaginations" (Howells 32). As Valerie Sweeney Prince points out, "White Americans read the presence of African American domestic workers as a sign of their own domestic security. Nearly a hundred years after the collapse of the slave economy, home for white people continued to be stabilized at the expense of black laborers" (114, n. 2). Additionally, the fact that help was hard to find heightened the experience of living on the suburban "frontier"— a frontier that was hardly beyond (white) civilization's reach.

Later masculine domestic and suburban fiction—such as John Updike's second Rabbit novel, *Rabbit Redux* (1971)—complicates the Africanist presence within white suburbia. While the character Skeeter also provides, at best, "something wilder" or local color to Rabbit's story, he also functions more clearly as a disruptive, dodgy character over which the white male protagonist has no control. Unlike Mrs. Johnson, Skeeter is not domesticated; he is dangerous. He makes the neighbors so nervous they make it clear to Rabbit that Skeeter needs to leave (Updike, *Rabbit Redux* 249–54). When he does not, the house mysteriously burns down, sparing Skeeter, Rabbit, and Rabbit's son, but killing Jill. The community's fear of Skeeter, however, should not suggest that Skeeter merely presents or represents physical violence in the novel. Key scenes in the novel involve Skeeter educating Rabbit's temporarily reconfigured family—Rabbit, Rabbit's son, Skeeter, and the runaway Jill— during living room teach-ins. What is particularly interesting about such scenes is that they bring the civil rights movement and the sexual revolution smack-dab into the middle of Rabbit's suburban living room. One especially intense and bizarre scene involves Rabbit reading aloud, at Skeeter's request, from *The Life and Times of Frederick Douglass*.[8] By contrast, Howells's *Suburban Sketches* positions the "external" workers who make the suburban home possible in clearly domesticated and "foreign" (not fully American) roles.

The narrator in *Suburban Sketches*, in fact, initially revels in the domestic tranquility and reliability that the suburban space produces: "Breakfast, dinner, and tea came up with illusive regularity, and were all the most perfect of their kind; and we laughed and feasted in our vain security" (13). Here the narrator describes the conventional model home of security and comfort. *Suburban Sketches* goes on to describe a sundry list of homemaking activities and suburban personalities and activities. As the narrator prepares to move from Charlesbridge in the final sketch, he discusses the labor involved, the effect the moving process has on domestic possessions and life, the preparation of the final meal in the old house, and the first meal in the new home. During this transition a less idealistic view of suburbia, which is more readily apparent in modern suburban fiction (such as Updike's Rabbit novels), begins to emerge, disrupting the family's "vain security" (Howells 13).

In the final chapter, the home's security—or the narrator's reliance on this security—gives way to a more masculine mobility—or "lighting out for new territory."[9] This early sketch about the flight from home develops the concept of American domestic mobility. The final sketch about the move, "Flitting," begins with the narrator's negotiation between a "beset manhood" that requires the rejection of home—particularly the maternal home—and a desire for home and security. The expression of these conflicting desires in the late nineteenth century simultaneously advances an imperial absorption of new territories and a solidification of homeland security amidst change and cultural diversity. It is also a precursor to what Jurca calls "sentimental dispossession," the sense of homelessness expressed in modern suburban fiction.

The following passage from "Flitting" succinctly outlines the narrator's negotiation between domestic security and mobility:

> I would not willingly repose upon the friendship of a man whose local attachments are weak. I should not demand of my intimate that he have a yearning for the homes of his ancestors, or even the scenes of his own boyhood; that is not in American nature; on the contrary, he is but a poor creature who does not hate the village where he was born; yet a sentiment for the place where one has lived two or three years, the hotel where one has spent a week, the sleeping car in which one had ridden from Albany to Buffalo,—so much I should think it well to exact from my friend in proof of that sensibility and constancy without which true friendship does not exist. (Howells 241)

The narrator expresses a paradox: the rejection of the boyhood, ancestral home—which I take to be feminine/maternal, in the sense that the boyhood home is ruled by the mother's influence—and the embrace of the adult masculine/patriarchal home, a symbol of Christian virtue, stability, and prosperity. Notably, public residences like a hotel or sleeping car help define this transient, masculine sense of home.

The narrator reconciles his alienation from and desire for home by describing a characteristically American domestic mobility: the ability to make home anywhere. This story individualizes America's foundational mythology of discovery, settlement, and independence. Later in the final sketch, the narrator explicitly connects domestic mobility with being American: "If the reader is of a moving family,—and so he is as he is an American—he can recall the zest he found during childhood in the moving" (Howells 250–51). Although the narrator in *Suburban Sketches* only recommends moving to members of the "leisure" class, he suggests that mobility and a succession of homes embody American domesticity and identity (Howells 245). Literally progressive, this sense of mobile domesticity fits nicely with the American dream of upward mobility. Domestic mobility in this incarnation involves reconciling, on the one hand, the desire for change and freedom, and on the other hand, the desire for stability and security. By implication, the ability to find or make home in a variety of locations—from a home of a few years to a sleeping car or a hotel—becomes the required domestic skill for all Americans. As we have seen in the previous chapters, neodomestic fiction that focuses on women—such as Barbara Kingsolver's *The Poisonwood Bible*, Leslie Marmon Silko's *Gardens in the Dunes*, and Toni Morrison's *Paradise*—recycles this American drive and narrative. These neodomestic fictions point to the edges where the two gendered sides of the domestic coin meet.

Thus, we can begin to see in *Suburban Sketches* the blueprint of twentieth-century suburban and neodomestic fiction. Howells's text anticipates later, more sardonic, suburban novels, and ends on a somber but assuring note. After four years of living in Charlesbridge, the narrator begins to see suburbia's flaws: "Many of the vacant lots abutting upon Benicia and the intersecting streets flourished up, during the four years we knew it, into fresh-painted wooden houses, and the time came to be when one might have looked in vain for the abandoned hoop-skirts which used to decorate the desirable buildings-sites. The lessening pasturage also reduced the herds which formerly fed in the vicinity" (Howells 242). Developed suburbia no longer provides the ideal mix of city and country. As suburbia develops, nature disappears. Additionally, the suburb frequently lacks the city's comforts and services. In the first sketch the narrator notes that while he "paid a heavy tax" and "never looked upon Charlesbridge as in any way undesirable for residence," his street lacks many conveniences: "Our street was unlighted. Our street was not drained nor graded; no municipal cart ever came to carry away our ashes; there was not a water-butt within half a mile to save us from fire, nor more than the one thousandth part of a policeman to protect us from theft" (16). A more oblique critique of the lack of municipal services appears in the final sketch. Howells describes how the sidewalks, poorly constructed and not maintained, quickly return to a "Nature" of the wrong sort (Howells 242). This lack of services and planning was a common problem in nineteenth- and twentieth-century suburban developments (Hayden, *Building Suburbia* 115; 128; 136–37).

While Howells's sketches are instructive for their early portrait of white, middle-class suburban space and domestic masculinity, they do not narrate the full extent of suburbia's diversity. By the latter half of the twentieth century, a more diverse presentation of suburban spaces and experiences emerged. For example, John Edgar Wideman's Homewood trilogy, which includes *Damballah* (1981), *Hiding Place* (1981), and *Sent for You Yesterday* (1983), depicts a frequently understudied location: the African American suburb.[10] As Andrew Wiese explains, "The truth is . . . historians have done a better job excluding African Americans from the suburbs than even white suburbanites. Scholarly neglect notwithstanding, African Americans lived in and moved to suburbs throughout the twentieth century, and black communities served as a social and spatial basis for expanded suburbanization over time" (5). Stereotypically, the term "suburban" evokes Protestant whiteness; however, as productive as this stereotype can be in regard to noting exclusionary development practices, it ignores suburbia's historical, present, and literary cultural diversity. Wiese, a historian of black suburbia, writes, "By the end of the [twentieth] century, suburbia, once a symbol of white supremacy and exclusion, had become a fundamental setting for African American life" (10). Wiese's observations hold true for other racial and ethnic minorities.

Dolores Hayden similarly points out in *Building Suburbia* that "some affluent suburban communities remain almost entirely white and Protestant, but there are also Irish-American suburbs, African-American suburbs, Polish-American suburbs, and Chinese-American suburbs, as well as older streetcar suburbs like Boyle Heights in Los Angeles, a place that has welcomed successive waves of new immigrants from Mexico, Russia, and Japan" (13). Hayden also notes suburbia's long history as a home for a variety of socioeconomic groups:

> Although the history of the suburbs includes countless examples of exclusion implemented through developers' deed restrictions, bankers' red-lining, realtors' steering, government lending policies, and other discriminatory practices, not all nineteenth-century [or twentieth-century] suburban residential areas were white, Protestant, and elite. From about 1870 on, many working-class and lower-middle-class families were attracted to the periphery of the city, where land was cheap and houses might be constructed with sweat equity. (*Building Suburbia* 12)[11]

Although not generally considered suburban literature, Wideman's Homewood trilogy, which takes place in the Homewood neighborhood outside of Pittsburgh, has clear suburban roots, particularly in the sweat equity connected with domestic masculinity.[12] Significantly, the Homewood trilogy memorializes home, especially one's ancestral home. For example, when John French in *Sent for You Yesterday* tries to explain why his troublemaking friend Albert Wilkes returns to Homewood, where he surely will be murdered for sleeping with a white woman, he says, "The man needs to come home" (84). The sentiment packed into this sentence emphasizes that men's identities are as deeply rooted in home as are women's. Additionally, when Mother Bess burns down her house in *Hiding Place*, she leaves her home or hiding place—a cross between a haven and a trap—to enter the world (158). The Homewood trilogy explores both women's and men's investments in home.

This abbreviated literary and spatial history of suburban fiction and domestic masculinity opens the discussion for how distinctly gendered characteristics produce related but unique domestic genres and politics. Literary history demonstrates that domestic masculinity presents the home as a haven and a trap; however, domestic mobility keeps the narratives from becoming overtly or problematically feminine. Looking across the spectrum of domestic fictions reveals distinct landmarks that signal a novel's gendered identity.

Domesticity's Gendered Landmarks

To analyze the domestic novel's gender politics more thoroughly, this section outlines three gendered facets that consistently appear in (neo)domestic fiction and that play key roles in determining a novel's gendered identity: (1) the presentation of gendered domestic space, (2) the main characters' domestic labor, and (3) the novel's understanding of the home's spiritual geography. Examining these characteristics helps identify how a novel "performs" its gender. Neodomestic fiction often blurs these gendered boundaries and may include both genders within the narrative for contrast or for merging: neodomestic fiction may carry a strong gender association or continually play with such conventions. Outlining the American home's gendered spatial contexts enriches our understanding of this so-called separate sphere and its connection to raced, classed, and sexualized space.

Gendered Space
The Den, the Parlor, and the Remodeled Suburb

Gender plays a key role in the home's social and economic organization. As married women for the most part could not legally own property in most states until the mid-nineteenth century, early domestic narratives featuring women understandably focus less on ownership and property relations.[13] Rather, they focus on achieving marriage and maintaining the family in order to acquire and keep a physical house. Women's home management roles contribute to the house's status as a private–public feminine space: the home traditionally reflects a woman's private–public housekeeper role. For men the home conventionally functions as private property, symbolizing their ability to provide for and protect their families. Because of the home's general association with femininity, men often carve out distinctly masculine spaces within the domestic sphere. The den and later the home office, garage, and workshop epitomize such masculine domestic spaces.

In the nineteenth century, according to Milette Shamir, the den functioned as the male's private domestic retreat and the parlor provided a public-private domain for women. We see such gendered spatial contours in Nathaniel Hawthorne's *The House of Seven Gables* (1851) where the den is an important setting. For example, key male deaths in the novel take place there. The study also houses a lost property deed. In this novel and for masculine domesticity generally, private property and the den are "sacrosanct [for] the romantic individual, demarcating the boundary between what he chose to hide and what he chose to display, between his private self and his public persona" (Shamir 446). In the twentieth century, gendered domestic space remains, but the den's and the parlor's significance and layouts undergo remodeling. For example, the lawyer Henry Rios in Michael Nava's mystery *Rag and Bone* (2001) designs his home office for specific effects consistent with conventional masculinity:

> Unlike the rest of my house, furnished, as John said, with mismatched pieces bought on sale, this room was formal and deliberate. The walls were forest green; the bookshelves, the file cabinets and the long table I used as my desk were mahogany. On the wall above the black leather sofa was the usual collection of degrees and admissions to various courts, including the United States Supreme Court. My tall desk chair was of the same black

leather. Since I never met clients at my house, the businesslike furnishings of the room were strictly for my own benefit; their conventional severity put me into work mode even if I stumbled in wearing a bathrobe and slippers. (Nava 79)

While designed for Henry's private use, his office also structures his personal relationships. His lover Josh "had hated this room and told me he never entered it without expecting to be cross-examined" (79). Henry's niece experiences a similar sensation. The furnishings, therefore, successfully embody legal authority (read "masculine authority"). The dark wood, leather, and certificates symbolize stereotypical masculine authority and space. Such spaces offer male characters a retreat and a position of power within an otherwise typically feminine domestic domain—even when no women live in the home, as in Henry Rio's case.

In contrast to the den, the parlor offers little, if any, private space. As a result, women rarely experience the home as a private space. The young protagonist Ellen in *The Wide, Wide World* provides a case in point. Ellen does not have privacy within the home: she has no control over her mail (Warner 146; 488–93) or over Nancy Vawse, who invades her room and privacy while Ellen is ill (Warner 207–12). As a poor orphan, she has no home, so she seeks her aptly named Aunt Fortune for a home. Aunt Fortune literally embodies Ellen's initial means to gain access to "fortune" or domestic property in the form of a house. Ellen negotiates family relations as she grows up; she does not seek formal employment or other means of obtaining money for subsistence. Ellen, moreover, never owns land; her material property consists of carefully selected possessions, such as her Bible, a writing desk, and articles of clothing.[14] The novel clearly indicates that Ellen's most precious "property" is the state of her soul and her search for "that home where parting cannot be" (Warner 64). Without a retreat, Ellen's "private" morality is open to public scrutiny: "The virtues now attributed to the 'valiant' woman—self-sacrifice, the ability to maintain intimacy, and social responsibility—are precisely those that are shown to endanger privacy" (Shamir 435).

The bedroom of a middle- or upper-class girl or woman provided some privacy in the nineteenth century; it was a space where she could literally and figuratively loosen the corset strings. Unlike the den, women could not fortify this space against intrusions by other family members or servants. In *The House of Seven Gables*, Colonel Pyncheon retreats to his study, leaving orders that he is not to be disturbed (Hawthorne 32–34). His servants dare not disturb him: "My master's orders were exceeding strict; and, as your worship knows, he permits of no discretion in the obedience of those who owe him service" (Hawthorne 33). Ellen, by contrast, has little—if any—control over access to her bedroom or private affairs.

In the twentieth century, architectural changes in home design and the middle-class (white) woman's relationship to the public sphere and to formal (paid) employment dramatically influenced women's relationship to domestic property and privacy. In one sense, (white, middle-class) women's relationship to domestic privacy began to resemble men's more closely. Baym explains this shift in *Women's Fiction*: "The liberal women who began their writing careers after the Civil War found the redemptive possibilities of enlightened domesticity to be no longer credible. . . . Home now became a retreat, a restraint and a constraint, it had not appeared to be earlier; to define it as woman's sphere was now unambiguously to invite her to absent herself permanently from the world's affairs" (50). Women seemingly gained privacy at the expense of connections to the world. White women writers, such as Elizabeth Phelps and Edith Wharton, began to characterize the home as a trap—like their male counterparts—or they idealized the home as a retreat from the public sphere.[15]

The contemporary home's literary and material designs reflect the social changes experienced by women in the public and private spheres. Architecturally, parlors changed to living rooms, but these public, social rooms still frequently showcase the family's (and its homemaker's) domesticity. Family rooms, where the television set is frequently located, became the family's private social space (and portal to the public world via the television). Living rooms—frequently unused space unless visitors were present—emerged as architectural and social remnants of the public/private parlor. In the late twentieth century, the (re)turn to the "great room" as a popular architectural feature further complicated feminine domestic space, because the great room follows seventeenth- and eighteenth-century housing designs that also incorporated a great room: "Overall, then, the seventeenth- and eighteenth-century interior was largely a communal space that made few accommodations for individual privacy and shaped open, visible spaces shared by the nuclear family and its adjuncts" (Shamir 437). Such spaces, scholars argue, are not clearly gendered, especially in comparison to nineteenth-century architectural designs.

Daphne Spain maps one version of this narrative of the home's architectural development through the nineteenth and twentieth centuries in her chapter "From Parlor to Great Room": "New housing forms reflect changing family ideals and with them new ideas of women's and men's proper places. Emphasis on family rooms and master bedroom suites in magazines illustrates the decreasing force of the older ideals of separate male and female spheres" (132). According to Spain, the modern home's open plan suggests a more egalitarian sociospatial design. Spain concludes, "The home is now indicative of more egalitarian gender relations" (140). Given these architectural and cultural changes in American domesticity, neodomestic fiction's emergence appears to follow and reflect a logical, historical progression toward "radical openness" (hooks, *Yearning* 148). However, further investigation reveals that American domestic history, culture, and architecture do not line up so neatly.

First, not everyone lives in such homes with ostensibly "more egalitarian gender relations," and not everyone can remodel living space in this fashion, even if everyone wished to do so. Additionally, the great room floor plan, as Shamir notes in regard to the seventeenth and eighteenth centuries, also effectively reduces private space—a spatial change that does not necessarily produce egalitarian relations. The great room locates personal privacy within individual bedrooms, which perhaps explains why with the reemergence of the great room we also see couches and reading chairs along with small kitchen suites appearing in the master bedroom. Where else would parents find private space? There is also no evidence that architectural changes have produced or reflect substantial changes in heterosexual women's and men's household roles and labor (Domosh and Seager 2). Furthermore, in the early twenty-first century, gendered domestic space made a comeback in the form of the "man cave" or "mantuary." The DIY Network launched a program, *Man Caves*, devoted to this design phenomenon, which may be situated in the basement, garage, outdoor shed, or even in rented storage units. According to the DIY Network's *Man Caves* Web site, "Every guy needs a space to call his own . . . a sanctuary where boys can be boys, where life essentials include a wet bar, a poker table and a place to watch the game with the fellas." Like the den, the man cave is a gendered space that supposedly harkens back to masculinity's primal instincts and need to escape the feminine domestication that pervades the rest of the residence.

A fixation on the home's (gendered) designs in and of themselves, though, does not fully illuminate the larger sociospatial positing of gender and family in the twenty-first century. Dolores Hayden, for example, situates the contemporary housing crisis by downplaying such design concerns and highlighting the need to recycle existing out-of-date structures like suburban tract housing: "The question of how to sustain or divide our seven-room suburban houses is not the problem itself, but a symptom of a larger, underlying demographic shift. Americans have established a national fabric of single-family housing that needs updating" (*Redesigning* 224). Therefore, while gendered space continues to shape contemporary literature and domestic culture, the question of the value of the single-family dwelling also requires our attention.

Hayden locates many contemporary housing problems in the single-family dwelling's monolithic status. She also suggests that our contemporary housing problems share much with those experienced by Americans in the 1870s (*Redesigning* 222–24). Hayden explains,

> The adaptation of suburban house forms to new uses is as inevitable as was the adaptation of brick row houses and brownstones and the introduction of mixed uses, higher densities, and new building types that accompanied it. This adaptation can be carried out brilliantly or half-heartedly. Housing stock can deteriorate or it can be correctly preserved; multifamily neighborhoods can create fear and unease or generate a better context for new kinds of units. These choices reverberate with implications for the larger public domain. (*Redesigning* 224)

Lourdes, Rufino, and Pilar Puente's Brooklyn home in Cristina Garcia's *Dreaming in Cuban* (1992) exemplifies neodomestic recycling and the remodeling of domestic space that Hayden describes.

The Puente family lives in the back of a warehouse. Pilar, the daughter, explains that her father, Rufino, "bought the warehouse from the city for a hundred dollars when I was in third grade." According to Pilar, the warehouse

> had lots of great junk in it until Mom made [Rufino] move it out. There were a vintage subway turnstile and an antique telephone, the shell of a Bluebird radio, even the nose fin of a locomotive. . . . Dad tells me the place was built in the 1920s as temporary housing for out-of-town public-school teachers. Then it was a dormitory for soldiers during World War II, and later the Transit Authority used it for storage. (Garcia 29–30)

Pilar's description highlights several neodomestic characteristics. First, the Puente family literally lives in recycled housing. In characteristic neodomestic fashion, the building flexibly exchanges human cargo for transit castoffs and then becomes family housing. The description implies that the building's transitions—it houses teachers, soldiers, equipment, and eventually, the Puente family—were fairly easy. The home also directly connects domesticity with commerce and mobility; the Transit Authority once used the building for storage. Significantly, "puente" means "bridge" in Spanish, which further emphasizes the relational aspects of the "bridge home." *Dreaming in Cuban* thus constructs a neodomestic spatial paradigm.

The Puentes' home also remains an ambivalent, unstable space—making it both flexible and potentially insecure. A Cuban family in New York living in a warehouse—a temporary storage place—is deeply significant. Where will they go next? Will they return to Cuba? The Puentes' home recycles the warehouse to craft a home with positive and negative features. While the mother maintains control of domestic space—she tells her husband to get rid of the junk—twenty-first-century neodomestic fiction does not generally produce the "divided plots" that Shamir describes as significant to the nineteenth century. Hybrid commercial-domestic spaces like the Puentes' home better characterize neodomestic space.

The conclusion to Chang-rae Lee's *Aloft* (2004) also remodels the suburban home in neodomestic fashion. Jerry Battle, the novel's narrator, owns a modest suburban ranch house on Long Island. His grown children have developed housing practices at two extremes. His daughter, Theresa, and her partner, Paul, still rent: "Theresa [is] perfectly content with whatever postdoc-style housing she and Paul can flop in each academic autumn with their fold-up Ikea furniture" (69). Theresa and Paul model a transient domesticity. His son, Jack, on the other hand, has a hefty mortgage and a large debt due to his McMansion:

> The house that Jack built is in a gated development called Haymarket Estates, a brand-new luxury "enclave" that sits on what was a patch of scrubby land a few exits east of where I live. . . . The proportion is really the opposite of my place, where my modest ranch house sits right smack in the middle of the property (just over an acre), so that I have plenty of trees and shrubs and lawn to buffer me from my good neighbors. (Lee 64–65)

Jerry, in fact, spends several pages describing the details of Jack's house. The home's opulence, however, is not sustainable—a truth played out in the novel and in the real downturn in the American housing market. Because of financial trouble, Jack rents his Haymarket home: "Jack found a Danish corporate executive on assignment to take a three-year lease on the place for $6000 a month, fully furnished, which will cover the mortgage and taxes plus" (334). The renter seems fantastical given the real housing crisis and falling dollar, but perhaps he is not entirely unrealistic as he is a *foreign* executive; Lee's novel portrays the real trend of foreigners taking advantage of increased buying power and a weak dollar by scooping up U.S. properties.[16] Investing in American real estate, particularly in urban areas like New York City and Miami, is a global enterprise. Furthermore, the global economy plays a significant role in American housing: "Nearly one in three buyers now are recent immigrants. . . . 30 percent of new U.S. homes since 2005 are being built by foreign-sourced labor," and large, publicly traded American home builders have seen "big infusions of foreign investment" (Wasserman).

However, *Aloft* pays less attention to the globalization of the American housing market than to the renovation of Jerry's suburban home. Jerry begins the novel living alone in his suburban three-bedroom house; by the novel's end, he has added a bedroom suite and a swimming pool, and he is living with seven family members, including his eighty-five-year-old father, his son-in-law (his newborn grandson will soon join them), and Jack's family. His long-time girlfriend, who left him at the beginning of the novel, has returned and spends time at the house. This racially, generationally, and ethnically mixed family and living situation redefines the conventional suburban home. In Jack's words, "I'll go solo no more, no more" (328), suggesting that he has changed from a rugged and alienated individualist to a happily domesticated man. Rather than devolve into decay and violence, this racially, ethnically, and mixed-age family and living situation redefine and reinvigorate the conventionally segregated, single-family suburban home.

As these examples from *Dreaming in Cuban* and *Aloft* suggest, neodomestic fiction aims to represent more routes to (and floor plans of) home and to scrutinize women's and men's relationships to domesticity. The homes and homemaking practices outlined above only begin to suggest the ways in which neodomestic fiction expands, remodels, and forges alternative routes to domestic enfranchisement. Nevertheless, as women today still lag behind men as homeowners, the conventional routes to access home and hearth—routes that deemphasize private property and ownership—remain relevant for women today.[17] Until women's legal and cultural relationship to property changes, realistic domestic fiction that focuses on women necessarily continues to construct domesticity through marriage or other family ties, not through private property relations. Furthermore, as women still spend more time than men on home maintenance, especially within the private interior of the home, gendered spatial and social domestic relationships remain largely unchanged in the twenty-first century. Thus, while neodomestic fiction mixes and merges domestic fiction's gendered traditions, these gendered conventions remain powerful spatial and social markers. The protagonists' professions and their homeownership status often emphasize gender's powerful structuring role within the domestic sphere and beyond.

Domestic Labor, Domestic Property

The protagonist's profession also plays a large role in gendering a text and identifying or disqualifying it as a domestic fiction. In domestic fiction that focuses on women, non-wage-earning caregivers are common central characters or narrators. In these stories, non-wage-earning caregivers are often daughters, mothers, and wives, though these characters may also have wage-earning professions in formal or informal sectors of the labor force. We see such characters in *Paradise* (the 8-rock wives and the Convent women), *The Poisonwood Bible* (Orleanna), and *Gardens in the Dunes* (Indigo and her sister). As cultural norms still predominantly assign women to domestic caretaking roles, (neo)domestic fiction reflects these norms. Compared to domestic novels that focus on male characters, domestic fiction that focuses on women disproportionately describes women's unpaid or informal domestic labor.

In masculine domestic fiction, key characters more frequently have a paid profession related to the domestic sphere. They are, for example, real estate agents, developers, cooks, architects, and home builders. The main characters in David Wong Louie's *The Barbarians Are Coming* (2000) and Richard Russo's *Empire Falls* (2001) are a professional chef and a cook, respectively. Joe Stratford from Jane Smiley's *Good Faith* and Frank Bascombe from *Independence Day* are real estate agents. Will Navidson from *House of Leaves* is a professional photographer engaged in capturing his family's life on film. Rachel Price, a hotel proprietor in *The Poisonwood Bible*, could also be viewed as a character that subscribes to domestic masculinity's value system, even as the novel overall is more closely associated with a feminine neodomestic tradition. *The Poisonwood Bible*, therefore, also demonstrates neodomesticity's hybrid form by combining masculine and feminine domestic paradigms. In fact, as helpful as it is to note the novels' depiction of informal and formal economies, such gendered economic spheres are often blurred and complicated in neodomestic fiction.

For instance, while the Homewood trilogy offers some fairly traditional depictions of domestic duties and labor, some of its characters are mavericks who emphasize homemaking's possibilities. For example, the elder generation represented in John French's family follows the conventional roles of male provider (John French) and female caretaker (John French's wife, Freeda). John's domestic duties do not include cooking or cleaning. He is a professional domestic laborer, an independent contractor who hangs wallpaper. The next generation (the narrator's parents, aunts, and uncles), does not follow such gender roles as strictly. For example, Lucy Tate's bold sexuality and her unconventional life offset her traditional caretaker role. Lucy and her long-time lover Carl never marry. Carl, furthermore, cooks dinner. Thus, we can begin to see in this trilogy from the early 1980s what later novels emphasize to greater degrees: the mixing, recycling, or hybridizing of conventional feminine and masculine domestic traditions and roles.

If the characters in masculine domestic fiction do not have a domestically orientated profession, then frequently the characters' conflicts revolve around ownership, property, or both. Smiley's *Good Faith* involves a real-estate-agent protagonist and property conflicts. Andre Dubus III's *House of Sand and Fog* (1999) and Walter Mosley's mystery novel *Devil in a Blue Dress* (1990) also use homeownership as a central motivating factor and as a source of conflict for their characters, especially for the male protagonists.[18] In *House of Sand and Fog*, a dispute over homeownership leads to violence. A contested tax payment results in the recovering addict Kathy Nicolo's loss of her inherited family home. As a result, the Persian immigrant Massoud Amir Behrani, a former colonel in the Iranian air force, seemingly achieves the American dream when he buys Nicolo's home at an auction. Tensions quickly escalate between Kathy and the Behrani family about the home's sale.

Homeownership—the attainment of the American dream's material accoutrements—does not bring happiness for the characters in *House of Sand and Fog*. The novel's final scenes bring the characters to breaking points. Kathy attempts suicide and her lover kidnaps the Behrani family to force a reversal of the home's sale. After police mistakenly shoot and kill Behrani's son, Behrani rejects the American dream that he fought so hard to attain: "I spit upon these people. I spit upon this country and all of its guns and automobiles and homes" (Dubus III 328). After Behrani leaves the hospital and his dead son, he attempts to kill Kathy and succeeds in killing his wife, saving her from suffering the news of her son's death. Behrani then commits suicide. He understands his family's terrible fate as a punishment for vanity and greed. Like Icarus, "For our excess we lost everything" (Dubus III 329). In Behrani's case, the pursuit and fulfillment of the American dream brings tragedy.

The story's strong pathos connects the neodomestic *House of Sand and Fog* to a feminized sentimental tradition, while the source of this dispute (property ownership and control) emerges from domestic masculinity. When the problems over the home's ownership first begin to intensify in *House of Sand and Fog*, Behrani's wife confronts her husband: "You want this home for you. *You*. You could never live in the street because there no one would respect you, Behrani, and you need everyone to respect you, even strangers must respect you" (Dubus III 285; emphasis in original). Mrs. Behrani's remarks emphasize that property is a prerequisite for Mr. Behrani's masculine sense of self-respect. Daddy Glenn from Dorothy Allison's *Bastard Out of Carolina* (1992) also seeks suburban tract rental houses (which are usually in worse condition and more expensive than the other available types of housing) as a means to represent his worth to his family. Homeownership and the types of homes that men provide for their families help define the characters' successful or unsuccessful domestic masculinities.

Homeownership, of course, is significant to female protagonists, too. Ownership is important to Kathy in *House of Sand and Fog*. Keeping her home represents not letting her family down; she especially does not want to disappoint her deceased father, who worked so hard for the house. Kathy, who is a house cleaner, emphasizes her ownership of the property throughout the novel. Her profession and homemaking practices emphasize domestic masculinity. When Kathy sees Behrani attempting to sell the house for a profit, she yells, "He can't sell you that house! He doesn't own it! He's trying to fucking *steal* it! He's trying to sell you a *stolen* house" (Dubus III 149; emphasis in original). Kathy shares with domestic masculinity an intense focus on the home's economic value. Thus, once again, we see how a character's sex is not a reliable indicator of the gendered practices that help define domestic space. Analyzing the home's spiritual geography helps to flesh out further the suggestive tensions between masculine and feminine domesticities and the ways in which these differences define neodomestic fiction's politics.

Domestic Ghosts
Haunting Gender Distinctions

> *Indeed, it's worth asking again: is there any cause to think a place—any place—within its plaster and joists, its trees and plantings, in its putative essence* ever *shelters some spirit ghost of us as proof of its significance and ours?*
>
> —Frank Bascombe from Richard Ford's Independence Day.
> (emphasis in original)

Frank Bascombe, the divorced real estate agent and narrator of *Independence Day*, questions near the end of the novel whether homes remember, whether some trace of the inhabitant's spirit remains in a place. The ways in which Frank Bascombe's question contrasts with both Morrison's ending to *Paradise* and Kingsolver's ending to *The Poisonwood Bible* further clarify domestic masculinity's unique characteristics and masculine domestic fiction's distinctive but related flip side of literary domestic history. The recourse to a viable spiritual geography in the Homewood trilogy, *Paradise*, and *The Poisonwood Bible* suggests that feminine neodomestic fiction connects more directly with romantic, sentimental, or gothic fictions rather than the realist tradition. As Kathryn Hume writes in *American Dream, American Nightmare*, a collection of contemporary novels "do not belong to the realist tradition" and rather "start from the belief that mainstream American culture has no spiritual dimension, and all seek ways of reinscribing the realm of the spirit in the imagination of their readers" (113). According to Hume, such novels craft a "spiritual reality" where "characters sense or experience some form of reality beyond the strictly material, and the author treats this without irony or skepticism. In other words, the novel constructs reality in a fashion that differs from secular and scientific reality and invites readers to reconsider the validity and human efficacy of the strictly phenomenal explanation" (113). This spiritual geography or "spiritual reality" is largely absent or resisted in nineteenth- and twentieth-century domestic masculinity. Conversely, Protestant morality in the nineteenth century and a secular spirituality or panspirituality in the late twentieth and twenty-first centuries have often defined the feminine forms of domestic fiction.

Hume includes John Updike's Rabbit series in her discussion of spiritual reality. *Rabbit at Rest* can be seen as a masculine domestic novel that deploys and recycles elements of religious sentiment and memory in its domestic ruminations. For example, in *Rabbit at Rest* Harry Angstrom's final flight from home takes him on a musical road trip from Pennsylvania to Florida. Oldies stations on the radio take Rabbit down memory lane. Even though Rabbit can no longer "get it up for Him" like he did "when God hadn't a friend in the world, back there in the Sixties," the road trip set to the soundtrack of his life provides a kind of spiritual, reflective space for Rabbit (*Rabbit at Rest* 373).[19]

Wideman's Homewood trilogy more thoroughly blends a feminized spiritual geography and a domestic masculinity, literally reimagining the Pittsburgh neighborhood that the novels invoke. Wideman creates a spiritual geography with his trilogy that spans the 1840s to the 1970s. The neighborhood's description also clarifies how home extends beyond four physical walls: "Homewood wasn't bricks and boards. Homewood was them singing and loving and getting where they needed to get. They made these streets" (*Sent for You Yesterday* 198). The neighborhood's people and history construct the novel's spiritual sense of home.

Spiritual geography in Wideman's Homewood trilogy, furthermore, emphasizes the neighborhood's relational connection to other spheres. The description below moves from the street (Cassina Way), to the neighborhood (Homewood), to the city (Pittsburgh), and to the region (the North), demonstrating the novel's relational connections across geographic scales:

> The life in Cassina Way was a world apart from Homewood and Homewood a world apart from Pittsburgh and Pittsburgh was the North, a world apart from the South, and all those people crowded in Cassina Way carried

the seeds of these worlds inside their skins, black, brown and gold and ivory skin which was the first world setting them apart. (21)

This passage emphasizes the home's translocal, yet isolated, sense of place. That is, while the passage maintains an emphasis on the homes located on a particular street, Cassina Way, and within the specific neighborhood of Homewood, it also recognizes the ways in which the regional overlaps the local and vice versa. Additionally, it recognizes the body as a home—"these worlds inside their skins"—or a location that helps determine one's place in the world. These connections are largely invisible ("words inside") but for the color of "their skins" (21). In this case, the text marks a specifically racial and class-conscious location, a "first world" that helps determine the characters' relationships with the outside world. This passage "results in redrawing the domestic space as the space of the normalizing, pastoralizing, and individuating techniques of modern power and police: the personal-*is*-the-political; the world-*in*-the-home" (Bhabha, *Location* 11; emphasis in original). The landscape's power is embedded ("seeded") in the body (Wideman 21).

Wideman's Homewood trilogy does not follow domestic masculinity's conventional practices that frequently posit a profoundly absent, alienated space and reject a reinscription or recycling of the (feminine) domestic novel's religious or spiritual geography. Don DeLillo's *White Noise* (1984) also follows the neodomestic form I have described in the previous chapters, but its irony and alienation distinguish it from novels like Wideman's Homewood trilogy, Morrison's *Paradise*, and Kingsolver's *The Poisonwood Bible*.[20] *White Noise*'s suburban family drama blends sentiment and satire in its characterization of a postmodern family created by multiple marriages. Living in a world where the television is always on, Jack Gladney, chair of the Department of Hitler Studies at the local Middle America liberal arts college, loves his children and wife fiercely. During a disaster that threatens the town, Jack reflects,

> I wanted to be near the children, watch them sleep. Watching children sleep makes me feel devout, part of a spiritual system. It is the closest I can come to God. If there is a secular equivalent of standing in a great spired cathedral with marble pillars and streams of mystical light slanting through two-tier Gothic windows, it would be watching children in their little bedrooms fast asleep. Girls especially. (147)

DeLillo recycles feminine domestic fiction's connection between religion and the home for a secular postmodern culture. Notably, "girls especially" become associated with this "spiritual system," heightening its femininity (DeLillo 147).

Alienation from such moments of "genuine" feeling weaves between such sentiments and limits (or at least calls into question) the novel's spiritual moments. The passage before this paragraph discusses humanity's persistence in manufacturing hope, hinting that Jack is manufacturing hope when he watches his children sleep. The passage following this one engages Jack in a discussion with his son Heinrich about alienation from labor and technology. Then, Jack finds a university colleague talking to a busload of sex workers. Finally, the brilliant sunsets punctuating the novel epitomize a spiritual geography tinged with irony and alienation. The sunsets may be made so striking due to air pollution: "Certainly there is awe, it is all awe, it transcends previous categories of awe, but we don't know whether we are watching in wonder or dread" (324). "Wonder" and "dread" succinctly characterize the shifting domestic spaces found in Mark Z. Danielewski's *House of Leaves*.

Domestic Instability
Mark Z. Danielewski's *House of Leaves*

Mark Z. Danielewski's *House of Leaves* (2000) also recycles spiritual geography while testing the limits of domestic instability. While the novel mixes masculine and feminine traditions, it also—like *White Noise*—continues to emphasize a masculine domesticity. As a result, its neodomestic politics function distinctively, emphasizing instability but without as clear of a recourse to the spirituality and spiritual geography that tend to prevail in feminine domestic fictions. Danielewski's *House of Leaves* fits the masculine tradition's multilayered "intellectual" tenor and combines it with a destabilized home and a gothic haunted-house tale. The novel, a postmodern, Deleuzian successor to Henry James's psychological domestic short story "The Jolly Corner" (1908), constructs increasingly complicated relationships between the home's inhabitants, the text's construction, and domestic space. Instead of exploring a mysterious force located within the attic space of the family home, as Spencer Brydon does in "The Jolly Corner," the characters in *House of Leaves* investigate a frighteningly unstable home whose dimensions expand and contract without warning.[21] A mysterious and profoundly empty space materializes within the home. Additionally, where "The Jolly Corner" begins with a confirmed bachelor and ends with his commitment to Alice Staverton, the house on Ash Tree Lane in *House of Leaves* renders already unstable minds and lives more insecure.

Although the novel defies easy summary, an attempt clarifies how *House of Leaves* participates in the (arguably masculine) postmodern discourses of fluid subjectivity and spatiality, vis-à-vis a Deleuzian schizophrenic subject, and an absent center, à la Jean Baudrillard's copy of a copy.[22] Ostensibly, the novel describes and analyzes a film, *The Navidson Record*, which probably exists only in the mind of another character, Zampanò. A famous photographer, Will Navidson, supposedly made the film to record his family's move to the house on Ash Tree Lane. Layered with this story about the Navidson family and their unusual home (the narratives are literally "layered," as the novel itself is a palimpsest) are Zampanò, who provides commentary on *The Navidson Record* and may, in fact, have fabricated its existence, and Johnny Truant, who gives order to Zampanò's scattered notes and comments on Zampanò's writing. Unnamed editors, who provide a brief "foreword," also apparently organized all the materials and put together the text that we, the reader, receive as *House of Leaves*, complete with a table of contents, appendixes by Zampanò and Johnny Truant, an appendix that provides "contrary evidence," an index, credits, and a poem-like final page called "Yggdrasil." The text indicates different contributions by using distinct fonts, the footnotes and index are narratives in and of themselves, and the spatial arrangement of the text generates yet another layer of meaning or level(s) of interpretation. As N. Katherine Hayles suggests, "the story's architecture is envisioned not as a sequential narrative so much as alternative paths within the same immense labyrinth of fictional space-time that is also, and simultaneously, a rat's nest of inscription surfaces" (784).

What I hope this description begins to suggest is that while there may be infinite ways to read *House of Leaves*, there remains, in the end, one basic way to understand it—through the lens of or as a commentary upon postmodern theories, especially as they relate to identity and space.[23] What concerns me here is the juxtaposition of this "high theory" experimental novel (often read as a masculine aesthetic) with the "popular" (feminine) domestic tale about the Navidson house that forms—in Johnny Truant's words—the book's "heart" (Danielewski xx). Navidson's documentary relates the domestic tale that produces the commentary surrounding and penetrating its telling. The editors share with us Navidson's explanation of his film's original sentimental goal: "'It's funny,' Navidson tells us at the outset. 'I just want to create a record of how Karen and I bought a small house in the country and moved into it with our children. Sort of see how everything turns out. No gunfire, famine, or flies. Just lots of toothpaste, gardening and people stuff. . . . I just thought it would be nice to see how people move into a place and start to inhabit it" (8–9). The home's instability keeps him from documenting the family's habitation. The central narrative about the Navidson's house explores the home's unprecedented absent-presence that haunts the family and all who read about their mysterious and frightening experiences.

The novel's narrative "heart" examines the house's mysterious labyrinth structure. One particularly unusual feature about the house on Ash Tree Lane is that its interior dimensions exceed its exterior ones: "The width of the house inside would appear to exceed the width of the house as measured from the outside by 1/4'" (30). Like the narrative itself, the house resists "coherent mapping" (Hayles 784). During Tom's "Exploration A," which brings him into a hallway that mysteriously appeared in the Navidson's living room, he discovers just "how big Navidson's house really is" (64) and uncovers how fast the home can change dimensions: "Absolutely nothing visible to the eye provides a reason for or even evidence of those terrifying shifts which can in a matter of moments reconstitute a simple path into an extremely complicated one" (Danielewski 68–69). The home resists, as Hayles points out, the assumption "that the contained must be smaller than the container" (788). The home's instability and the mysterious hallway's complete emptiness produce horror and fear.

House of Leaves magnifies and embodies domestic instability to such an extent that it produces a gothic home of unprecedented proportions and complexity, shaped as a mysteriously cold, labyrinthine hallway that expands and contracts at will. Hayles remarks on the home's hallway, also noting its extraordinary emptiness: "'The absence at the center of this space is not merely nothing. It is so commanding and absolute that it paradoxically becomes an especially intense kind of presence" (788). Notably, when the family discovers the home's core instability and emptiness, relationships deteriorate. (We see a similar relationship between family and house structures in Poe's "The Fall of the House of Usher.") For example, when a door in the living room mysteriously appears that leads to the enormous interior hallway, fissures in the Navidson family intensify: "Without sound or movement but by presence alone, the hallway creates a serious rift in the Navidson household" (Danielewski 60).

Gothic fiction and ghosts who inhabit houses have long challenged domestic stability. Chapter 9 of *The Navidson Record* in *House of Leaves* shows awareness of this literary tradition and explores the film's gothic elements (146–47). The film's closing shots, additionally, take place on Halloween (527–28). *House of Leaves*, therefore, emphasizes that if neodomesticity celebrates such instability, it must also confront instability's potential disadvantages. Can a family survive, let alone prosper, in an unstable, fluid, and flexible environment? If the core or heart of the family home is profoundly empty, what are the consequences? Where the feminine forms of neodomestic fiction we have discussed suggest a productive instability based on a spirited, relational geography, *House of Leaves*'s instability generates horror and familial breakdown by juxtaposing a profoundly empty core with unstable space.

Instability combined with emptiness or *unheimlich*, which literally means "not at home," produces a horror story of vast proportions in *House of Leaves*, cautioning against instability's liberating powers.[24] Karen, Navidson's wife, eventually leaves Navidson because he continues to explore the mysteriously empty hallway, despite the clear dangers it poses to physical safety and mental stability (322). As she packs up her belongings in the bedroom, the house attacks, collapsing the bedroom walls (341). All told, the home kills at least three people, including Navidson's brother, Tom (371). These flexible, unstable boundaries are no kinder than clearly defined oppositions. The home's vast absent-presence, which can occasionally be heard growling in the background, represents danger, not the potential for regeneration, transformation, or renewal.

As in James's "The Jolly Corner," a woman eventually saves the male protagonist from this frighteningly unstable position. In the end of *The Navidson Record*, Karen returns to the house on Ash Tree Lane to retrieve her husband. When she does, the house dissolves (524). Although her husband is crippled after his hallway explorations, the family is back together again at *The Navidson Record*'s conclusion (527). Thus, the narrative concludes with reunion and apparent family stability. During the Victorian age, gothic novels often narrated a "cultural haunting" that derived from class or economic origins; these novels similarly ended with stability restored. Where female protagonists ordered domestic space in nineteenth-century domestic fiction, male protagonists similarly took on this role through the conceit of fighting a ghost, as Lara Baker Whelan argues in "Between Worlds: Class Identity and Suburban Ghost Stories, 1850–1880."

Although she focuses on British Victorian writers, Whelan's argument about the relationship between suburban ghost stories and class anxieties also holds true for an American context. As in Britain, the nineteenth century was a period of suburban growth that disrupted classed and gendered spaces—these new, unstable suburban spaces needed to be "normalized" or interpolated into the national imagination. Whelan argues that, like domestic fiction, the suburban ghost story "is also concerned with ordering and 'normalizing' domestic space. Unlike domestic fiction, however, where female agency is emphasized, the Victorian suburban ghost narrative provides a middle-class male hero the opportunity to order the space of a haunted house that has been disrupted by a specter, and through a fantasy of excluding the specter, to reassert (the readers') middle-class values" (134). Stories such as "The Jolly Corner" appear to follow this logic—the male protagonist orders his life and finds a mate by fighting a ghost.

House of Leaves undercuts *The Navidson Record*'s concluding domestic stability and, thereby, deconstructs the stabilizing model that Whelan attributes to gothic fiction. The novel's narrative ends with a tree that is "ten thousand feet high / But doesn't reach the ground. Still it stands. / Its roots must hold the sky" (709).[25] Just as the rest of the novel plays with inversions, the final lines turn gravity upside down. The stability at the heart of this postmodern novel, after all, is most likely a fiction, not a reality. The tree in *House of Leaves*'s final poem refers to the sacred ash tree (Yggdrasil) from Norse mythology. The ending explicitly gestures to this spirited, mythological location. According to Gloria W. Lannom, "Yggdrasil (IG-drah-sil) stood at the center of the earth, where Odin discovered that its falling twigs formed the runic alphabet" (40). The tree connects various regions (including the earth, heaven, and hell) and provides a "life force" (Lannom 40). Significantly, the Navidson's house is located on Ash Tree Lane. The house on Ash Tree Lane becomes, like Yggdrasil, a "life force" portal between worlds. Additionally, both the records of the house on Ash Tree Lane and Yggdrasil connect to runic language. Part of *House of Leaves*'s dangerous and seemingly magical potential includes its mysterious ability to produce obsession in those who encounter its papers. If the reader did not catch the sacred ash tree symbolism previously, the final lines spell out the connection. This "life force," however, seems more destructive than life giving. Therefore, what the sacred tree really explains about the novel remains unclear. Are the connections between the mythological Yggdrasil and the house on Ash Tree Lane sacred and spiritual, or are they both fictions, mythologies? If they are both set up as mythologies, is the conclusion a final critique of the home as sacred space and as the family's "life force"? The final lines do not provide a clear roman à clef for the novel—beyond the fact that the novel clearly references (recycles) this Norse myth. As this chapter's epigraph suggests, domestic geographies that clearly embrace or reject spirituality more clearly outline the politics at stake. Other masculine suburban novels more strongly reject the home's spiritual geography and clarify why such a rejection generally follows patriarchal rather than feminist principles.

Comparing Gendered Approaches to Spiritual Geographies

While both *The Poisonwood Bible* and *Paradise* invoke ghosts or spirits in their conclusions, Richard Ford's Frank Bascombe gives up the ghost at the end of his tale: "ghosts ascribed to places where you once were only confuse matters" (*Independence Day* 442). The ghostly memories that potentially haunt Frank Bascombe's old residence, including memories of his deceased son, ultimately lack "corroborating substance" (442). If fostered or held onto, these haunting memories would contribute to a reduction of feeling—a freezing and loss of a piece of his heart. Rather than offer peace or even some well-deserved haunting, a place's spirit becomes a joke and needless anxiety for Frank. Like Rachel Price in *The Poisonwood Bible*, Frank's willful amnesia, his letting go of the past, allows him to get on with—or perhaps *pass through*—his life.

In Richard Ford's *Independence Day*, the novel's domestic politics hearken back to earlier (white) masculine domestic models such as those represented by William Dean Howells's *Suburban Sketches*. Frank Bascombe's domestic practices and politics in Ford's novels hold more in common with the narrator in *Suburban Sketches* than with his literary contemporary Orleanna in *The Poisonwood Bible*. Both Howells and Ford, though writing over one hundred years apart, present the lasting power of the home (its spiritual geography) as worth defeating. *Suburban Sketches*'s narrator writes, "As to the house which one has left, I think it would be preferable to have it occupied as soon as possible after one's flitting. Pilgrimages to the dismantled shrine are certainly to be avoided by the friend of cheerfulness" (252). Frank Bascombe comes to the same conclusion in *Independence Day*.

Frank responds to his own question about the home's potential "spirit ghost" (442) by concluding that ghosts do not inhabit places:

> The truth is—and this may be my faith in progress talking—my old Hoving Road house looks more like a funeral home now than it looks like my house or a house where any past of mine took place. And this odd feeling I have is of having passed on (not in the bad way) to a recognition that ghosts ascribed to places where you once were only confuse matters with their intractable lack of corroborating substance. I frankly think that if I sat here in my car five more minutes, staring out at my old house like a visitant to an oracle's flame, I'd find that what felt like melancholy was just a prelude to bursting out laughing and needlessly freezing a sweet small piece of my heart I'd be better off to keep than lose. (442)

Suburban Sketches similarly advises, "Yes, the place must always be sacred, but painfully sacred; and I say again one should not go near it unless as a penance. . . . Let some one else, who had also escaped from his past, have your old house; he will find it new and untroubled by memories, while you, under another roof, enjoy a present that borders only upon the future" (Howells 254–55). *Suburban Sketches* and *Independence Day*'s shared emphasis on progression, (a "faith in progress") and on the future characterizes (white) domestic masculinity's rejection of the home's lasting spirit (Ford 442).

Frank and the *Suburban Sketches* narrator move on from their pasts. Frank specifically moves on from the loss of his son and marriage. He remains whole, whereas Sethe in Morrison's *Beloved* must reassemble her past to become whole. Frank and the *Suburban Sketches* narrator believe they must "pass on"—move beyond—to a present and future that can only be confused or damaged by the past, "needlessly freezing a sweet small piece of my heart I'd be better off to keep than lose" (Ford 442). The narrator likewise concludes that his present "borders only upon the future" (Howells 255). Thus, Frank and the *Suburban Sketches* narrator contentedly bury and forget their ghosts. Conversely, Sethe uses the ghost Beloved to help her "pass on," in the dual sense of remember and move forward (Morrison, *Beloved* 274–75). Beloved's story, which emphasizes and plays on the meanings of "pass on," is both not a story to forget and not a history to repeat.

Houses in particular do not serve as memorials to Frank or the narrator in *Suburban Sketches*. Matthew Guinn suggests that in *Independence Day*, "Frank's comments about the dubious 'mystery' of certain places reveal an anti-essentialist conception of place, a notion of setting as empty of transcendent or definitive character" (202). Guinn characterizes Frank's postmodern landscape and sensibility: "For the postmodern individual such as Frank, a new conception of place is in order: a sense of place as literal, straightforward, and knowable—with no mystery to complicate things beyond the tangible, no character beyond the commercial. In short, a postregional landscape" (202). A more spiritual domestic politics, as seen in Morrison's *Beloved*, Kingsolver's *The Poisonwood Bible*, and Wideman's Homewood trilogy, suggest that this sense of landscape does not (always) adequately deal with the loss of history required to produce such a "blank" place. These novels support Salazar's argument about spiritual geography's "three fundamental functions": spiritual geographies value non-Western perspectives, reveal history's influence on the present, and connect the community and the individual (400).

However, Frank's final descriptions of his spirituality are not clearly patriarchal. His spiritual ambiguity connects *The Lay of the Land* (2006), Ford's final novel in the Frank Bascombe series, to *House of Leaves*. *The Lay of the Land* continues Frank's exploration of home and its spiritual force. Near the end of *The Lay of the Land*, Frank's estranged wife Sally writes a letter to him about his sense of spirituality: "I think everybody needs a definition of spirituality, Frank (you have one, I believe). You wouldn't want to go on a quiz show, would you, and be asked your definition of spirituality and not know one" (383). Frank does ponder his definition of spirituality. After a near death experience, Frank admits that he "possibly . . . could stand an improved sense of spirituality" (476). He goes on to quote several passages from the Dalai Lama and concludes,

> I am not a poet, though I've read plenty of them and find their books easy to finish. But in the most purely personal-spiritual vein—since I took two slugs four inches above my own—the best motivational question in the spirituality catechism, and one seeking an answer worth remembering, may *not* be "Am I good?" (which is what my rich Sponsorees often want to know and base life on), but "Do I have a heart at all?" Do I see good as even a possibility? The Dalai Lama in *The Road to the Open Heart* argues I definitely do. And I can say I think I do, too. But anymore—as they say back down in New Jersey—anymore than that is more spiritual than I can get. (*Lay of the Land* 476; emphasis in original)

This optimism, if not confidence, in the possibility of goodness in the world defines Frank's spirituality. "Anymore than that," the passage above suggests, would be unreasonable, entering a spiritual geography that does not hold water with practical New Jersey residents like Frank. This practicality is what Frank goes on to emphasize: "A working sense of spirituality can certainly help. But a practical acceptance of what's what, in real time and down-to-earth, is as good as spiritual if you can finagle it. I thought for a time that practical acceptance, the final certifying 'event' and extra beat for me had been my breathless 'yes, yes,' to my son Ralph Bascombe's death, and that I would never again have to wonder if how I feel now would be how I'd feel later on. I felt sure it would be. *Here* was necessity" (*Lay of the Land* 484; emphasis in original). Frank's practical spiritual geography is more physically grounded than the amorphous women that conclude Morrison's *Paradise*.

Ford's series of suburban domestic novels about Frank Bascombe emphasizes that suburban literature and suburban space more generally do not readily foster spirited places. Rather than a site of regeneration and renewal, the suburban home is frequently characterized as a soulless or spiritless dystopia. The literary portrayal has roots in material suburban space. According to Dolores Hayden in *Building Suburbia*, by the 1970s and 1980s, architects and urban theorists "largely ignored suburbs or lambasted them as banal areas of tract houses. Artists and writers tended to agree, perhaps because television, films, and advertising often represented American family life in comfortable suburban houses as a mindless consumer utopia. Synonyms for 'suburb' in the 1970s included 'land of mediocrity,' 'middle America,' and 'silent majority'" (Hayden 15). Not surprisingly, given this divisive attitude, no apparitions appear at the end of *Independence Day* or *The Lay of the Land*. Ghosts, furthermore, are not usually ironic tropes. The two potential ways to understand *Beloved* and *Paradise*'s conclusions, one providing a rational explanation and another supporting the spirits' existence, emphasize that a belief in spirits requires faith, a quality much of the literature focused on masculine middle-class America seems to disregard, lack, or discourage.

While neodomestic authors such as Kingsolver, Morrison, and Wideman do not reinscribe an "old-school" Protestant religion into their neodomestic fictions, they do maintain "spirituality" in a broad sense and support a living sense of history. Morrison's *Beloved* is especially relevant to these comparisons between the spiritual geographies found in feminine and masculine domestic fiction because of the ways in which *Beloved* plays with the meanings of "pass on," the home's spirit, and memory (*Beloved* 274–75). Where Sethe works at "re-membering"—both in the sense of dealing with her past and of collecting or re-membering her self—*Independence Day*'s Frank Bascombe and the narrator of *Suburban Sketches* work at forgetting in order to keep themselves intact. The ghost/person Beloved is one of the characters who help Sethe through her "re-membering" process.

The Poisonwood Bible's ghostly conclusion also offers an instructive comparison to the negative space described in *House of Leaves* and *House of Sand and Fog*. The Price women at the end of *The Poisonwood Bible* embark on a second family pilgrimage to Africa in search of their old home and Ruth May's grave (Kingsolver 538–43). The Price family's second pilgrimage also fails. The women cannot cross the border, and when they question a local merchant about their old village she insists, "There is no such village. The road doesn't go past Bulungu. . . . There has never been any village on the road past Bulungu" (Kingsolver 542). This "absent presence" in *The Poisonwood Bible* functions as part of the story's mystery—as part of the truth of the place that never existed. As Kingsolver explains, fictional place "exists in your heart and your imagination. So long as its truth sustains you from one page to the next, while a new way of looking at the world settles in beside your own, it's true enough" (Kingsolver, "Q&A"). The spirit and memory of the place matters—regardless of what the woman tells the Price family in the marketplace. As in Naylor's *Mama Day*, the spirit place constitutes the novel's final voice and eyes.

Sent for You Yesterday's conclusion particularly reveals a spirit that follows in the feminine tradition invoked by *Paradise* and *The Poisonwood*

Bible. Sent for You Yesterday concludes with the dead (specifically Brother Tate and Albert Wilkes) returning to the Tates' living room. The dead men are summoned by music. The final scene repeats a scene in which the narrator, John Lawson—now a grown man visiting the old neighborhood—took his first steps as a toddler while listening to the blues song "Sent for You Yesterday and Here You Come Today." Although the closing scene features a different song—the narrator John Lawson, his uncle Carl French, and Lucy Tate are listening to Smokey Robinson's "Tracks of My Tears"—the music emphasizes Homewood's *soul*. The epigraph to *Sent for You Yesterday* clarifies the significance of the novel's final scene in which the dead and the living commune: "Past lives live in us, through us. Each of us harbors the spirits of people who walked the earth before we did, and those spirits depend on us for continuing existence, just as we depend on their presence to live our lives to the fullest." The paraphrased versions, "past places live in us" or "past places place us," also ring true for this trilogy and for feminine, relational, neodomestic fiction that recycles the home's spirit. Not so different from the women at the end of *Paradise*, these spirits—ancestors—at the end of *Sent for You Yesterday* partake in the living's daily lives. Furthermore, as a trilogy enmeshed in traditional African religious practices—*Damballah*, for example, is a serpent god—the Homewood trilogy not surprisingly pays homage to the community's ancestors.[26] The connections among Morrison's, Kingsolver's, and Wideman's novels suggest that fiction focusing on women and minorities remains invested in history whereas white (male) privilege seeks to move on from the past. However, Richard Russo's *Empire Falls* complicates this schema.

Empire Falls clearly draws from and plays up the foundational narrative of "beset manhood" and entrapping femininity; however, it does so in a neodomestic fashion that also allows a space for reconciliation with the past. *Empire Falls*—with its likeable, white, divorced, suburban dad as its protagonist—presents an extreme example of anxious domestic masculinity. Francine Whiting and Miles Roby present revised versions of dictatorial femininity and anxious masculinity. Francine owns the entire town and controls the protagonist's life—hence, Miles Roby's "beset manhood." Francine—part of a long line of Whiting wives who contribute to the Whiting males' "*lives of marital torment*" (15; emphasis in original)—has agreed to bequeath Miles the restaurant, where he previously took over as a cook in order to be near his dying mother (Russo 36–38). The novel's final image is of Francine and her female cat, Timmy. Francine is literally sent down the river in a torrential flood—her ferocious feline power highlighted in her spiteful cat, who ends the novel hanging on to the owner's corpse for dear life: "Together, dead woman and living cat bumped along the upstream edge of the straining dam, as if searching for a place to climb out and over. Bumping, nudging, seeking, until finally a small section of the structure gave way and they were gone" (Russo 483). In the tradition of Mark Twain's *The Adventures of Huckleberry Finn*, Francine presents an extreme and often comedic portrait of domineering female power—and its eventual fall.

Like *Independence Day*'s optimistic ending, *Empire Falls* ends with the possibility that even broken families can be fixed. However, Miles's "beset manhood" and flight from home is not cured by Francine's death, as one might expect according to patriarchal power's antidomestic logic. While Francine certainly gets her "due," her death does not provide the linchpin for Miles's change. In neodomestic fashion, *Empire Falls* clearly mixes the feminine and masculine narrative traditions. In the closing scene, just moments before learning of Francine's death, Miles "awoke a man," which meant, "It was time to return to Empire Falls, to his life. Better to be a man there, his 'Sojourner' dream has shown him, than a boy here [on Martha's Vineyard]" (471; 472). Unlike *Independence Day*, Miles learns from a ghostly experience, specifically a dream in which he meets his mother's dead lover, and they discuss why the lover never returned for her.

No longer haunted by his past, Miles grows up and embarks on his journey home as an adult. At the novel's end, the reconfigured family includes Miles; his estranged father, Max; his daughter, Tick; and his ex-wife, Janine, who recently separated from her second husband. After Miles calls to inform Janine, "'We're on our way back, if that's all right with you,'" Janine replies, "'There's plenty of room at the house'" (Russo 472). The novel concludes with an optimistic outlook that with whatever else comes, "anything could be fixed" (Russo 473). Given domestic masculinity's—particularly the suburban male's—connection to "do-it-yourself" domesticity, this outlook (expressed by the handyman grandfather, Max) provides a fitting capstone for this analysis of contemporary domestic masculinity.

Significantly, the absence of a viable spiritual geography does not necessarily exclude domestic masculinity from a neodomestic politics. Like the endings to Marilynne Robinson's *Housekeeping* and Joy Williams's *Breaking and Entering*, endings without recourse to a spiritual geography also confirm that not all alternatives to conventional domesticity may be uniformly freeing or fully realized; domestic instability carries its own set of restrictions, determined in part by the specific historical and present conditions recycled by the neodomestic narrative. Perhaps it is a (gender/race/class) privilege to not seek redemption or recourse to spirituality. And, perhaps the "empty" geography persistent in novels featuring (white) domestic masculinity also marks a distinctly liberal, democratic politics that enjoys and demands a space to refuse recourse to religion or spirituality—an outlook that promises no cure or redemption. The refusal to (re)invent or recycle a spiritual system follows, at least in part, the logic of a post-Nietzschean, postmodern world. Just as a reinscription of spirituality or a moral imperative holds the unsavory potential to reproduce rather than recycle imperial practices, (white) domestic masculinity's tendency to privilege the future over the past leads to a potentially explosive politics. As a result, feminine domesticity, coming out of didactic and (proto)feminist traditions, does not usually reject but rather recycles for a (post)modern world the conventional domestic novel's spiritual geographies and didactic ambitions.

Unlike the haunting conclusions found in *Sent for You Yesterday*, *Beloved*, *Paradise*, and *The Poisonwood Bible*, *Independence Day* ends with Frank Bascombe looking forward to "The Permanent Period," which would put an end to the "the Existence Period" (Ford 450; 10). Caught up in the crowd enjoying the Fourth of July parade, Frank comments, "It is not a bad day to be on earth" (*Independence Day* 450). Jurca understands such examples of Frank's optimistic "poignant ambivalence" as distinct from a characteristic "suburban victimization" (Jurca 170). Clearly, Frank (like the narrator in William Dean Howells's *Suburban Sketches*) does not position himself as a victim or a martyr—whereas Rabbit and Rachel Price remain alienated martyrs and victims of their domestic environments. Nevertheless, his attitude is also part and parcel of the typical suburban male character that simply endures. *The Lay of the Land* chronicles Frank's "Permanent Period" (31) and the "different necessities" that put this period to "its sternest test" (55). The Permanent Period, according to Frank, offered "a blunt break with the past and provided a license to think of the past only indistinctly" (*Lay of the Land* 54). He enjoys this "durable" stage of his life until cancer puts a wrench in the works and "everything got all fucked up" (*Lay of the Land* 55). As the above discussion suggests, Frank copes with such obstacles largely by rejecting both the past and his home's lasting spirit (buying a new house on the shore marks the start of the Permanent Period)—which, furthermore, suggests in this case a desire for a more conventional *permanence* versus a neodomestic *instability*.

Conclusions
The Spirited Politics of Masculine Domesticity

Both a representative and a unique character, Frank Bascombe demonstrates how and why the past does not haunt conventional masculine domesticity.

Masculine domestic fiction, especially suburban fiction, is not often aligned with feminine domestic fiction's moralizing, didactic tradition (examples of which include *The Wide, Wide, World* and *Little Women*). Rather, masculine domestic fiction's frequently antidomestic literary history connects it more with the exposure of the home as a trap. Such masculine domestic novels remain ambivalent toward, if they do not outwardly critique, the responsibility to offer redemption or to reinscribe a spiritual geography. Like Rachel Price, Frank's ability to leave the past behind marks his privilege as a white, middle-class American. Frank's letting go of the past and resistance to such haunting also follows in a masculine gothic tradition that seeks stability. This tradition, in turn, often aligns itself with patriarchy.

Feminist politics coming out of and shaping the feminine domestic tradition bump against a masculine, progressive, "American" domestic politics because feminist analysis has a responsibility to the past. Feminist analysis associates such flights from history with "the logic of patriarchy" that discourages relational spatial constructions (Davis and Gilligan 58). My analysis of these masculine suburban fictions, an analysis that follows and is committed to feminist praxis, should not be misunderstood as a dismissal of suburban fiction, masculine domestic fiction, or of the subjectivity that the fiction explores. Rather, this critique seeks to put spiritual geography's gendered approaches in conversation to flesh out the embedded politics. How critics understand the turn to or away from spiritual geographies constitutes an important part of these politics.

Jonathan Franzen's essay "Why Bother?" offers a rubric for understanding these novels' alternative endings and addresses the resistance to reinscribe a spiritual geography. The essay defines good, substantial fiction as similar to "a particularly rich section of a religious text": good fiction is a text in which "the answers aren't there, there isn't closure. The language of literary works gives forth something different with each reading. But unpredictability doesn't mean total relativism. Instead it highlights the persistence with which writers keep coming back to fundamental problems" (82). According to this definition of "good fiction," the absence or presence of a spiritual geography still resonates as contemplatively rich and unstable. As long as "the answers aren't there, there isn't closure" (82). The endings to the (neo)domestic fictions that I discuss follow this definition. The unclear status of the women at *Paradise*'s conclusion and Frank Bascombe's final remarks at the conclusion of *The Lay of the Land* resist narrative closure. Our understanding of Enid at the conclusion of *The Corrections*, as I discuss in the next chapter, also leaves more questions than answers.

However, Franzen also states earlier in his essay that "good" novels do not provide "Medicine for a Happier and Healthier World," which he believe is frequently an ambition in "the work of women and of people from nonwhite or nonhetero cultures" ("Why Bother?" 79). Here, we begin to see the ways in which literary analysis is itself influenced by gendered and racial practices and paradigms. Franzen's remarks imply a resistance to feminine domestic fiction's didactic turn and to the spiritual geographies often associated with this didacticism or "medicine." As both masculine and feminine neodomestic fictions fundamentally value a politics of instability, we can begin to see the value and risks of a "both/and" rather than an "either/or" politics. Hybrid novels that combine these gendered strands especially challenge our generic and political categories as well as our aesthetic standards. In the next chapter, I explore in more detail such hybrid texts, their circulation in the public sphere, and the implications associated with the resistance to and embrace of a spiritual geography. I pay special attention to how authors and novels frequently become distinctly gendered—or, as Foucault might say, become disciplined into gendered categories.

5

Performing Domesticity

Anxious Masculinity and Queer Homes

> *Am I a social novelist, or am I sort of an old-fashioned domestic novelist?*
> —Jonathan Franzen, quoted in Lorraine Adams's "Literary Life without Oprah"

Jonathan Franzen's confusion about how to define his writing points to a more general confusion about masculine domesticity and its literary and cultural place. Reviewers of Franzen's *The Corrections* characterize it as a hybrid novel that combines the feminine family saga with the ironic masculine edge associated with suburban fiction. Benjamin Svetkey in *Entertainment Weekly*, for example, not only described *The Corrections* as a "domestic drama" but also as "a big, ambitious, unwieldy hybrid of a book" (85). Jesse Berrett writing for *The Village Voice* characterizes Franzen as "half brainiac hipster, half traditionalist" (72). Such celebratory reviews could have heralded a new age for American literature, announcing a happy reconciliation between the long-estranged masculine intellect and feminine sentiment. However, this literary marriage between high art and domestic drama did not last long. The "Franzen Affair," the public spectacle tipped off by the author's snide remarks about Oprah's Book Club that led to his appearance being pulled from the show, reestablished the old boundaries and, as a result, provides valuable insight into the gendered and classed tensions that surround and inhabit twenty-first-century American domestic fiction.[1] The affair suggests that little has changed since Nathaniel Hawthorne complained about "a d—d mob of scribbling women," many of whom wrote popular domestic fiction in the nineteenth century (304).

This chapter examines the textual and cultural anxieties produced when masculine and feminine forms mix. As explained in the previous chapter, domestic masculinity especially heightens our awareness of "the 'unnatural' [that] might lead to the denaturalization of gender as such," because conventional gender roles consider masculinity already outside, unnatural, or foreign to domesticity (Butler, *Gender Trouble* 149). According to *The Oxford English Dictionary Online*, for instance, the word "cotquean" refers to "a man that acts the housewife, that busies himself unduly or meddles with matters belonging to the housewife's province" (def. 3). Thus, by its "undue" incorporation of domesticity, domestic masculinity especially highlights gender's denaturalization and performative aspects. As Homi K. Bhabha explains in "Signs Taken for Wonders," hybridity represents "that ambivalent 'turn' of the discriminated subject into the terrifying, exorbitant object of paranoid classification—a disturbing questioning of the images and presences of authority" (174). Like Bhabha, I am interested in how this "terrifying" hybridity—particularly in the form of domestic masculinity—gets classified and causes "trouble" in twenty-first-century American culture.

My discussion of these hybrid, recycled novels demonstrates that while individual neodomestic fictions may lean more toward a masculine or feminine association, they ultimately trouble or "queer" conventional dualistic gender paradigms. As a result, they also are often regendered by readers and critics rather than read as queer novels. Nayan Shah in *Contagious Divides* defines "queer domesticity" as a category that resists the conventional model home: "Rather than viewing the term *queer* as a synonym for homosexual identity, I use it to question the formation of exclusionary norms of respectable middle-class, heterosexual marriage. The analytical category of queer upsets the strict gender roles, the firm divisions between public and private, and the implicit presumptions of self-sufficient economics and intimacy in the respectable domestic household" (13–14). Shah's definition clarifies that queer domesticity offers another way of describing the neodomestic novel's recycling of gender roles and spaces, referring specifically to homemaking practices that produce "an alternative articulatory space of gender and sexuality" (Parikh 863). Thus, neodomesticity's hybridity does not erase gender distinctions but rather attempts to "trouble" their stability.

Judith Butler describes "trouble" as "inevitable, and the task, how best to make it, what best way to be in it" (*Gender Trouble* vii). Neodomestic novels provide various models of making and being in "gender trouble." As we have seen in the previous chapters, unlike conventional rhetoric that stabilizes boundaries, neodomestic novels "trouble the gender categories that support gender hierarchy and compulsory heterosexuality" (Butler viii). That is, neodomestic fiction understands "gender is an identity tenuously constituted in time, instituted in an exterior space through a *stylized repetition of acts*" and that these "tenuous acts" carry significant stabilizing power (Butler 140; emphasis in original). Neodomestic "local strategies" produce "subversive repetitions" within gender's stylized (conventional domestic) categories; thus, neodomesticity provides models to trace the movement "From Parody to Politics" (Butler 149; 146).

Butler's performance model emphasizes that "the task is not whether to repeat, but *how to repeat*" (148; my emphasis). As we have seen throughout this study, Rosemary Marangoly George's notion of historically conscious recycling provides one model of "how to repeat" (Butler 148). As neodomestic novels challenge and recycle conventional domestic structures—both in terms of domestic space and fictional tropes—the speculative limits of gender's flexibility or fluidity come to light. Just as Judith Fetterley and Marjorie Pryse map out regionalism's queer space in *Writing Out of Place: Regionalism, Women and American Literary Culture*, this chapter provides a blueprint for neodomesticity's queer homesteads—the emergent home territories appearing across a more fluid gender terrain: "The analysis of 'queer domesticity' emphasizes the variety of erotic ties and social affiliations that counters normative expectations" (Shah 13). The Franzen-Oprah miff highlights that "unadulterated" masculinity still receives high prestige in American literature and culture; however, the queer homes discussed in the final section pose serious challenges to this policing of neodomestic fiction's reception.

This Is Not a Chick Book!
Jonathan Franzen's *Corrections*

As I discussed in the previous chapter, a variety of tropes within a novel help establish its gendered identity. A text's marketing, readership, and reception also contribute to its gendered identity. Jonathan Franzen's remarks about his novel's selection as "an Oprah book" highlight how literary and social hierarchies continue to exclude or degrade women and femininity. These patriarchal hierarchies reproduce gender distinctions that differentiate the so-called niche category of women's fiction from genres coded as more "universal," well respected, and frequently more masculine. As Eva Illouz points out regarding Oprah's Book Club, "The cultural objects that irritate taste and habits are the very ones that shed the brightest light on the hidden moral assumptions of the guardians of taste. Such cultural objects make explicit the tacit divisions and boundaries through which culture is classified and thrown into either the trash bin or the treasure chest" (4). In this case, feminine culture as represented in *The Oprah Winfrey Show* creates an anxious masculine culture that must separate itself from the program's feminizing properties.

Just what did Franzen say or imply that led Oprah to call off her invitation and for reporters, writers, and publishers to spill untold amounts of ink over the tiff? On October 12, 2001, *The Oregonian* published Franzen's remarks about the Oprah's Book Club logo: "I see this as my book, my creation, and I didn't want that logo of corporate ownership on it" (Franzen, qtd. in Baker 5). Franzen remarked three days later on the National Public Radio show *Fresh Air* that "more than one reader" expressed to him that they were "put off by the fact that it is an Oprah pick" (Franzen, "Novelist"). He also said of Oprah: "She's picked some good books, but she's picked enough schmaltzy, one-dimensional ones that I cringe, myself" (Franzen, qtd. in Jacoby A19).[2] Shortly after these remarks, Oprah canceled Franzen's appearance, disinviting Franzen on October 22, 2001.[3]

Newsweek caught up with Franzen shortly after the cancellation. Franzen explained his controversial remarks by positioning himself as a writer detached from mass culture: "'The Oprah Show,' like almost everything on TV, is not really quite real to me because I don't see it,' he said [referring to the fact that he does not own a television set]. 'I think if it had been more real to me I would have realized, 'Hey, watch what you're saying'" (Giles 68). Franzen's explanation does not suggest that he did not mean what he said about Oprah's Book Club, only that he did not realize that he should have been more careful about what he said in public. Like his initial critique of Oprah's "corporate logo" and his disquiet about the wide range of texts endorsed by Oprah, these rhetorical gymnastics serve, at least in part, to position his work as "high art," allegedly beyond or outside corporate sponsorship. Franzen went on to say, "I feel as if I'm not the first writer to have experienced some minor discomfort over the selection. I'm just the first one who was unwise and insensitive enough to mention some of that discomfort in public" (qtd. in Giles 68). The economic implications of Oprah's "corporate sponsorship" are indeed phenomenal. According to Jeff Jacoby, reporter for the *Boston Globe*, Oprah's endorsement of *The Corrections* "prompted Farrar, Straus & Giroux to increase their print run from 65,000 to 600,000. . . . The added sales, it is said, will swell Jonathan Franzen's royalties by more than $1.5 million" (A 19). *Entertainment Weekly* reported that Oprah's endorsement prompted Farrar, Straus & Giroux to increase the print run from 90,000 to 800,000 copies (Burr 167). Whatever the exact numbers, selection for Oprah's Book Club is a financial jackpot for writers and publishers.

Franzen's postquarrel essay "Meet Me in St. Louis" (published in *The New Yorker* in December 2001) also attempted to diffuse and explain his criticism of *Oprah*. The essay begins by emphasizing his midwestern compulsion to please and the "so fundamentally bogus" filming that he was required to participate in as part of the *Oprah* appearance (70). However, Franzen's 1996 *Harper's* essay, "Perchance to Dream"—which he revised and retitled "Why Bother?" for his 2002 collection, *How to Be Alone*—provides the context for many reviewers' remarks and persistent questions about *The Corrections*'s place within American literary history and culture. Franzen writes in the introduction to *How to Be Alone* that after the publication of *The Corrections*, "My interviewers were particularly interested in what they referred to as 'the *Harper's* essay.' . . . Interviews typically began with the question: 'In your *Harper's* essay in 1996, you promised that your third book would be a big social novel that would engage with mainstream culture and rejuvenate American literature; do you think you've kept that promise with *The Corrections*?'" (3). The *Harper's* essay did set up *The Corrections* within the masculine tradition of the postmodern social novel, epitomized by the work of authors such as Don DeLillo and Thomas Pynchon who engage both high and low cultures. Nevertheless, for his essay collection Franzen decided to revise the *Harper's* essay because he thought its argument was not clear and because he no longer agreed with the "very angry and theory-minded person" who wrote the essay "from this place of anger and despair, in a tone of high theoretical dudgeon that made me cringe a little now" (*How to Be Alone* 4; 5).

What was once an ivory tower of escape from mass culture now is a trap in the form of a "high theoretical dudgeon." Significantly, both his pretentious *Harper's* essay and his invitation to appear on *Oprah* made Franzen "cringe." One grimace results from an association with "schmaltzy low novels" and the other from theory-minded elitism. Franzen's "double-consciousness" of high and low, and masculine and feminine, puts him at war with himself. His critics tend to agree. As Joanna Smith Rakoff points out in her profile of Franzen, "he embodies both the humble charm and earnestness of the Midwesterner and the haughty superiority of the New Yorker. And, I suppose, it's no surprise that such oppositions—which clearly coexist in Franzen himself—are at the heart of *The Corrections*" (31). Written before Oprah selected *The Corrections* for her book club, Rakoff's article presents these contradictions as producing interesting tensions—both within the author himself and within his work. After the *Oprah* blowup, however, both Franzen and his critics seem unable to envision Franzen's work or personality as both sentimental and intellectual. Franzen's specific concerns arise not only out of an anxiety about confusing high and low cultures, but also from the ways that "Oprahfication" specifically genders and races that blurring.

The fact that Franzen's snobbery played such a large role in the press suggests that many writers, journalists, and readers do worry about how popular, commercial success can affect a writer's long-term reputation. Several commentaries on the Franzen Affair considered this dilemma between high art status and popular, commercially successful readership.[4] David Mehegan characterizes Franzen's problem as something that "many fiction writers, past and present" have grappled with: "He wants to be famous and sell a lot of books, but he also wants to be honored in his tribe. And he's not sure he can be both" (F1). "Tribe" is an especially curious and apt word. "Tribe" implies elite white male writers without requiring Mehegan to spell out the specific gendered and racial paradigm for his readers. Mehegan may also be subtly referring to Franzen's *Harper's* essay, "Perchance to Dream," in which Franzen describes straight white men as a "tribe" that is "much more susceptible to technological addictions than women are" (52).

How is it that Oprah's invitation produced such consternation among Franzen's "tribe"? While John Seabrook suggests that "culture and marketing" merge at a zero point called "nobrow," he also recognizes that the publishing industry houses a last guard of "genteel tastemakers" who remain invested in the "old High-Low" hierarchy (199). Seabrook also points out that we increasingly live in an age when what is popular is considered "good"; consequently, these "genteel tastemakers" confront a new dilemma: "How do you let the Buzz into the place, in order to keep it vibrant and solvent, without undermining the institution's moral authority, which was at least partly based on keeping the Buzz out?" (64). What happens, in other words, when good literature—or art generally—becomes popular?

Rather than reconciling popularity and quality, much literary and cultural criticism has responded by continuing to invest in their separation. If "quality, once the exclusive property of the few, has slowly and inexorably become available to the many," how do readers determine a novel's literary worth? (Seabrook 166). Rather than developing new strategies or methods of evaluation, a vocal contingent responding to the Franzen case has continued to suggest that the old ways of determining literary worth are still the best. According to this formula, Winfrey and her ilk cannot read serious fiction. While a novel may blur high/low and masculine/feminine forms and be praised for its postmodern blending of these dichotomies, the trained critic/reader continues to examine sales as a key means to distinguish genuine literature from a cheap knockoff. If a lot of people are reading it (and especially if those readers are women), then the novel simply cannot be that good—or those readers certainly will not get the story's importance.

Thus, we can begin to see that while much American (post)modern fiction may blur the boundaries between high and low cultures, the evaluation process remains invested in solidifying the separation between these classes and their gendered implications. For example, novelist Allan Gurganus goes so far as to suggest that it is doubtful whether *The Corrections* would have been selected as a National Book Award finalist if Winfrey had selected the novel earlier: "You are not nominated for certain prizes if you have had huge critical success. It's not an unmixed blessing" (Gurganus, qtd. in Mehegan F1). Joseph Epstein concurred in *Commentary*, taking the joining of high art and obscurity to the next level. Epstein praises Richard Russo's *Empire Falls* (2001) because, unlike Franzen's novel, neither Winfrey nor the National Book Award singled it out (37).[5]

The possibility of "Oprahfication," thus, promises a triple whammy: high sales, a feminine domestic readership, and the possibility that the novel could be read not as a novel engaged in questioning the status quo (compared with the critique offered by the social novel) but as yet another *Oprah* novel (or sentimental woman's fiction) that provides "Medicine for a Happier and Healthier World" (Franzen, "Why Bother?" 79). The conscious and unconscious acts by Franzen and various critics emphasize, as John Seabrook observes, how "people become more obsessed than ever with status" when "the old High-Low hierarchy" becomes blurred or absent (168). Ironically, the spectacle of the Franzen Affair reestablishes the gendered boundaries that *The Corrections* blurs.

The Corrections, at least in part, sets out to recycle the narrative of "beset manhood" through the character Chip Lambert, introduced in a section called "The Failure." Chip's character arc begins with labeling his parents "killers," a clear rejection of the home, and concludes with the prodigal son returning and reconciling himself to family, home, and responsibility (Franzen 15).[6] Chip's disastrous screenplay is even shaping up nicely by the novel's conclusion. However, unlike Chip, Franzen cannot escape or recycle his role in the "beset manhood" narrative so easily. For example, *Entertainment Weekly* writer Ty Burr reproduces distinctions between art and women's fiction in his commentary: "If some of Oprah's book choices tend to fall out of art and into earnest, womanly fiction, is it enough that she's getting people ready?" (167). Such comments reveal that while Franzen mixes and recycles genres in *The Corrections*, his own and his critics' remarks suggest that the author and the public are less than comfortable with this hybrid form, especially its popular, feminine component.

In the contemporary American fiction world, Oprah's Book Club is often understood as emphasizing a text's feminine qualities, both in terms of content and readership. These connotations are almost universally negative. For example, Philip Hensher, writer for *The Spectator*, characterizes "typical" *Oprah* selections and the divisive attitudes that her club has inspired: "[*Oprah* selections are] heartrending tales of love prevailing over circumstances, kitsch guff about the human spirit, epics about hoeing in Wyoming and smutty reconstructions of the lives of strong women during the American Civil War" (44). Eva Illouz's more positive analysis of Oprah's Book Club also emphasizes the club's feminine choices: "the genre of novels chosen by Oprah is [the detective novel's] feminine and therapeutic counterpart" (167). These "chick books," or, broadly defined, domestic fictions, must be defined *against* not *with* Franzen's *The Corrections*, lest the novel is taken outside the realm of "serious" (masculine) fiction.[7]

Franzen's defenders also frequently emphasize that their critique of Oprah's Book Club stems from the way that books are read on the show—Winfrey's "emotional" reading method. Janice Radway disagrees with this critique, "She's criticized by high-art critics or even cultural-studies scholars, because they say when she picks a book like *Beloved*, she's not looking at its aesthetic complexity—she's making it sentimental, confessional. That seems like a pointless criticism to me. When you write a book and put it out, that book can be read in many ways by many different people" (qtd. in "A Novelist" B4). Radway emphasizes that Winfrey's method is one of many. Critics following a Frankfurt School mentality suggest that the combination of Winfrey's popularity and power makes her "dangerous" to literary studies—a threat that stems in part from fears that her popularization of literature will "dumb down" literary critique. In this vein, Thomas R. Edwards, writing in the *Raritan*, goes so far as to hint that the book club is a sham: "Oprah, or her panel of referees, pricked up their ears at the sound of this one [*The Corrections*] even before they read it, assuming they did" (78). He goes on to characterize the club's "prevailing taste" as "schmaltzy," "female," and "one-dimensional or at best middlebrow" (78). According to Edwards, Winfrey's sentimental reading may be one of many but it is clearly one of the worst. Significantly, Cecilia Konchar Farr argues in *Reading Oprah: How Oprah's Book Club Changed the Way America Reads* that Winfrey's emotional reading of novels has been overemphasized and oversimplified in the criticism. Countering such selective analysis of the book club's reading methods, Farr demonstrates how Winfrey leads her readers through "all three modes—reflective, empathic, and inspirational" (50). However, reviewers and critics rarely address this point.

The harsh critiques of Winfrey's book club selections help contextualize the "unseemly tinge" that the Oprah's Book Club logo represents to Franzen and general readers who may feel uncomfortable—at least in the (masculine) public sphere—about reading or liking an *Oprah* pick. As John Young suggests, "The 'Oprah' editions are thus less 'authentic,' in Walter Benjamin's terms, than the first editions" (182). The *Oprah* sticker, like a movie-version book cover, renders texts less "literary." To retain status, some readers avoid *Oprah* picks or explain that they read a novel *before* it was an *Oprah* selection. Scott Stossel reports, "Several people I know refuse to read an Oprah-selected book—or if they do read it, they decline to read it in public—not out of principled objection to what Oprah is doing or what she represents (in fact, each of these people say, as Franzen did, that they admire and support what she does), but because they feel embarrassed to be publicly associated with an Oprah-selected book." In fact, some readers went so far as to request editions of *The Corrections* without the *Oprah* sticker. Farr clarifies in *Reading Oprah*, "So when Farrar, Strauss [& Giroux] put the Oprah seal into the cover art of Franzen's *The Corrections*, it became a different book. It became a mass-produced, popular choice rather than a marker of distinction and taste. And elite readers began to insist on unmarked covers" (88). Kathleen Rooney also reports in her study *Reading with Oprah: The Book Club That Changed America* how some readers went even further by establishing anti-*Oprah* book clubs.[8]

Why does this elitism expressed by the author, critics, and some of *The Corrections*'s readers exist when Nobel Prize–winning author Toni Morrison has appeared on the show several times? Farr reminds us, "For Americans, artistic standards come trailing shrouds of an aristocratic Western cultural tradition, where real art is supposed to be underappreciated, reserved for a discriminating few" (80). In this light, Franzen—unlike Toni Morrison—may be perceived to be "selling out" if he appears on *Oprah* because white male writers have not "historically been excluded from both the market and the canon" (Young 185). Nevertheless, Franzen claims after his fallout with Winfrey that he did not have "any preconceptions about what kind of reader makes a good reader for my work" (Franzen, qtd. in Giles 69), and he was hesitant to claim that "the work I'm doing is simply better than [Michael] Crichton's" (Franzen, qtd. in Wood 3).

Tellingly, Franzen does not cite Toni Morrison in his remarks that attempt to reconcile himself with Winfrey and her supporters. While Michael Crichton never appeared on Oprah's Book Club, Crichton seems to represent the club's supposed "lowbrow" popular taste. Interestingly, like the club's supposed reductive reading methods, this lowbrow or middlebrow reputation persists despite the club's emphasis on "the transforming possibilities of serious fiction" (Hall 655). Moreover, Crichton's novels are not associated with women's fiction, a female readership, or an analysis of oppression—three commonly cited hallmarks of Winfrey's picks.[9] Franzen plays it safe and tries to deflect the racial and gendered implications by comparing his work with that of another white male author—at most, Crichton and Franzen occupy distinctive literary positions.

Thus, we can begin to see how part of Franzen's discomfort may stem from the ways in which Winfrey's work promotes African American heritage and black women's cultural practices.[10] As Sherryl Wilson points out, Winfrey's celebrity is associated with "an African American tradition of thought" (180). Wilson explains, "black feminism and African American thought in which self is constructed in relation to community and significant others" constitutes one of the show's important traditions (94). R. Mark Hall notes that the book club promotes literacy in order to achieve cultural uplift (655). Winfrey, thus, blurs categories by her careful cultivation of "her success, wealth and celebrity—with all of the connotations of consumption and commercialism—whilst being simultaneously considered 'down home'" (Wilson 157). To insert Franzen into this context would mean that he would be out of his "natural" cultural element—forced to participate in a discourse and environment associated with both feminized consumer culture and African American rhetorical and cultural traditions. Rather than embrace this opportunity to cross or blur boundaries, Franzen balks and then Winfrey forecloses the possibility by canceling his appearance on the show. Franzen eventually does clarify that he and Winfrey are on the same team: "Both Oprah and I want the same thing and believe the same thing, that the distinction between high and low is meaningless" (qtd. in Epstein 34). Franzen also did not turn up his nose at selling the film option for *The Corrections* and later appeared as a guest for the *Today Show*'s book club.[11]

The femininity that Oprah's Book Club represents is not just a dilemma for white male writers like Franzen. Nor, as the narrative of "beset manhood" illustrates, does masculine anxiety toward femininity appear only on the public stage; it erupts within fiction as well. One of the most curious passages in regard to masculinity, white femininity, and the home appears in David Wong Louie's *The Barbarians Are Coming* (2000). In the following scene, Sterling Lung, the twenty-six year-old protagonist, has sex with the home—actually a ladies' club, not a residence—where he works as a chef. This perverse sexual scene seeks to reassert masculinity and male power—to get Sterling out from under the thumb of his female employers. Like the Franzen Affair, this fictional passage amplifies masculine anxiety about feminine power in particularly telling ways.

> I slide off the bed, onto the Oriental rug, seeking friction commensurate with my hardness and longing. My hand is too soft and familiar for this strange urgency. I fuck the rug some more, then the brass bedpost, the armoire, the back of the overstuffed chair; eventually I fuck the entire bedroom. Still unsatisfied, I fuck the runner in the dark hallway, the moldings, the telephone and its stand just outside the bathroom. I fuck the banister, the stairs, the dining room table, where the ladies are most intimately acquainted with me. I leave droplets of myself everywhere, the sticky residue of my love—they won't even know how we've communed, each time they turn a knob, pull up a chair, raise a fork to lips. I fuck the front door like crazy, then the shabby mat at the threshold. (Louie 32)

By literally screwing the home, Sterling figuratively fucks his white female employers. His transgression challenges white authority and reworks stereotypical Asian submissiveness and asexuality. Crystal Parikh suggests in "'The Most Outrageous Masquerade': Queering Asian-American Masculinity" that such textual "perversions" challenge and rework "the heteronormative logic through which Asian-American masculinity has been formulated" (863). This passage in particular confronts the relationship between Asian American masculinity and white femininity, revealing "the schisms in the purportedly unitary and normative formations of gender and nation in the US" (Parikh 863). Sterling's remarks near the end of the novel clarify these gender, racial, and national connections: "I embraced school because school wasn't home, European cuisine because Escoffier wasn't home, Bliss because she wasn't home" (323). Following this logic, he fucks the ladies' club because it is the (white) home he desires. Sterling's othering of white culture both serves as an oppressive rejection of his own heritage (home) and a transgressive means of control and mastery of the dominant culture. Furthermore, his acts invoke rape and sexual violation because they are committed without consent.

Significantly, Sterling positions his transgression in relation to the female body and domestic space, even as his transgression challenges stereotypical formulations of Asian American masculinity. While the reader may have little sympathy for the women Sterling works for—they treat Sterling more like a pet than a person—Sterling recovers his masculinity, if only temporarily and imaginatively, through an act of sexual violence against unaware "foreign" women. While clearly exaggerated, this textual eruption provides an important example and reminder of how conventional masculinity frequently depends on the (violent) repression of the feminine. Franzen and the critics' rhetorical violations of Oprah's intellectual integrity compose another part of this patriarchal logic. In this case, Oprah's race, gender, and status as a popular (that is, not intellectual) television host make her a prime target for Franzen and his supporters to reassert a patriarchal masculinity.

In Franzen's case, reestablishing his authorial masculinity—correcting his novel's status so potential readers understand that his book would *not* appear on *Oprah*—stabilizes cultural norms about the differences between high and low art forms as well as between masculine and feminine aesthetics and tastes. As querying American masculinity seemingly demands queering it, Franzen must assume a "tough guise" against popular or feminine culture to "straighten out" his place in the literary canon. Thus, even as fictions break apart gendered binaries, real authors and critics frequently correct any confusion and reestablish clear gender differences.

Returning to Franzen and turning to the novel itself, we see that like *House of Leaves* and *Independence Day*, *The Corrections*'s domestic politics are decidedly masculine in their ambivalent, progressive principles. Yet, there are also clear feminine elements recycled throughout this hybrid novel. Like *The Lay of the Land*, which hinges on gathering Frank's family for Thanksgiving dinner, *The Corrections*'s plot pivots on getting the entire Lambert family together for one last Christmas. John Mullan points out that *The Corrections* also features meals throughout the novel. As the homemaking mother and the person responsible for calling the family together, Enid Lambert plays a central role in shaping *The Corrections*'s domestic politics.

Like the other mothers I have discussed thus far—Orleanna in *The Poisonwood Bible*, Sethe from *Beloved*, and Mrs. March from *Little Women*—Enid plays a pivotal role in determining the home's construction. Enid, in fact, gets the last line. Her "correction" comes at age seventy-five. After her husband's death, Enid decides that "she was going to make some changes in her life" (568). After suffering under her husband's domineering rule, Enid is finally free. The novel's conclusion, thus, recalls the ending of *Rabbit at Rest*, in which Rabbit's wife Janice, waiting to see her husband after his heart attack, thinks that "she should pray for Harry's recovery, a miracle, but when she closes her eyes to do it she encounters a blank dead wall. . . . With him gone, she can sell the Penn Park house. *Dear God, dear God,* she prays. *Do what You think best*" (Updike 423). Like Enid, Janice's blossoming seems to come with her husband's demise.

There are at least two schools of thought about *The Corrections*'s ending. For some, the ending is genuinely hopeful: Enid "embod[ies] the prevailing [American] myth that one can start over again, or at the very least live for a better day tomorrow" (Filkins 231). Valerie Sayers argues that the novel's conclusion holds the most promise—"in its last third, the novel shifts from a condemnation of contemporary American materialism to the possibility of family (and, by implication, human) forgiveness" (Sayers 23). Others read the ending as ironic: Enid's triumph at age seventy-five is too little, too late; her dogged belief in the American dream is a farce. Joseph Epstein complains that by the ending the Lamberts "have long since lost their color by having been thoroughly rinsed in contempt" (Epstein 35). Looking more specifically at Enid's character suggests that while the novel leans more toward the latter reading, which follows an ironic masculine tradition, it clearly mixes gendered traditions. *The Corrections*'s ending is ambivalent, although of a decidedly different sort than what we encounter in *Paradise* or *The Poisonwood Bible*'s more ghostly, uncertain conclusions.

Knowing a little about Enid's relationship with her husband helps us understand the significance of Enid's concluding statement. For example, early in her pregnancy with their daughter, Denise, Enid initiates sexual contact with her husband. Enid does so with a mind to influence a financial investment that Alfred refuses to make because of his ethical business principles. However, she explicitly protests vaginal intercourse because she fears that it may hurt the baby. Alfred ignores her protests and commits spousal rape (Franzen 279–82). To justify his actions, Alfred tells himself that "he was a man having lawful sexual intercourse with his lawful wife" (280). Enid submits to her husband and cries herself to sleep. She does not change Alfred's mind about the investment.

Although she is not always satisfied by her marriage, leaving is never a feasible option for Enid. Like Orleanna Price, Enid is portrayed as a woman from "another country." Her generation of women was not permitted to conceive of other options and, as a result, rarely saw divorce as viable. All Enid can do is exclaim, "Oh, I'm so unhappy about this!" and cook unpleasant dinners that she knows Alfred hates (281). While Enid is clearly the victim of spousal rape, her manipulative behavior toward her husband and children prevents us from casting her only as a victim of Alfred's domineering personality. Nevertheless, her manipulations come to nothing; she never succeeds in correcting Alfred: "All of her correction had been for naught. He was as stubborn as the day she'd met him" (568). Alfred's death frees her to change her own life at the novel's conclusion: "She felt that nothing could kill her hope now, nothing" (568). Alfred's death seemingly produces a late regeneration for Enid. Her remarks echo *Suburban Sketches*'s forward thinking; Enid envisions—whether read ironically or seriously—a life that focuses on the future and not the past.

Enid's fear of instability furthers our understanding of her character and of the novel's neodomesticity. Unlike the neodomestic women discussed in the previous chapters, Enid continues to fight against rather than embrace instability, especially in regard to her domestic life. Her manipulative behavior can in part be explained by her overwhelming fear of domestic instability. While talking with Sylvia, a woman whom Enid meets on a cruise, Enid envisions a house of tissue, an image that serves as a metaphor for her anxiety and fears:

> To Enid at this moment came a vision of rain. She saw herself in a house with no walls; to keep the weather out, all she had was tissue. And here came the rain from the east, and she tacked up a tissue version of Chip and his exciting new job as a reporter. Here it came from the west, and the tissue was how handsome and intelligent Gary's boys were and how much she loved them. Then the wind shifted, and she *ran* to the north side of the house with such shreds of tissue as Denise afforded: how she'd married too young but was older and wiser now and enjoying great success as a restaurateur and hoping to meet the right young man! And then the rain came blasting up from the south, the tissue disintegrating even as she insisted that Al's impairments were very mild and he'd be fine if he'd just work on his attitude and get his drugs adjusted, and it rained harder and harder, and she was so tired, and all she had was tissue— (310; emphasis in original)

Rather than embracing this radically open structure, as we have seen other neodomestic protagonists do, Enid attempts to construct walls (lies). Enid realizes here that the flimsy stories (lies) that she tells others and herself about her children and husband cannot withstand the blasting storms pummeling her family. Her job as caretaker depends on her ability to construct a home that will weather such storms, but fabricated stories are unstable building materials.

The home that Enid attempts to construct, eventually revealed as a house of tissue, looks very familiar: it is Protestant, white, and suburban. Enid fixates on this vision of the perfect home. Unlike Frank Bascombe, "Enid reliably experienced the paroxysmal love of *place*—of the Midwest in general and suburban St. Jude in particular—that for her was the only true patriotism and the only viable spirituality" (118; emphasis in original). Enid attempts to construct home as a spiritual haven. Even though Enid no longer really believes in God or nation, "at a Saturday wedding in the lilac season, from a pew of the Paradise Valley Presbyterian Church, she could look around and see two hundred nice people and not a single bad one" (118). St. Jude weddings, in fact, remind Enid of the upstanding young men and women produced by a town like St. Jude: "Enid's heart would swell at the sight of yet another sweetly charitable Root girl now receiving, as her reward, the vows of a young man with a neat haircut of the kind you saw in ads for menswear, a really super young fellow who had an upbeat attitude and . . . who came from a loving, stable, traditional family and wanted to start a loving, stable, traditional family of his own" (118). Enid reflects, "Most important of all was that the bride and groom themselves match: have similar backgrounds and ages and educations" (119). Through Enid's character, Franzen focuses the ironic, masculine domestic fiction lens on conventional domesticity's sacred home.

Reality is much different for Enid. Going to St. Jude weddings allows Enid to participate vicariously in the lives she wishes for her children. Her divorced, lesbian daughter, Denise; her unmarried, philandering son, Chip; and her married but clinically depressed son, Gary, do not fit the St. Jude mold like other people's children: "Her children wanted radically, shamefully other things" (122). While Enid understands that midwestern St. Jude weddings are not "elegant," the "lack of sophistication" nonetheless assures her that "for the two families being joined together there were values that mattered more than style" (119). Notably, when Denise marries her boss, who is Jewish and much older, Denise elopes to Atlantic City (120). When Denise announced her divorce, Enid stews: "The effort she made to be a good sport and cheerleader, to obey Alfred and receive her middle-aged son-in-law cordially and not say *one single word* about his religion, only added to the shame and anger she felt five years later when Denise and Emile were divorced . . . she felt that the least Denise could have done was stay married" (123; emphasis in original). She echoes here the put-upon white male suburban character. Enid, constructing herself as a martyr and victim of her children's poor choices, bites her tongue and gives advice to her children in an attempt to keep her house of tissue intact.

Enid's unrealistic desires for her family produce shame. These feelings make the shame-blocking drug, Aslan, attractive to her. Nancy Berlinger suggests that Enid's shame is representative of her American Protestant heritage: "Her sense of shame is part of her cultural identity, to the extent that she has vague religious scruples about allowing Dr. Hibberd to ex(or)cise shame from her personality, . . . Thanks to 'Aslan's effect on the chemistry of shame,' Enid will be released from a key aspect of her American Protestant heritage" (18). By naming the drug Aslan, Franzen is surely referencing C. S. Lewis's lion Aslan, who is an allegory for Christ, from *The Lion, the Witch and the Wardrobe*. Christ or redemption, in this sense, becomes a pill—a sly critique that the novel levels at both organized religion and the pharmaceutical industry. Enid's use of the shame-blocking drug verges on addiction, but she ultimately decides not to continue taking it. Enid explains to her daughter, "'I want the real thing or I don't want anything'" (530). She does not appear to be released from her American Protestant heritage (her shame) until the moment her husband dies. Widowhood frees Enid from duty to her husband and any shame she may have felt for not being able to care for him. As Enid also sees Alfred as a lion, this sets him up as a Christ figure; it follows that Alfred dies so she can live.

In this light, we see that the novel produces a certain amount of hope—a kind of secular, ironically charged spirituality that follows in the tradition established by Updike's Rabbit novels, DeLillo's *White Noise*, and Ford's Frank Bascombe series. This ironically charged spiritual geography constructs and deconstructs itself. For example, when Chip, the middle Lambert child, returns to St. Jude for Christmas, he notes how the Lambert house is "saturated with an aura of belonging to the family. The house felt more like a body—softer, more mortal and organic—than like a building" (541). His response and changed demeanor after his near-death experiences in Lithuania provide additional evidence that the novel has taken a hopeful turn. After returning home, Chip initially moves into his parents' house to help care for his father who suffers from Parkinson's disease, and he eventually marries. Chip turns his selfish life around, recognizing the spiritual geography of the Lambert home and becoming a responsible caretaker.

Yet, while some circumstances have changed, Enid and her construction of home remain the same in many respects. Her narrow Protestant outlook still leads her to find fault with herself and others. In this sense, Franzen's recycling in *The Corrections* emphasizes the flaws rather than selects only the best domestic qualities to be reused. For example, the following passage demonstrates that the more things change, the more they stay the same in *The Corrections*:

> But when Chip informed her that he was going to be the father of twins with a woman he wasn't even married to, and when he then invited Enid to a wedding at which the bride was *seven months pregnant* and the groom's current "job" consisted of rewriting his screenplay for the fourth or fifth time and the majority of the guests not only were extremely Jewish but seemed *delighted* with the happy couple, there was certainly no shortage of material for Enid to find fault with and condemn! (566; emphasis in original)

These remarks make the reader suspicious of the type or degree of life changes that Enid contemplates in the concluding line a few pages later. Enid's chance to correct her own life comes so late, only with her husband's death, and with no clear direction. The novel uses this ambivalence to conclude ironically.

The Corrections's ironic masculine tone and ambivalent ending—its assertion of instability combined with the critique of religion, specifically Protestantism—renders the novel's drama in the public sphere all the more curious. In many respects, Franzen should not have needed to defend his novel's masculinity. The tremendous response to the Franzen Affair demonstrates that Franzen's anxieties by no means represent an isolated or individual artistic quirk. The affair's resolution suggests that domestic novels—especially those written by and focused on men—have clear stakes in establishing a masculine identity. In the aftermath of the scandal, Franzen pondered whether he was a "social novelist" or "an old-fashioned domestic novelist" rather than framing his role along genre- and gender-bending terms (qtd. in Adams C01). These anxieties regarding the feminine present one of the greatest challenges to neodomestic politics. Furthermore, a neodomestic fiction that is more fully invested in a spiritual geography does not simply prescribe a guaranteed route for spreading the good news. Neodomestic fiction's lessons, as the novels I discuss below demonstrate, model hybrid identities and conclusions that are less anxious and ironic.

Queer Eyes for Homespun Guys
Viable Neodomestic Masculinity

> *The guy who put this house together is an artist*
> —Henry Rios from Michael Nava's Rag and Bone

The Corrections's ensemble cast of male and female characters does not allow it to study masculine domesticity, let alone male domestic artists, in great detail. Male domestic artists, like the character that Henry Rios refers to in the mystery *Rag and Bone* (2001), are a rare breed in contemporary American literature. Unlike their female contemporaries, heterosexual male characters are not generally known for their domestic artistry and faculty. They are, in this sense, doubly queer by virtue of their rarity and their domestic talents. In the specific case of *Rag and Bone*, the characters are also queer due to their sexuality. A reductive reading of Michael Nava's mystery novel would simply place Henry Rios's remark as a sign of the popularized queer eye. Gay men, according to this stereotype, have a feminized proclivity for fashion, interior design, and mass consumption.

Like the undeveloped gay male characters in Jane Smiley's *Good Faith*, who have "so many friends. . . . With so much money," gay men, according to this stereotype, demonstrate an uncanny eye for economic profit and domestic style (Smiley 55). In rather stereotypical fashion, the gay couple in *Good Faith*, David Pollock and David John, provide sympathetic ears to the main (heterosexual) characters' affairs, demonstrating their feminine listening skills, while simultaneously performing a very masculine do-it-yourself project—ripping up kitchen tile (Smiley 84–87). While the other characters lose money in *Good Faith*, "the Davids" come out on top: "True to form, they [David Pollock and David John] tripled their investment" (Smiley 415). In fact, much like a drag queen can be said to outperform femininity at its own game, the queer eye may be said to outdo a woman's domestic touch.

However, Henry's remark that serves as this section's epigraph does not place his lover's masculinity or femininity under erasure. This is not a "Queer Eye for the Straight Guy" but rather a queer eye for the domestic guy, whose bisexuality transgresses boundaries and defies stable definitions. If Franzen's novel ironically repeats conventional domestic structures as its mode of critique, the novels in this section reverently and irreverently challenge gender constructions through their tweaked performances. Such neodomestic representations of domestic masculinity craft alternative narratives to the "melodramas of beset manhood" that often require a rejection of home and frequently condone violence against women and foreigners. The range of queer domesticities surveyed here begins to map domestic masculinity's "social variety" frequently masked by "a narrow expectation of domestic, social, and sexual arrangements" conventionally considered "acceptable, plausible, recognizable, and knowable" (Shah 15).

In *Rag and Bone*, John, the bisexual house artist whom Henry refers to above, built and designed his home. The passage below underscores that John embodies feminine homemaking and masculine do-it-yourself characteristics. As a professional builder, furthermore, John's character follows the masculine domestic tradition of having a formal profession related to the domestic sphere. John balances conventionally masculine and feminine characteristics. Henry's remark about John's unique housekeeping and homemaking highlight his hybrid, bisexual domesticity:

> The walls of the kitchen were painted a warm orange, the tile was blue and white. On the stove was a skillet with rice and peas in tomato sauce. A handpainted ceramic bowl on the counter held a green salad. There was a second, glass bowl in which two pieces of fish were marinating in a clear oil. A door opened out to the deck, where there was a grill and a small wrought-iron table set with pale green plates and blue glasses. I was

aware that the things in John's house had not been chosen at random, but the effect was casual rather than calculated, and though the eye that had arranged them was masculine, it was also capable of delicacy. (112–113)

Nava's passage carves out a nonpatriarchal, "delicate" domestic masculinity.[12] The passage praises John's domestic arts while not denying his masculine sensuality. Patriarchal masculinity allows little, if any, room for domestic masculinity beyond protector and provider roles. Additionally, it assumes that such roles will occur within a heterosexual relationship. *Rag and Bone* successfully, as Ralph Rodríguez argues, "scratches *familia*," or "reinvent[s] it so as to think past what Michel Foucault identifies as the poverty of relational possibilities that saddle us" (76).

Nava's *Rag and Bone* queers domesticity. This queer, neodomestic fiction details the minutiae involved in making and keeping a home and unsaddles the white, Protestant, heterosexual, and masculine norm. Michael Cunningham's *A Home at the End of the World* (1990) similarly rewrites patriarchal, heteronormative domesticity. The novel narrates the lives of "the Hendersons," which includes adolescent friends and lovers, Bobby and Jonathan, and Jonathan's roommate Clare. The trio's personal and sexual relationships shift throughout the novel. The name "the Hendersons" emerges after Bobby and Jonathan stop their adolescent affair but before Bobby and Clare begin seeing each other. (Bobby and Clare do not marry, but they do eventually date and have a daughter, Rebecca.)

The name "the Hendersons" recycles or reperforms the conventional family for the characters' unconventional situation. Bobby explains the name's origin and what it connotes: "We took to calling ourselves the Hendersons. I don't remember how it started—it was part of a line tossed out by Clare or Jonathan, and it stuck. The Hendersons were a family with modest expectations and simple tastes. They liked going to the movies or watching TV. They liked having a few beers in a cheap little bar. . . . Clare came to be known as Mom, I was Junior, and Jonathan was Uncle Jonny" (Cunningham 155–56). The characters repeat these roles with ironic twists:

> Mom was the boss. She wanted us to mind our manners and sit up straight, she clicked her tongue if one of us swore. Junior was a well-intentioned, shadowy presence, a dim-witted Boy Scout type who could be talked into anything. Uncle Jonny was the bad influence. He had to be watched. "Junior," Clare would say, "don't sit too close to your Uncle Jonny. And he doesn't need to go into the bathroom with you, you're big enough now to manage just fine on your own." (Cunningham 156)

These familial roles represent exaggerated aspects of each character's personality and also play-up their stereotypical implications. For example, the "caretaker" Mom (Clare) must watch the "dangerous" homosexual Uncle Jonny (Jonathan) when he's around the "innocent" Junior (Bobby). Rather than simply conform to stereotypically gendered and sexualized family roles, the characters recycle and reinvent them as shorthand for their (un)conventional family. I hesitate here to label the Hendersons simply unconventional because this label too easily assigns the normative, "natural" familial role to heterosexual "conventional" families. Part of what Bobby, Clare, and Jonathan accomplish is to reassign and rethink the conventional family unit.

The protagonists form a close-knit family, bonding as friends and lovers better than they were able to connect with their biological families. Like any other family unit, all of the members must participate to form a family. Bobby explains that Uncle Jonny's role is particularly important: "But without Uncle Jonny, the Hendersons didn't work. Without our bad uncle we were too simple—just bossy Mom and the boy who always obeyed. We needed all three points of the triangle. We needed mild manners, perversity, and a voice of righteousness" (156). Jonathan, the element of "perversity," adds an atypical element to this "ideal" family. In this context, perversity provides a necessary "imperfection"—the queer element that makes the family, in the end, a "normal," cohesive unit.[13]

The family, however, does not stay together just as it is. By the novel's conclusion, a fifth member (in addition to Clare and Bobby's daughter) has joined the family: Erich, who is dying of AIDS and who was one of Jonathan's lovers. At the end of the novel, Clare leaves the family, taking her daughter with her. Even though Bobby is the biological father, he understands: "Clare has taken Rebecca to the world of the living—its noise and surprises, its risk of disappointment. . . . We [Jonathan and Bobby] are here in the other world, a quieter place, more prone to forgiveness" (331). The concluding geography of the "home at the end of the world" embodies a spiritual, otherworldly nature. A reference to a spirit also appears briefly at the novel's conclusion. For a moment, Bobby thinks that Clare has returned. He realizes that he was mistaken: "Clare isn't back. What I saw was just the wind blowing. It was either the wind or the spirit of the house itself, briefly unsettled by our nocturnal absence but too old to be surprised by the errands born from the gap between what we can imagine and what we in fact create" (Cunningham 336). This domestic space is more materially grounded than the spaces that conclude *The Poisonwood Bible* and *Paradise*, but it is also, as the remarks above suggest, not completely "real." Like the Convent in *Paradise*, the house functions as a place where outsiders can find home on the margin. This frontier, however, is not like the suburban frontier defined by Howells and his successors.

This home, unlike the home we see in *Suburban Sketches*, does not border on the future but "maintain[s] a present, so people can return to it when their futures thin out on them" (Cunningham 336). This "home at the end of the world" provides a haven, a "place to escape" and a place to escape from: "This is ours; we have it to run from and we have it to return to" (336). It is the haven and the trap, incorporating and gender-bending masculine and feminine domestic narratives. Furthermore, sexual relations are not the foundation of the haven that Jonathan and Bobby create. Their homemaking remains platonic and stereotypically feminine in its nurturing selflessness. In this story Clare, not Bobby or Jonathan, finds it necessary to leave home—to light out for new territory. Domestic masculinity forms the foundation for Bobby and Jonathan's home: "Jonathan and I are here to maintain a present, so people can return to it when their futures thin out on them. We've been on our way here for a long time" (Cunningham 336). Bobby and Jonathan's home mixes masculine and feminine features, demonstrating that their home and their lives do not have to follow one gendered model; they negotiate various roles to produce a hybrid space and gendered identities.

Making Home
Spiritual Geographies and Masculine Domesticity

Explicitly homosexual or bisexual characters are not masculine domesticity's only homemakers. Chang-rae Lee's *A Gesture Life* (1999) also queers stereotypical masculine suburban space by positioning the reclusive, heterosexual Japanese (Korean) Franklin "Doc" Hata as its narrator.[14] Although his narration remains reluctant to move beyond surfaces, the small details of Doc Hata's habits and home combined with wartime flashbacks of Hata serving as a medic in the Japanese army during World War II accumulate to form a fuller, deeper picture of Doc Hata's complex domestic masculinity and his queer homemaking. Similar to Quentin Compson, Doc Hata attempts to resist the haunting of his violent past and finds that he cannot. Rather than commit suicide, Doc Hata attempts to make a home after World War II in the American suburban town of Bedley Run. The novel recycles suburban and Asian American literary conventions, producing a neodomestic suburban masculinity that ultimately accounts for its haunting history and the home's spirit.[15]

A Gesture Life addresses the challenges associated with occupying traditionally white spaces; the "race house" that Doc Hata encounters emerges from his own experience as an ethnic Korean adopted by a Japanese family and the broader sociohistorical contexts that inform the Asian American experiences of making home in America after World War II. Cindy I-Fen Cheng explains, "While postwar suburbanization has come to typify the retreat of whites and European immigrants into the suburbs, sociological and historiographical studies, along with newspaper and magazine articles published during the early cold war years from 1946 to 1965, highlighted how many Chinese also sought residence in the suburbs" (1067). While not Chinese, Doc Hata's experiences relate to Cheng's findings. Although Doc Hata maintains his "deviant bachelor society," he still models a "conformity to the domestic ideal of suburban, middle-class heterosexual, nuclear families" through his perfect suburban home and adopted daughter (Cheng 1068). As a result, he "mitigate[s] the alterity that racial difference pose[s] to white society" (Cheng 1068). The price Doc Hata and his mixed raced daughter Sunny pay for his gestures or performances of domestic conformity composes much of the novel's plot.

Isolation is one of the consequences of living in a predominately white suburb, where "it seemed people took an odd interest in telling me that I wasn't *un*welcome" (Lee 3; emphasis in original). Unlike other suburban characters who express alienation or isolation, Doc Hata embraces his solitary position: "Save the time that Sunny spent with me, I've known myself best as a solitary person, and although I've always been able to enjoy the company of others, I've seen myself most clearly when I'm off on my own, without others in the mix" (Lee 68). Rather than producing a trap, suburban space's isolation seemingly suits Doc Hata.

In part, suburban space fails to trap Doc Hata because he owns his own home and because of the particular homemaking practices he follows. *A Gesture Life* straightforwardly recycles the masculine suburban focus on ownership but crafts homeownership into something almost spiritual. Doc Hata explains,

> I cannot help but feel blessed that I have as much as I do, even if it is in the form of box hedge and brick and paving stone. There is, I think, a most simple majesty in this, that in regarding one's own house or car or boat one can discover the discretionary pleasures of ownership—not at all conspicuous or competitive—and thus have another way of seeing the shape of one's life, how it has transformed and, with any luck, multiplied and grown. (Lee 137)

Doc Hata's measured materialism allows for the "discretionary pleasures of ownership" but does not condone conspicuous consumption. His views on homeownership also begin to suggest that where he tweaks suburban alienation to his advantage, he reproduces suburban control. Like Rachel Price in *The Poisonwood Bible*, Doc Hata considers his home "a lovely place of my own making" (Lee 24).

When Doc Hata repaints his estranged, adopted daughter's bedroom, his penchant for control, perfection, and, by implication, domestic security emerges: "I remember patching and repainting the ceiling and walls, making sure to fix all the mars in the plaster. There were larger pocks, into which I found it easy enough to spade the filler. But it was the smaller ones, particularly the tack holes, which seemed to number in the hundreds. . . . It wasn't until much later, as I'd drift into the room to inspect for missed holes, running my hand over the surfaces, that the whole project was quite satisfactorily done" (Lee 14–15). Doc Hata's housework reveals his obsessive maintenance that smoothes out all imperfections and cracks in the surface. His meticulous patching technique presents a clear contrast to the cracked tile that provokes the mother's realization in *Geographies of Home* that "nothing was stable—nothing" (Pérez 293). Instead of letting the evidence stand, Doc Hata attempts to make it seem as though the holes never existed. Unlike Baby Suggs's renovations in *Beloved*—renovations that reverse race house expectations—Doc Hata's renovations produce a "lovely, standing forgery" of conventional white domesticity (Lee 352).

The problem with Doc Hata's reproduced suburban homemaking is that it appears "just as though I have not lived there [in his home] every day for the last thirty years of my life" (Lee 119). The lack of dirt and scratches leaves no trace of its inhabitants. As Witold Rybczynski so aptly puts it, "Hominess is not neatness" (17). Doc Hata's perfect homemaking certainly does not create a homey atmosphere. In fact, his daughter Sunny hates the house (Lee 26). Doc Hata explains, "Sunny felt no more at home in this town, or in this house of mine, or perhaps even with me, than when she very first arrived at Kennedy Airport, accompanied by a woman from the agency" (55). Significantly, while both Sunny and her father possess a home, they feel homeless. As feminist geographer Linda McDowell points out, "At one time, the stereotypical homeless person was a rather romanticized version of the hobo or the tramp: a masculine figure who was unable to settle down and shoulder the responsibilities of home and work" (90). In contrast to this romantic masculine figure, Doc Hata represents the immigrant who finds himself homeless regardless of his material possessions.[16]

Doc Hata's "gesture life" relates to the aspects of control and perfection in his homemaking and domestic design. By living a life of gestures, Doc

Hata remains on the outside. Doc Hata's suburban homemaking embodies nonpatriarchal nonviolence but not simply. In fact, his daughter Sunny suggests, "You burden with your generosity" (95). As seen in *The Poisonwood Bible*, present actions, such as Doc Hata's generosity, and the past, particularly his military duty during World War II, burden the characters and Doc Hata in particular. According to Doc Hata, because he has "seen what no decent being should ever look upon and have to hold in close remembrance," he should be "left to the cold device of history, my likeness festooning the ramparts of every house and town and district of man" (345–46). Instead of living in "broad infamy," Doc Hata "persist[s], with warmth and privilege accruing to me unabated, ever securing my good station here, the last place I will belong" (345; 346). The use of the future tense—"the last place I will belong"—underscores Doc Hata's persistent homelessness and counterfeit domestic life.

Doc Hata's "habitation" forges new territory and rehearses old (352). Similar to Rachel Price and Frank Bascombe, Doc Hata attempts to ignore the bad, especially the heavy burden of his past, in order to "pass on" with his life. Like Orleanna Price in *The Poisonwood Bible*, however, Doc Hata eventually realizes that there is no outside to his responsibilities and that he cannot slough off his role in events: "I see now, I was in fact a critical part of events, as were K and the other girls, and the soldiers and the rest. Indeed the horror of it was how central we were, how ingenuously and not we comprised the larger processes, feeding ourselves and one another to the all-consuming engine of the war" (Lee 299). While his military outpost was not near combat, Doc Hata still considers himself and those around him as central to the war. He eventually understands, like Orleanna, that local actions can have national and global repercussions.

Also similar to Orleanna, Doc Hata's privileges influence the position that he occupies and creates. Like the characters in *Paradise*, Doc Hata occupies a vexed space. On the one hand, he is privileged; in Japan, his adoption by a Japanese family led to material and social prestige. In America, he owns a beautiful home and occupies an important position in his community: "Doc Hata *is* Bedley Run. He is what this place is about" (Lee 136; emphasis in original). On the other hand, his ethnic identity in Japan burdens him and needs to be hidden (Lee 112). He lives a dream life but not in a positive sense: "I feel I have not really been living anywhere or anytime, not for the future and not in the past and not at all of-the-moment, but rather in the lonely dream of an oblivion, the nothing-of-nothing drift from one pulse beat to the next, which is really the most bloodless marking-out, automatic and involuntary" (Lee 320–21). Furthermore, his American home is an "oddly unsatisfying museum" (139). As these passages suggest, the ghost in *A Gesture Life* is Doc Hata.

Doc Hata's ghostly existence is emphasized throughout the novel. While driving through Bedley Run, for example, Doc Hata notes, "I feel precipitously insubstantial behind the wheel, like an apparition who has visited too long" (Lee 192). In another passage, Doc Hata's friend and realtor, Liv Crawford, leads him through his home so he can examine the renovations that she supervised after a house fire damaged his living room. During the tour, Doc Hata has "the peculiar sensation that this inspection and showing is somehow postmortem, that I am already dead and a memory and I am walking the hallways of another man's estate, leaning into rooms to sniff what lingering notes of his person may remain, the tang of after-shave or slivers of soap, the old wool of his coats and leather shoes, the dust and spice of the cupboards" (Lee 138–39). Doc Hata's "museum house" entombs lifelessness.

Doc Hata creates this space as much as he finds himself lifelessly marking time. For instance, he explains how he makes his home: "I've always believed that the predominant burden is mine, if it is a question of feeling at home in a place. Why should it be another's? How can it? So I do what is necessary in being complimentary, as a citizen and colleague and partner. This is almost never too onerous. If people say things, I try not to listen. In the end, I have learned I must make whatever peace and solace of my own" (135). Doc Hata ignores racial slurs and attempts to control life by focusing on his "predominant burden"—what he can control: his own personal space (135). Franklin Hata—if not an oblique reference to Benjamin Franklin, it works all the same—follows an "exact scale of ... appropriate response" in order to maintain a "delicate and fragile balance" (Lee 44).[17]

Like Benjamin Franklin's measured work ethic described in *The Autobiography of Benjamin Franklin*, Doc Hata's "Scheme of Order" attempts to keep his house in order and the past at bay (Franklin 288). However, it appears that Franklin Hata experiences what Benjamin Franklin warns against: "That such extreme Nicety as I exacted of myself might be a kind of Foppery in Morals, which if it were known would make me ridiculous; that a perfect Character might be attended with the Inconvenience of being envied and hated; and that a benevolent Man should allow a few Faults in himself, to keep his Friends in Countenance" (Franklin 290). When Sunny explains to her father, "You burden with your generosity," she expresses the frustration caused by his perfection, a perfection that will not "keep his Friends in Countenance" (Lee 95). She also emphasizes that his housekeeping does not successfully make a home.

Doc Hata's domestic practices account for much of the trouble he encounters with his rebellious daughter. A key scene that highlights the novel's queer, "perverse" domesticity, especially as it relates to Sunny and her father, occurs in the middle of the book when Doc Hata recalls going out to look for Sunny at a friend's house. The home is foul, and yet Sunny decides to live there instead of with her father. In the home Doc Hata spies his daughter with two men—Jimmy and another man named Linc (Lee 112–116). This scene breaks a social, familial taboo, exposing the daughter's sexual life to her father. Significantly, this scene is juxtaposed against memories of the women who were under Doc Hata's care as a medic during the Pacific war. The women under his care worked in the "Comfort House" and were forced into sexual slavery for the Japanese military (Lee 105–112).

The intervening scene with his daughter underscores that Doc Hata does not understand her chosen relationship with these unsavory, violent men who are involved with drugs: "I didn't wish to think that it was she who had initiated this moment but there was nothing to indicate otherwise. They weren't forcing her, or even goading her, or doing anything to coerce" (Lee 115). Doc Hata does not understand his daughter's choices, given the sexual violence he witnessed committed against the women in the Comfort House.

What Doc Hata fails to understand is that Sunny rebels by not being polite, by not being a "model minority." Sunny complains to her father, "You make a whole life out of gestures and politeness" (95). Doc Hata's seemingly perfect housekeeping—his ability to be "active and vigilant" and keep at bay "the ever-threatening domestic entropy and chaos"—produces a daughter who hates her father's house (Lee 196). His neighbor, lover, and friend Mary Burns questions his relationship with Sunny: "It's as if she's a woman to whom you're beholden, which I can't understand. I don't see the reason. You're the one who wanted her. You adopted her. But you act almost guilty, as if she's someone you hurt once, or betrayed, and now you're obliged to do whatever she wishes" (60). Hata's reparations for what he did not do to help the women trapped in sexual slavery during the war, especially the woman K, do not ease his guilt. Doc Hata's reparations include his adoption of Sunny and helping the Hickey family by buying back his business.

In the end, Doc Hata, like Frank Bascombe, decides to sell his beloved home. While Doc Hata does not wish to haunt the residence, he wishes that there could be some way for the new owners to know who he was:

> And yet it seems nearly wrong that the next people will never know what sort of man walked the halls within, or know the presences of his daughter and his lady friend, or wonder about the other specters of his history.

Of course I don't wish them to be haunted. But if they might be somehow casually informed, whispered to that this man was nothing special or extraordinary but, as Mary Burns suggested, particular to himself, I would feel a certain sentence had been at least transferred, duly passed. (352–53)

Here, the haunting becomes about a particular communication about the past—about this "particular" loner, Doc Hata. Doc Hata hopes to be remembered, to pass on some sense of himself.

Home, by contrast, remains a more grounded concept to the middle-aged Frank Bascombe in *The Lay of the Land*. Reflecting on Haddam, the home he left for his "chosen new life" in Sea-Clift, Frank Bascombe muses,

> What is home then, you might wonder? The place you first see daylight, or the place you choose for yourself? Or is it the someplace you just can't keep from going back to, though the air there's grown less breathable, the future's over, where they really don't want you back, and where you once left on a breeze without a rearward glance? Home? Home's a musable concept if you're born to one place, as I was (the syrup-aired southern coast), educated to another (the glaciated mid-continent), come full stop in a third—then spend years finding suitable "homes" for others. Home may only be where you've memorized the grid pattern, where you can pay with a check, where someone you've already met takes your blood pressure, palpates your liver, slips a digit here and there, measures the angstroms gone off your molars bit by bit—in other words, where your primary care-givers await, their pale gloves already pulled on and snugged. (14)

Written in the conditional, Frank's meditation on home emphasizes familiarity and routine more than sentiment or spirit. The passage also eschews the didactic through its initial use of questions. Not defined or haunted by the past, home as a place is defined by the present: it is the place "where your primary care-givers await" (14).

In contrast, near the end of *A Gesture Life* a ghost appears to Doc Hata. The ghost is K, one of the women who was under his care and with whom he fell in love. At this moment, Doc Hata explains, "I think I feel at home" (Lee 286). However, my description of K as a ghost is not quite right. She is no more clearly a ghost in this novel than the ghostly women who conclude *Paradise*. Hata clarifies, "I was almost sure she was a spectral body or ghost. But I am not a magical man, and never have been.... And as deeply as I wished she were some wondrous, ethereal presence, that I was being duly haunted, I knew that she was absolute, unquestionably real, a once-personhood come wholly into being" (Lee 286). In this mysterious scene, K asks Doc Hata when they will leave Bedley Run. He questions her about why they should leave when "we have everything that we require. And much more. . . . Everything is in delicate harmony. And yet still you seem dissatisfied" (Lee 287). K replies that she knows she will not die in Bedley Run, "and sometimes, sir, I so wish to" (287). Leaving Bedley Run, however, does not mean that Doc Hata finally has the courage to do what he could not do in Japan.

Doc Hata flees home not because it is a trap, but because his own past prevents him from creating home, at least in any conventional sense. Doc Hata can only gesture toward home. As he prepares to leave his home, Doc Hata reveals, "But I think it won't be any kind of pilgrimage. I won't be seeking out my destiny or fate. I won't attempt to find comfort in the visage of a creator or the forgiving dead" (356). Doc Hata does not recycle the "melodrama of beset manhood" to seek out his fortune or his "destiny." He also does not look to embark on a "Pilgrim's Progress." He just seems to go on yet another walk.

The novel's final sentences emphasize that Doc Hata remains paradoxically outside of yet constituted by domestic masculinity's framing. *A Gesture Life* recycles and queers the alienated suburban home and the narrative of "beset manhood":

> Let me simply bear my flesh, and blood, and bones. I will fly a flag. Tomorrow, when this house is alive and full, I will be outside looking in. I will be already on a walk someplace, in this town or the next or one five thousand miles away. I will circle round and arrive again. Come almost home. (Lee 356)

Mike Crang, explaining the work of Michel de Certeau, suggests that "walking is thus to create non-sites and haunted geographies" (150). Doc Hata embodies de Certeau's tactic of walking; his "almost home" is a haunting "non-site." This approximate space, "almost home," in many ways epitomizes queer neodomesticity. It suggests a "third space" that is neither fully material nor fully spiritual. It never achieves what home "should be," yet it provides a space in which the characters can live.

Jonathan and Bobby in *A Home at the End of the World* and Doc Hata in *A Gesture Life* settle into this type of hybrid, ambivalent space. The Convent women at the end of *Paradise* may also be said to inhabit an unstable "third space." This space also describes the "lost" village at *The Poisonwood Bible*'s conclusion and the beautiful gardens that the protagonists return to at the conclusion of *Gardens in the Dunes*. As Jonathan in *A Home at the End of the World* remarks, "I wouldn't say I was happy. I was nothing so simple as happy. I was merely present, perhaps for the first time in my adult life. The moment was unextraordinary. But I had the moment, I had it completely. It *inhabited* me" (Cunningham 342–43; my emphasis). Jonathan describes, like Doc Hata above, a queer homecoming—a feeling of being not quite out of place anymore.

6

Conclusions
The Territory Ahead

> *Serious intellectual work would seem to have much in common with housework.*
> —Toril Moi, "What Is a Woman? Sex, Gender, and the Body in Feminist Theory"

Just as Jonathan Franzen claims in "Why Bother" that good literature resists closure, Toril Moi suggests that serious scholarship poses questions that demand constant work. Domestic scholarship likewise requires endless housekeeping. Just when we think we have finally caught up, another pile of novels appears, and we must start the process over again. Dust, laundry, and novels accumulate. Before outlining the territory ahead, let me first briefly review the terrain covered in the previous chapters. I will then summarize what this literary map of domesticity suggests for lived experience.

Neodomestic American Fiction's contribution to the study of American literature is threefold: first, it traces and extends domestic fiction's time period into the twenty-first century; second, it redefines the genre so it includes male as well as female authors and protagonists; and finally, it adds another lens with which to define and interpret this genre, providing a spatial rather than an exclusively plot- or character-based analysis of the fiction. This analysis defines a new subgenre, which I call neodomestic fiction, and demonstrates a shift in the politics of home from stability to instability. I locate this shift in the 1980s, pointing to the threshold neodomestic novels *Housekeeping* and *The House on Mango Street* as landmark texts that mark neodomestic fiction's emergence with their revised conception of model domesticity. The preceding chapters identified and analyzed the three primary characteristics that define neodomestic fiction: mobility, home renovation or redesign, and relational domestic space.

(Neo)domestic fictions share intense attention to the domestic sphere and self-conscious homemaking. The geographic lens focused on domestic space and the processes of homemaking plots neodomestic fiction's queer, recycled, and unstable domestic territories. Understanding these changes in the context of nineteenth-, twentieth-, and twenty-first-century fiction and culture reveals that neodomestic fiction does not represent a radical break but rather a recycling and reordering of domestic tropes, practices, and spaces. Particularly complex are the ways in which neodomestic fiction recycles and queers raced and gendered spaces. Neodomestic fiction intervenes in what Cheryl I. Harris describes as "Whiteness as Property," or "the legal legitimation of expectations of power and control that enshrine the status quo as a neutral baseline, while masking the maintenance of white privilege and domination" (1715). Like Harris's legal analysis, my analysis of (neo)domestic fictions demonstrates that the "origins of whiteness as property lie in the parallel systems of domination of Black and Native American peoples out of which were created racially contingent forms of property and property rights" (1714). Neodomestic fiction addresses and remodels the resulting "race house," as Toni Morrison labels it.

Neodomestic fiction also complicates the distinctly gendered binary between domestic fiction's gendered strands. This aspect of my analysis places my own study in a potentially awkward position. I frequently emphasize gender distinctions in my chapter divisions while simultaneously explaining how neodomestic fiction blurs such boundaries. At first glance, I may appear to reproduce the very discourses that neodomestic fiction and my research questions. In other words, the gendered map that my chapters create seemingly participates in the disciplining of gender. However, rather than disciplining gender, the chapters embody gender's relational dynamics. In Janet R. Jakobsen's terms, the gendered chapters aim "to queer . . . [or] rely on and trouble norms" (530). Domesticity emerges from this gendered binary and has developed along two distinct but related tracks; maintaining gendered chapters represents the norm's power and clarifies masculine and feminine domestic fiction's distinct and common tropes and politics. Furthermore, while neodomestic fiction troubles these gendered traditions, it does not eliminate them or present a postgendered genre. Neodomestic fiction heightens rather than erases gendered spatial awareness. My "queer" analysis, thus, seeks "to engage the complex of uneven relations among norms" (Jakobsen 520). Gender performances in the fiction and in my analysis operate across a spectrum of masculine and feminine behaviors.

The analysis of these gendered fictions reveals that both strands offer viable neodomesticities because of their shared emphasis on domestic instability. However, I also want to be clear about how difference—differences that are often grounded in gendered notions about spiritual geography—functions. Neither difference nor sameness is constructed on neutral ground. American culture and literature suggest that masculine and feminine spaces and genres are different but certainly not equal. They espouse distinct politics, and feminist geography makes a case for why a relational (feminine) spatial politics might serve us better than an oppositional (masculine) spatial politics. My analysis of the literature contributes to arguments against oppositional spatial relationships and spaces that deemphasize, if not attempt to erase, the past.

Here we might keep in mind what Homi Bhabha explains in "DissemiNation" about how nation formation emerges from a violent forgetting. A conventional strand of masculine and feminine domesticity follows this forgetful course. Neodomestic fiction—particularly those novels that emphasize "historically conscious recycling"—attempts to construct different routes to home and nation (George, "Recycling" 2–3). As we saw in *The Poisonwood Bible, Paradise, Gardens in the Dunes,* and *A Gesture Life,* in its most intense forms, this historically conscious recycling process materializes the past in the form of a spiritual geography. Domestic fiction's literary history demonstrates that the novels engaged in this project tend to emerge out of the feminine tradition, whereas masculine domestic fiction, following an oppositional and patriarchal spatial organization, tends to break with history. As we saw in *Suburban Sketches* and *Independence Day,* masculine domestic fiction's most intense forms reject the past in favor of the present and the future.

This project demonstrates that there are historical drives, gendered/raced/classed incentives, and political consequences related to the rejection or embrace of a spiritual or a historically relational domestic geography. Neodomestic fiction that espouses an incorporation rather than a rejection of ghosts—who function in much of the fiction as "specters of history"—more clearly and consistently aligns itself with a feminist and antiracist politics. Feminism, in this sense, agrees with Gaston Bachelard's statement, "An entire past comes to dwell in a new house" (5). Neodomestic fiction finds ways to reintroduce funk—those "problematic" eruptions from the past—into American housekeeping and homemaking and to craft relational rather than oppositional bonds to the past and/or other "foreign" entities. It espouses the critical, historically grounded queer foundations that feminism demands.

Consequently, to argue that fictions that reject ghosts and fictions that embrace ghosts are simply different types of fiction fails to consider seriously the politics inscribed in these distinct spatial narratives. If scholars, like myself, who further a politics of difference, hybridity and multiplicity, want to be heard, we also need to clarify the politics of the difference that we seek. In other words, like Homi Bhabha, I believe that the critic has political responsibilities: "For the critic must attempt to fully realize, and take responsibility for, the unspoken, unrepresented pasts that haunt the historical present" (*Location* 12). Novels such as *Gardens in the Dunes*, *A Home at the End of the World*, and *Beloved* represent neodomestic fictions of strong persuasion—fictions in which a spiritual geography becomes an integral part of the narrative. DeLillo's *White Noise* and Franzen's *The Corrections* provide a more realist, hybrid presentation of spiritual geography, shifting between (feminine) sentiment and (masculine) irony. For instance, Wilder's wild ride across the highway in his tricycle at the end of *White Noise* perhaps confirms a force larger than ourselves: "[Wilder] began to pedal across the highway, mystically charged" (DeLillo 322). Or his survival may simply be dumb luck or even a testament to "lame-brained determination" (DeLillo 323). As Ann Douglas argues, "Sentimentalism provides a way to protest a power to which one has already in part capitulated" (12). The suggestive strength of masculine neodomestic novels such as DeLillo's *White Noise*, Franzen's *The Corrections*, and Ford's *Lay of the Land* lies in the possibility that their irony counters this capitulation. While my own analysis suggests that there is little to gain from embracing a forgetting of history—an analysis that other feminists share—future research in literary and cultural studies may seek other routes to answer the question: does killing such ghosts necessarily reproduce patriarchal logic?[1]

As such, my research, like neodomestic fiction itself, seeks—as Elaine Neil Orr describes in *Subject to Negotiation: Reading Feminist Criticism and American Women's Fiction*—"to contribute ... to a progressive shift in feminist discourse," a shift

> from a criticism of subversions—the dominant mode of American feminist criticism from Judith Fetterley's *The Resisting Reader* to Alicia Ostriker's poetics of theft—to a criticism of negotiations, a form of work that emerges where feminist readers and intellectuals argue for productive relations at the crossroads of difference and opposition. (Orr 2)

Rather than argue for women's subversive domestic powers—powers that merely allow Enid to punish her husband by cooking bad meals—neodomestic fiction encourages domesticity's unstable, productive differences that consider normativity's "interrelational complexity in the hope of establishing a different type of network" (Jakobsen 529). It aims to "engage" domestic norms' "complex field rather than . . . reverse or oppose the norm" (Jakobsen 518). It places in dialogue or *in negotiation* the past, present, and possible future constructions of and theories about home. It aims, as Hortense J. Spillers writes in regard to the "female social subject," to construct an *"insurgent ground"* (80; emphasis in original).

The architect Aldo van Eyck aptly describes neodomesticity's goal: "Architecture need do no more, nor should it ever do less, than assist man's [and woman's] homecoming" (qtd. in Hertzberger, Roijen-Wortmann, Stauven 65). Eyck directs us to another fundamental implication of my project—the influence that such narratives have on or reflect for lived experience. Until now, this aspect of my research has remained, for the most part, at the margins of my analysis. Census statistics, architectural design, and historical research ground my readings of the fiction, but what does the fiction suggest about lived experience? How does neodomestic fiction's architecture, to paraphrase Eyck, facilitate homecoming? I will now look more closely at what neodomestic fiction and its politics reveal about lived American domestic experience.

To Be Really Domestic
Lived American Neodomesticity

> *Domestic architecture mediates social relations, specifically those between women and men. Houses are the spatial context within which the social order is reproduced. . . . The history of American housing design indicates a gradual reduction in the gendered spaces creating, and created by, gender stratification. . . . The home is now indicative of more egalitarian gender relations.*
>
> —Daphne Spain, Gendered Spaces

There are numerous encouraging examples of lived neodomesticity, suggesting, as Daphne Spain writes, that "the home is now indicative of more egalitarian gender relations" (140). For example, the innovative program CoAbode refashions conventional domesticity's geography by connecting single mothers who are in search of other single moms to share housing; such programs help widen women's access to housing. Indicative of American domesticity's changing and unstable legal definition is the fact that gay marriages began being officially recognized in 2004 in Massachusetts and San Francisco, albeit they were also immediately contested. Also apropos of Spain's conclusions about contemporary American housing design is the fact that today's American women are fastening around their waists the traditionally masculine tool belt more than ever before.

American Demographics reports that women currently favor home improvement projects over shopping or cooking as their preferred leisure activity (Gallop-Goodman 14). Additionally, according to Home Improvement Research Institute's product purchase tracking study, "Women's fix-it-yourself purchases jumped from 32 percent in 1997 to 37.6 percent in 1999" (Gallop-Goodman 14). The percentages quantify changes in America's domestic arrangements. Home improvement and do-it-yourself projects, traditionally men's forte, now find women their fastest growing market, indicating that American (heterosexual) homemaking is undergoing fundamental changes.

Additionally, the term "metrosexual" has emerged to revise our understanding of men who engage in traditionally feminine activities like shopping and paying careful attention to grooming.[2] The term attempts to craft a positive word for a "feminine male." According to the *Oxford English Dictionary*, the term "metrosexual" refers to "a man (esp. a heterosexual man) whose lifestyle, spending habits and concern for personal appearance are likened to those typical of a fashionable, urban, homosexual man" (def. A). Mark Simpson coined the term in 1994, according to the online dictionary *The Word Spy*, to refer to a "gay, straight or bisexual" man who is "not afraid to embrace his feminine side" ("Metrosexual"). While it is unclear what effects the metrosexual has had, if any, on domestic relationships, it has clearly influenced the marketplace. Jean-Marc Carriol, director of the fashion company Trimex, goes so far as to suggest that feminism directly brought about this change for men: "The feminist movement has been the biggest contributor to the men's market since it has developed.... The success of that push has fundamentally altered the way men and women interact within the workplace. Appearance and grooming are really important" (qtd. in "Rise of the Metrosexual"). Fashion is an opening, though clearly not an end point, for feminist intervention. As Janet R. Jakobsen points out, even "non-normative" terms like "*lesbian* . . . can become a specific regime of the normal" (521; emphasis in original). The metrosexual challenges male heterosexual norms evens as it affirms norms scripted for homosexual men and a feminized American consumer culture.

Material spaces also engage the norm of the single family, privately owned home while actualizing new architectures. The Rural Studio, Auburn

University's community architecture program founded by the late Samuel Mockbee, provides one of, if not *the* best, material examples of neodomestic architectural standards.³ The Rural Studio asks its students

> to cross the threshold of misconceived opinions to create/design/build and to allow students to put their educational values to work as citizens of a community. The Rural Studio seeks solutions to the needs of the community within the community's own context, not from outside it. Abstract ideas based upon knowledge and study are transformed into workable solutions forged by real human contact, personal realization, and a gained appreciation for the culture. ("Mission")

As the mission statement begins to explain, the Rural Studio seeks to provide livable, sustainable designs for low-income families and communities. The buildings use local and unique materials to keep economic and environmental costs low (by making houses out of recycled carpet tiles and hay bales, for example). Recently, they have also begun to recycle buildings for new purposes. At the same time that they aim to keep initial construction and long-term maintenance costs low, the Rural Studio's designs also seek "to raise the spirits of the rural poor through the creation of homes and community facilities that aspired to the same set of architectural ideals and virtues as those buildings which have substantial budgets and prosperous clientele" (King 50; 52). For example, one particular challenge that the Rural Studio tackles is the design and building of "20K" homes, or dwellings whose materials and labor cost no more than twenty thousand dollars.

The Rural Studio's attention to smaller living and community spaces, local materials, economic and environmental sustainability, and vernacular architecture clarifies its differences from the extreme dream homes and the portrayal of the American dream in renovation shows like *Extreme Makeover: Home Edition* and *This Old House*.⁴ Additionally, while the Rural Studio has enjoyed its share of the media limelight, Mockbee advised architects to "help those who aren't likely to help you in return, and do so even if nobody is watching!" (qtd. in Polter 42). Krista Tippett's radio show, *Speaking of Faith*, featured a segment on the Rural Studio, "Rural Studio: An Architecture of Decency." The segment explores the material and spiritual ways that Rural Studio designs affect their communities. The Rural Studio emphasizes (like the neodomestic fiction I have defined and analyzed) the sense of cultural history embedded in the local geography, particularly the history of slavery. Mockbee, in fact, hoped that the Rural Studio would help complete the unfinished reconstruction of the South.⁵

Not Living the American Dream
Failures to Change

As suggestive as these changes are for how neodomesticity emerges within lived experience, there are also problematic aspects to these popular hybrid constructions. Who has access to the egalitarian homes Spain describes and to the neodomestic ideology explored in this book? More specifically, to what extent is the "metrosexual" man the same person packaged in a different, albeit Armani, outfit? Carriol's suggestion that feminism has brought fashion to men carries dubious egalitarian politics. For example, attention to grooming and vanity perpetuate a youth- and body-obsessive culture that feminism has long fought against. Furthermore, while the term "metrosexual" increases attention to men's "lifestyles," it does not dramatically or explicitly challenge the unequal division of domestic labor. The metrosexual does not, for good or bad, foster an interest in laundry, childcare, or eldercare. Fundamental feminine domestic roles (as caretakers and house cleaners) do not enjoy this same "sexy" hybridity, which is primarily available to middle- and upper-class single or childless men.[6] Until real changes occur in the hours that men and women devote to domestic labor, the home will remain women's special domain.

Women's embrace of do-it-yourself projects also carries as much predicament as promise. One positive aspect of this trend is its reflection and encouragement of women's independence and confidence. Barbara's Way markets their Barbara K! line of tools, for example, as "a comprehensive lifestyle brand whose mission is to provide solutions for women through innovative products that help eliminate the fear factor in areas where women may lack confidence or knowledge." Companies like Barbara's Way and Tomboy Tools market tools and do-it-yourself services that are designed for women. Some of the tools offer colors intended to appeal to female consumers as well as grips and other features designed to fit women's smaller hands; some work gloves, for example, "accommodate long fingernails" (McCann G07).

These tools for women suggest more about the enforcement of gender differences and an anxiety about women taking on these new roles than they suggest about a fulfillment of women's need for speciality tools. For instance, Herbert G. McCann reports the "Wisconsin-based RotoZip Tool Corp. introduced the Solaris, a bright red power saw, a smaller version of the company's original black model" (G07). According to the company's spokeswoman, "many women found the original too big and heavy. The new model is one pound lighter and has less power, which gives the user more control" (McCann G07). Tools designed for gender differences in hand size or upper body strength hold merit, but companies seemingly ignore the fact that men will also benefit from a wider range of tool sizes.

Consumer remarks about these products designed for women confirm deeply entrenched ideas about femininity, masculinity, home improvement, and domestic roles. For example, one woman commented that she was not sure if she would buy power tools, even if they were designed for women, because "a lot of men won't let you use it. They say it's too dangerous" (qtd. in McCann G07). Another woman, while shopping with her husband for "drywall, flooring and a book on wiring" remarked that "she wasn't sure about the tools either, especially if they were more expensive. 'As a woman, I'd probably be more likely to adapt to what he wants. . . . It's true, I'm more used to adapting'" (McCann G07). The women's remarks suggest the appearance of these products and services does not necessarily indicate radical changes in gender roles. Whether a marketing trick or an attempt to recognize that "universal" tools do not fit the needs of all, these tools and services designed for women do not clearly measure up to more egalitarian gender roles.

Building companies' marketing to single women also confirms that the more things change on the domestic front, the more they stay the same. Julie V. Iovine, for example, describes an advertisement produced by a Colorado builder that targets single female homebuyers. The advertisement's visual and verbal rhetoric, which features a young woman and her dog, recycles a familiar fairy tale, *Cinderella*. According to Iovine, "The message is clear: Why wait for your prince to come? You can afford a home now—and 'Woof! woof!' surely beats a husbandly whine" (3). Owens Corning also reuses the fairy tale *Sleeping Beauty* to market its products: the "Chicago-based manufacturer of building materials, introduced a television ad campaign called 'Siding Beauty' in which a damsel awakens after 100 years to find that the vinyl siding covering her palace has outlasted them all. Subliminal message: Men may come and go, but good siding is hard to find" (Iovine 3).

These advertisements suggest that even as women take on different roles, there are clear attempts to recontain and repackage these changes in old narratives. Conversely, the advertisements' humor suggests that they consciously recycle the old narratives to appeal to a new generation of women who increasingly do not wait until after marriage to buy a home: "Thanks to delayed marriages, profitable careers, higher divorce rates and longer lives, the number of women living alone has increased by more than a third in the past 15 years" (Iovine 3). Along these lines, another recent trend involves older women who are increasingly planning their retirement with their female friends: "This friends-helping-friends model for aging is gaining momentum among single, widowed or divorced women of a certain age.

The census does not tabulate households like these, and experts say it would be too early to see large numbers of older women living with friends, since few baby boomers, born from 1946 to 1964, have retired yet. But sociologists and demographers say the interest is growing" (Gross A). What discourages older single men from developing similar strategies? Men clearly also have much to gain in the revision and recycling of domestic roles, but as the Franzen Affair suggests, the troubling of domestic masculinity's norms releases powerful anxieties.

Therefore, while the twentieth and twenty-first century's "new normal" indicates some transformations in men's and women's roles and domestic settings, other domestic statistics encourage considerably less optimism about the emergence and establishment of more egalitarian domestic relations. For example, where male householders have a median net worth of $16,346 ($7,375 excluding home equity), female householders have a median net worth of $14,949 ($4,400 excluding home equity) (Davern and Fisher xvi). Such numbers indicate that women rely more on their homes for economic security than their male counterparts do: home equity composes about 70 percent of women's median net worth, where home equity comprises about 50 percent of men's median net worth. And, while neither married households nor female householders experienced a significant change in household net worth between 1993 and 1995, the median net worth of male householders rose from $14,219 to $16,346 during this same period (Davern and Fisher xvi). Men continue to hold distinct economic advantages over women. It follows, therefore, that gay male households would be better off financially than lesbian households. Gentrification's association with the gay male community furthers this hypothesis. However, more data collection and research needs to be done on gay households and homemaking.[7]

One positive aspect of America's love affair with the single-family, detached home is the fact that the "abundant supply [of privately owned housing stock] makes it relatively easier for American families to adjust their housing circumstances to changes in needs than is true of most European countries with larger social housing sectors" (Stegman 86). However, as we have seen played out in the fiction, the questions of access and material impact become especially significant when one considers homeownership differences among a range of gender, class, and racial groups. Black and Hispanic homeowners remain economically disadvantaged. And those individuals and families who rent are truly left out in the cold—especially when one considers that homes account for an average of 44 percent of household wealth (Luckett 1). Thus, masculine domestic fiction's focus on property and economics remains an important area of inquiry. Fiction addressing homelessness, such as Marge Piercy's *Longings of Women* (1994), Nami Mun's *Miles from Nowhere* (2009), and Helena María Viramontes's *Their Dogs Came with Them* (2007), and fiction addressing migrant families, such as Helena María Viramontes's *Under the Feet of Jesus* (1995), also contribute to the widening awareness and understanding of the domestic sphere's uneven geographic development.

Extreme Makeover
Sponsoring Faith in the Bankrupt American Dream

The persistent problem from the nineteenth to the twenty-first century with the popularization of a limited vision of American model domesticity is that such popularizations effectively impede alternative models from gaining larger visibility. In the twenty-first century, the American dream's corporate sponsorship in the popular ABC television program *Extreme Makeover: Home Edition* powerfully illustrates the amount of capital needed to keep the American dream alive in the public sphere. The weekly reality program chronicles the renovation of a needy family's home. In most episodes, the old residence is demolished and the crew has only a week to build the family an entirely new, fully furnished and landscaped home. The experience of watching *Extreme Makeover* teaches viewers what the model home looks like in its extreme and resuscitates a narrow vision of the American dream in the face of harsh ownership realities and increased obstacles in the road to homeownership.

While its title does not explicitly invoke a nationalistic focus, *Extreme Makeover*'s storyline frequently uses the American myth of exceptionalism. This familiar European-based story places America as a New World where immigrants find a wealth of opportunities unavailable elsewhere, including private home ownership and upward mobility. In season 3, episode 25, of *Extreme Makeover*, for example, a family of immigrants—the Peter family—encounters troubles that are juxtaposed with the familiar narrative that hard work will bring success in the United States, regardless of religion or social status. This aspect of the American dream, the host Ty Pennington admits in this episode, is what he loves most about America. Pennington's claim, however, exists in tension with the fact that all the families featured in *Extreme Makeover* are hard working and yet still have fallen on hard times that merit extreme measures.

The repressed subtext is that hard work alone is often not enough to keep or maintain your own home. While American exceptionalism, especially regarding homeownership, remains a central part of our contemporary American identity, "the relative advantage of the New World has declined: ownership levels are now much the same in North America and Britain" (Harris and Hamnett 184). Although the research conducted by geographers Richard Harris and Chris Hamnett does not consider the relative advantages for modern non-European or non-first-world immigrants, the material advantages that lead to more opportunities in the New World are largely gone: we no longer enjoy the "higher incomes, abundant land, and early suburban growth, [that] gave working families a real economic advantage in the New World" in the late nineteenth century (Harris and Hamnett 185).[8] Not surprisingly, given this context, the show frames the families' problems as a kind of "bad luck."

Therefore, the Peter family is both representative of the American dream and unique because the family's "special" circumstances interrupted the "normal" course of achieving the dream. *Extreme Makeover*'s Web site explains that this poor Hindu family from Guyana falls just short of "achieving the American dream, when tragedy struck" ("Peter Family"). Had the house not caught fire, the family would have been okay. The program, furthermore, reinforces and capitalizes on the American dream by condensing its achievement into a seven-day miracle makeover.

The critics agree that *Extreme Makeover* is more than just another reality show: it is a miracle that creates a new world for a family in seven days. Unlike God, though, the staff and volunteers usually need the *full* seven days to complete the project. *Extreme Makeover* also employs Christian-style rhetoric and philanthropy to elevate its goals. Ann Oldenburg, writing for *USA Today*, emphasizes the program's religious power. She writes, "What may have seemed at first to be an updated version of *This Old House* has become a spiritual happening, more revival meeting than TV taping. With its charitable sensibilities and ability to mobilize entire communities with a single episode, *EM: HE* is setting a standard for a new genre: Good Samaritan television" (E1). Stephen Johnson, who received an *Extreme Makeover* house, tellingly remarks, "It was a gift from God and ABC" (qtd. in Oldenburg E1). While a few families express concerns about construction practices and their ability to pay taxes and upkeep costs after appearing on the show, almost all of the families profusely thank the volunteers and businesses who helped. Many businesses, furthermore, continue to volunteer their services and supplies. *Extreme Makeover* masks the corporate privatization of the American dream by invoking Christian charity as a key element to the American dream's achievement.

Notably, *Extreme Makeover* airs on Sunday evenings. While not overtly

Pentecostal, the program's religious "spiritual" aspects explicitly play into the show's format. Julie Polter, a writer for *Sojourners Magazine*, observes, "I find something almost biblical in the abundance the crew pours out on families and the genuine delight they appear to take in bringing some fantasy and lushness into modest spaces" (41). In one episode, for example, not one but *two* subzero refrigerators outfit a gourmet kitchen to help support a mother's burgeoning catering business. The gifts keep coming in every episode in the form of new vehicles, family entertainment and workout rooms, and lavish, if not outlandish, decors, courtesy of *Extreme Makeover* and Sears (as well as other national and local sponsors). This commercialized spiritual geography contrasts with the historically and culturally grounded spiritual geographies that are central to many neodomestic novels.

The numerous material gifts overwhelm the family members and the audience. In some cases, the families are literally overwhelmed—teasers for the program frequently play and replay family members ecstatically collapsing on the ground when they see their new home for the first time. Hands are thrown in the air and clasped in prayer. The recipients invoke God. In the words of the Koepke family, "You are all a blessing from God." The hosts graciously give the new home to the family, receive their thanks, and share hugs and tears. The show's format emphasizes the extreme contrasts with "before" images juxtaposed against the dramatic new results. And, to ensure that the results are dramatic, the homes selected for the program are never larger than two thousand square feet. Once lost, but then found by *Extreme Makeover*, the participants are truly saved. Thus, (Christian) faith legitimizes and elevates the volunteers' call to action, and families attest that their faith has been rewarded through their appearance on the program.

Like the nineteenth-century texts that precede it, *Extreme Makeover* highlights society's duty to help the needy. In fact, Beecher and Stowe's chapter entitled the "Homeless, Helpless, and Vicious" could very well be a subtitle for *Extreme Makeover*. A leaked March 2006 memo written by Charisse Simonian, *Extreme Makeover*'s director for family casting, acknowledges the show's emphasis on sensational tragedy. The memo, sent to several ABC affiliates, contains a specific "wish list" of diseases and tragedies that *Extreme Makeover* would like to feature, including families with members who have Down syndrome, skin cancer, muscular dystrophy, or amyotrophic lateral sclerosis (Simonian). The memo also expresses interest in families who have lost children to a drunken driving accident and families who have been victims of hate crimes (Simonian). The memo placed the show's sentimental politics under close scrutiny, at least for a few days. The mainstream media quickly picked up the story; CNN's *Showbiz Tonight*, for example, featured an interview with Tom Forman, executive producer of *Extreme Makeover*, and Andrew Goldberg from *The Smoking Gun*, the Web site that initially published the leaked memo. Forman defended the memo and emphasized the program's goal of helping people. Goldberg reminded viewers that reality television "looks to exploit people in order to commercialize people's woe in order to sell ads and make money" (*Showbiz Tonight*). The incident raised questions about the show's primary motivation: does it aim to help people or to market products?

Extreme Makeover piques audience interest by invoking foundational American myths, featuring sensational family tragedies, and subconsciously playing on our fears of homelessness. After all, stuck families seeking a way out of their American nightmares are increasingly more the norm than the exception. The suspense and relief that we participate in as viewers hits home during a time of record foreclosures and falling home prices. *Extreme Makeover* provides a fantasy of domestic security for our post-9/11, post-Katrina, and credit card debt-infused age.

Not all viewers and reviewers of *Extreme Makeover* celebrate the program's philanthropy. Paul Farhi points out that the "designers and builders call constant attention to their own act of charity, as if the whole exercise were really about enhancing their self-esteem" (C1). Farhi goes on to quote host Ty Pennington and to provide context for Pennington's remark: "'It's been said a million times—"it's better to give than to receive"—but I never thought about that more than I did this week.' . . . Amid sad piano music, another crew member adds, 'They [the featured family] didn't have anyone to turn to, and that's why we're here'" (C1). Farhi sarcastically adds his reading of *Extreme Makeover*'s presentation of their purpose, "Oh, thank you, kindly millionaires at ABC. Thank you" (C1). Farhi's remarks emphasize that America's streets may no longer be paved with gold (if they ever were); the United States is now a country where *Oprah*, *Extreme Makeover*, and any number of media outlets and corporations sponsor a few American dreams.

Also like its white nineteenth-century predecessors, *Extreme Makeover* privileges middle-class heterosexual whiteness. For example, while *Extreme Makeover* has featured a variety of blended, single-parent, multiethnic, and multigenerational families, the show has yet to feature an openly gay parent.[9] When the program came under fire from gay rights groups for allowing the antigay, Christian group Focus on the Family to sponsor an episode aired on October 2, 2005, "ABC denied any bias and said it would 'absolutely' consider featuring a gay family on the show" (Allen 18). The roots of *Extreme Makeover*'s conservative vision of the American dream and the origins of its philanthropic hypermaterialism that keeps the dream alive can be found in this exclusionary but powerfully conservative vision of the model home.

Extreme Makeover reveals how the achievement of the American dream remains tied to a conservative, middle-class whiteness. A family's "uncivilized" dwelling becomes a tasteful dream home. While the children in *Extreme Makeover* often receive extravagantly themed rooms—designed with the individual interests and dreams of each child in mind—the living areas and master bedroom uniformly conform to mainstream notions of "good taste." The new landscaping lacks such folksy touches as an old tire filled with dirt to create a raised flowerbed. The interiors include new furnishings of largely classic and contemporary design—no mirrored headboards, hula girl lamps, or velvet artwork. Valuing or representing ethnic diversity becomes a design challenge. Ethnic touches, such as those designed for the Native American Piestewa family, reflect "a decorator's delight . . . if it can be done in time" ("About the Show").[10] Notably absent are liquor cabinets, wine cellars, and ashtrays, as apparently all family members are nondrinkers and nonsmokers. The viewers, at least, never see a family member drink or light up. Former addicts, however, are allowed to grace the screen (Sadie Holmes from season 3, episode 21, for example).

In fact, one of the tips included in the show's application packet suggests that family members not chew gum while taping their application video (*Extreme Makeover* 19). Editors need to select tape that will encourage the audience to sympathize with a family's plight. If families smack gum or display other such "distasteful" habits, the editors' task becomes more difficult. To put it bluntly, while these families may be poor or while they may have fallen on hard times, they should not exhibit "trashy" or "low-class" habits or tastes. Rather than overtly claiming that the designers civilize the needy homeowners, the program reverses this rhetoric by explicitly emphasizing how the family makes the volunteers more human. When we take into account the burdens associated with the gifts, we see that the half-million-dollar homes help the sponsors and perhaps even the volunteers more than the recipients.

Perhaps the vernacular architecture significant to projects like Auburn University's Rural Studio or the green building practices that create both sustainable and ecofriendly structures are not regularly implemented in *Extreme Makeover* because they would eat into too much of the seven-day time limit. But this seems unlikely considering all of the other technological innovations and design elements each home includes. While more recent episodes often emphasize green options, any focus on a real reduction in size and consumption goes against *Extreme Makeover*'s formula of more is better—even when the resources to support the excess are not readily available. *Extreme Makeover* replaces Beecher and Stowe's call for thrift with a call for extreme excess.

As the economic downturn plays out, it will be interesting to see whether the program adjusts its rhetoric and practices, whether its popularity continues because of its appeal to fantasy and sentiment, or whether the show's sponsors and viewers withdraw support. For our current moment—just as in the late nineteenth century—building a handful of lavish homes certainly does not address America's housing crisis. Little wonder that *Extreme Makeover* receives more than fifteen thousand applications each week ("FAQ" 80). In this light, both *Extreme Makeover* and neodomestic fiction ultimately fail us. We have yet to popularize the domestic models that truly fulfill this extreme need and live up to the promise of the American dream.[11]

Historian Andrew Wiese celebrates the positive changes in suburban space for African Americans during the course of the twentieth century. However, he concludes his history, *Places of Their Own: African American Suburbanization in the Twentieth Century*, on a somber note, emphasizing "the persistence of racial inequality" and the challenges that disenfranchised populations still have to overcome:

> As Nobel laureate Toni Morrison has remarked, a central issue facing African Americans in the modern United States is how to overcome racism without losing or denying racial identity, how to build a 'race-specific yet non-racist home' from the building materials of a race-troubled society. For black suburbanites, this challenge was always more than figurative. In making places of their own in the margins of the city, they negotiated not only the hurdles of building homes and communities, but lines of color, class, and power embedded in the world around them. (Wiese 292)

Neodomestic fiction like Morrison's *Paradise* interrogates exactly these questions. While the fiction does not necessarily provide solutions or answers to these issues, it demonstrates the advantages of relational spatial politics and helps us frame alternatives to the conventional model home within the arguably more manageable space of the novel.

Neodomestic fiction carves out spaces for alternative domestic geographies that both reflect and theorize lived realities. Americans' lived domestic experiences provide clear material evidence—if there was any doubt in the first place—that sexism, classism, and racism remain lodged in the domestic geography of American culture. In other words, not everyone lives within and benefits from the contemporary egalitarian homes that Daphne Spain praises and from which she draws her conclusions. Masculine domestic fiction significantly emphasizes this frequently overlooked aspect of the American dream. Additionally, feminine domestic fiction frequently emphasizes that the material house is only part of the equation. Like the dwellings designed and built by the Rural Studio, neodomestic fiction provides a "vernacular architecture" engaged in "dreaming, moving forward and beyond the limits and confines of fixed locations" (hooks, "Black Vernacular" 400).

A Woman's Work Is Never Done
Conclusions and Remaining Chores

Women—from Jane Addams, who devoted her life to Hull-House, to Jane Jacobs, who reconceptualized how we view the city—are frequently at the forefront of alternative housing initiatives.[12] My analysis of feminine and masculine (neo)domestic fiction reflects this trend as well. Women's leadership in this area is not surprising given that women's identities are still more strongly associated with the home, that their time investment in the home tends to exceed that of men, and that their economic well-being is more fully invested in their homes. A focus on instability and hybridity alone does not mark radical changes in cultures and everyday domestic space. Domestic fiction may be experiencing another renaissance, but we are far from a domestic revolution. Neodomestic fiction and American lived experience suggest that feminist politics still have much to do with home.

Thus, this study indicates that the long view is necessary. "Careful and effective reversals" take steps forward as well as steps back (Martin and Mohanty 306). Changes in the dominant, conventional politics of home—whatever "foreign" bodies it attempts to incorporate or exclude—come slowly. Unlike the popular home makeover show *Trading Spaces* (aired on the Learning Channel), where dramatic changes are achieved in a matter of days (and on a limited budget!), domestic fiction and culture cannot be renovated over the course of a few novels, even with expert designers such as Toni Morrison executing the task. Therefore, the chores ahead for domestic scholarship include more analysis of novels engaged in redesigning the home as well as those engaged in conventional constructions. As the housing crisis and foreign investment in American real estate continues to develop, writers will also continue to craft art that reflects and attempts to shape the shifting geography of the American dream.

Furthermore, remapping American domesticity involves the critics as much as the literature and culture. The novels surveyed here emphasize that the study of domestic fiction should occupy a more central position in American literary history. While a spatial redefinition of the genre more readily includes a range of writers and homes, this remapping of the genre does not eliminate domesticity's taint within critical spheres. Hawthorne's oft-repeated curse against such fiction continues to set the tone for its critical analysis. Mary Kelley points out in "The Sentimentalists: Promise and Betrayal of Home" how "Leslie Fiedler's ridicule of 'the purely commercial purveyors of domestic sentiments'" extends Hawthorne's complaint into the twentieth century (434). The now infamous remarks made by Jonathan Franzen about Oprah's selection of *The Corrections* for her book club further suggests that the labels "women's fiction" and "domestic fiction" continue to pack a negative punch. As long as domestic fiction continues to occupy territory outside the realm of serious literature and scholarship, our criticism normalizes women's marginality and men's dearth of domestic responsibility.

While scholars have made some progress in complicating the "separate spheres," such divisions still seem to function in the production of American literary histories. Dana Heller, for example, explains how men's writing about domesticity occupies a separate sphere within American literary history:

> Such irony is compounded by the recognition that a reification of the American literary tradition has occurred, in this century, largely in accord with a critical tendency—most impressively demonstrated by Eric Sundquist's *Home as Found*, Richard Chase's *The American Novel and Its Tradition*, and Leslie Fielder's *Love and Death in the American Novel*—to concentrate on the male American writer's ambiguous, yet powerfully romantic attachments to this domestic space and the concept of origin. (226)

Neodomestic fiction challenges us to revise such gendered mapping of American domesticity. As projects like the Rural Studio indicate, this remapping need not be confined to literature. We can find instructive examples in other art forms, including the visual arts.

Photographer and multimedia artist Clarissa Sligh in particular interrogates what constitutes normative gendered and raced family roles and domestic space.[13] Her book *What's Happening with Momma* (1987), for example, is shaped like a house. Lisa Gail Collins describes another series, *Reading Dick and Jane with Me*, as a project that "captures the pain and contradiction of poor African American children internalizing the American Dream" (50). Sligh's work addresses domestic violence, incest, and colonialism and is also deeply engaged in the relationships between the present and the past: "From the perspective of the artist as participant-observer, Sligh considers the voices of the past and uses them to create imagery that is both provocative and historically introspective" (Willis 11). Collins goes on to explain that Sligh's approach

> critique[s] the ideal. She incorporates pictures from her own family albums and school yearbooks to dramatize the gap between the world represented by watercolor illustrations in the [Dick and Jane] primers and the one represented in her black and white photographs. Drawing from her own photographic archive, she sets the mythic vision of the reader against the material reality of the children who lived in her neighborhood and attended her segregated school. (50)

Her neodomestic visual images (which often incorporate text) blur the lines between the past and the present as well as the personal and the universal, questioning and repositioning cultural norms and taboos.

Her series *The Men* examines men's relationship to the domestic sphere and masculinity. The domestic masculinity in *The Men* provides a visual representation of what neodomestic fiction such as Nava's *Rag and Bone* accomplishes. For example, *Ron Ironing, Dallas, Texas, 1986*, which serves as the cover image for the book, provides an instructive visual image. In the portrait the man is barefoot and ironing in a garage or some other space full of bicycles. Three bicycles appear in the background; two hang on the wall and one stands just behind the subject—on the right side of the image—in front of what appears to be a metal filing cabinet. A closed window also appears in the background. The subject is placed in the center of a triangle produced by the right and left walls and the length of the ironing board. The crossed ironing board's legs reproduce the triangle shape. The circles (repeated with the bikes' wheels) and the window's rectangle fill out the composition's visual depth and interest.

The photograph is particularly interesting for the ways it juxtaposes the stereotypically feminine (completing domestic chores while barefoot, if not pregnant) and the stereotypically masculine (working in a garage among symbols of athleticism). The feminine chore transforms the masculine space and vice versa. Rather than reinforce gender norms, the image blurs them. The subject's steadfast gaze challenges the viewer to see him as an embodiment of a nonanxious, domestic masculinity. The other images in this series similarly ask the viewer to engage with images that destabilize our conventional understandings of masculinity and femininity. Sligh's oeuvre, like neodomestic fiction, "is an ongoing investigation and reinterpretation of our perceptions of normality and the role of the individual within the various frameworks that shape her or him, such as the family, society, one's gender group, and one's ethnicity" (Williams 3).

Thus, the work ahead will continue Biddy Martin and Chandra Mohanty's project of determining "What's Home Got to Do with It?" Undoubtedly, the heart of such inquiries will require a discussion about the relationships among power, place, and history. Jane Tompkins writes that "domestic fiction is preoccupied, even obsessed with the nature of power" (160). My own work confirms her statement. Determining the various incarnations and meanings of domestic power constitutes the territory ahead.

WHILE ENGAGED in the process of remapping the study of domestic fiction, I was reminded of how my brother teased me in high school after I became president of my high school's local chapter of the Future Homemakers of America. He poked fun that I was actually leading the charge of the Future Home-Wreckers of America. As much as it pains me to admit, but in the best possible ways, I hope this project proves that he was right. From the model's fragments may we continue to seek ways to recycle ecologically and socially viable homes and homemaking practices. We have only begun to scour the range of America's domestic geographies.

Appendix

Major Neodomestic Authors and Novels—Chronological Order

Marilynne Robinson's *Housekeeping* (1981)
Joy Williams's *Breaking and Entering* (1981)
John Crowley's *Little, Big* (1981)
John Edgar Wideman's Homewood trilogy:
    Damballah (1981)
    Sent for You Yesterday (1981)
    Hiding Place (1983)
Sandra Cisneros's *The House on Mango Street* (1984)
Don DeLillo's *White Noise* (1984)
Gloria Naylor's *Linden Hills* (1985)
Richard Ford's *The Sportswriter* (1986)
Toni Morrison's *Beloved* (1987)
Gloria Naylor's *Mama Day* (1988)
Michael Cunningham's *A Home at the End of the World* (1990)
Anne Tyler's *Saint Maybe* (1991)
Dorothy Allison's *Bastard Out of Carolina* (1992)
Cristina Garcia's *Dreaming in Cuban* (1992)
Toni Morrison's *Jazz* (1992)
Marge Piercy's *The Longings of Women* (1994)
Richard Ford's *Independence Day* (1995)
Louise Erdrich's *Tales of Burning Love* (1996)
Lan Cao's *Monkey Bridge* (1997)
Toni Morrison's *Paradise* (1997)
Barbara Kingsolver's *The Poisonwood Bible* (1998)
Danzy Senna's *Caucasia* (1998)
Andre Dubus III's *House of Sand and Fog* (1999)
Loida Maritza Pérez's *Geographies of Home* (1999)

Leslie Marmon Silko's *Gardens in the Dunes* (1999)
Chang-rae Lee's *A Gesture Life* (1999)
Mark Z. Danielewski's *House of Leaves* (2000)
Ernesto Quiñonez's *Bodega Dreams* (2000)
Jonathan Franzen's *The Corrections* (2001)
Richard Russo's *Empire Falls* (2001)
Michael Nava's *Rag and Bone* (2001)
Toni Morrison's *Love* (2003)
Jane Smiley's *Good Faith* (2003)
Chang-rae Lee's *Aloft* (2004)
Richard Ford's *The Lay of the Land* (2006)
Richard Russo's *Bridge of Sighs* (2007)
Helen María Viramontes's *Their Dogs Came with Them* (2007)
Randa Jarrar's *A Map of Home* (2008)
Marilynne Robinson's *Home* (2008)
Toni Morrison's *A Mercy* (2008)
Joseph O'Neill's *Netherland* (2008)
Nami Mun's *Miles from Nowhere* (2009)
Eric Puchner's *Model Home* (2010)
Gabrielle Zevin's *The Hole We're In* (2010)

Notes

Introduction

1. In geography, the terms "space" and "place" have distinct histories. See their respective entries in *A Feminist Glossary of Human Geography* for a brief overview of the various ways in which these terms are used and debated in geographic literature. Unless otherwise noted, I use "place" and "space" relatively interchangeably, though "place" tends to refer to a more specific location; for example, gendered, raced, and classed space may be used to describe the home ("place"). As this and the next chapter outline in greater detail, my use of these terms is informed by feminist geography that understands place as relational and space as inextricable from time. See Doreen Massey's *Space, Place, and Gender* for arguments against place's bound nature and discussions of space's relationship with time and gender.

2. For a reconsideration of Armstrong's arguments, see Leila Silvana May, "The Strong-Arming of Desire: A Reconsideration of Nancy Armstrong's *Desire and Domestic Fiction*."

3. I explore this relationship in greater detail in my article, "Renovating *The American Woman's Home*: American Domesticity in *Extreme Makeover: Home Edition*."

4. I would like to thank an anonymous reader for helping me identify many of the counterhegemonic examples from the nineteenth century.

5. Rethinking nineteenth-century texts' domestic politics constitutes a growing and exciting field of scholarship. For example, Elizabeth Moss's *Domestic Novelists in the Old South: Defenders of Southern Culture* (1992) discusses the "ideological warfare" produced by southern women writers in the nineteenth century. *The Cambridge Companion to Nineteenth-Century American Women's Writing* (2001), edited by Dale M. Bauer and Philip Gould, provides an overview of recent (re)appraisals of nineteenth-century American women's writing. Recent scholarship by Claudia Tate, Lora Romero, and Amy Kaplan read alongside earlier work by Susan K. Harris, Nina Baym, and Judith Fetterley were most influential in my characterization and understanding of nineteenth-century domesticity.

6. Recent modernist studies of domesticity and domestic fiction include Guy Reynolds, "Re-making the Home, 1909–33" and "Modernist Geographies," in *Twentieth-*

Century American Women's Fiction: A Critical Introduction (1999); Thomas Foster, *Transformations of Domesticity in Modern Women's Writing: Homelessness at Home* (2002); Jennifer Haytock, *At Home, At War: Domesticity and World War I in American Literature* (2003); Betsy Klimasmith, *At Home in the City: Urban Domesticity in American Literature and Culture, 1850–1930* (2005); and Susan Edmunds, *Grotesque Relations: Modernist Domestic Fiction and the U.S. Welfare State* (2008).

7. While I am the first to redefine the genre primarily according to its spatial politics, I am not the first scholar to move the study of domestic fiction into the twentieth century. For further reading on contemporary American domestic fiction, consult Valerie Sweeney Prince, *Burnin' Down the House: Home in African American Literature*; Robert Beuka, *SuburbiaNation: Reading Suburban Landscape in Twentieth-Century American Fiction and Film*; Marilyn R. Chandler, *Dwelling in the Text: Houses in American Fiction*; Jeannette Batz Cooperman, *The Broom Closet: Secret Meanings of Domesticity in Postfeminist Novels by Louise Erdrich, Mary Gordon, Toni Morrison, Marge Piercy, Jane Smiley, and Amy Tan*; Catherine Jurca, *White Diaspora: The Suburb and the Twentieth-Century American Novel*; Geoffrey Kain, ed., *Ideas of Home: Literature of Asian Migration*; Helen Fiddyment Levy, *Fiction of the Home Place: Jewett, Cather, Glasgow, Porter, Welty, and Naylor*; Ann Romines, *The Home Plot: Women, Writing and Domestic Ritual*; Roberta Rubenstein, *Home Matters: Longing and Belonging, Nostalgia and Mourning in Women's Fiction*; and Catherine Wiley and Fiona R. Barnes, eds., *Homemaking: Women Writers and the Politics and Poetics of Home*.

While not focused on the contemporary American domestic novel specifically, Sara Blair's "Cultural Geography and the Place of the Literary" and Rosemary Marangoly George's *The Politics of Home: Postcolonial Relocations and Twentieth-Century Fiction*, as well as her edited collection, *Burning Down the House: Recycling Domesticity*, influenced my research and approach to contemporary domestic fiction.

8. I first encountered the phrase "spatial narrative" in Mary Pat Brady's analysis of Chicana literature, *Extinct Lands, Temporal Geographies*.

9. For a more detailed introduction to reading space as a social process, see David Harvey, *Justice, Nature and the Geography of Difference*, especially pages 316–24.

10. This idea—that a place can shape its inhabitants as much as inhabitants can shape a place—should be distinguished from nineteenth-century theories of architectural determinism, which emphasize a "top down" power hierarchy. Proponents of architectural determinism worried about the ways that places, especially urban places, could shape inhabitants. Architectural determinists did not explore the potential of the inhabitants to influence the spaces in which they lived and worked.

11. The post–September 11 "credit-card patriotism" has undergone some analysis (Solomon 43). Theda Skocpol, for instance, reminds us of the context and content of the Bush administration's "managerial coordination" after September 11:

> President Bush did not launch any big new civic effort [after 9/11], such as mandatory national service for young Americans. Instead, for weeks after 9/11, his most prominent appeals were commercial rather than civic. The Travel Industry Association of America estimated that two-thirds of Americans saw the President starring in a television advertisement calling for people to express "courage" by taking more trips. And the president repeatedly asked people to go shopping to stimulate the economy.

While distinct from the civic responsibilities demanded of, for example, the World War I and II eras, these domestic-commercial attitudes have a long history, at least as long and deep as nineteenth-century American domesticity. For instance, Ellen's mother in *The Wide, Wide World* takes her daughter shopping to prepare her for their tragic separation. The exquisite details of the shopping trips with her mother allow the reader to enjoy vicariously the successful procurement of new goods. When Ellen shops by herself, as is the case when Ellen looks for muslin, the reader experiences the unease associated with a young girl shopping alone in the masculine public sphere (Warner 44–52). While Catharine E. Beecher promoted thrift, she also encourages her readers in *Treatise on Domestic Economy*, to purchase "superfluities" in order "to spend for the welfare of mankind" (Beecher 182). Furthermore, "The link between retail therapy and warfare is not as incongruous as it sounds. After Hiroshima and Nagasaki, stores on Fifth Avenue sold atomic jewellery, the Atomic Undergarment Company took off, a cereal maker offered atomic trinkets in return for 15 cents and a breakfast flakes box top and Lowell Blanchard released his popular country single, 'Jesus Hits Like an Atom Bomb'" (Riddell). See Simon J. Bronner's edited collection, *Consuming Visions: Accumulation and Display of Goods in America 1880–1920* for an overview of the development of American consumer culture.

12. Numerous articles and books address the American housing crisis in detail. Works that helped shape my own understanding include Andres Duany et. al., *Suburban Nation: The Rise of Sprawl and the Decline of the American Dream*; Dolores Hayden, *Redesigning the American Dream: Gender, Housing, and Family Life*; James Howard Kunstler, *The Geography of Nowhere: The Rise and Decline of America's Man-Made Landscape*; Leslie Kanes Weisman's *Discrimination by Design;* and Witold Rybczynski, *Last Harvest*. For a look at how gender influences housing issues that are pertinent primarily to America and Britain, see Rose Gilroy and Roberta Woods's edited collection, *Housing Women*. The U.S. Census Bureau's Web site, http://www.census.gov, hosts numerous articles and statistics on America's housing. My final chapter discusses the American housing crisis in more detail.

Chapter 1

1. Both Amy Kaplan and Rosemary Marangoly George point out the genre's imperial origins and influence to reinforce imperialism. Carolyn Vellenga Berman explores the genre's role in both abolishing slavery and establishing the nuclear family in her study *Creole Crossings: Domestic Fiction and the Reform of Colonial Slavery*.

2. See Dianne Chisholm's *Queer Constellations* for a more sustained definition and discussion of queer (urban) space.

3. Just as I am engaged in rethinking domesticity and domestic fiction, other scholars have asked us to reconsider our understanding of the sentimental and sentimental fiction. See, for example, June Howard's "What Is Sentimentality?"

4. Dana Heller's "Housebreaking History: Feminism's Troubled Romance with the Domestic Sphere" discusses in greater detail, and in a literary context, post–World War II feminism's reluctant relationship with the home. Her essay analyzes "a convergence of discursive trajectories driven by American feminism's anxieties about its historical relationship to the ideology of separate social spheres, the family romance of classical psychoanalysis, and the semiotics of popular culture's focus on the domestic" (219). For a more detailed exploration of the feminist movement's reluctant embrace of home, see

Judith Newton's "Feminist Family Values; or, Growing Old—and Growing Up—with the Women's Movement" and Rachel Bowlby's "Domestication."

5. See Edward W. Soja's *Postmodern Geographies: The Reassertion of Space in Social Theory* for a discussion of how time is being replaced by space.

6. McCullough cites Houston A. Baker Jr. and Richard Yarborough as examples of critics who dismiss African American women's appropriation of the sentimental form. See footnote 6 in McCullough's chapter "Slavery, Sexuality, and Genre: Pauline E. Hopkins's Negotiations of (African) American Womanhood" for an extensive list of critics that charge *Contending Forces* with assimilation (298–99).

7. Jane Tompkins's afterword to the Feminist Press edition of *The Wide, Wide World* claims, "No novel written in the United States had ever sold so well" (584).

8. See Nancy Armstrong's "Why Daughters Die: The Racial Logic of American Sentimentalism."

9. President George W. Bush made these remarks in regard to gay marriage's legality.

10. While the Breedlove apartment in Morrison's *The Bluest Eye* (1970), like the Puente home in *Dreaming in Cuban*, recycles a commercial space for domestic use, it unsuccessfully crafts a neodomestic home. The Breedlove's "abandoned store" apartment is a serviceable structure in the sense that it provides shelter, but the apartment fails to provide a home because it lacks comfort: "Without it [comfort], our dwellings will indeed be machines instead of homes" (Rybczynski 232). As a recycled structure that has housed gypsies, a real-estate office, a Hungarian baker, and a pizza parlor, the apartment is a versatile "machine" but ill adapted for family *home* life. The apartment and rooms, for example, are not cozy. Described as an eyesore that is "both irritating and melancholy" (33), the "unimaginative" (34) living quarters consist of only two rooms (*Bluest Eye* 34–35). "Festering together in the debris of a realtor's whim," the Breedlove family decays rather than flourishes in this destructive environment (*Bluest Eye* 34). Unlike the Puente family's warehouse home, the home in *The Bluest Eye* (re)produces a domestic trap rather than recycling a new route to home.

11. Sian Mile and Jean Wyatt have also argued that *Housekeeping* presents an ambivalent view of the characters' potential liberation.

12. Cisneros discusses the inspiration for *Mango Street* in an interview with Feroza Jussawalla and Reed Way Dasenbrock (301–2).

13. See Amy Kaplan, *The Anarchy of Empire in the Making of U.S. Culture*, 43–44.

14. During an interview on National Public Radio conducted by host John Ydstie for "All Things Considered," Natalie Pace, a CoAbode client, gave the motto "until better times do us part," referring to her arrangement provided through the nonprofit service (qtd. in Ydstie).

15. To flesh out this discussion more completely, I would need to look closely at the nineteenth century's "Boston marriages," which carved out a socially acceptable space for women to live together for mutual economic benefit. See Shannon Jackson's *Lines of Activity: Performance, Historiography, Hull-House Domesticity* (2000), which provides a fuller discussion of queer domesticity in the nineteenth century.

16. While walled cities have been around since Roman times, "gated communities remained rarities until the advent of the master-planned retirement developments of the late 1960s and 1970s" (Blakely and Snyder 4). See *Fortress America: Gated Communities in the United States* (Edward J. Blakely and Mary Gail Snyder) and *Behind the Gates: Life, Security, and the Pursuit of Happiness in Fortress America* (Setha Low).

Chapter 2

1. Sarah A. Leavitt also underscores conventional domesticity's racial and class implications in her chapter "Americanization, Model Homes, and Lace Curtains." Leavitt writes that at the turn of the century, immigrant women were the primary targets of much domestic advice (75). She also notes that "most domestic-advice texts left out black women. For domestic advisors, black women existed only as servants" (Leavitt 75).

2. J. K. Gibson-Graham deploys the term along these lines in *The End of Capitalism (As We Knew It): A Feminist Critique of Political Economy* (see 139–45). For additional discussion of queer space, see Lauren Berlant and Michael Warner's scholarship, especially "Sex in Public," and Judith Halberstam's *In a Queer Time and Place: Transgender Bodies, Subcultural Lives.*

3. *Little Women* begins by revealing each of the March girl's flaws, which they in turn plan—as in John Bunyan's *The Pilgrim's Progress* (1678)—to resolve. *Little Women*, in this sense, narrates the March girls' journeys toward recognizing, accepting, and correcting their burdens and flaws. See chapters 1 and 2 in *Little Women*, "Playing Pilgrims" and "A Merry Christmas."

4. Rachel Price and Amy March also resemble each other because both are guilty of misusing language; Rachel's frequent malapropisms and Amy's mispronunciations connect their characters.

5. Regarding Amy's "disability," Alcott writes, "If anybody had asked Amy what the greatest trial of her life was, she would have answered at once, 'My nose.' When she was a baby, Jo had accidentally dropped her into the coal-hod, and Amy insisted that the fall had ruined her nose forever" (42).

6. Domestic "faculty" is a nineteenth-century term that refers to the collection of skills that make "a housekeeper of exemplary competence" (Romines 4).

7. G. M. Goshgarian's *To Kiss the Chastening Rod: Domestic Fiction and Sexual Ideology in the American Renaissance* examines domestic fiction's "(im)piety," complicating a straight reading of the domestic protagonists' selflessness (xi).

8. Although beyond the scope of this chapter, *The Poisonwood Bible* also works a subtle critique of the African domestic sphere into the narrative. Ruth May, for example, describes a conversation she overhears about a "Circus mission," and Leah notes how the women in Kilanga marry young (271; 107). Rachel and Orleanna record the toll the body, especially the female body, endures in part as a result of those early marriages (53–54; 126). The novel also balances this subtle critique with Mama Tataba, an icon of domestic prowess who "cursed our mortal souls as evenhandedly as she nourished our bodies" (94).

9. Kaplan's term "manifest domesticity" plays on the term "manifest destiny" and its imperial connotations; it refers to the "pervasive imperial metaphor" in the nineteenth century, linking domesticity "to the contemporaneous geopolitical movement of imperial expansion" (Kaplan, "Manifest Domesticity" 583).

10. Biddy Martin and Chandra Mohanty similarly outline "the consolidation of the white home in response to a threatening outside" as the rhetoric of home's dark underbelly (303). The series of foreign and domestic policy initiatives undertaken after September 11 add even greater magnitude to Orleanna's, Benhabib's, and Martin and Mohanty's remarks. America frequently uses violence to respond to the backlash against its privileged position within the global community.

11. Kaplan suggests in "Manifest Domesticity" that "the expansionist logic of domestic-

ity . . . turns an imperial nation into a home by producing and colonizing specters of the foreign that lurk inside and outside its ever shifting borders" (602).

12. I am indebted to Kaplan's essay "Manifest Domesticity" for first connecting nineteenth-century American domesticity to Morrison's notion of the "Africanist presence" (602).

13. My emphasis here on the "Africanist presence" should not discount Barbara Kingsolver's political agenda to make her readers aware of American involvement in the Congo, especially in terms of America's role in Patrice Lumumba's assassination.

14. The Price's luggage symbolizes the (un)packing of their imperial burdens, or the dual predicament and promise embedded in their revised domestic pilgrimages. Whereas the March girls in *Little Women* take up their burdens and learn to carry them in order to establish a "Celestial City," the Price family's burdens initially bury them in cultural baggage. As missionaries in the Belgian Congo during the latter half of the twentieth century, the Price family ostensibly continues a tradition of cultural imperialism, furthering the "civilizing" reach of the "White House." However, *The Poisonwood Bible*'s historically conscious recycling tweaks the conventional narrative of *Pilgrims' Progress*.

15. See George, "The Authoritative Englishwoman" (50–56) in *The Politics of Home*, for a detailed discussion of the colonial home's replication of empire.

16. To describe Rachel as both child-like and sexual may seem contradictory; however, I would argue that this paradox defines the "dumb blonde" personality.

17. My favorite malapropism spoken by Rachel is this: "He [Axelroot] has a hundred and one reasons not to marry the cow so he can buy the milk for free" (403). This section written from Johannesburg, South Africa, also notes Rachel's fluency in three languages (402). While it is unclear what exactly constitutes "fluency," she can at least recite John 3:16 in English, Afrikaans, and French. Clearly this novel engages language in ways that extend beyond the scope of this chapter. (Adah's fascination with palindromes also comes to mind.) In Rachel's case, at least, her ability to speak three languages highlights a kind of "boutique multiculturalism"—akin to bragging about how "one of my very close friends happens to be from Paris, France" (402). Thank you to Brandon Kempner and Deborah Clarke for pointing out the language connections to my overall project.

18. While beyond the scope of this chapter, a fuller reading of this passage would interrogate how African children of white and black parents fit into both African and American societies.

19. "Cultural impersonation" is Minnie Bruce Pratt's term, as Martin and Mohanty note.

20. Baym in *Woman's Fiction* does not argue that women's fiction before the Civil War advanced the home as a separate sphere or facilitated its retreat from the world (48). But after the Civil War, Baym suggests, "the Gilded Age affirmed profit as the motive around which all of American life was to be organized. Home now became a retreat, a restraint and a constraint, as it had not appeared to be earlier" (50). My use of the term "retreat" more broadly encompasses the security sought by women's narratives during both the antebellum and post–Civil War periods.

21. Rachel expresses a similar frustration with the Price home in "Bel and the Serpent": "I think our house gave me the worst willies of all. That house was the whole problem, because it had our family in it. I was long past the point of feeling safe huddling under my parents' wings" (358).

22. Orleanna expresses the most grief about the loss of Ruth May; she does not appear to suffer as much angst about her other daughters who remain in Africa. She refers to Ruth May as the baby that she can't put down (382): "My little beast, my eyes, my favorite

stolen egg" (385). Ruth May's eyes are the eyes of judgment: "If you are the eyes in the trees, watching us as we walk away from Kilanga, how will you make your judgment? Lord knows after thirty years I still crave your forgiveness, but who are *you?*" (385; emphasis in original). Orleanna conflates Ruth May with the jungle in this passage; more broadly, the "you" also refers to the Congo.

23. Although not to the same extent as *Gardens in the Dunes*, *The Poisonwood Bible* also uses bird, snake, and garden symbolism to convey its message about American domesticity's links to colonialism.

Chapter 3

1. Domestic space in *The Bluest Eye* crafts a house-home dichotomy rather than deconstructing and recycling it. See chapter 1, footnote 10.

2. For a reading of the home metaphor as it appears in twentieth-century African American literature, see Valerie Sweeney Prince's *Burnin' Down the House: Home in African American Literature* (2005). Prince's study examines the concept of home in five novels: *Native Son*, *Invisible Man*, *The Bluest Eye*, *Corregidora*, and *Song of Solomon*.

3. I was unable to locate housing figures for black households in 1940. The first housing census was taken in 1940, but the U.S. Census Bureau did not begin to collect race-specific data until 1950. According to the Bureau, 31 percent of houses in 1940 had no running water, 18 percent needed major repairs, and 44 percent lacked a built-in bathtub or shower for the exclusive use of its occupants (U.S. Census, "Tracking" 1). In Ohio—the setting of *The Bluest Eye*—black homeownership was at 36 percent in 1950, above the national average for blacks (34.5 percent), but still well below the total national average of 55 percent (U.S. Census Bureau, "Historical Census").

4. Practical arguments for having an external kitchen included keeping smoke and food smells out of the main part of the home and keeping the house cooler during the summer by placing the cook stove outside the main house.

5. Strictly speaking, Morrison's trilogy follows a chronology that places *Jazz* between *Beloved* and *Paradise*. Morrison clarifies the year, 1976, on page 49 in *Paradise*. Peter Widdowson's "The American Dream Refashioned: History, Politics and Gender in Toni Morrison's *Paradise*" describes in greater detail the various clues that place the novel's start on July 4, 1976.

6. See Nell Irvin Painter's *Exodusters: Black Migration to Kansas after Reconstruction* for additional information on the Exoduster movement.

7. See Peter Widdowson, "The American Dream Refashioned: History, Politics and Gender in Toni Morrison's *Paradise*"; Katrine Dalsgård's "'The One All-Black Town Worth the Pain': (African) American Exceptionalism, Historical Narration, and the Critique of Nationhood in Toni Morrison's *Paradise*"; and Jill C. Jones's "The Eye of a Needle: Morrison's *Paradise*, Faulkner's *Absalom, Absalom!*, and the American Jeremiad."

8. See Rob Davidson's "Racial Stock and 8-Rocks: Communal Historiography in Toni Morrison's *Paradise*" and Philip Page's "Furrowing All the Brows: Interpretation and the Transcendent in Toni Morrison's *Paradise*."

9. The novel's most notoriously inscrutable detail appears on the first page: "They shot the white girl first." The woman's identity remains a mystery, despite various clues throughout the story as to the identities of the women residing at the Convent. In this vein, Philip Page suggests that Patricia Best Cato burns her papers and charts because

she finally discovers a similar false method of interpretation embedded in her genealogy. Page suggests that in Morrison's novel the "quest for facts, for closed answers" will always frustrate and thwart the reader and the characters (641).

10. See footnotes 7 and 8. The essays listed in these footnotes outline, to various degrees, the patriarchal nature of the 8-rock story. In addition to these essays, Michael K. Johnson interprets *Paradise*'s critique of patriarchy in light of the frontier myth in *Black Masculinity and the Frontier Myth in American Literature* (see especially pages 59–68).

11. The gardens do benefit the butterflies, who "journeyed miles to brood in Ruby" (90).

12. See, for example, Katrine Dalsgård's "The One All-Black Town Worth the Pain: (African) American Exceptionalism, Historical Narration, and the Critique of Nationhood in Toni Morrison's *Paradise*."

13. Peter Widdowson draws this connection in his essay "The American Dream Refashioned: History, Politics and Gender in Toni Morrison's *Paradise*."

14. See Holly Flint, "Toni Morrison's *Paradise*: Black Cultural Citizenship in the American Empire," for a discussion of the imperial narrative rewritten by *Paradise*.

15. Nell Irvin Painter writes that a significant portion of Exodusters traveling to Kansas hailed from Mississippi, Louisiana, Texas, and Tennessee ("Acknowledgments").

16. For historical information on prominent all-black Oklahoma towns, see George O. Carney's "Oklahoma's All-Black Towns" and William Loren Katz's "Oklahoma: A Black Dream Crushed."

17. According to Kenneth Marvin Hamilton, the column "Come Prepared or Not At All" appeared in the *Herald* throughout 1891 and 1892 (104). William Loren Katz explains that the *Herald* printed both "propaganda and caution" (260). As the *Herald* was first published on May 23, 1891, Morrison does not strictly follow the historical record in having her characters be aware of the Langston City newspaper and this column in particular. The 8-rock families travel and found Haven just as Langston City itself was being established in 1890.

18. Hamilton also notes, "When the acting governor proposed assistance to a colony of five hundred poor blacks settling in Oklahoma during November 1891, the *Herald* deplored his proposal, asserting that it was 'a mistake for any but self-supporting people to come' to Oklahoma" (104).

19. Peter Widdowson suggests that gender ultimately trumps race as "the key defining characteristic and the crucial potential source of destabilizing change" within the novel (329). Widdowson suggests that "what the Convent women partly represent is 'Out There,' or Misner's 'the whole world' which the exclusive paradise of Ruby must perforce 'live in.' The Convent's apparent separation from, but contiguity with, the town underpins this paradox" (329). I will examine momentarily the gendered geopolitics of this conflict more specifically in my discussion of the Convent and the interactions between the Convent and Ruby.

20. The Five Civilized Tribes were so named "because they possessed more European characteristics than any of the other North American tribes. Many of them could read and write English and had a basic understanding of U.S. Institutions" (Hamilton 133, n2).

21. Carney suggests several related reasons for why many real all-black towns in Oklahoma did not survive. ("By the post-World War II period," Carney notes, "only nineteen of the original twenty-eight [all-black towns] remained" [152].) Carney suggests, for instance, that all-black towns "never totally escaped their dependence on an economic system essentially controlled by whites. Furthermore, they experienced many of the same problems faced by all small town rural market centers, black or white" (151). These

problems included being bypassed by highway networks, residents traveling farther distances for goods and services as a result of the increased mobility brought about by the automobile, younger generations moving away for better employment opportunities, and insufficient funding for schools and roads (Carney 151–52). Additionally, "Low cotton prices and the agricultural recession of the 1920s, followed by the Great Depression of the 1930s, severely affected farming communities" (Carney 152).

22. *Culture of Fear* (1999) is the title of Barry Glassner's sociological critique of American culture. Documentary filmmaker Michael Moore draws from Glassner's work in *Bowling for Columbine* (2002), which also argues what I am suggesting here: fear often drives American policy. As the short animated film within *Bowling for Columbine* suggests, a cursory overview of American history contextualizes this deep fear of the "foreign" and the escalating violence associated with it.

23. Gigi's military-like attire is described on page 310.

Chapter 4

1. See Massey, 9–11, for a discussion of some common gendered understandings of place (for example, masculinity and the universal, femininity and the local).

2. Unlike Steven M. Gelber, I use the term "domestic masculinity" broadly—to refer to both conventionally feminine homemaking practices, which Gelber calls "masculine domesticity," and to traditionally masculine domestic tasks, which Gelber defines as the practices and spaces in the suburban home "that had been the purview of professional (male) craftsmen" (73). While there is not an exact equivalent for femininity, Judith Halberstam's *Female Masculinity* (1998) troubles femininity and masculinity just as "domestic masculinity" troubles these categories. My work examines how domesticity is not women's exclusive domain; likewise, Halberstam questions "the privileged reservation of masculinity for men" and looks at various sites of "masculinity without men" (xii; 1).

3. Catherine Jurca notes the following authors as key to the development of suburban fiction: "Sinclair Lewis, James M. Cain, Sloan Wilson, Richard Yates, John Updike, Frederick Barthelme, and Richard Ford" (4). While Jurca does consider some women writers, her work focuses on texts in which male protagonists play a central role. The notable exception is Jurca's chapter on James M. Cain's *Mildred Pierce* (1941).

A list of contemporary female American authors significant to the study of suburban fiction might include Marge Piercy, Joyce Carol Oates, Anne Tyler, Jane Smiley, and Ann Beattie.

4. Gelber suggests, "One would have to go back to an even earlier time, before there were suburbs, when most people lived on farms, in order to find husbands" who had more than an economic relationship to the daily running and functioning of their households (67). I discuss in the final chapter how women are increasingly taking part in traditionally masculine do-it-yourself projects.

5. Martin and Mohanty make the opposite point about Minnie Bruce Pratt's narrative in "Feminist Politics: What's Home Got to Do With It?" They discuss a passage where Pratt realizes she cannot abnegate responsibility for her father's history/privilege (Martin and Mohanty 301–2).

6. While I agree that twenty-first century suburban fiction that focuses on white men may continue to reflect and generate this attitude, the fact that new American immigrants increasingly make the suburb their first entry point suggests that the long view may

indeed hold changes (Hayden, *Building Suburbia* 12). For a discussion of how suburbia produces white privilege, see James S. Duncan and Nancy G. Duncan's *Landscapes of Privilege: The Politics of the Aesthetic in an American Suburb* (2004). For a discussion of African Americans and suburbia, see Andrew Wiese's *Places of Their Own: African American Suburbanization in the Twentieth Century* (2004).

7. My thanks to Jamie Ebersole for pointing out these gendered histories.

8. See part 3, "Skeeter," (183–293) in Updike's *Rabbit Redux*.

9. Fetterley and Baym go further to suggest that mobility in such cases functions not only to define masculinity but also it defines a fundamental tenant of what it means to be "American." Therefore, as Fetterley argues, women's domestic fiction is "not in the least American." See Fetterley and Baym's essays for fuller readings of the gendered logic of what gets labeled "American." Amy Kaplan's recent work uncovers the mobility and "foreign" spaces in much (white women's) domestic fiction, problematizing the "limited scope" nineteenth-century domestic fiction by women presents for its audience.

10. Other novels in this diverse tradition include Gloria Naylor's *Linden Hills* (1985) and Stephen L. Carter's *The Emperor of Ocean Park* (2002), both set in affluent African American suburban neighborhoods. *Linden Hills* fictionalizes the emergence of an African American self-built neighborhood. Rather than celebrating black suburbia, Naylor's harsh "appraisal of black mobility . . . portrays life in a black middle-class suburb as an allegory for Dante's descent into Hell" (Wiese 287). Significant parts of Carter's novel take place in the family's summer home, the Vineyard House, located on Ocean Park in Oak Bluffs on Martha's Vineyard. While Carter's thriller does not have an intense focus on domestic masculinity, it does spend some time outlining the significance of the homes presented in the novel. The Vineyard House's suburban history is explained in the opening prologue: "My parents like to tell how they bought the house for a song back in the sixties, when Martha's Vineyard, and the black middle-class colony that summers there, were still smart and secret" (Carter 3). Sandra Tsing Loh's humorous depictions of suburban life in *If You Lived Here, You'd Be Home By Now* (1997) and *A Year in Van Nuys* (2001) and Chang-rae Lee's novels *A Gesture Life* and *Aloft* also expand suburban literature's range beyond white suburbia.

11. Langston Hughes's poem "Little Song on Housing" also addresses the barriers African Americans often face when buying a home. Racial and gender discrimination occurred in a range of practices involving suburban development. This history of exclusionary practices includes outright racial segregation and exclusion, redlined mortgages, unequal housing subsidies, and highway development that disproportionately destroyed low-income and minority neighborhoods. More recently, higher-priced and riskier mortgages have been connected to higher foreclosure rates among Hispanic and black homeowners (See Kochhar, Gonzalez-Barrera, and Dockterman). All of these practices continue to have long-term effects on female and minority homeownership. See Dolores Hayden's *Building Suburbia* (68; 125; 135; 147; 166) and Wiese's *Places of Their Own*. See also Wiese's index, specifically the entry "housing discrimination," for additional reading.

12. "Sweat equity" here includes the practice of self-building homes and suburbs as well as do-it-yourself home improvements. See Hayden's *Building Suburbia* (111–114) and Andrew Wiese's *Places of Their Own*. See also Wiese's index, specifically the entry "owner building," for additional reading.

13. Joan Hoff-Wilson explains in *Law, Gender, and Injustice* that after the Civil War, laws were passed that helped equalize property law for wives. The laws "ranged from the simple ability of wives to write wills with or without their husbands' consent, to granting

feme sole status to abandoned women, to allowing women some control over their own wages, to establishing separate estates for women, to protecting land inherited by widows from their husbands' creditors, to allowing widows legal access to their husbands' personal estates" (Hoff-Wilson 128). Morrison's *A Mercy* explores the anxiety around the loss of a white male homeowner and the perilous position in which his death places his female and male dependents during the colonial period. See Spain's "From Parlor to Great Room" (137–38) in *Gendered Spaces* for a succinct overview of property control in American law.

14. See chapter 3 in *The Wide, Wide World* for the description of Ellen and her mother's shopping excursions.

15. Recent fiction that follows the haven model includes much of Jan Karon's fiction, especially about the fictional town Mitford, and fiction by Thomas Kinkade and Katherine Spencer, especially the "Cape Light" novels. Mitford, for example, is described as a world "you won't want to leave" because "It's easy to feel at home in Mitford. In these high, green hills, the air is pure, the village is charming, and the people are generally lovable." (These quotations come from the back cover of Karon's *At Home in Mitford*, 1996 Penguin paperback edition.)

16. Foreign buyers have played a significant role in major urban areas in the United States since 2005 and perhaps earlier. See Ron Scherer's article "House Not Home: Foreigners Buy Up American Real Estate." The subprime mortgage crisis, falling housing prices, and a weak dollar have made American real estate even more attractive to foreign buyers.

17. Recall, as I noted in the introduction, that 25 percent of female-headed households could afford a modestly priced house in 2004 versus 36 percent of male-headed households (Savage 4). Seventy percent of married couples could afford the same moderately priced home (Savage 4).

18. While Mosley's novel could not be considered a full-fledged version of domestic fiction, it does contain the crucial element of homeownership driving its narrative. The novel clearly and significantly integrates the mystery form with a fundamental element of domestic fiction. Mosley's novel *The Man in My Basement* (2004) deepens this exploration—exploring the relationship between a black man in danger of losing his home and a white man who offers a lot of money to live in—actually, to be imprisoned in—the other man's basement.

19. See Updike's *Rabbit at Rest* (361–85) for the description of his final flight and road trip to Florida.

20. *White Noise* is not necessarily representative of DeLillo's oeuvre. *Underworld* (1997), for example, does not share the same intense and sustained focus on family and homemaking.

21. As the home's changes also seem to reflect the inhabitants' psyches, *House of Leaves* also can be seen as an American literary successor to the British novel *The Picture of Dorian Gray* (1891) by Oscar Wilde.

22. Space does not permit me to clarify the distinct ways in which Gilles Deleuze and Félix Guattari (particularly in "What Is a Minor Literature?" and *A Thousand Plateaus*) and Jean Baudrillard (in *Simulacra and Simulation*) have influenced this novel. I gesture to them here to offer a sense of the novel's overall flavor rather than to engage their theories in any detail.

Feminism generally requires some reworking of postmodern theory. See Doreen Massey's "Flexible Sexism" for a representative feminist critique of postmodern theory as well as Rosi Braidotti's *Nomadic Subjects: Embodiment and Sexual Difference in Contem-*

porary Feminist Theory, Caren Kaplan's "Deterritorializations: The Rewriting of Home and Exile in Western Feminist Discourse," and Rosemary Marangoly George's chapter "Home-Countries: Narratives Across Disciplines" in *The Politics of Home*.

23. See N. Katherine Hayles's article "Saving the Subject: Remediation in *House of Leaves*" for a representative postmodern interpretation.

24. *House of Leaves* specifically discusses Heidegger's definition of the uncanny, or *unheimlich*, in chapter 4 (Danielewski 24–28). A fictional Harold Bloom mentions it as well in his interpretation of the film (Danielewski 364). Also see footnote 330 in *House of Leaves* (Danielewski 359).

25. While I do not explore this connection, the tree can also be read as "arborescence," given the novel's nod to Deleuze and Guattari. See the introduction to *A Thousand Plateaus* for Deleuze and Guattari's description of this concept.

26. The practice of ancestor worship appears in many African traditional religions and some form of these practices sometimes carries over into African American religious practices. See Toni Morrison's "Rootedness: The Ancestor as Foundation" and Trudier Harris's entry "Ancestors" in *The Oxford Companion to African American Literature*.

Chapter 5

1. *Publisher's Weekly* referred to the flap as "Oprahgate."

2. This line was edited from the permanent web version interview and transcript available from NPR: http://www.npr.org/templates/story/story.php?stor Id=1131456. Current as of 21 May 2010.

3. *The Complete Review*'s "A Book, an Author, and a Talk Show Host: Some Notes on the Oprah-Franzen Debacle" has a detailed outline of the unfolding events and links to publication materials at http://www.complete-review.com/quarterly/vol3/issue1/oprah.htm.

4. See James Wood, "It's Not Tolstoy, But It Does Belong to High Literature," and David Mehegan, "Franzen Not Alone in Oprah Dilemma."

5. *Empire Falls* did win the Pulitzer Prize in 2002—an award granted after the publication of Epstein's article.

6. Not surprisingly, given the domestic novel's use of plots involving journeys to or away from home, the prodigal son trope appears in several neodomestic novels, including, for example, Marilynne Robinson's *Home* and Richard Russo's *Bridge of Sighs*. The prodigal son (or daughter) trope also works well with the narrative of "beset manhood," as it takes the wayward protagonist back home.

7. The chick lit community is very aware of its status and the Franzen Affair. (Thank you to April Kent at New Mexico Highlands University for making me aware of this fact.) For example, Candace Bushnell's *Trading Up* (New York: Hyperion, 2003) lampoons Franzen's snobbery through the character Craig Edgers, author of *The Embarrassments* (consult pages 187–88; 192; 202–4). Another popular chick lit author, Plum Sykes, takes a quick jab at Franzen in *Bergdorf Blondes* (New York: Hyperion, 2004) (consult page 208).

8. See chapter 2 of Kathleen Rooney's book, *Reading with Oprah: The Book Club That Changed America*.

9. My remarks should not imply that Crichton's novels are apolitical. His recent novel, *State of Fear*, for example, engages the debate about global warming.

10. R. Mark Hall, for example, suggests that Oprah's Book Club "supports traditional female identities. In short, even as Winfrey frames reading in terms of female empower-

ment, 'Oprah's Book Club' depends upon fundamentally conservative forces in the history of literacy sponsorship for women in this country" (Hall 661). Paul Street's essay "The Full Blown 'Oprah' Effect: Reflections on Color, Class and New Age Racism" provides a representative analysis of Winfrey's celebrity and what it represents to black and white American communities.

11. Producer Scott Rudin optioned *The Corrections* and David Hare is writing the screenplay. Hare also wrote *The Hours*'s screenplay for Rudin. See Karen Valby, "Correction Dept."

12. For a fuller reading of *Rag and Bone*'s domestic politics, see Ralph Rodríguez's "A Poverty of Relations: On Not 'Making *Familia* from Scratch,' But Scratching *Familia*."

13. A contemporary British neodomestic novel that queers family in wonderfully perverse ways is Katherine Dunn's *Geek Love* (1983).

14. Doc Hata is Japanese by nationality and Korean by birth (ethnicity); his poor Korean parents give him away to a wealthy Japanese family. His parents entrust their son to this other family in order to improve their son's station in life: "No one of my family's circumstance could expect to change his station, at least without a lifetime of struggle" (Lee 72).

15. Although my reading here does not address this reference, one of the foundational suburban texts that *A Gesture Life* specifically recycles is John Cheever's short story "The Swimmer." *A Gesture Life* also continues a distinct Asian American literary tradition that addresses masculinity, immigration/assimilation, and home. Novels in this tradition include Louis Chu's *Eat a Bowl of Tea* (1961), John Okada *No-No Boy* (1976), and Frank Chin's *Donald Duk* (1991).

16. See Rosemary Marangoly George's chapter "'Traveling Light': Home and the Immigrant Novel" in *The Politics of Home* for a fuller reading of exile and homelessness in immigrants' novels (171–197).

17. Young-Oak Lee also connects Franklin Hata to Benjamin Franklin in "Gender, Race, and Nation in *A Gesture Life*": "Because 'Franklin' evokes Benjamin Franklin, one of the Founding Fathers of the United States and also the creation for Americans of lives loaded with the myth of success, the irony of his adoptive name foreshadows his failure to become a new person" (153).

Chapter 6

1. Another means to address this question might trace more particularly the theoretical debates invested in the relationship between haunting, memory, space, and history. Such analysis might engage Walter Benjamin's "Thesis on the Philosophy of History," Martin Heidegger's *Being and Time*, Karl Marx and Friedrich Engels's invocation of a "specter haunting Europe" in *The Communist Manifesto*, and subsequent analyses, such as Jacques Derrida's *Specters of Marx: The State of the Debt, the Work of Mourning, and the New International* and Dick Howard's *The Specter of Democracy*. Further exploration of Michel de Certeau's haunted geographies or an analysis of what Michel Foucault calls in *Madness and Civilization* the "geography of haunted places" would enrich this understanding of place, haunting, memory, and history.

2. While the terms are not usually connected, the "metrosexual" seems to be a younger and specifically male incarnation of what David Brooks defines as the "bourgeois bohemian." This hybrid class identity mixes the "bourgeois world of capitalism and the bohemian counterculture" (Brooks 10).

3. The Rural Studio was founded in 1993. Mockbee died in 2001.

4. *This Old House* recently broke this trend. To celebrate its thirtieth anniversary, *This Old House* partnered with the affordable housing nonprofit Nuestra Comunidad to renovate "a foreclosed 1870s Second Empire in Boston's Roxbury neighborhood" (Pandolfi).

5. For a complete list of projects and a description of the program, see the Rural Studio's homepage http://www.cadc.auburn.edu/rural-studio. Krista Tippett's *Speaking of Faith* segment on the Rural Studio, "Rural Studio: An Architecture of Decency," also offers a wealth of information. The segment's website is located at http://speakingoffaith.publicradio.org/programs/ruralstudio.

6. Metrosexuals tend to be young heterosexual men, such as soccer star David Beckham. Michael Flocker's book *The Metrosexual Guide to Style: A Handbook for the Modern Man*, in fact, specifically defines the metrosexual as heterosexual. By and large, the term "metrosexual" provides heterosexual men with an acceptable justification for their interest in fashion and grooming. It also perpetuates a double standard: men are praised for being vain, but vain women are considered "narcissistic" or "high maintenance."

7. See Judith Halberstam's *In a Queer Time and Place*, Wayne D. Myslik's essay "Renegotiating the Social/Sexual Identities of Places: Gay Communities as Safe Havens or Sites of Resistance?" and J. W. Paris and R. E. Anderson's article "Faith-Based Queer Space in Washington, DC: The Metropolitan Community Church–DC and Mount Vernon Square" for an introduction to the blossoming research on queer space.

8. A 2003 U.S. Census Bureau report based on data collected between 1994 and 2002 found that minority naturalized-citizen householders were more likely than native-citizen minorities to achieve homeownership (Callis 2). There was also a correlation between place of birth and the likelihood of homeownership for naturalized citizens: "In 2002, naturalized-citizen householders born in Europe reported higher homeownership rates (74.5 percent) than those born in Asia (69.9 percent) or Latin America (61.7 percent)" (Callis 3). The housing report did not speculate why these discrepancies existed.

9. Accurate through season 7.

10. This description is no longer available on the *Extreme Makeover: Home Edition* Web site. See http://abc.go.com/shows/extreme-makeover-home-edition/about-the-show for the current description (as of 23 May 2010).

11. Habitat for Humanity and the six-part Sundance series *Architecture School*, which "follows a group of students at Tulane University's prestigious School of Architecture as they submit competing designs for an affordable home in Katrina-battered New Orleans," offer compelling "old" and "new" solutions to America's ongoing housing crisis ("About"). Habitat for Humanity was founded in 1976 and *Architecture School* first aired in August 2008.

12. See Shannon Hayes, *Radical Homemakers*; Dolores Hayden, *The Grand Domestic Revolution: A History of Feminist Designs for American Homes, Neighborhoods, and Cities*; Jane Jacobs, *The Death and Life of Great American Cities*; and Jane Addams, *Twenty Years at Hull-House*.

13. There is also an established tradition within the visual and performance arts that reconceptualizes domestic culture. The early twentieth-century American tradition includes the impressionist painter Mary Cassatt (1844–1926), the surrealist painter Dorothea Tanning (1910–), and the landscape and portrait painter Alice Neel (1900–1984). Each of these artists' work depicts the home in conventional and unconventional ways. In addition to Clarissa Sligh's work, other key pieces from the latter half of the twentieth century include Judy Chicago's *Womanhouse* (1971–72), Martha Rosler's video *Semiotics of the Kitchen* (1975), and photographer Carrie Mae Weems's *Kitchen Table Series* (1990).

Works Cited

"About." *Architecture School*. 17 Aug. 2008. http://www.sundancechannel.com/architecture-school/#/about.

"About the Show." *Extreme Makeover: Home Edition*. 4 Sept. 2006 http://abc.go.com/primetime/xtremehome/show.html. (Link no longer available)

Adams, Lorraine. "Literary Life Without Oprah." *The Washington Post*. 19 Nov. 2002: C01.

Alcott, Louisa May. *Little Women*. 1868. Boston: Little, Brown and Company, 1994.

Al-Hindi, Karen Falconer. "Feminist Critical Realism: A Method for Gender and Work Studies in Geography." *Thresholds in Feminist Geography: Difference, Methodology, Representation*. Eds. John Paul Jones III, Heidi J. Nast, and Susan M. Roberts. New York: Rowman & Littlefield Publishers, Inc., 1997. 145–64.

Allen, Dan. "*Extreme Makeover* Too Extreme?" *The Advocate* 8 Nov. 2005: 18.

Allison, Dorothy. *Bastard Out of Carolina*. New York: Dutton, 1992.

Anzaldúa, Gloria. *Borderlands/La Frontera: The New Mestiza*. 1987. San Francisco: Aunt Lute Books, 1999.

Armstrong, Nancy. *Desire and Domestic Fiction: A Political History of the Novel*. New York: Oxford, 1987.

———. "Some Call It Fiction: On the Politics of Domesticity." *Feminisms: An Anthology of Literary Theory and Criticism*. Eds. Robyn R. Warhol and Diane Price Herndl. New Brunswick: Rutgers University Press, 1997. 913–930.

———. "Why Daughters Die: The Racial Logic of American Sentimentalism." *Burning Down the House: Recycling Domesticity*. Ed. Rosemary Marangoly George. Boulder: Westview Press, 1998. 23–46.

Arnold, Ellen L. "Listening to the Spirits: An Interview with Leslie Marmon Silko." *Conversations with Leslie Marmon Silko*. Ed. Ellen L. Arnold. Jackson: University Press of Mississippi, 2000. 162–195.

Bachelard, Gaston. *The Poetics of Space*. Trans. Maria Jolas. New York: Beacon Press, 1964/1994.

Baker, Jeff. "Oprah's Stamp of Approval Rubs Writer in Conflicted Ways." *The Oregonian* (12 Oct. 2001): Arts and Living 5.

Barbara K! Solutions for Women. "Our Company." Barbara K Enterprises, Inc. 25 May 2004. http://www.barbarak.com/company.html. (Link no longer available)

Barthelme, Frederick. *Natural Selection*. 1990. New York: Penguin Books, 1991.

Baudrillard, Jean. *Simulacra and Simulation*. Trans. Sheila Faria Glaser. Ann Arbor: University of Michigan Press, 1994.

Baym, Nina. "Melodramas of Beset Manhood: How Theories of American Fiction Exclude Women Authors." *American Quarterly* 33.2 (Summer 1981): 123–39.

———. "Re: Query About Domestic Fiction." E-mail to the author. 29 June 2004.

———. *Woman's Fiction: A Guide to Novels By and About Women in America, 1820–1870*. 1979. Ithaca, Cornell University Press, 1980.

Beecher, Catharine E. and Harriet Beecher Stowe. *American Woman's Home*. 1869. New Brunswick: Rutgers University Press, 1998.

Beecher, Catharine E. *Treatise on Domestic Economy*. 1841. New York: Schocken Books, 1977.

Benhabib, Seyla. "Sexual Difference and Collective Identities: The New Global Constellation." *Signs* 24.2 (Winter 1999): 335–61.

Bent, Geoffrey. "Less Than Divine: Toni Morrison's *Paradise*." *The Southern Review* 35.1 (Winter 1999): 145–49.

Berlant, Lauren, and Michael Warner. "Sex in Public." *Critical Inquiry* 24 (Winter 1998): 547–66.

Berlinger, Nancy. "Listening to Aslan*." *Hastings Center Report* Mar./Apr. 2003: 17–18.

Berman, Carolyn Vellenga. *Creole Crossings: Domestic Fiction and the Reform of Colonial Slavery*. Ithaca: Cornell University Press, 2006.

Berrett, Jesse. "Family Man." *The Village Voice* 46.38 (25 Sept. 2001): 72.

Beuka, Robert. *SuburbiaNation: Reading Suburban Landscape in Twentieth-Century American Fiction and Film*. New York: Palgrave Macmillan, 2004.

Bhabha, Homi. *The Location of Culture*. New York: Routledge, 1994.

———. "The Third Space: Interview with Homi Bhabha." *Identity: Community, Culture, Difference*. Ed. J. Rutherford. London: Lawrence and Wishart, 1990.

———. "DissemiNation." *Nation and Narration*. Ed. Homi Bhabha. London: Routledge Press, 1990.

———. "Signs Taken for Wonders: Questions of Ambivalence and Authority under a Tree Outside Delhi, May 1817." *"Race," Writing, and Difference*. Ed. Henry Louis Gates Jr. and Anthony Appiah. Chicago: University of Chicago Press, 1986: 163–84.

Blair, Sara. "Cultural Geography and the Place of the Literary." *American Literary History* 10.3 (Fall 1998): 544–67.

Blakely, Edward J., and Mary Gail Snyder. *Fortress America: Gated Communities in the United States*. Washington, D.C.: Brookings Institution Press, 1997.

"A Book, an Author, and a Talk Show Host: Some Notes on the Oprah-Franzen Debacle." *The Complete Review: A Literary Saloon & Site of Review* 3.1 (Feb. 2002). 18 August 2008. http://www.complete-review.com/quarterly/v013/issue1/oprah.htm.

Bowlby, Rachel. "Domestication." *Feminism Beside Itself*. Eds. Diane Elam and Robyn Wiegman. New York: Routledge, 1995: 71–91.

Bowling for Columbine. Dir. Michael Moore. MGM, 2002.

Brady, Mary Pat. *Extinct Lands, Temporal Geographies: Chicana Literature and the Urgency of Space*. Durham: Duke University Press, 2002.

Brogan, Kathleen. *Cultural Haunting: Ghosts and Ethnicity in Recent American Literature*. Charlottesville: University Press of Virginia, 1998.

Brooks, David. *Bobos in Paradise: The New Upper Class and How They Got There.* 2000. New York: Touchstone, 2001.
Burr, Ty. "A Smart Writer's Dumb Move." *Entertainment Weekly* 625/626 (16 Nov. 2001): 167.
Bush, George. "Transcript of Bush Statement: Feb. 24, 2004." CNN.com. 25 Feb 2004. http://www.cnn.com/2004/ALLPOLITICS/02/24/elec04.prez.bush.transcript/index.html.
Butler, Judith. *Bodies That Matter: On the Discursive Limits of "Sex."* New York: Routledge, 1993.
———. *Gender Trouble.* New York: Routledge, 1990.
Callis, Robert R. "Moving to America—Moving to Homeownership: 1994–2002." *Current Housing Reports.* US Census Bureau. September 2003.
Callis, Robert R. and Linda B. Cavanaugh. "Census Bureau Reports on Residential Vacancies and Homeownership." *United States Department of Commerce News.* Bureau of the Census. 27 April 2009.
Cao, Lan. *Monkey Bridge.* New York: Viking, 1997.
Carbonell, Armando. *Smart Growth: Form and Consequences.* Eds. Armando Carbonell and Terry S. Szold. Cambridge: Lincoln Land Institute, 2002.
Carney, George O. "Oklahoma's All-Black Towns." *African Americans on the Western Frontier.* Eds. Monroe Lee Billington and Roger D. Hardaway. Niwot, CO: University Press of Colorado, 1998. 147–59.
Carter, Stephen L. *The Emperor of Ocean Park.* New York: Random House, 2002.
Caver, Christine. "Nothing Left to Lose: *Housekeeping*'s Strange Freedoms." *American Literature* 68.1 (Mar. 1996): 11–37.
Cheng, Cindy I-Fen. "Out of Chinatown and into the Suburbs: Chinese Americans and the Politics of Cultural Citizenship in Early Cold War America." *American Quarterly* 58.4 (2006): 1067–1090.
Chicago, Judy. *Womanhouse.* 10 Aug. 2010 http://womanhouse.Refugia.net.
Chisholm, Dianne. *Queer Constellations: Subcultural Space in the Wake of the City.* Minneapolis: University of Minnesota Press, 2005.
Cisneros, Sandra. *The House on Mango Street.* 1984. New York: Vintage Books, 1991.
Clark, Suzanne. *Sentimental Modernism: Women Writers and the Revolution of the Word.* Bloomington: Indiana University Press, 1991.
Cohen, Emily Jane. "Kitchen Witches: Martha Stewart: Gothic Housewife, Corporate CEO." *The Journal of Popular Culture* 38.4 (2005): 650–77.
Collins, Lisa Gail. "Brown Crayons and Black Dolls: The Art of Coming of Age." *Exposure* 33.1/2 (2000): 43–52.
"Cotquean." Def. 3. *The Oxford English Dictionary Online.* 2nd ed. 1989. 19 May 2004. http://dictionary.oed.com.
Crang, Mike. "Relics, Places and Unwritten Geographies in the Work of Michel de Certeau (1925–86)." *Thinking Space.* Eds. Mike Crang and Nigel Thrift. New York: Routledge, 2000. 136–53.
Crenshaw, Kimberlé Williams. "Demarginalizing the Intersection of Race and Sex: A Black Feminist Critique of Antidiscrimination Doctrine, Feminist Theory, and Antiracist Politics." *Critical Race Feminism: A Reader.* 2nd ed. Ed. Adrien Katherine Wing. New York: New York University Press, 2003. 23–33.
Cunningham, Michael. *A Home at the End of the World.* New York: Picador USA, 1990.
Dalsgård, Katrine. "'The One All-Black Town Worth the Pain': (African) American Exceptionalism, Historical Narration, and the Critique of Nationhood in Toni Morrison's *Paradise.*" *African American Review* 35.2 (Summer 2001): 233–48.

Danielewski, Mark Z. *House of Leaves*. New York: Pantheon Books, 2000.

Davern, Michael E., and Patricia J. Fisher. "Household Net Worth and Asset Ownership." *Current Population Reports: The Survey of Income and Program Participation*. U.S. Census Bureau. Feb. 2001.

Davidson, Cathy and Jessamyn Hatcher, eds. *No More Separate Spheres!: A Next Wave American Studies Reader*. Durham: Duke University Press, 2002.

Davidson, Rob. "Racial Stock and 8-Rocks: Communal Historiography in Toni Morrison's *Paradise*." *Twentieth-Century Literature* 47.3 (Fall 2001): 355–73.

Davis, Peggy Cooper, and Carol Gilligan. "Reconstructing Law and Marriage." *The Good Society* 11.3 (2002): 57–67.

"Decline in Black Home Ownership Poses a New Barrier to Higher Education." *The Journal of Blacks in Higher Education* (1994): 19–20.

DeLillo, Don. *White Noise*. 1984. New York: Penguin, 1985.

DeMarr, Mary Jean. *Barbara Kingsolver: A Critical Companion*. Westport, CT: Greenwood, 1999.

Domosh, Mona, and Joni Seager. *Putting Women in Place: Feminist Geographers Make Sense of the World*. New York: Guilford Press, 2001.

Douglas, Ann. *The Feminization of American Culture*. 1977. New York: Farrar, Straus and Giroux, 1998.

Dubus III, Andre. *House of Sand and Fog*. New York: W.W. Norton & Company, 1999.

Duggan, Lisa. *The Twilight of Equality? Neoliberalism, Cultural Politics, and the Attack on Democracy*. Boston: Beacon Press, 2003.

Duncan, James S., and Nancy G. Duncan. *Landscapes of Privilege: The Politics of the Aesthetic in an American Suburb*. New York: Routledge, 2004.

DuPlessis, Rachel Blau. *Writing beyond the Ending*. Bloomington: Indiana University Press, 1985.

Edmunds, Susan. *Grotesque Relations: Modernist Domestic Fiction and the U.S. Welfare State*. New York: Oxford University Press, 2008.

Edwards, Thomas R. "Oprah's Choice." *Raritan* 21.4 (Spring 2002): 75–86.

Elliott, Jane. "O is For the Other Things She Gave Me: Jonathan Franzen's *The Corrections* and Contemporary Women's Fiction." *Bitch: Feminist Response to Pop Culture* 16 (Spring 2002): 70–74.

Epstein, Joseph. "Surfing the Novel." *Commentary* Jan. 2002: 32–37.

Espiritu, Yen Le. *Home Bound: Filipino American Lives Across Cultures, Communities, and Countries*. Berkeley: University of California Press, 2003.

Extreme Makeover: Home Edition 2009 Family Application. 1–19. 30 May 2010. http://a.abc.com/media/primetime/xtremehome/apply. (Link no longer available)

"FAQ on *Extreme Makeover: Home Edition*." *Inside TV*. 7–13 Nov. 2005: 80.

Farhi, Paul. "Makeover Madness: Suddenly the Mirrors All Have Remotes." *The Washington Post*. 9 May 2005: C1.

Farr, Cecilia Konchar. *Reading Oprah: How Oprah's Book Club Changed the Way America Reads*. Albany: State University of New York Press, 2005.

Fern, Fanny. *Ruth Hall*. New York: Mason Brothers, 1855. Ed. Joyce W. Warren. New Brunswick: Rutgers University Press, 1999.

Fetterley, Judith. "'Not in the Least American': Nineteenth-Century Literary Regionalism." *College English* 56 (1994): 877–95.

Filkins, Peter. "All In the Family." *The World & I* 17.2 (Feb. 2002): 231.

Flint, Holly. "Toni Morrison's *Paradise*: Black Cultural Citizenship in the American Empire." *American Literature* 78.3 (Sept. 2006): 585–612.

Flocker, Michael. *The Metrosexual Guide to Style: A Handbook for the Modern Man.* New York: DaCapo Press, 2003.
Forcey, Blythe. "Domestic Fiction." *The Oxford Companion to Women's Writing in the United States.* Eds. Cathy N. Davidson and Linda Wagner-Martin. New York: Oxford University Press, 1995. 253–54.
Ford, Richard. *Independence Day.* 1995. New York: Vintage Contemporaries, 1996.
———. *The Sportswriter.* 1986. New York: Vintage Contemporaries, 1995.
———. *The Lay of the Land.* New York: Alfred A. Knopf, 2006.
Foster, Thomas. *Transformations of Domesticity in Modern Women's Writing: Homelessness at Home.* New York: Palgrave Macmillan, 2002.
Foucault, Michel. *Discipline & Punish: The Birth of the Prison.* 1977. New York: Vintage Books, 1979.
———. *Madness and Civilization: A History of Insanity in the Age of Reason.* 1967. Trans. Richard Howard. New York: Vintage Books, 1988.
———. "Of Other Spaces." *diacritics.* Trans. Jay Miskowiec. 16.1 (Spring 1986): 22–27.
———. *Power/Knowledge.* Trans. Colin Gordon. New York: Pantheon Books, 1980.
Franklin, Benjamin. *The Autobiography [Part Two].* 1868. *The Norton Anthology of American Literature.* Shorter Seventh Edition. Vol. 1. Ed. Nina Baym. New York: W.W. Norton & Company, 2008. 276–92.
Franzen, Jonathan. *The Corrections.* New York: Farrar, Straus and Giroux, 2001.
———. *How To Be Alone.* New York: Farrar, Straus and Giroux, 2002.
———. "Meet Me in St. Louis." *The New Yorker* 77. 44 (Dec. 24–31, 2001): 70–75.
———. "Novelist Jonathan Franzen." Interview by Terry Gross. *Fresh Air.* National Public Radio. WHYY, Philadelphia. 15 Oct. 2001. Radio.
———. "Perchance to Dream: In the Age of Images, a Reason to Write Novels." *Harper's Magazine* 292.1751 (April 1996): 35–54.
———. "Why Bother?" *How To Be Alone.* New York: Farrar, Straus and Giroux, 2002. 55–97.
Friedman, Ellen G. "Postpatriarchal Endings in Recent U.S. Fiction." *Modern Fiction Studies* 48.3 (Fall 2002): 693–712.
Frieswick, Kris. "The Job without Benefits." *The Boston Globe Magazine.* 11 March 2007: 30.
Gallop-Goodman, Gerda. "Ms. Fix-it." *American Demographics* 22.9 (Sept. 2000): 14–16.
Garcia, Cristina. *Dreaming in Cuban.* 1992. New York: Ballantine Books, 1993.
Gates, Anita. "These Old Houses: A TV Genre Is Built." *New York Times.* 11 Feb. 2005: E1+.
Gathorne-Hardy, Flora. "Home." *A Feminist Glossary of Human Geography.* Eds. Linda McDowell and Joanne P. Sharp. London: Arnold Publishers, 1999. 124–25.
Gelber, Steven M. "Do-It-Yourself: Constructing, Repairing and Maintaining Domestic Masculinity." *American Quarterly* 49.1 (1997): 66–112.
George, Rosemary Marangoly, ed. "Recycling: Long Routes to and From Domestic Fixes." *Burning Down the House: Recycling Domesticity.* Boulder: Westview Press, 1998. 1–20.
———. *The Politics of Home: Postcolonial Relocations and Twentieth-Century Fiction.* Berkeley: University of California Press, 1996.
Gibson-Graham, J. K. *The End of Capitalism (As We Knew It): A Feminist Critique of Political Economy.* Cambridge: Blackwell Publishers, 1996.
Giles, Jeff. "Errors and 'Corrections.'" *Newsweek* 138.19 (5 Nov. 2001): 68–69.
Goshgarian, G. M. *To Kiss the Chastening Rod: Domestic Fiction and Sexual Ideology in the American Renaissance.* Ithaca: Cornell University Press, 1992.

Gottschalck, Alfred. O. "Net Worth and the Assets of Households: 2002." *Current Population Reports.* US Census Bureau. April 2008.

Griffith, Michael A. "'A Deal for the Real World': Josephine Humphreys's *Dreams of Sleep* and the New Domestic Novel." *Southern Literary Journal* 26.1 (Fall 1993): 94–108.

Gross, Jane. "Older Women Team Up to Face Future Together." *The New York Times* 27 Feb. 2004: A1.

Guinn, Matthew. "Into the Suburbs: Richard Ford's Sportswriter Novels and the Place of Southern Fiction." *South to a New Place: Region, Literature, Culture.* Eds. Suzanne W. Jones and Sharon Monteith. Baton Rouge: Louisiana State University Press, 2002. 196–207.

Halberstam, Judith. *Female Masculinity.* Durham: Duke University Press, 1998.

———. *In a Queer Time and Place: Transgender Bodies, Subcultural Lives.* New York: New York University Press, 2005.

Hall, R. Mark. "The 'Oprahfication' of Literacy: Reading 'Oprah's Book Club.'" *College English* 65.6 (July 2003): 646–67.

Hamilton, Kenneth Marvin. *Black Towns and Profit: Promotion and Development in the Trans-Appalachian West, 1877–1915.* Urbana: University of Illinois Press, 1991.

Hansberry, Lorraine. *A Raisin in the Sun.* 1959. New York: Vintage Books, 1994.

Harris, Cheryl I. "Whiteness as Property." *Harvard Law Review* 106.8 (June 1993): 1707–1791.

Harris, Richard and Chris Hamnett. "The Myth of the Promised Land: the Social Diffusion of Home Ownership in Britain and North America." *Annals of the Association of American Geographers* 77.2 (June 1987): 173–90.

Harris, Susan K. *19th-Century American Women's Novels: Interpretive Strategies.* 1990. New York: Cambridge University Press, 1992.

Harvey, David. *Justice, Nature, and the Geography of Difference.* Malden, MA: Blackwell Publishers, 1996.

———. *Spaces of Hope.* Berkeley: University of California Press, 2000.

Hawthorne, Nathaniel. *The House of Seven Gables.* 1851. New York: Dell, 1960.

———. "To William D. Ticknor." (19 January 1855) In *The Centenary Edition of the Works of Nathaniel Hawthorne.* Vol. XVII, eds. William Charvat, Roy Harvey Pearce, and Claude M. Simpson. Columbus: The Ohio State University Press, 1962. 304.

Hayden, Dolores. *Building Suburbia: Green Fields and Urban Growth, 1820–2000.* New York: Pantheon Books, 2003.

———. *The Grand Domestic Revolution: A History of Feminist Designs for American Homes, Neighborhoods, and Cities.* Cambridge, The MIT Press, 1985.

———. *Redesigning the American Dream: Gender, Housing, and Family Life.* New York: W.W. Norton & Company, 2002.

Hayes, Shannon. *Radical Homemakers: Reclaiming Domesticity from a Consumer Culture.* Richmondville, NY: Left to Write Press, 2010.

Hayles, N. Katherine. "Saving the Subject: Remediation in *House of Leaves.*" *American Literature* 74.4 (Dec. 2002): 779–806.

Haytock, Jennifer. *At Home, At War: Domesticity and World War I in American Literature.* Columbus: Ohio State University Press, 2003.

Heller, Dana. "Housebreaking History: Feminism's Troubled Romance with the Domestic Sphere." *Feminism Beside Itself.* Eds. Diane Elam and Robyn Wiegman. New York: Routledge, 1995. 217–33.

Hensher, Philip. "Writing Beyond his Means." *The Spectator* 24 Nov. 2001. 44–45.

Hertzberger, Herman, Addie van Roijen-Wortmann, and Francis Stauven. *Aldo van Eyck: Hubertushuis*. Amsterdam: Stichting Wonen/Van Loghum Staterus, 1982.

Hetherington, Kevin. *The Badlands of Modernity: Heterotopia and Social Ordering*. London: Routledge, 1997.

Higgins, Therese E. *Religiosity, Cosmology, and Folklore: The African Influence in the Novels of Toni Morrison*. New York: Routledge, 2001.

Hoff-Wilson, Joan. *Law, Gender, and Injustice*. New York: New York University Press, 1991.

Hogan, Michael. "Built on the Ashes: The Fall of the House of Sutpen and the Rise of the House of Sethe." *Unflinching Gaze: Morrison and Faulkner Re-Envisioned*. Eds. Carol A. Kolmentan, Stephen M. Ross, and Judith Bryant Wittenberg. Jackson: University Press of Mississippi, 1997. 167–80.

hooks, bell. "Black Vernacular: Architecture as Cultural Practice." *Visual Rhetoric in a Digital World: A Critical Sourcebook*. Ed. Carolyn Handa. Boston: Bedford/St. Martin's, 2004. 395–400.

———. *Yearning: Race, Gender, and Cultural Politics*. Boston: South End, 1990.

Howard, June. "What Is Sentimentality?" *American Literary History* 11.1 (Spring 1999): 63–81.

Howells, William Dean. *Suburban Sketches*. New and Enlarged Edition. Boston: James R. Osgood and Company, 1872.

Hughes, Langston. "Little Song on Housing." *The Panther and the Lash: Poems of Our Times*. New York: Knopf, 1967. 79–80.

Hulbert, Ann. "All in the Family." *New Republic* 3649 (24 Dec. 1984): 36–39.

Hume, Kathryn. *American Dream, American Nightmare: Fiction since 1960*. Urbana: University of Illinois Press, 2000.

Illouz, Eva. *Oprah Winfrey and the Glamour of Misery*. New York: Columbia University Press, 2003.

Iovine, Julie V. "'Handy Ma'am'/ Men Beware: More Single Women Become Weekend Warriors of Home-Improvement." *Houston Chronicle* 14 Nov. 1999: 3.

Irving, Washington. "Rip Van Winkle." *The American Short Story and Its Writer*. Ed. Ann Charters. Boston: Bedford/St. Martin's, 2000. 35–48.

Jackson, Shannon. *Lines of Activity: Performance, Historiography, Hull-House Domesticity*. Ann Arbor: University of Michigan Press, 2000.

Jacobs, Harriet. *Incidents in the Life of a Slave Girl*. 1861. *The Classic Slave Narratives*. Ed. Henry Louis Gates, Jr. New York: Penguin, 1987. 333–515.

Jacobson, Kristin J. "Renovating *The American Woman's Home*: American Domesticity in *Extreme Makeover: Home Edition*." *Legacy* 25.1 (2008): 105–27.

Jacoby, Jeff. "Too Good for Oprah." *Boston Globe* 1 Nov. 2001. A19.

Jakobsen, Janet R. "Queer Is? Queer Does? Normativity and the Problem of Resistance." *GLQ* 4.4 (1998): 511–536.

Jarrar, Randa. *A Map of Home*. New York: Other Press, 2008.

Jeffery, Craig. "Third Space." *A Feminist Glossary of Human Geography*. Eds. Linda McDowell and Joanne P. Sharp. London: Arnold Publishers, 1999. 274.

Johnson, Michael K. *Black Masculinity and the Frontier Myth in American Literature*. Norman: University of Oklahoma Press, 2002.

Joint Center for Housing Studies of Harvard University. *The Remodeling Market in Transition: Improving America's Housing 2009*. President and Fellows of Harvard College, 2009. 18 May 2010. http://www.jchs.harvard.edu/publications/remodeling/remodeling 2009/index.htm

Jones, Carolyn M. "Southern Landscape as Psychic Landscape in Toni Morrison's Fiction." *Studies in the Literary Imagination* 31.2 (Fall 1998): 37–48.

Jones, Jill C. "The Eye of the Needle: Morrison's *Paradise*, Faulkner's *Absalom, Absalom!*, and the American Jeremiad." *The Faulkner Journal* 17.2 (Spring 2002): 3–23.

Jurca, Catherine. *White Diaspora: The Suburb and the Twentieth-Century American Novel.* Princeton: Princeton University Press, 2001.

Jussawalla, Feroza, and Reed Way Dasenbrock, eds. "Sandra Cisneros." *Interviews with Writers of the Post-Colonial World.* Jackson: University Press of Mississippi, 1992. 287–306.

Kaplan, Amy. *The Anarchy of Empire in the Making of U.S. Culture.* Cambridge: Harvard University Press, 2002.

———. "Manifest Domesticity." *American Literature* 70.3 (September 1998): 581–606.

Kaplan, Caren. "Deterritorializations: The Rewriting of Home and Exile in Western Feminist Discourse." *Cultural Critique* 6 (Spring 1987): 187–98.

Karon, Jan. *At Home in Mitford.* New York: Penguin, 1996.

Katz, William Loren. "Oklahoma: A Black Dream Crushed." *The Black West.* 3rd ed. William Loren Katz. Seattle: Open Hand Publishing INC, 1987. 245–64.

Kelley, Mary. "The Sentimentalists: Promise and Betrayal of Home." *Signs* 4.3 (Spring 1979): 434–46.

Kerouac, Jack. *On the Road.* 1955/57. New York: Viking, 1997.

King, Maggie. "Shelter for the Soul." *Ecologist* 37.3 (April 2007):48–53.

Kingsolver, Barbara. *Animal Dreams.* New York: Harper Perennial, 1990.

———. "Barbara Kingsolver FAQ on *The Poisonwood Bible*." Harper Collins Publishers. 17 May 2010. http://www.harpercollins.com/author/microsite/Readingguide.aspx?authorID=5311&displayType=essay&articleId=7456.

———. *The Bean Trees.* New York: Harper Perennial, 1988.

———. *Pigs in Heaven.* New York: HarperCollins, 1993.

———. *The Poisonwood Bible.* 1998. New York: Harper Perennial, 1999.

———. *Prodigal Summer.* New York: HarperCollins Publishers, 2000.

———. "Q&A with Barbara Kingsolver." HarperCollins Publishers. 21 May 2010. http://harpercollins.com/author/microsite/Readingguide.aspx?authorID=5311&displayType=essay&articleId=7460.

———. *Small Wonder.* New York: HarperCollins Publishers, 2002.

Klimasmith, Betsy. *At Home in the City: Urban Domesticity in American Literature and Culture, 1850–1930.* Durham, NH: University of New Hampshire Press, 2005.

Knopp, Laura. "Queer." *A Feminist Glossary of Human Geography.* Eds. Linda McDowell and Joanne P. Sharp. London: Arnold Publishers, 1999. 225–26.

Kochhar, Rakesh, Ana Gonzalez-Barrera, and Daniel Dockterman. "Through Boom and Bust: Minorities, Immigrants and Homeownership." Pew Hispanic Center. 12 May 2009.

Koepke family. "Koepke Family-Campbellsport, WI." *Extreme Makeover: Blog Edition.* 1 March 2007. 24 March 2007. http://blogs.abc.com/emhe/2007/03/koepke_family_c.html.

Köhler, Angelika. "'Our human nature, our human spirit, wants no boundaries': Leslie Marmon Silko's *Gardens in the Dunes* and the Concept of Global Fiction." *Amerikastudien/American Studies* 47.2 (2002): 237–44.

Kowalski, Michael. "Domestic Fiction and Mid-Nineteenth Century Literature." *Encyclia* 62 (January 1985): 60–65.

Koza, Kimberly A. "The Africa of Two Western Women Writers: Barbara Kingsolver and Margaret Laurence." *Critique* 44.3 (Spring 2003): 284–94.

Lannom, Gloria W. "Yggdrasil, the sacred ash tree." *Calliope* 13.5 (Jan. 2003): 40.
Leavitt, Sarah A. *From Catharine Beecher to Martha Stewart: A Cultural History of Domestic Advice*. Chapel Hill: The University of North Carolina Press, 2002.
Lee, Chang-rae. *Aloft*. New York: Riverhead Books, 2004.
———. *A Gesture Life*. New York: Riverhead Books, 1999.
Lee, Young-Oak. "Gender, Race, and Nation in *A Gesture Life*." *Critique* 46.2 (Winter 2005): 146–59.
Lefebvre, Henri. *The Production of Space*. Oxford: Balckwell, 1991.
Leslie, D. A. "Femininity, Post-Fordism and the 'New Traditionalism.'" *Space, Gender, Knowledge: Feminist Readings*. Eds. Linda McDowell and Joanne P. Sharp. London: Arnold, 1997. 300–17.
Levy, Helen Fiddyment. *Fiction of the Home Place: Jewett, Cather, Glasgow, Porter, Welty, and Naylor*. Jackson: University Press of Mississippi, 1992.
Lorde, Audre. *Sister Outsider*. Berkeley: The Crossing Press, 1984.
Louie, David Wong. *The Barbarians Are Coming*. New York: G.P. Putnam's Sons, 2000.
Low, Setha. *Behind the Gates: Life, Security, and the Pursuit of Happiness in Fortress America*. New York: Routledge, 2003.
Luckett, Sandra. "Did You Know? Homes Account for 44 Percent of All Wealth: Findings from the SIPP." *Household Economic Studies. Current Population Reports*. U.S. Census Bureau. May 2001. 1–5.
"Man Caves." DIY Network. 21 July 2008. http://www.diynetwork.com/diy/shows_dmcv/.
Manrique, Jaime. *Latin Moon in Manhattan*. New York: St. Martin's Press, 1992.
Marcus, Sharon. *Apartment Stories: City and Home in Nineteenth-Century Paris and London*. Berkeley: University of California Press, 1999.
Marshall, Paule. *Brown Girl, Brownstones*. 1959. New York: The Feminist Press, 1981.
Martin, Biddy, and Chandra Talpade Mohanty. "Feminist Politics: What's Home Got to Do with It?" *Feminisms: An Anthology of Literary Theory and Criticism*. Eds. Robyn R. Warhol and Diane Price Herndl. New Brunswick: Rutgers University Press, 1997. 293–310.
Marx, Karl, and Friedrich Engels. *The Communist Manifesto*. 1848/1888. Trans. Samuel Moore. New York: Penguin Books, 2002.
Massey, Doreen. *Space, Place, and Gender*. Minneapolis: University of Minnesota Press, 1994.
Massey, Doreen, and Pat Jess, eds. *A Place in the World? Places, Cultures and Globalization*. Oxford: The Open University, 1995.
May, Leila Silvana. "The Strong-Arming of Desire: A Reconsideration of Nancy Armstrong's *Desire and Domestic Fiction*." *ELH* 68 (2001): 267–85.
McCann, Herbert G. "Hardware Makers Come to Grips with Female Do-It-Yourselfers." *The Washington Post* 19 Aug. 2000. G07.
McCullough, Kate. *Regions of Identity: The Construction of America in Women's Fiction, 1885–1914*. Stanford: Stanford University Press, 1999.
McDowell, Linda. *Gender, Identity and Place: Understanding Feminist Geographies*. Minneapolis: University of Minnesota Press, 1999.
———. "Spatializing Feminism: Geographic Perspectives." *BodySpace: Destabilizing Geographies of Gender and Sexuality*. Ed. Nancy Duncan. New York: Routledge, 1996.
McGinn, Daniel. *House Lust: America's Obsession with Our Homes*. New York: Currency, 2008.
McKee, Patricia. "Geographies of *Paradise*." *The New Centennial Review* 3.1 (Spring 2003): 197–223.

———. "Spacing and Placing Experience in Toni Morrison's *Sula*." *Modern Fiction Studies* 42.1 (1996): 1-30.
Mehegan, David. "Franzen Not Alone in Oprah Dilemma." *Boston Globe* 10 Nov. 2001: F1.
"Metrosexual" Def. A. *The Oxford English Dictionary Online*. Draft Entry. March 2008. 26 July 2009. http://dictionary.oed.com.
"Metrosexual." *The Word Spy*. 7 May 2004. www.wordspy.com.
"Mission." *Rural Studio*. Homepage. Auburn University. 18 Aug. 2008. www.ruralstudio.com.
Mixon, Bobbie. "Chore Wars: Men, Women and Housework." National Science Foundation. 28 April 2008. 21 July 2008. http://www.nsf.gov/discoveries/disc_summ.jsp?cntn_id=111458.
Moi, Toril. "What Is a Woman? Sex, Gender, and the Body in Feminist Theory." *What Is a Woman? And Other Essays*. Toril Moi. Oxford: Oxford University Press, 1999. 3-120.
Morrison, Toni. *Beloved*. 1987. New York: Penguin Books, 1988.
———. *The Bluest Eye*. 1970. New York: Penguin Books, 1994.
———. "Home." *The House That Race Built*. Ed. Wahneema Lubiano. New York: Pantheon Books, 1997. 3-12.
———. *Jazz*. 1992. New York: Plume, 1993.
———. *Love*. New York: Random House, 2003.
———. *A Mercy*. New York: Knopf, 2008.
———. *Paradise*. 1997. New York: Random House, 1998.
———. *Playing in the Dark: Whiteness and the Literary Imagination*. Cambridge: Harvard University Press, 1992.
———. "Rootedness: The Ancestor as Foundation." *Black Women Writers (1950-1980): A Critical Edition*. Ed. Mari Evans. New York: Anchor Press, 1984: 339-45.
———. *Song of Solomon*. 1977. New York: Plume, 1987.
———. *Sula*. 1973. New York: Plume, 1982.
———. *Tar Baby*. 1981. New York: New American Library, 1987.
Mullan, John. "Elements of Fiction: Dysfunctional Feasts." *The Guardian* 7 Dec. 2002: 40.
Myslik, Wayne D. "Renegotiating the Social/Sexual Identities of Places: Gay Communities as Safe Havens or Sites of Resistance?" *BodySpace: Destabilizing Geographies of Gender and Sexuality*. Ed. Nancy Duncan. New York: Routledge, 1996. 159-69.
Nava, Michael. *Rag and Bone*. 2001. New York: Berkley Prime Crime, 2002.
Newton, Judith. "Feminist Family Values; or, Growing Old—and Growing Up—with the Women's Movement." *Generations: Academic Feminists in Dialogue*. Eds. Devoney Looser and E. Ann Kaplan. Minneapolis: University of Minnesota Press, 1997. 327-43.
"A Novelist, a Talk-Show Host, and Literature High and Low." *The Chronicle of Higher Education* 48.14 (30 Nov. 2001): B4.
Oldenburg, Ann. "Reality TV with Heart." *USA Today* 22 April 2005: E1.
Olivares, Julián. "Sandra Cisneros' *The House on Mango Street*, and the Poetics of Space." *Americas Review* 15.3-4 (Fall/Winter 1987): 160-70.
Orr, Elaine Neil. *Subject to Negotiation: Reading Feminist Criticism and American Women's Fiction*. Charlottesville: University Press of Virginia, 1997.
Page, Philip. "Furrowing All the Brows: Interpretation and the Transcendent in Toni Morrison's *Paradise*." *African American Review* 35.4 (2001): 637-49.
Painter, Nell Irvin. *Exodusters: Black Migration to Kansas after Reconstruction*. 1976 New York, W.W. Norton & Company, 1986.
Pandolfi, Keith. "Roxbury House Project." *This Old House*. 3 June 2010. http://www.thisoldhouse.com/toh/tv/house-project/overview/O,,20277827,00.html.

Parikh, Crystal. "'The Most Outrageous Masquerade': Queering Asian-American Masculinity." *Modern Fiction Studies* 48.4 (Winter 2002): 858–98.

Paris, J. W., and R. E. Anderson. "Faith-based Queer Space in Washington, DC: The Metropolitan Community Church-DC and Mount Vernon Square" *Gender, Place and Culture* 8.2 (2001): 149–68.

Parker-Pope, Tara. "Gay Unions Shed Light on Gender in Marriage." *The New York Times*. 10 June 2008: F1.

Pérez, Loida Maritza. *Geographies of Home*. New York: Viking, 1999.

Perry, Donna. "An Interview with Barbara Kingsolver." *Backtalk: Women Writers Speak Out*. Ed. Donna Perry. New Brunswick: Rutgers University Press, 1993. 145–68. Gale Literary Database. 21 September 2000. http://www.galenet.com.

"Peter Family." *Extreme Makeover: Home Edition*. 23 May 2010. http://abc.go.com/shows/extreme-makeover-home-edition/episode-guide/peter-family/101392.

Petry, Ann. *The Street*. 1946. New York: Houghton Mifflin Company, 1991.

Philips, Deborah. "Keeping the Home Fires Burning: The Myth of the Independent Woman in the Aga-Saga." *Women: A Cultural Review* 7.1 (1996): 48–54.

Polter, Julie. "Extreme Community." *Sojourners Magazine* 34.1 (Jan. 2005): 38–39; 41–42.

Prince, Valerie Sweeney. *Burnin' Down the House: Home in African American Literature*. New York: Columbia University Press, 2005.

Rakoff, Joanna Smith. "Making *The Corrections*: An Interview with Jonathan Franzen." *Poets & Writers* (Sept./Oct. 2001): 27–33.

Riddell, Mary. "If in Doubt, Go Shopping." *The Observer*. 30 Sept. 2001. Guardian Unlimited. 10 March 2004. http://observer.guardian.co.uk/waronterrorism/story/0,1373,560567,00.html.

"Rise of the Metrosexual." *The Age*. 11 March 2003. 7 May 2004. http://www.theage.com.au/articles/2003/03/10/1047144914842.html.

Robinson, Marilynne. *Home*. New York: Farrar, Straus and Giroux, 2008.

———. *Housekeeping*. 1981. New York: Bantam Books, 1987.

Rodriguez, Denise. "'Where the Self that had No Self Made Its Home': The Reinscription of Domestic Discourse in Toni Morrison's *Beloved*." *Griot* 20.1 (Spring 2001): 40–51.

Rodriguez, Ralph E. "A Poverty of Relations: On Not 'Making *Familia* from Scratch,' But Scratching *Familia*." *Velvet Barrios: Popular Culture and Chicana/o Sexualities*. Ed. Alicia Gaspar De Alba. New York: Palgrave Macmillan, 2003.

Romero, Lora. *Home Fronts: Domesticity and Its Critics in the Antebellum United States*. Durham: Duke University Press, 1997.

Romines, Ann. *The Home Plot: Women, Writing and Domestic Ritual*. Amherst: University of Massachusetts Press, 1992.

Rooney, Kathleen. *Reading with Oprah: The Book Club that Changed America*. Fayetteville: The University of Arkansas Press, 2005.

Russo, Richard. *Empire Falls*. 2001. New York: Vintage Contemporaries, 2002.

Rybczynski, Witold. *Home: A Short History of an Idea*. New York: Viking, 1986.

———. *Last Harvest*. New York: Scribner, 2007.

Salazar, Inés. "Can You Go Home Again? Transgression and Transformation in African-American Women's and Chicana Literary Practice." *Postcolonial Theory and the United States: Race, Ethnicity and Literature*. Eds. Amritjit Singh and Peter Schmidt. Jackson: University Press of Mississippi, 2000. 388–411.

Savage, Howard A. "Who Could Afford to Buy a House in 2004?" *Current Housing Reports*. U.S. Census Bureau. May 2009.

Sayers, Valerie. "Caffeinated Realism." *Commonweal* 21 Dec. 2001: 23-24.
Schenk, Susan J. "Protest or Pathology: The Politics of Madness in Contemporary Domestic Fiction." *Women's Studies* 21 (1992): 231-41.
Scherer, Ron. "House Not Home: Foreigners Buy Up American Real Estate." *The Christian Science Monitor*. 15 July 2005. 2 July 2008. http://www.csmonitor.com/2005/0715/p01s03-ussc.html.
Scruggs, Charles. "The Invisible City in Toni Morrison's *Beloved*." *Arizona Quarterly* 48.3 (1992): 95-132.
Seabrook, John. *Nobrow: The Culture of Marketing, the Marketing of Culture*. New York: Vintage, 2001.
Shah, Nayan. *Contagious Divides: Epidemics and Race in San Francisco's Chinatown*. Berkeley: University of California Press, 2001.
Shamir, Milette. "Divided Plots: Interior Space and Gender Difference in Domestic Fiction." *Genre* 29.4 (Winter 1996): 429-72.
Showbiz Tonight. CNN. 28 March 2006. Transcript. *LexisNexis Academic*. Stockton College. 4 Sept. 2006. http://web.lexis-nexis.com.
Silko, Leslie Marmon. *Gardens in the Dunes*. New York: Simon & Schuster, 1999.
———. *Yellow Woman and a Beauty of the Spirit: Essays on Native American Life Today*. 1996. New York: Touchstone, 1997.
Simonian, Charisse. "Note from *Extreme Makeover: Home Edition* Casting Department." E-mail to Phinel PetitFrere. 10 March 2006. "ABC's 'Extreme' Exploitation." 27 March 2006. *The Smoking Gun*. http://www.thesmokinggun.com/archive/0327062extreme1.html.
Skocpol, Theda. "Will 9/11 and the War on Terror Revitalize American Civic Democracy?" *American Political Science Association Online*. 10 March 2004. http://www.apsanet.org/content_13152.cfm.
Sligh, Clarissa. *Ron Ironing, Dallas, Texas, 1996*. 25 May 2004. http://www.clarissasligh.com/selected_works/series/popumig/imgaa.html.
Smiley, Jane. *Good Faith*. New York: Alfred A. Knopf, 2003.
Solomon, Alisa. "Shirts Off Their Backs." *The Village Voice* 46.49 (11 Dec. 2001): 40.
Spain, Daphne. *Gendered Spaces*. Chapel Hill: The University of North Carolina Press, 1992.
Spillers, Hortense J. "Mama's Baby, Papa's Maybe: An American Grammar Book." *Diacritics* 17.2 (Summer 1987): 64-81.
Stegman, Michael A., with Joanna Brownstein and Kenneth Temkin. "Home Ownership and Family Wealth in the United States." *Housing and Family Wealth: Comparative International Perspectives*. Eds. Ray Forrest and Alan Murie. New York: Routledge, 1995. 86-107.
Stossel, Scott. "Elitism for Everyone." *The Atlantic Online* 29 Nov. 2001 http://www.theatlantic.com/past/docs/unbound/polipro/pp2001-11-29htm.
Street, Paul. "The Full Blown 'Oprah' Effect: Reflections on Color, Class and New Age Racism." *The Black Commentator*. 127.24 Feb. 2005.http://www.blackcommentator.com/127/127_oprah.html.
Svetkey, Benjamin. "Domestic Drama." *Entertainment Weekly*. 14 Sept. 2001: 85.
Tate, Claudia. *Domestic Allegories of Political Desire: The Black Heroine's Text at the Turn of the Century*. New York: Oxford University Press, 1992.
———. "Toni Morrison." *Conversations with Toni Morrison*. Ed. Danielle Taylor-Guthrie. Jackson: University of Mississippi, 1994: 156-70.
Tippett, Krista. "Rural Studio: An Architecture of Decency." *Speaking of Faith*. 15 Nov.

2007. http://speakingoffaith.publicradio.org/programs/ruralstudio/index.shtml.
Tomboy Tools. Tomboy Tools, Inc. 25 May 2004. http://www.tomboytools.com.
Tompkins, Jane. "Afterward." *The Wide, Wide World.* Susan Warner. New York: The Feminist Press, 1987. 584–608.
———. *Sensational Designs: The Cultural Work of American Fiction, 1790–1860.* New York: Oxford University Press, 1985.
Updike, John. *Rabbit at Rest.* 1990. New York: Fawcett Crest Publications, 1991.
———. *Rabbit is Rich.* 1981. New York: Fawcett Crest Publications, 1982.
———. *Rabbit Redux.* 1971. New York: Fawcett Crest Publications, 1972.
———. *Rabbit, Run.* New York: Fawcett Columbine, 1996.
U.S. Census Bureau. "Historical Census of Housing Tables—Ownership Rates." 21 April 2000. http://www.census.gov/hhes/www/housing/census/historic/ownrate.html.
———. "Tracking the American Dream: The First Fifty Years of the Census of Housing, 1940–1990." Series H-121, no. 94-1.
Valby, Karen. "Correction Dept." *Entertainment Weekly* 679 (25 Oct. 2002): 23.
Vlach, John Michael. *Back of the Big House: The Architecture of Plantation Slavery.* Chapel Hill: The University of North Carolina Press, 1993.
Warner, Susan. *The Wide, Wide World.* 1850. New York: The Feminist Press, 1987.
Wasserman, Jim. "Home Front: House Building Taps the Global Economy." *McClatchy—Tribune Business News* 9 Nov 2007. ProQuest. 21 July 2008. http://proquest.umi.com.
Weems, Carrie Mae. *The Kitchen Table Series.* 1990. Houston: Contemporary Arts Museum, 1996.
Weisman, Leslie Kanes. *Discrimination by Design: A Feminist Critique of the Man-Made Environment.* Urbana: University of Illinois Press, 1992.
Welter, Barbara. *Dimity Convictions: The American Woman in the Nineteenth Century.* Athens: Ohio University Press, 1976.
Whelan, Lara Baker. "Between Worlds: Class Identity and Suburban Ghost Stories, 1850 to 1880." *Mosaic* 35.1 (Mar. 2002): 133–48.
Widdowson, Peter. "The American Dream Refashioned: History, Politics and Gender in Toni Morrison's *Paradise.*" *Journal of American Studies* 35.2 (2001): 313–35.
Wideman, John Edgar. *Damballah.* 1981. New York: Houghton Mifflin Company, 1998.
———. *Hiding Place.* 1981. New York: Vintage, 1988.
———. *Sent for You Yesterday.* New York: Houghton Mifflin Company, 1983.
Wiese, Andrew. *Places of Their Own: African American Suburbanization in the Twentieth Century.* Chicago: The University of Chicago Press, 2004.
Williams, Carla. "Reading Deeper: The Legacy of Dick and Jane in the Work of Clarissa Sligh." *Image* 38.3-4 (1995): 3–15.
Williams, Joy. *Breaking and Entering.* 1981. New York: Vintage, 1988.
Williamson, Judith. "Woman Is an Island: Femininity and Colonization." *Studies in Entertainment.* Ed. Tania Modleski. Bloomington: Indiana University Press, 1986. 99–118.
Willis, Deborah. "Clarissa Sligh." *Aperture* 138 (1995): 4–11.
Willis, Susan. "Eruptions of Funk: Historicizing Toni Morrison." *Black American Literature Forum* 16.1 (Spring 1982): 34–42.
Wilson, Sherryl. *Oprah, Celebrity and Formations of Self.* New York: Palgrave, 2003.
Wood, James. "It's Not Tolstoy, But It Does Belong to High Literature." *The Guardian* 9 Nov. 2001: 3.
Wright, Gwendolyn. "Prescribing the Model Home." *Social Research* 58.1 (Spring 1991): 213–25.

Yates, Richard. *Revolutionary Road*. 1961. New York: Vintage Contemporaries, 1989.
Ydstie, John. Interview: Carmel Sullivan, founder of Co-abod.org, and satisfied client. *All Things Considered*. National Public Radio. 6 March 2004. Transcript.
Young, Iris Marion. "The Ideal Community and the Politics of Difference." *Feminism/Postmodernism*. Ed. Linda J. Nicholson. New York: Routledge, 1990. 300–23.
Young, John. "Toni Morrison, Oprah Winfrey, and Postmodern Popular Audiences. *African American Review* 35.2 (2001): 181–204.
Zeller, Tom. "Two Fronts: Promoting Marriage, Fighting Poverty." *The New York Times* 18 Jan. 2004. 4.3.

Index

Adams, Lorraine, 153, 169
African Americans: and black towns, 92–93, 98–102, 212n16, 212n21; Crenshaw, Kimberlé Williams, 113; home, 78, 80–82, 86, 88, 99–100, 105, 112–13, 121–22, 125, 183, 197, 199–200, 209n1; homeownership, 1, 34, 37, 80–81, 93, 135, 191, 211n3, 213n6, 214nn11–12, 215n18; race house, 79–103, 106, 110–11, 173–75, 183; space, 86–87; suburban space, 121–22, 125–26, 197, 214nn11–12; Vlach, John Michael, 13, 86–87, 90, 112; Wiese, Andrew, 81, 88, 100, 125, 197, 213n6, 214nn10–12. *See also* kitchens: slavery
African American literature: and domestic fiction, 21, 25–26, 42, 79–113, 206n7, 211n2. *See also* Jacobs, Harriet; Marshall, Paule; Morrison, Toni; Mosley, Walter; Naylor, Gloria; Petry, Ann; Senna, Danzy; Wideman, John Edgar
Africanist presence. *See* Morrison, Toni
aga-saga, 2
Alcott, Louisa May: *Little Women,* vii, 6, 24, 26–27, 41, 46, 51–53, 55, 60–61, 63, 68, 71, 151, 164, 209n3, 209n5, 210n14. *See also The Poisonwood Bible* (Kingsolver)

Al-Hindi, Karen Falconer, 9
alienation. *See* masculinity
Allen, Dan, 195
Allison, Dorothy: *Bastard Out of Carolina,* 39, 135–36, 203
Aloft (Lee). *See* Lee, Chang-rae
American dream, 1, 10, 33–35, 76, 93, 99, 124, 135, 165, 188–99. *See also* assimilation; homeownership
ancestor worship. *See* religion
Anderson, R. E., 218n7
Animal Dreams (Kingsolver). *See* Kingsolver, Barbara
antidomestic, 8, 13, 20, 32, 48, 118–20, 123–25, 149, 151, 153, 155–69. *See also* domesticity; masculinity
Anzaldúa, Gloria, 30
Architecture School, 218n11
Armstrong, Nancy, 4–5, 11, 205n2, 208n8
Arnold, Ellen L., 48
Asian Americans: homeownership, 1, 174–75, 213n6
Asian American literature: and domestic fiction, 162–63, 173–80, 217n15. *See also* Cao, Lan; Jarrar, Randa; Lee, Chang-rae; Mun, Nami; Zevin, Gabrielle
assimilation, 28, 107, 208n6, 217n15; and heteronormativity, 5, 11, 17, 36–37,

233

50–51, 163, 170–71, 195. See also American dream

Bachelard, Gaston, 33, 184
Baker, Jeff, 156
Barbara K!, 189
Barnes, Fiona R., 206n7
Barthelme, Frederick, 213n3; *Natural Selection*, vii, 3
Bastard Out of Carolina (Allison). See Allison, Dorothy
Baudrillard, Jean, 140, 215n22
Bauer, Dale M., 205n5
Baym, Nina, 13, 19–20, 118, 205n5, 214n9; *Woman's Fiction*, 15, 19, 23, 54, 62, 129, 210n20. See also beset manhood
The Bean Trees (Kingsolver). See Kingsolver, Barbara
Beattie, Ann, 213n3
bedrooms, 128–30, 133, 138, 142, 163, 175, 196
Beecher, Catherine E., 5, 28, 35–40, 55, 194, 197, 206n11
Beloved (Morrison), 9, 13, 78–79, 81, 100–103, 160, 185, 203, 211n5; haunted house, 35, 111–12, 145, 147, 150; remodeling, 79, 81–92, 106, 175; Sethe, 54–55, 90–91, 106; 108, 145, 147, 164. See also Morrison, Toni
Benhabib, Seyla, 58, 60, 209n10
Benjamin, Walter, 103, 161, 217n1
Bent, Geoffrey, 82, 109–10
Berlant, Lauren, 209n2
Berlinger, Nancy, 167
Berman, Carolyn Vellenga, 25, 30–31, 54, 207n1
Berrett, Jesse, 153
beset manhood, 13, 20–21, 118–19, 123, 148–49, 159, 162, 170, 180, 216n6. See also Baym, Nina
Beuka, Robert, 206n7
Bhabha, Homi K., 4, 18–19, 103, 138, 154, 184–85. See also third space
blacks. See African Americans
black towns, 92–93, 98–102, 212n16, 212n21. See also *Paradise* (Morrison)

Blair, Sara, 206n7
Blakely, Edward J., 38, 208n16
The Bluest Eye (Morrison). See Morrison, Toni
Boston marriage. See gay marriage
Bowlby, Rachel, vii, 207n4
Bowling for Columbine (Moore), 213n22
Brady, Mary Pat: and spatial narrative, 206n8. See also spatial narrative
Braidotti, Rosi, 215n22
Breaking and Entering (Williams). See Williams, Joy
Brogan, Kathleen: and cultural haunting, 22, 142
Bronner, Simon J., 206n11
Brooks, David, 217n2
Bunyan, John: *The Pilgrim's Progress*, 180, 209n3
Burr, Ty, 156, 159
Burton, María Amparo Ruiz de, 26, 42
Bush, George W., 28, 36, 206n11, 208n9
Bushnell, Candace, 216n7
Butler, Judith: 14, and gender performance, 115, 154–55

Callis, Robert R., 1, 218n8
Cao, Lan: *Monkey Bridge*, 16, 38–39, 203
Carney, George O., 212n16, 212n21
Carter, Stephen L., 214n10
Cassat, Mary, 218n13
Caucasian. See whites
Caver, Christine, 32, 35
Certeau, Michel de, 180, 217n1
Chandler, Marilyn R., 206n7
Cheng, Cindy I-Fen, 174
Chesnutt, Charles: *The House Behind the Cedars*, 6
Chicago, Judy, 218n13
Chicano/as. See Hispanics/Latino/as
chick lit, 2, 155, 160, 216n7
Chisholm, Dianne, 207n2
Christianity. See religion
Cisneros, Sandra: *The House on Mango Street*, 12, 31–35, 48, 203, 208n12
Clark, Suzanne, 15
class, 23, 25, 29, 36, 48, 100, 106, 184; and gated communities, 37–38, 66,

106, 132, 208n16; Marx, Karl/communism, 69, 217n1; metrosexual, 187, 189, 217n2, 218n6; middle-class home, 1–2, 5, 7, 10–11, 17, 55, 60–61, 77–78, 119–20, 125, 128–29, 138, 142, 147, 153–54, 174, 209n1, 214n10; poverty, 36, 55, 62, 100–101, 128, 188, 193, 196, 199, 212n18, 217n14; privilege, 57–71, 149–51, 191, 195–97; space, 77, 126, 142, 205n1; upper class (bourgeoisie), 5, 25, 28, 62–64, 72, 77, 107, 128, 189, 217n2; white trash, 39–40. *See also* domestic labor; homeownership; white privilege
CoAbode, 37, 186, 208n14
Cohen, Emily Jane, 28
Collins, Lisa Gail, 199–200
colonialism. *See* (post)colonialism
conclusions: and death, 27, 49, 135, 149, 164–65; domestic fiction, 54–55, 60; marriage, 4, 26–27, 54, 60; neodomestic fiction, 3, 9, 35, 51, 54–55, 90–91, 110–12, 132, 142–44, 147–51, 159, 164–65, 169, 172, 180–81. See also *Paradise* (Morrison); *The Poisonwood Bible* (Kingsolver)
conventional domestic fiction. See conventional domesticity
conventional domesticity, 6, 26–28, 209n1; and appropriation of ideals, 6, 26; contemporary conventional domestic novels, 11; cult of true womanhood, 55–56, 62–63, 65; family values, 5, 35–36, 38, 41, 72, 99, 195–96; heteronormativity, 5, 11, 17, 36–37, 50–51, 163, 170–71, 195; middle-class home, 1–2, 5, 7, 10–11, 17, 55, 60–61, 77–78, 119–20, 125, 128–29, 138, 142, 147, 153–54, 174, 209n1, 214n10; neodomesticity and neodomestic fiction, 17, 26–40, 46–47, 52–71, 75, 110–11, 149–50, 155, 167, 170, 186; Protestant, 5, 11, 26, 28, 39, 42, 50, 52, 125, 137, 147, 166–69, 171. See also *Extreme Makeover: Home Edition;* home: conventional and unconventional; race house

Cooperman, Jeannette Batz, 206n7
The Corrections (Franzen), 13, 21, 151, 153–69, 185, 199, 204, 217n11; and Enid 151, 164–69, 185; gender performance, 153–69; Oprah's Book Club, 16, 23, 118, 153, 153–64, 199; reception 153; Winfrey, Oprah, 155–62. *See also* Franzen, Jonathan
Crang, Mike, 180
Crenshaw, Kimberlé Williams, 113
Crowley, John: *Little, Big,* 203
cult of true womanhood, 55–56, 62–63, 65
cultural haunting. *See* Brogan, Kathleen
Cunningham, Michael, 13; *A Home at the End of the World,* 16, 171–73, 180–81, 185, 203

Dalsgård, Katrine, 211n7, 212n12
Danielewski, Mark Z: *House of Leaves,* 16, 134, 139–43, 145, 147, 164, 204, 215n21, 216nn23–24
Dasenbrock, Reed Way, 208n12
Davern, Michael E., 191
Davidson, Cathy, 11, 14
Davidson, Rob, 103, 105, 211n8
Davis, Peggy Cooper, 118, 151
Deleuze, Gilles, 139–40, 215n22, 216n25
DeLillo, Don: 157, 215n20; *White Noise,* 13, 138–39, 168, 185, 203
DeMarr, Mary Jean, 53–54
den, 127–28, 130
Derrida, Jacques, 217n1
didactic fiction: and (neo)domestic novel, 2, 4, 12, 30, 41, 82, 150–52, 179
disability: and family, 78; *Little Women* (Alcott), 209n5; *The Poisonwood Bible* (Kingsolver), 73
do-it-yourself (DIY). *See* home improvement
domestic fiction: and characteristics/definition of, 2–12, 15–26, 183–86; historical-cultural context, 1–2, 15–16, 35–40, 42, 66, 77–78, 80–85, 116–17, 120, 125, 130–31, 161, 174, 183–86; origin of term, 2–3, 19–20; stability, 2, 6, 10–12, 14, 27, 31, 40,

51, 57, 60, 63–64, 69, 71–72, 76, 117, 120, 123–24, 141–43, 151, 154, 182. *See also* African American literature; Asian American literature; conclusions; conventional domesticity; didactic fiction; gendered forms (domestic fiction); Hispanic/Latino/a American literature; journey structure; literary history (domestic fiction); Native American literature; protagonists; (post)colonialism
domesticity: and homemaking, 2–3, 5, 7–9, 16–17, 20–21, 24, 26–27, 30–32, 34, 39–40, 47–51, 53, 56, 58–75, 94, 104–109, 114–34, 136, 154, 164, 170, 173–78, 183–84, 187, 191, 201, 208n11, 213n2; house vs. home, 7, 80, 84, 106; masculinity, 13–14, 20–21, 114–15, 117–26, 134–38, 145, 148–50, 154–55, 162–64, 169, 173–81, 191, 200–201, 213n2, 214n10. *See also* antidomestic; conventional domesticity; queer domesticities; recycled domesticities
domestic labor, 61, 97, 122, 126, 133–36, 175, 182; formal economy, 21, 40, 129, 134, 170; gender and housework, 97, 116, 133–36; informal economy, 36, 128, 134; women as domestic icons/workers, 28–29, 36–37, 75, 78, 116, 127, 133–34, 186–87, 189–91, 198. *See also* housekeepers
domestic romance, 2–4
domestic sentimentalism, 2, 19
domestic stability. *See* domestic fiction: stability
domestic violence: and homeownership, 135; Morrison, Toni (novels), 79–81, 93, 103, 106, 109–11; oppositional space, 83, 94–103, 108–10; sexual violence, 163, 178; women/foreigners, 20, 37, 79–81, 122, 133, 170, 199, 209n10
Domosh, Mona, 36, 60, 130
doorways. *See* thresholds
Douglas, Ann, 185
Dreaming in Cuban (Garcia). *See* Garcia, Cristina

Duany, Adres, 207n12
Dubus III, Andre: *House of Sand and Fog*, 13, 21–22, 135–36, 147, 203
Duggan, Lisa, 10
Duncan, James S. and Nancy G., 213n6
Dunn, Katherine: *Geek Love*, 217n13
DuPlessis, Rachel Blau, 4

economy: formal, 21, 40, 129, 134, 170; informal, 36, 128, 134. *See also* domestic labor
Edmunds, Susan, 15, 205n6
Edwards, Thomas R., 160
Empire Falls (Russo). *See* Russo, Richard
endings. *See* conclusions
Epstein, Joseph, 159, 162, 165, 216n5
Erdrich, Louise, 203
Espiritu, Yen Le, 24
ethnicity. *See* hybridity; *and specific ethnic identities*
Extreme Makeover: Home Edition, 5, 14, 188, 192–98, 205n3, 218n10; charity, 193, 195; complaints, 193; Koepke Family, 194; Peter Family, 192–93
Eyck, Aldo van, 186

family romance, 2, 23, 207n4
family values, 3, 5, 35–36, 207n4; conservative, 5, 35–36, 38, 41, 72, 99, 195–96; feminist, vii, 3, 12, 23, 151, 198, 207n4. *See also* conventional domesticity
Farhi, Paul, 195
Farr, Cecilia Konchar, 160–61
femininity, 14, 20–22, 33, 127, 139, 148, 155, 162–63, 170, 190–91, 200, 213nn1–2; cult of true womanhood, 55–56, 62–63, 65; home improvement, 187, 190. *See also* gender; gendered forms (domestic fiction); women
feminism, vii, 19–20, 50, 60, 75, 162, 184, 187, 189, 207n4, 215n22; second-wave, 3, 19–20, 36. *See also* family values; feminist geography
feminist geography, 8–10, 60, 71, 175,

184, 205n1; relational space, 4, 9, 14, 18, 29, 47–50, 75, 83–85, 92, 94, 109–10, 112–13. *See also* Domosh, Mona; gendered space; Massey, Doreen; McDowell, Linda; Seager, Joni
Fern, Fanny: *Ruth Hall,* 27–29
Fetterley, Judith, 20, 118, 155, 185, 205n5, 214n9
Filkins, Peter, 164
Flint, Holly, 212n14
Flocker, Michael, 218n6
Forcey, Blythe, 2, 15
Ford, Richard, 13, 168, 213n3; *Independence Day,* 13, 16, 21, 114–17, 134, 136, 143–47, 149–50, 164, 184, 203; *The Lay of the Land,* 21, 145–47, 150–51, 164, 179, 185, 204; *The Sportswriter,* 21, 203
foreclosures. *See* homeownership
Foster, Thomas, 28, 205n6
Foucault, Michel, 4, 18, 85, 152, 171; *Discipline & Punish,* 83; *Madness and Civilization,* 217n1; "Of Other Spaces," 24, 41; *Power/Knowledge,* 82
Franklin, Benjamin: *Autobiography,* 177, 217n17
Franzen, Jonathan, 11, 52, 153–69; gender performance, 153–69; *How to Be Alone,* 157; "Meet Me in St. Louis," 157; "Perchance to Dream," 157–58; "Why Bother?," 151–52, 157, 159, 182; Winfrey, Oprah and Book Club, 16, 23, 118, 153–69, 191, 199, 216nn2–4; 216n7. *See also The Corrections* (Franzen)
Freeman, Mary E. Wilkins, 6
Friedan, Betty, 119
Friedman, Ellen G., 94
Frieswick, Kris, 116

Gallop-Goodman, Gerda, 187
Gap Creek (Morgan). *See* Morgan, Robert
Garcia, Cristina: *Dreaming In Cuban,* 16, 29–30, 131–33, 203, 208n10
gardens, 73, 88, 97–98, 105, 140, 211n23, 212n11. See also *Gardens in the Dunes* (Silko)

Gardens in the Dunes (Silko), 9, 12, 16, 42–52, 76, 116, 134, 184–85, 204, 211n23; and gardens, 97–98, 105, 180; historical/cultural context, 44–45; mobility, 46–47, 124; plot summary/structure, 43–44, 53; recycling, 39, 42–43, 51; relational space, 47–50; renovation, 50–52; space/time, 44–45. *See also* Silko, Leslie Marmon
gated communities, 37–38, 66, 106, 132, 208n16
Gates, Anita, 78
Gathorne-Hardy, Flora, 29
gay marriage, 36, 186–87, 208n9; Boston marriage, 208n15. *See also* marriage
Gelber, Steven M., 118–19, 213n2, 213n4
gender: and construction of, 115, 154–55, 189–91, 199–201 (*see also* Butler, Judith; gender performance); genre, 2–3, 6–8, 13–14, 20–22, 28, 41–42, 114–84, 199, 214n9; housework, 97, 116, 133–36; intersectionality, 113; power, 23–24, 50, 57, 92, 94, 106, 111–13, 116, 149, 184, 191–92, 212n19, 214n11; space, 17, 29, 60, 79, 92, 94, 99, 106, 111–12, 126–33, 142, 154, 183, 186, 205n1, 207n12, 213n1, 214n13; spiritual geography, 136–52, 168–69, 173–81, 184–85. *See also* femininity; masculinity
gendered forms (domestic fiction): and bedrooms, 128–30, 133, 138, 142, 163, 175, 196; den, 127–28, 30; feminine, 8, 22, 27, 41, 48, 111, 115–16, 119, 138–40, 142, 150–52, 154, 158–59, 173, 183–84, 198; male authorship, 6–7, 11–12, 23–25, 115–16, 158, 161–62, 182; masculine, 8, 19, 21, 111, 115, 117–27, 134–39, 144, 147, 150–51, 153, 167, 169–71, 173, 184, 191, 197–98, 213n2; parlor, 127–29; women writers, 2–4, 11, 19–20, 22, 25–26, 36, 40, 42, 92, 129, 152–53, 205n5, 213n3. *See also* protagonists; sexuality: (neo)domestic fiction
gendered space, 17, 29, 60, 79, 92, 94, 99, 106, 111–12, 126–33, 142, 154, 183,

186, 205n1, 207n12, 213n1, 214n13. See also separate spheres
gender performance, 115, 154–55, 170–71, 174, 183; and Franzen, Jonathan, 153–69; neodomestic masculinity, 169–75, 180, 183–85. See also Butler, Judith
genre: and gender, 2–3, 6–8, 13–14, 20–22, 28, 41–42, 114–84, 199, 214n9; gothic fiction, 3, 136, 139, 141–43, 151; neo-genre, 4, 7, 9; novel as bourgeois form, 5, 25–26. See also domestic fiction; neodomestic fiction; suburban fiction
Geographies of Home (Pérez). See Pérez, Loida Maritza
geography. See feminist geography; Harvey, David; Soja, Edward W.; space; spiritual geography
George, Rosemary Marangoly, 59, 67, 206n7, 207n1, 210n15, 215n22, 217n16; and recycling, 17–18, 42, 71, 74–75, 155, 184
A Gesture Life (Lee). See Lee, Chang-rae
ghosts. See spiritual geography
Gibson-Graham, J. K., 209n2
Giles, Jeff, 156, 161
Gilligan, Carol, 118, 151
Gilman, Charlotte Perkins: *Herland*, 48; "The Yellow Wallpaper," 47
Gilroy, Rose, 207n12
Glassner, Barry: *Culture of Fear*, 213n22
Goshgarian, G. M., 209n7
gothic fiction, 3, 136, 139, 141–43, 151
Gottschalck, Alfred. O., 1
Gould, Philip, 205n5
great room, 129–30
green design. See home
Griffith, Michael A., 5
Gross, Jane, 191
Guattari, Félix, 215n22, 216n25
Guinn, Matthew, 145

Habitat for Humanity, 218n11
Haggard, Ted, Rev., 37
Halberstam, Judith, 209n2, 213n2, 218n7
Hall, R. Mark, 161–62, 216n10

Hamilton, Kenneth Marvin, 100, 212nn17–18, 212n20
Hamnett, Chris, 5, 193
Hansberry, Lorraine: *A Raisin in the Sun*, 88
Harris, Cheryl I., 183
Harris, Richard, 5, 193
Harris, Susan K., 22–23, 205n5
Harris, Trudier, 216n26
Harvey, David, 7, 85: *Justice, Nature, and the Geography of Difference*, 12, 84, 206n9; *Spaces of Hope*, 8, 18, 75–76, 80; spatiotemporal utopias, 18, 80
Hatcher, Jessamyn, 11, 14
haunting. See spiritual geography
Hawthorne, Nathaniel, 16, 20, 153, 199; *The House of Seven Gables*, 6, 127–29
Hayden, Dolores, 28–29, 34–35, 40, 120–21, 125, 130–31, 146–47, 207n12, 213n6, 214nn11–12, 218n12
Hayes, Shannon: *Radical Homemakers*, 218n12
Hayles, N. Katherine, 140–41, 216n23
Haytock, Jennifer, 8, 27, 205n6
Heidegger, Martin, 216n24, 217n1
Heller, Dana, 23, 199, 207n4
Hensher, Philip, 160
heterosexuality. See sexuality
heterotopia, 4, 18. See also Foucault, Michel
Hetherington, Kevin, 18
Higgins, Therese E., 94
Hispanics/Latino/as: homeownership, 1, 33, 191, 213n6, 214n11
Hispanic/Latino/a American literature: and domestic fiction, 84–85, 206n8. See also Burton, María Amparo Ruiz de; Cisneros, Sandra; Garcia, Cristina; Lopez, Erika; Manrique, Jaime; Nava, Michael; Pérez, Loida Maritza; Quiñonez, Ernesto; Viramontes, Helena María
Hoff-Wilson, Joan, 214n13
Hogan, Michael, 91
home: and assimilation, 28, 107; bedrooms, 128–30, 133, 138, 142, 163, 175, 196; Christianity, 27, 37, 55–57, 95, 123, 193–94; conventional and

Index | **239**

unconventional, 10–11, 17, 27–28, 31–32, 36, 62, 68, 75, 186, 208n14, 209n1, 215n15; den, 127–28, 130; gardens, 73, 88, 97–98, 105, 140, 211n23, 212n11; great room, 129–30; green design, 78, 196–97; as haven and/or trap, 6, 13, 20–21, 24, 30–35, 46–48, 51, 55, 62, 72, 78–79, 85, 89, 91–92, 94, 117–21, 126, 129, 151, 157, 166, 173–74, 180, 208n10, 215n15; kitchens, 31, 38, 70, 120–22, 130, 170, 194, 218n13; model home, 4–6, 26–29, 33–40, 50–52, 54, 56, 58–76, 122, 154, 192, 196–97; outside(rs) or Out There, 4, 9, 14, 20, 29–35, 39–40, 48, 62, 65, 67, 71–72, 75, 87–90, 92–94, 101–10, 121, 154, 172, 176, 180, 209nn10–11, 212n19; parlor, 127–29. *See also* American dream; domesticity; home improvement; homeownership; suburban space; *and specific racial and ethnic identities*
"Home" (Morrison). *See* Morrison, Toni
Home (Robinson). *See* Robinson, Marilynne
A Home at the End of the World (Cunningham). *See* Cunningham, Michael
home improvement, 35, 50–52, 77–78, 190, 214n12; Barbara K!, 189; *Beloved* (Morrison), 79, 81–92, 106; men, 118–19, 130, 133, 149, 170, 213n4; neodomestic fiction, 4, 9, 11–12, 29–30, 50–52, 77–113, 131–33, 175, 182–83; *Paradise* (Morrison), 78–85, 92–94, 197; spending trends, 77–78, 187; *This Old House*, 188, 193, 218n4; Tomboy Tools, 189; women, 187, 190. See also *Extreme Makeover: Home Edition*
homemaking. *See* domesticity
home office. *See* den
homeownership, 1, 5, 35, 77, 135–36, 191–93, 218n8; and African Americans, 1, 34, 37, 80–81, 93, 135, 191, 211n3, 213n6, 214nn11–12, 215n18; Asian Americans, 1, 174–75; foreclosures, 1–2, 195, 214n11; globalization, 132–33; Hispanics/Latino/as, 1, 33, 191, 214n11; immigrants, 33, 125, 132–33, 135, 174–75, 192–93, 213n6; married couples, 1, 81, 215n17; men, 1, 21, 133, 135–36, 191; mortgage crisis, 132, 214n11, 215n16; net worth, 1, 191; *Paradise* (Morrison), 21, 134; single households, 37, 186, 190; whites, 1, 81; women, 1, 37, 133, 136, 190–91, 214n11; 214n13. *See also* American dream; home improvement; Rural Studio
homosexuality. *See* sexuality
hooks, bell, 4, 13, 29–30, 46, 75, 78, 81, 83–86, 88, 90–91, 105, 111–12, 130, 198
Hopkins, Pauline E., 25–26, 42, 208n6
Hopkins, Sara Winnemucca, 42
house. *See* domesticity; home
The House Behind the Cedars (Chesnutt). *See* Chesnutt, Charles
housekeepers, 41, 61, 121–22, 127, 209n6. *See also* domestic labor
Housekeeping (Robinson). *See* Robinson, Marilynne
House of Leaves (Danielewski). *See* Danielewski, Mark Z.
House of Sand and Fog (Dubus). *See* Dubus III, Andre
The House of Seven Gables (Hawthorne). *See* Hawthorne, Nathaniel
The House on Mango Street (Cisneros). *See* Cisneros, Sandra
housework. *See* domestic labor
housing market. *See* homeownership
Howard, Dick, 217n1
Howard, June, 207n3
Howells, William Dean: *Suburban Sketches*, 13, 120–25, 144–45, 147, 150, 165, 173, 184
Hughes, Langston, 214n11
Hulbert, Ann, 5
Hume, Kathryn, 111, 136–37
Hurricane Katrina, 36
hybridity, 18–19, 48–49, 105, 117, 132, 134, 152–154, 159, 164, 169–73, 180, 185, 189, 198, 217n2. *See also* Bhabha, Homi K.

Illouz, Eva, 155, 160
imperialism. *See* (post)colonialism
Independence Day (Ford). *See* Ford, Richard
instability. *See* neodomestic fiction
Iovine, Julie V., 190
irony: and masculinity, 109, 119, 137–39, 147, 153, 165, 167–70, 185. *See also* antidomestic; suburban fiction
Irving, Washington, 13, 20, 117–18

Jackson, Shannon, 208n15
Jacobs, Harriet, 6, 26, 42
Jacobs, Jane, 198, 218n12
Jacoby, Jeff, 156
Jakobsen, Janet R., 183, 186–87
James, Henry, 20; "The Jolly Corner," 139, 142–43; *Washington Square*, 6
Jarrar, Randa, 204
Jeffery, Craig, 18, 48
Jess, Pat, 37
Johnson, Michael K., 94, 96, 102, 109, 111, 212n10
Joint Center for Housing Studies of Harvard University, 77
"The Jolly Corner" (James). *See* James, Henry
Jones, Carolyn M., 83, 112
Jones, Jill C., 211n7
journey structure, 33, 43, 45–46, 49, 51, 54–55, 58, 74, 137, 149, 209n3, 216n6; literal, 46; metaphoric, 46. *See also* beset manhood
Jurca, Catherine, 20, 114, 117, 119–20, 123, 150, 206n7, 213n3
Jussawalla, Feroza, 208n12

Kain, Geoffrey, 206n7
Kaplan, Amy, 30, 205n5, 207n1, 208n13, 214n9; and manifest domesticity, 12, 14, 23, 27, 56, 61, 209n9, 209n11, 210n12
Kaplan, Caren, 215n22
Karon, Jan, 215n15
Katz, William Loren, 212nn16–17
Kelley, Mary, 19, 199

Kerouac, Jack, 20
King, Maggie, 188
Kingsolver, Barbara, 11, 52–53, 82, 113, 147–48; *Animal Dreams*, 66; *The Bean Trees*, 53–54; *Pigs in Heaven*, 54; *Small Wonder*, 30. *See also The Poisonwood Bible* (Kingsolver)
Kinkade, Thomas, 215n15
kitchens, 31, 38, 70, 120–22, 130, 170, 194, 218n13; and slavery, 86–88, 96–97, 211n4
Klimasmith, Betsy, 6, 205n6
Knopp, Laura, 50
Kochhar, Rakesh, 1, 214n11
Koepke family, 194
Köhler, Angelika, 42
Kowalski, Michael, 3–4
Koza, Kimberly A., 57
Kunstler, James Howard, 207n12

Lannom, Gloria W., 143
Latino/as. *See* Hispanics/Latino/as
The Lay of the Land (Ford). *See* Ford, Richard
Leavitt, Sarah A., 209n1
Lee, Chang-rae, 52; *Aloft*, 132–33, 204, 214n10; *A Gesture Life*, 13–14, 16, 35, 173–81, 184, 204, 214n10, 217nn14–15, 217n17
Lee, Young-Oak, 217n17
Lefebvre, Henri, 4
Leslie, D. A., 38
Levy, Helen Fiddyment, 206n7
Linden Hills (Naylor). *See* Naylor, Gloria
literary history (domestic fiction), 2, 6, 15–16, 21–22, 25, 115, 117–26, 151, 157, 184, 199; death of genre, 15–16; literary reputation/reception, 13, 15–16, 118, 153, 155–64, 199. *See also* modernism; nineteenth-century domestic fiction
Little Women (Alcott). *See* Alcott, Louisa May; disability
Loh, Sandra Tsing, 21, 214n10
Lopez, Erika, 21
Lorde, Audre, 4, 99
Louie, David Wong, 16, 134, 162–63

Low, Setha, 208n16
luck. *See* white privilege
Luckett, Sandra, 191

Mama Day (Naylor). *See* Naylor, Gloria
man caves, 130
manifest domesticity, 12, 14, 23, 27, 56, 61, 209n9, 209n11. *See also* Kaplan, Amy
margin, 4, 25, 30, 37, 39–40, 73, 80–84, 87, 89–92, 98–99, 101–3, 111, 121, 172–73, 197, 199. *See also* hooks, bell
marriage, 17, 51, 68, 73, 101, 116, 127, 133, 138, 154, 165, 190, 209n8; conclusions, 4, 26–27, 54, 60; marriage initiative, 36–37. *See also* gay marriage
Marshall, Paule, 26; *Brown Girl, Brownstones*, 33–34
Martin, Biddy, 23, 61, 69, 75, 78–79, 104, 106, 198, 201, 209n10, 210n19, 213n5
Marx, Karl. *See* class
masculinity, 127, 130, 155, 190, 213n1, 214n9, 217n15; and alienation, 119–20, 123–24, 138–39, 174–75; authorship, 6–7, 11–12, 23–25, 115–16, 158, 161–62, 182; domesticity, 13–14, 20–21, 114–15, 117–26, 134–38, 145, 148–50, 154–55, 162–64, 169, 173–81, 191, 200–201, 213n2, 214n10; home improvement, 118–19, 130, 133, 149, 170, 213n4; irony, 109, 119, 137–39, 147, 153, 165, 167–70, 185; man caves, 130; neodomesticity, 169–73, 180, 183–85. *See also* antidomestic; gendered forms (domestic fiction); patriarchy
Massey, Doreen, 9, 37, 48, 50, 60, 71, 84–85, 108–11, 205n1, 213n1, 215n22
May, Leila Silvana, 205n2
McCann, Herbert G., 189–90
McCullough, Kate, 25–26, 208n6
McDowell, Linda, 9, 70, 175
McGinn, Daniel, 77
McKee, Patricia, 84, 95, 102–3, 107–8, 111
Mehegan, David, 158–59, 216n4

Melville, Herman, 20; *Moby-Dick*, 6
men: authorship, 6–7, 11–12, 23–25, 115–16, 158, 161–62, 182; homeownership, 1, 21, 133, 135–36, 191. *See also* masculinity; patriarchy
metrosexual, 187, 189, 217n2, 218n6
Mile, Sian, 208n11
Mixon, Bobbie, 116
mobility. *See* journey structure; neodomestic fiction: definition/characteristics
Mockbee, Samuel. *See* Rural Studio
model home, 4–6, 26–29, 33–40, 50–52, 54, 56, 58–76, 122, 154, 192, 196–97. *See also* conventional domesticity; neodomesticity
modernism: and domestic fiction, 6, 8, 15–16, 24–25, 27–28, 37, 119, 159, 205n6. *See also* Stein, Gertrude; Wharton, Edith
Mohanty, Chandra Talpade, 23, 61, 69, 75, 78–79, 104, 106, 198, 201, 209n10, 210n19, 213n5
Moi, Toril, 182
Monkey Bridge (Cao). *See* Cao, Lan
Morgan, Robert: *Gap Creek*, 11
Morrison, Toni, 11, 13, 22, 52, 77–113, 147–48, 161, 183, 197–98, 211n5; Africanist presence, 57, 61, 67, 113, 121–22, 210nn12–13; *The Bluest Eye*, 78, 81, 107, 208n10, 211nn1–3; domestic violence, 79–81, 93, 103, 106, 109–11; funk, 107–8; "Home," 4, 30, 51, 76–77, 79–85, 104, 113, 183, 197; *Jazz*, 81, 83, 203, 211n5; *Love*, 81, 204; *A Mercy*, 81, 204, 214n13; patriarchy, 16, 79, 92, 94–96, 98–99, 101, 103–6, 109, 212n10; "Rootedness," 216n26; *Song of Solomon*, 81, 112, 211n2; *Sula*, 81–82, 108; *Tar Baby*, 82; thresholds and definition of home, 4, 30, 51, 82–83, 89, 110. See also *Beloved* (Morrison); *Paradise* (Morrison); race house
mortgage crisis. *See* homeownership
Mosley, Walter, 135, 215n18
Moss, Elizabeth, 205n5
mothers. *See* protagonists

Mullan, John, 164
Mun, Nami: *Miles from Nowhere*, 192, 204
Myslik, Wayne D., 218n7

Native Americans, 42–44, 51, 53–54; and home, 60, 101, 183, 196, 213n6; narrative structure, 44–45; *Paradise* (Morrison), 98–99, 101
Native American literature: and domestic fiction, 42, 44–45, 53–54. *See also* Erdrich, Louise; Hopkins, Sarah Winnemucca; Silko, Leslie Marmon; Zitkala-Sa
Nava, Michael: *Rag and Bone*, 127–28, 169–71, 200, 204, 217n12
Naylor, Gloria: *Linden Hills*, 21, 203, 214n10; *Mama Day*, 9, 147, 203
Neel, Alice, 218n13
neodomestic fiction: and characteristics/definition of, 1–26, 29–31, 113–17, 124, 126, 133–34, 154–55, 169, 182–86, 197–201; conventional domesticity, 17, 26–40; early (threshold) novels, 31–35; historical-cultural context for, 12, 24–26, 35–40, 84–85, 130, 188; instability, 3–4, 6–7, 9–11, 18–19, 29–32, 89, 116–17, 150; mobility, 4, 29–30, 46–47, 124, 131, 182–83, 185–86; neo-genre, 4, 7, 9; recycling, 5, 7, 17–19, 29, 32, 38–76, 117, 131–32, 171–72; redesign/remodeling/renovation, 4, 9, 11–12, 29–30, 50–52, 77–113, 131–33, 175, 182–83; as spatial narrative, 3–4, 7–10, 16–17, 24, 44, 185, 206n8; thresholds within, 12, 30–35, 75, 182. *See also* conclusions; didactic fiction; neodomesticity; protagonists; queer domesticities; sexuality; spiritual geography
neodomesticity: and examples outside fiction, 186–88, 198–201; masculinity, 169–75, 180, 183–85; space, 7, 9, 17–19, 85, 132, 183–86. *See also* neodomestic fiction
neoliberalism, 10, 36

Newton, Judith, 207n4
nineteenth-century domestic fiction, 2, 4–8, 12–13, 15, 18, 19–20, 22–23, 25–28, 30–31, 33, 36, 41–43, 46, 52, 54, 56, 61, 119, 120, 127, 142, 205n5, 214n9; and thresholds, 30. *See also* Alcott, Louisa May; Burton, María Amparo Ruiz de; Chesnutt, Charles; Hawthorne, Nathaniel; Hopkins, Pauline; Hopkins, Sara Winnemucca; Howells, William Dean; Jacobs, Harriet; James, Henry; Melville, Herman; Zitkala-Sa
novel: bourgeois family/form, 5, 25–26; female authorship, 2–4, 11, 19–20, 22, 25–26, 36, 40, 42, 92, 129, 152–53, 205n5, 213n3; male authorship, 6–7, 11–12, 23–25, 115–16, 158, 161–62, 182. *See also* domestic fiction; neodomestic fiction

Oates, Joyce Carol, 213n3
Oldenburg, Ann, 193
Olivares, Julián, 33
O'Neill, Joseph: *Netherland*, 204
oppositional space. *See* space
Oprah's Book Club, 16, 23, 118, 153–64, 199, 216n8, 216n10. *See also* Winfrey, Oprah
Oprah Winfrey Show. *See* Winfrey, Oprah
Orr, Elaine Neil, 185
Ostriker, Alicia, 185
Other(ness), 18, 40, 42, 58, 60, 69, 76, 96, 101–12, 125, 163, 184, 201, 217n14; poverty, 36, 55, 62, 100–101, 128, 188, 193, 196, 199, 212n18, 217n14. *See also* home: outside(rs); margin, queer domesticities; white trash
Out There. *See* home

Page, Philip, 105, 211nn8–9
Painter, Nell Irvin, 99, 211n6, 212n15
Pandolfi, Keith, 218n4
Paradise (Morrison), 13, 16, 78–85, 92–114, 124, 203, 211n5, 211–12nn7–14, 212n19; conclusion/spiritual geog-

raphy, 35, 84, 94, 105–12, 116, 136, 138, 143, 146–48, 150–51, 165, 172, 176, 179–80, 184; homeownership, 21, 134; Native Americans, 98–99, 101; patriarchy, 94–96, 98–99, 101, 103–6, 109; remodeling the race house, 78–85, 92–94, 197; true home, 103–112. *See also* black towns; Morrison, Toni
Parikh, Crystal, 17, 154, 163
Paris, J. W., 218n7
Parker-Pope, Tara, 116
parlor, 127–29
patriarchy, 11, 23, 28–29, 32–33, 35, 44, 47, 49, 57, 64–65, 68, 72, 74, 118, 123, 143, 145, 149, 151, 155, 164, 171, 184–85; Morrison's fiction, 16, 79, 92, 94–96, 98–99, 101, 103–6, 109, 212n10; nonpatriarchal masculinity, 171, 176
Pérez, Loida Maritza: *Geographies of Home*, 10, 30, 55, 175, 203
Perry, Donna, 53
Peter Family. See *Extreme Makeover: Home Edition*
Petry, Ann, 26; *The Street*, 120
Phelps, Elizabeth Staurt, 21, 129
Philips, Deborah, 2
Piercy, Marge: *The Longings of Women*, 192, 203, 213n3
Pigs in Heaven (Kingsolver). *See* Kingsolver, Barbara
place. *See* space
The Poisonwood Bible (Kingsolver), 12, 16, 21, 35, 42, 52–76, 97, 124, 134, 175–76, 203; conclusion/spiritual geography, 110–11, 116, 136, 138, 143–45, 147–48, 150, 172, 180, 184; recycled homes, 59–75; recycling of *Little Women*, 52–53, 55–57, 60–63, 68, 71, 164–65; white privilege/imperialism, 40, 57–69, 72–73, 75, 89, 103, 113, 209n8, 210nn13–14, 211n23. *See also* disability; Kingsolver, Barbara
Polter, Julie, 188, 194
(post)colonialism, 60, 62, 73, 199; 206n7; colonialism/imperialism and domestic fiction, 16, 23, 27, 41, 43, 47, 49, 56–69, 72–73, 75, 101, 104–5, 123, 150, 199, 207n1, 209nn9–11, 210nn14–15, 211n23, 212n14. *See also* manifest domesticity; *The Poisonwood Bible* (Kingsolver)
postmodernism, 16, 28, 46, 50, 93, 138–40, 143, 145, 150, 157–58, 208n5, 215n22, 216n23.
Pratt, Minnie Bruce, 79, 210n19, 213n5
Prince, Valerie Sweeney, 122, 206n7, 211n2
protagonists, 5–8, 24–25, 30, 32, 39, 41, 55, 82, 112, 115, 172, 182, 216n6; female characters, 2–3, 8, 21, 26–27, 29–30, 33–34, 42, 46, 54–61, 78, 92, 110, 128, 165–69, 209n7; gender and profession, 8, 115, 133–36; (in)formal economy, 21, 36, 40, 128–29, 134, 170; male characters, 6–8, 21, 35, 114, 117, 122, 142–43, 148, 162–63, 213n3; mothers, 10, 34, 38–39, 56–59, 108, 132, 164–69, 175; neodomestic, 3, 5, 11–12, 24, 29–30, 33–35, 54–59, 75, 166
Protestant. *See* religion
Pryse, Marjorie: *Writing Out of Place*, 155
Puchner, Eric: *Model Home*, 204

queer domesticities, 13–14, 16–18, 47, 50–51, 154–55, 162–64, 169–173, 178, 180–81, 183–84, 208n15, 217n13. *See also* sexuality
queer space. *See* Chisholm, Dianne; space
Quiñonez, Ernesto: *Bodega Dreams*, 204

race. *See* hybridity; race house; space; women: erasure of women of color; *and specific racial identities*
race house, 79–103, 106, 110–11, 173–75, 183. See also *Paradise* (Morrison)
Rakoff, Joanna Smith, 157
rape. *See* domestic violence: sexual violence
recycled domesticities, 17–19, 38–76; and *Gardens in the Dunes* (Silko), 39, 42–43, 51; neodomestic fiction, 5, 7,

17–18, 29, 32, 38–39, 117, 131–32, 171–72. *See also* George, Rosemary Marangoly
relational space. *See* space
religion, 40, 138–39, 150, 192; and ancestor worship, 216n26; Protestant, 5, 11, 26, 28, 39, 42, 50, 52, 125, 137, 147, 166–69, 171. *See also* home: Christianity; spiritual geography
remodeling. *See* home improvement
Reynolds, Guy, 205n6
Riddell, Mary, 206n11
Robinson, Marilynne: *Home,* 204, 216n6; *Housekeeping,* 12, 29–33, 35, 149, 182, 203, 208n11
Rodriguez, Denise, 89, 91–92
Rodriguez, Ralph E., 171, 217n12
romance (genre), 3, 8, 28, 117
Romero, Lora, 6, 8, 117, 205n5
Romines, Ann, 27, 206n7, 209n6
Rooney, Kathleen, 161, 216n8
Rosler, Martha, 218n13
Roxbury house project (*This Old House*), 218n4
Rubenstein, Roberta, 206n7
Rural Studio, 14, 187–88, 196, 198–99, 218n3, 218n5
Russo, Richard: *Bridge of Sighs,* 204, 216n6; *Empire Falls,* 134, 148–49, 159, 204, 216n5
Ruth Hall (Fern). *See* Fern, Fanny
Rybczynski, Witold: *Home,* 74, 175, 208n10; *Last Harvest,* 38, 207n12

safe space. *See* space
Saint Maybe (Tyler). *See* Tyler, Anne
Salazar, Inés, 33, 84–85, 111, 145
Savage, Howard A., 1, 81, 215n17
Sayers, Valerie, 164–65
Schenk, Susan J., 2
Scherer, Ron, 215n16
Scruggs, Charles, 90, 92
Seabrook, John, 158–59
Seager, Joni, 36, 60, 130
Sears, 28, 194
Senna, Danzy: *Caucasia,* 203
sentimental fiction, 2, 8, 15, 19, 23, 25–26, 43, 54, 135–36, 157, 159–60, 185, 207n3, 208n6, 208n8
separate spheres, 6–7, 11, 20, 26, 117, 126, 199, 210n20
September 11th, 36, 78, 195, 206n11, 209n10
sexism. *See* patriarchy
sexuality: asexuality, 163; bisexuality, 170; heteronormativity, 5, 11, 17, 36–37, 50–51, 163, 170–71, 195; heterosexuality, 50–51, 130, 169, 173–74, 187, 195, 218n6; homosexuality, 17, 152, 170–73; homosocial bond, 96; metrosexual, 187, 189, 217n2, 218n6; (neo)domestic fiction, 29, 40, 78, 107–8, 134; queer, 17, 50, 154–55, 169–81. *See also* gay marriage
sexual violence. *See* domestic violence
Shah, Nayan, 17, 154–55, 170
Shamir, Milette, 8, 127–30, 132
Silko, Leslie Marmon, 11, 76, 82, 113; *Yellow Woman,* 44–45. See also *Gardens in the Dunes* (Silko)
Simonian, Charisse, 194
Skocpol, Theda, 206n11
slavery: *See* kitchen
Sligh, Clarissa, 14, 199–201, 218n13
Smiley, Jane, 13, 213n3; *Good Faith,* 134–35, 169–70, 204
Snakes, 45, 53, 211n23
Snyder, Mary Gail, 38, 208n16
social novel, 3, 117, 153, 157, 159, 169
Soja, Edward W., 208n5
Solomon, Alisa, 206n11
space: and African Americans, 86–87; ambivalence, 91, 93, 132, 169, 180–81, 208n11; Bachelard, Gaston, 33, 184; class, 77, 126, 142, 205n1; gated communities, 37–38, 66, 106, 132, 208n16; gender, 17, 29, 126–33, 142, 154, 183, 186, 205n1; heterotopia, 4, 18; history, 17–19, 44–45, 85; neodomestic, 7, 9, 17–19, 85, 132, 183–86; oppositional, 83, 94–103, 108–10; place, 205n1; queer, 50, 155, 169–81, 183, 207n2, 209n2, 218n7; race, 7, 13, 29, 33, 48, 57–58, 69, 77–85, 120, 126, 183, 197, 205n1; relational, 4, 9,

14, 18, 29, 47–50, 75, 83–85, 92, 94, 109–10, 112–13; safe, 71, 103, 109; Spain, Daphne, 110, 129–30, 186–87, 189, 197, 214n13; third space, 4, 18–19, 48, 116–17, 180; time, 24, 44–45, 51, 140, 205n1, 208n5, 209n2. *See also* feminist geography; home; margin; spatial narrative; suburban space

Spain, Daphne, 110, 129–30, 186–87, 189, 197, 214n13

spatial lens. *See* spatial narrative

spatial narrative, 4, 7–8, 16, 24, 44, 185, 206n8; and spatial lens, 12, 25, 93. *See also* Brady, Mary Pat

spatiotemporal utopias. *See* Harvey, David

Speaking of Faith. *See* Tippett, Krista

Spencer, Katherine, 215n15

Spillers, Hortense J., 28–29, 186

spiritual geography, 7, 84–85, 94, 105, 110–11, 116–17, 126, 136–39, 143–46, 149, 151–52, 168–69, 184–85, 194; and gender, 136–52, 168–69, 173–81, 184–85; ghosts/spirits, 22, 35, 49, 110–11, 136, 141–45, 147–49, 165, 177, 179–80, 184–85. See also *Paradise* (Morrison); *The Poisonwood Bible* (Kingsolver)

The Sportswriter (Ford). *See* Ford, Richard

stability. *See* domestic fiction

Stegman, Michael A., 191

Stein, Gertrude, 6, 26

Stewart, Martha, 5, 28

Stossel, Scott, 161

Stowe, Harriet Beecher, 5, 11, 27–28, 36–39, 55, 194, 197

Street, Paul, 216n10

suburban fiction, 3, 13, 20–21, 114–53, 213n3; literary history, 114–26, 213n6, 214n10. *See also* Jurca, Catherine; suburban space

Suburban Sketches (Howells). *See* Howells, William Dean

suburban space, 28, 117, 120–25, 142, 146–47, 173–74; African Americans, 121–22, 125–26, 197, 214nn11–12; frontier, 120–22, 172–73; gated communities, 37–38, 66, 106, 132, 208n16; masculinity, 119–20. *See also* Hayden, Dolores; Wiese, Andrew

suburbia. *See* suburban space

Svetkey, Benjamin, 153

Sykes, Plum, 216n7

Tanning, Dorothea, 218n13

Tate, Claudia, 25, 80, 205n5

third space, 4, 18–19, 48, 116–17, 180. *See also* Bhabha, Homi K.

This Old House, 188, 193, 218n4

Thoreau, Henry David, 20; *Walden*, 6

thresholds: and Morrison's definition of home, 4, 30, 51, 82–83, 89, 110; neodomestic fiction, 12, 30–35, 75, 182; nineteenth-century domestic fiction, 30

time. *See* space

Tippett, Krista, 188, 218n5

Tomboy Tools, 189

Tompkins, Jane, 201, 208n7

Trading Spaces, 198

Twain, Mark, 13, 48, 118, 149

Tyler, Anne, 213n3; *Saint Maybe*, 21, 203

Updike, John, 20–21, 123, 137, 168, 213n3; *Rabbit at Rest*, 137, 164, 215n19; *Rabbit Redux*, 122, 214n8; *Rabbit, Run*, 20

U.S. Census Bureau, 1, 80–81, 93, 186, 191, 207n12, 211n3, 218n8

utopian space. *See* Harvey, David

Valby, Karen, 217n11

violence. *See* domestic violence

Viramontes, Helena María, 16, 192, 204

Vlach, John Michael, 13, 86–87, 90, 112

Walden (Thoreau). *See* Thoreau, Henry David

Warner, Michael, 209n2

Warner, Susan: *The Wide, Wide World*,

26–27, 46, 54–55, 128–29, 151, 206n11, 208n7, 215n14
Washington Square (James). *See* James, Henry
Wasserman, Jim, 133
Weems, Carrie Mae, 218n13
Weisman, Leslie Kanes, 207n12
welfare, 36
Welter, Barbara, 26
Wharton, Edith, 21, 24, 26, 48, 129
Whelan, Lara Baker, 142–43
White Noise (DeLillo). *See* DeLillo, Don
white privilege, 29, 32, 36–37, 40, 46, 55–59, 61–69, 74, 113, 119, 148–51, 183, 195–96, 213n6; and luck, 65–67, 193. *See also* class: privilege; *The Poisonwood Bible* (Kingsolver)
whites, 92, 100–101, 120, 174, 212n21; and homeownership, 1, 81; whiteness, 64, 68–69, 71, 125, 183, 195–96. *See also* Kingsolver, Barbara; Robinson, Marilynne; white privilege; white trash
white trash, 39–40
Whyte, William H., 21, 119
Widdowson, Peter, 99, 105–6, 211n5, 211n7, 212n13, 212n19
Wideman, John Edgar, 13, 16, 21, 125–26, 137–38, 145, 147–48, 203; *Damballah*, 125, 148, 203; *Hiding Place*, 125–26, 203; *Sent for You Yesterday*, 125–26, 137, 147–48, 150, 203
Wiese, Andrew, 81, 88, 100, 125, 197, 213n6, 214nn10–12
Wilde, Oscar: *Picture of Dorian Gray*, 215n21
Wiley, Catherine, 206n7
Williams, Carla, 200–201
Williams, Joy: *Breaking and Entering*, 16–17, 19, 29, 32, 35, 149, 203

Williamson, Judith, 62–63
Willis, Deborah, 199–200
Willis, Susan, 107
Wilson, Harriet, 26
Wilson, Sherryl, 162
windows. *See* thresholds
Winfrey, Oprah: reading method, 160, 216n10. *See also* Franzen, Jonathan; Oprah's Book Club
Wood, James, 161, 216n4
Woods, Roberta, 207n12
women: as domestic icons/workers, 28–29, 36–37, 75, 78, 116, 127, 133–34, 186–87, 189–91, 198; erasure of women of color, 25–26, 113; gender/sex as category of analysis, 115; home improvement, 187–90; homeownership, 1, 37, 133, 136, 190–91, 214n11, 214n13; roles, 3–4; as writers, 2–4, 11, 19–20, 22, 25–26, 36, 40, 42, 92, 129, 152–53, 205n5, 213n3. *See also* domestic violence; femininity; patriarchy; women's fiction
women's fiction, 2, 6–7, 11, 15, 19–20, 22–23, 25, 28, 42, 54, 118, 129, 155, 159, 162, 199, 205n5, 210n20. *See also* women: as writers
Wright, Gwendolyn, 76
Wyatt, Jean, 208n11

Ydstie, John, 37, 208n14
Young, Iris Marion, 25
Young, John, 161

Zeller, Tom, 36–37
Zevin, Gabrielle, 21, 204
Zitkala-Sa, 42

www.ingramcontent.com/pod-product-compliance
Lightning Source LLC
Chambersburg PA
CBHW021838220426
43663CB00005B/293